FTTx Networks

FTTx Networks
Technology Implementation and Operation

James Farmer

Brian Lane

Kevin Bourg

Weyl Wang

AMSTERDAM • BOSTON • HEIDELBERG • LONDON
NEW YORK • OXFORD • PARIS • SAN DIEGO
SAN FRANCISCO • SINGAPORE • SYDNEY • TOKYO

Morgan Kaufmann is an imprint of Elsevier

Morgan Kaufmann is an imprint of Elsevier
50 Hampshire Street, 5th Floor, Cambridge, MA 02139, United States

Notices

Knowledge and best practice in this field are constantly changing. As new research and experience broaden our understanding, changes in research methods, professional practices, or medical treatment may become necessary.

Practitioners and researchers must always rely on their own experience and knowledge in evaluating and using any information, methods, compounds, or experiments described herein. In using such information or methods they should be mindful of their own safety and the safety of others, including parties for whom they have a professional responsibility.

To the fullest extent of the law, neither the Publisher nor the authors, contributors, or editors, assume any liability for any injury and/or damage to persons or property as a matter of products liability, negligence or otherwise, or from any use or operation of any methods, products, instructions, or ideas contained in the material herein.

Library of Congress Cataloging-in-Publication Data
A catalog record for this book is available from the Library of Congress

British Library Cataloguing-in-Publication Data
A catalogue record for this book is available from the British Library

ISBN: 978-0-12-420137-8

For information on all Morgan Kaufmann publications
visit our website at https://www.elsevier.com/

Working together
to grow libraries in
developing countries

www.elsevier.com • www.bookaid.org

Publisher: Todd Green
Acquisition Editor: Brian Romer
Editorial Project Manager: Jennifer Pierce
Production Project Manager: Punithavathy Govindaradjane
Cover Designer: Mark Rogers

Typeset by TNQ Books and Journals

Dedication

We dedicate the book to the innumerable geniuses who, over a bit more than 100 years, have built the telecommunications industry from nonexistent to what it is today. We and others would not be able to develop our modern fiber optic communications infrastructure were it not for these giants upon whose shoulders we stand.

Contents

About the Authors

Jim Farmer retired in August, 2013. He has enjoyed a 45-year career in communications technology. He has held CTO responsibilities in the cable television and FTTH industries.

He holds over 90 patents in the field of delivering video, voice, and data. He received the 1996 NCTA Vanguard Award in Technology, was inducted into the SCTE Hall of Fame in 1997, and was inducted into Cable Pioneers in 1998. Formerly the President of the IEEE Consumer Electronics Society and then editor of its newsletter for 11 years, Jim has served on the program committees for the NCTA, SCTE, and the IEEE International Conference on Consumer Electronics, and chaired the program committee for the FTTH Council from its inception through 2011. He was an early member of the SCTE Board of Directors and wrote its first certification tests for set-top converters. He was active on the NCTA Engineering Committee and participated in development of several standards and recommended practices. He has been on the FTTH Council's Board of Directors, was the first chair of its Technology Committee, and remained active on the Planning Committee until his retirement. Jim is a life member of SMPTE, a senior member of the SCTE, and a Life Fellow of the IEEE.

He coauthored two editions of *Modern Cable Television: Video, Voice and Data Communications*, which won the Cable Center 2000 Cable Book Award. *Broadband Cable Access Networks* was released in 2009. He has a number of publications with the FTTH Council, NCTA, SCTE, and IEEE and has been a columnist with several periodicals. Jim holds BSEE and MSEE degrees from the University of South Florida.

Brian Lane has held key technology and business management positions, in engineering, manufacturing/operations, and product management in the FTTx industry—focused on the development and support of FTTx products and technologies.

Brian has over 28 years of industry experience. Before getting into FTTH, he held various engineering and management positions in real-time, embedded software and critical systems development focusing on aircraft controls, avionics, satellite communications, and consumer communications product development.

Brian has a Bachelor of Science in Electrical Engineering from the University of Tennessee, Knoxville, and a Master of Science in Electrical Engineering from the University of Texas, Arlington, where his research thesis focused on control theory of unstable systems.

Kevin Bourg has over 20 years of industry experience in system engineering, software development, and sales in the telecommunication industry. Kevin is an active member of the FTTH Council Americas serving on the Technology and Planning Committees as well as Conference Chair for the 2012 Conference in Dallas, Texas. Kevin is a past Chairman of the Board for the Council and continues to serve as an active Board member.

He holds a Bachelor of Science degree in Computer Science with a minor in Business Administration from the University of Southwestern Louisiana and a Master of Science from Southern Methodist University.

Weyl Wang has more than 20 years of industry hands-on experience in metro transport and FTTH access broadband networks. He worked at several major labs on WDM devices and systems. For more than 10 years Weyl had been responsible for system testing of FTTx network equipment.

Dr. Wang holds a Ph.D. degree in Electronics Engineering from NCTU University in Taiwan. He holds more than 10 US patents in areas of optical transport, DWDM, OADM, switching components, and broadband access systems.

Acknowledgments

The authors are indebted to the team at Elsevier, and particularly to Amy Invernizzi, who patiently prodded and cajoled as we missed one deadline after another. We also appreciate the help of our reviewer, Kim Kersey, who made the book much better with his many suggestions. And of course we thank our families for their extra patience as we struggled to complete the project.

PART

1

Overview of FTTx

CHAPTER 1

Introduction

PHYSICAL TECHNOLOGIES FOR COMMUNICATION

People have had communications facilities into and out of their homes for over a century now, and in that time there have been at least three different media technologies used. The oldest, and still widely deployed, is twisted pair copper wire, used initially to support a single analog telephone line to the home, now often used to also transport digital data using a technology called *digital subscriber line* (DSL). As television became popular in the 1950s, companies began bringing TV signals into homes using coaxial cable from a master antenna somewhere in the area. These were initially called *community antenna television* (CATV) systems. That term is considered outdated today, because that same coaxial cable now transports not only signals from a local antenna (in many cases, getting a direct feed from the TV studio rather from the antenna), but even more TV signals delivered by satellite or other means, as well as providing voice and telephony services over the same cable. The technology has evolved from coaxial cable emanating from the central receive point (the *headend*), to *hybrid fiber-coax* (HFC) systems, in which fiber optic cable takes the signal part way from the headend or *hub* (a collection point for signals, described later) to a *node*, where the signals are put on coaxial cable for the journey the rest of the way to the subscribers' homes.

The advantage of fiber is that its signal loss is very low compared to that of coax, so it is possible to transport signals a very long distance without having to amplify them. This translates into better reliability, better quality, and lower operational expenses (op-ex). Early implementation of HFC networks (c. the late 1980s) supplied signals to 10 to 20 thousand homes from one node. As technology progressed and the cost of fiber optic equipment plummeted, the size of nodes continued to shrink as fiber was moved closer to the home. Today, few nodes being installed serve more than 500 homes passed, with many serving even smaller numbers of homes passed.

The logical extension of HFC to the smallest node, serving one home, brings us to the third technology, the subject of this book: *fiber-to-the-home* (FTTH). Typically, FTTH systems are built with only passive components from the origination

FTTx Networks. http://dx.doi.org/10.1016/B978-0-12-420137-8.00001-9

of the system to the home. This means that no power-using components are placed in the network. With no power-using components in the network, reliability is inherently better, and no provision must be made in the network for obtaining (and paying for) power from commercial sources, and back-up power is not needed. Hence, both capital and operational expenses are reduced, while reliability and quality of the received signals are enhanced. Operators who have gone from either twisted pair or HFC networks to FTTH have privately reported operational expense savings of 75–95% compared with their old plant.

PURPOSE OF THE BOOK

This book is intended to give practical advice for successfully selecting, installing, and using an FTTH network. It includes enough theory so that you will understand what you are doing, and so that you can logically trouble-shoot faults, but it is not intended to go deeply into the theory of how systems work.

TERMINOLOGY

If you come from a telephone background, you will call the point where signals are assembled to go to subscribers, a *central office* (CO). If you come from a cable TV background, you will call it a *headend*. Either way, it is the point at which communications of all types are assembled for transmission to the customer.

If you come from a telephone background, you might call a field-mounted terminal which converts signal formats and sends them the last distance to a home, a *digital subscriber line access multiplexer* (DSLAM). If you come from a cable telecommunications background, you will call it a *hub* (maybe a *node* would also fit that description—we shall define both below). We shall generally use cable TV terminology, though we tend to switch back and forth. In order to show how FTTH systems fit in, it is useful to show a high-level view of a modern cable TV HFC system, while understanding that this description could be of a telephone system with data and video.

Fig. 1.1 illustrates a high-level HFC system as it might be applied in a large metropolitan area. A primary headend gathers most or all TV content, and may be the interface point for data and voice services. An optional secondary headend, which mirrors the functions of the primary headend, may be placed in a geographically different part of the metropolitan area, so that if a disaster, such as a fire, occurs at the primary headend, the secondary headend can take over. The headend(s) are linked using fiber optic cables, to *hubs*, which may serve 10,000–20,000 customers. The hub may include certain data and maybe voice equipment, and will typically convert signals to the RF-modulated format

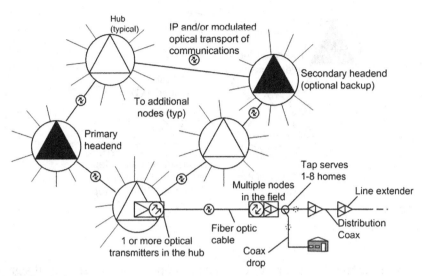

FIGURE 1.1
Metropolitan HFC network.

needed on the coaxial cable. The RF signals are in turn modulated onto optical carriers in *optical transmitters*. The output of these transmitters differs from that which you may have experience with for transmitting data. Rather than transmitting a digital signal, represented by light ON for a binary 1 and OFF for a binary 0 (or vice versa), the optical transmitter of Fig. 1.1 is a linear (analog) transmitter capable of transmitting a wide spectrum of RF signals (typically from 54 to 1002 MHz or more in North America), each signal carrying one of several types of content: One 6MHz (8MHz in many parts of the world) channel may carry one analog video signal (declining in use), or multiple digital TV signals, or time division multiplexed data including voice. These signals are assigned a frequency band, and many such signals can coexist at one time on one fiber optic transmitter.

The optical transmitter puts signals described above onto a fiber optic cable, which traverses most of the distance to a neighborhood to be served. At the neighborhood, a *node* demodulates the optical signal, turning it back into the RF-modulated carriers which went into the optical transmitter. From here, the signals are transported to homes through coaxial cable. RF amplifiers are usually needed to overcome signal loss, which loss may be attributed to two mechanisms. Each time a *tap* is used remove some signal power to serve one or more homes, conservation of energy dictates that less power is available to go further downstream to other homes. The second mechanism is loss in the coaxial cable itself, which can be significant. If the signal level gets too low, then analog channels get noisy ("snow" in the picture). If the digital signal gets

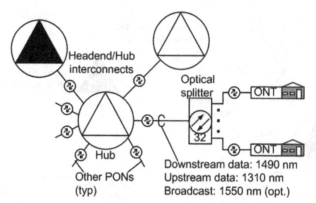

FIGURE 1.2
Typical hub serving PONs.

too low in amplitude, the picture or data disappears, with just a small signal level range where the picture breaks up.

Upstream signals are all RF-modulated carriers, returned over the coax by using lower frequencies on the coax (typically 5–42 MHz in North America). At the node they are modulated onto an optical carrier by an upstream transmitter, and then transmitted to the hub, usually on a dedicated fiber, but sometimes on the same fiber used for downstream, but on a different wavelength.

Many areas of the world use other transmission standards. In many locations, RF channels are 8 MHz wide rather than the 6 MHz used in North America, and carry upstream signal at frequencies up to about 65 MHz, with downstream signals being carried from about 85 MHz up. For many years there has been talk in North America about changing our split between upstream and downstream frequencies, but momentum and the market are hard things to overcome.

COMMON FTTH SYSTEMS

An HFC network may be contrasted to the most common type of FTTH system, called a *passive optical network* (PON). The PON starts at the hub (taking a lead from the example HFC system above), and serves, commonly, 32 homes. Some systems may serve 64 homes, and future systems are expected to serve more homes.

Fig. 1.2 illustrates one of the hubs of Fig. 1.1, but this hub serves a number of PONs. Each PON is defined by a single fiber strand feeding a passive optical splitter, which may be located in one place as shown, or which may be distributed. Each splitter serves, typically, 32 homes, with some serving 64 homes. There is interest in serving more homes per PON as the technology permits.

The splitter outputs each connect one home (or apartment building, or business, or whatever). An interface on the home is called the *optical network terminal* (ONT). The ONT is sometimes called the *optical network unit* (ONU). In the early days of FTTH, the term ONU was used generally to define a smaller, less capable termination, and the term ONT implied a more capable unit. Today these terms seem to be used pretty much interchangeably.

The ONT receives the optical signals and converts them to electrical signals useful in the home. The most basic electrical signal is Ethernet for data, and almost every ONT has one or more Ethernet ports. It may also have analog voice ports for *plain old telephone service* (POTS), and it may have one or more RF ports for video if the system uses RF video. The ONT is just about universally powered from the home, and the power supply may or may not include battery backup, depending on the services ordered and the policy of the operator.

Several wavelengths are used to transport optical signals on the PON. In the most common systems, 1490 nm is used for downstream data (1/2.5 Gb/s EPON and 2.5 Gb/s GPON). Ten Gb/s systems use 1577 nm for downstream data. Upstream data are transported at 1310 nm, or 1290 nm for 10 Gb/s links. When broadcast video is used, it is carried on a 1550 nm optical carrier. A variation on the termination equipment is the radio frequency over glass system (RFoG) used by some cable operators, which uses the same physical architecture as Fig. 1.2, but which puts all downstream signals, both video and data, on 1550 nm, and upstream modulated data on 1610 nm (1310 nm if the operator is not concerned about being compatible with other PONs).

The equipment used at the hub to handle the data signals is called an *optical line terminal* (OLT), and is covered in great detail later in the book. It plays a role analogous to a *cable modem termination system* (CMTS) in HFC networks, or a DSLAM in twisted pair networks, in that it has network interfaces, usually 1 Gb/s or 10 Gb/s Ethernet, and contains conditioning equipment to support the distribution protocol of choice.

OTHER FTTH PHYSICAL ARCHITECTURES

While most systems use the physical layer architecture of Fig. 1.2, some use a point-to-point (P2P) architecture in which a fiber is run directly from the hub to each subscriber. A single fiber is usually used, with downstream and upstream communications on different wavelengths. This technology is part of the IEEE Ethernet specification, and can operate to 1 Gb/s. The primary advantage usually cited for P2P networks is that there is no sharing of the "data pipe," so more bandwidth is available for each user. However, in the typical case, this perceived advantage is negated by data concentration at the switch in the hub. ONUs for P2P networks tend to be very low in cost because there is little need for the more complex protocols needed to support PON standards, and as we shall show just below, broadcast video is effectively out of the question for P2P networks, so there is no need for a broadcast receiver in the ONU.

The offsetting factors to lower ONU cost include the need for more fiber, and higher fiber splicing costs. While the OLT-side equipment is also less expensive than for a PON, 32 or 64 times as much equipment is needed, along with much more fiber management in the headend. As we shall see below, broadcast video is combined with the data in a *wave division multiplexer* (WDM), which tends to be too costly to deploy in a P2P network. Finally, with the greater amount of fiber leaving the hub and for a longer distance, any fiber cuts ("backhoe fades") will be more difficult to repair because more fiber is involved.

FTTH DATA LINK AND NETWORK PROTOCOLS

As we move up above the strictly physical level, we find a few different transport layer protocols in use. Much of this book is devoted to describing these protocols and how to best use them. So here we present a short overview of the PON protocols in use today.

Fig. 1.3 is an attempt to summarize the FTTH systems that are in use now, along with one or two included mainly for historical reasons. When we consider what we usually think of as FTTH systems, meaning binary data down- and upstream on the same fiber, optionally combined with broadcast, there are two chains of standards to follow. The earliest was the ITU's APON (**A**TM over **PON**) system specified in the 1990s. It established the general architectural elements of subsequent systems, and was deployed a little experimentally, but we know of no current systems in use. It was based on ATM (*asynchronous transfer mode*, a layer 2 protocol essentially competing with Ethernet), a protocol used and still in use extensively in the telephone industry, among others. There was no provision for broadcast video, and at the time IPTV (video transmitted using internet protocol) was not really feasible.

APON was modified to free the 1550nm wavelength for a broadcast video overlay, by putting the downstream data at 1490nm. This produced the BPON standard, which offered a maximum downstream speed of 622 Mb/s and an upstream speed of 155 Mb/s, and which has been deployed rather widely in much of Verizon's FiOS network, along with other installations.

Operators perceived the need for higher speeds and Ethernet was becoming the apparent winner of the layer 2 race, so the ITU ratified the G.984 GPON standard in 2004. It started with BPON, increased the maximum downstream speed to 2.488 (rounded to 2.5) Gb/s and the upstream to 1.2 Gb/s, and added Ethernet and TDM (T1/E1) transport to the ATM transport already

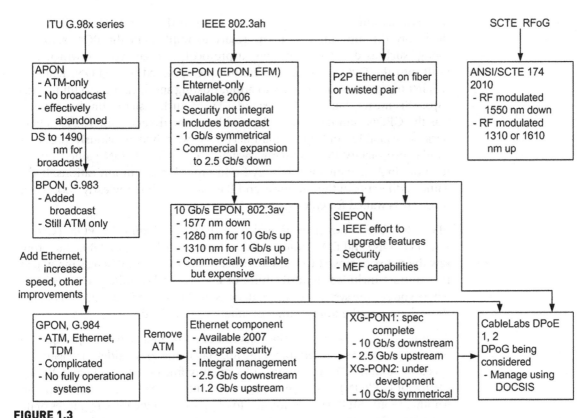

FIGURE 1.3

FTTH systems then and now.

in the standard. Adding these additional layer 2 transport standards, though, made implementation of the standard extremely complex, and as a consequence, not much happened commercially for a year or two. Then people realized that they really did not need all of these transport standards. Ethernet, which began as an enterprise standard for corporate data networking, had improved in many respects, and costs were dropping precipitously. So the Ethernet portion of GPON was built into chip sets, effectively abandoning the other parts. This made a commercially viable product possible, and since then a number of operators, many with telephone backgrounds, have deployed GPON.

Meanwhile, the 802.3 subcommittee of the IEEE, which was responsible for the Ethernet standard, had been adding its own version of FTTH to the Ethernet standard. The task force charged with developing the original standard was formally known as 802.3ah and at times you will see the standard so referenced. The standard was ratified in 2004 (the same year as GPON), and the next time the 802.3 Ethernet standard was updated, the 802.3ah work was incorporated into it. Typical of IEEE Ethernet work, the EPON standard specified only the minimum items necessary to implement the PON standard. Things such as detailed management protocols and encryption, which were built into the GPON standard, were not incorporated into EPON. Rather, it was left to commercial interests to adopt existing specifications to fill in these gaps. This meant that the EPON standard was much easier to implement than was the GPON standard, so by the middle of the decade chip sets for EPON became available, and some manufacturers, who had previously produced similar proprietary PON systems, switched to EPON. EPON gained quite a toe-hold in Asia, which was hungry for improved telecommunications. It also gained adherents in the Americas and Europe, though many early adopters in those areas waited for GPON.

EPON has been known by several other terms, including GE-PON (Gigabit Ethernet PON) and EFM, Ethernet in the First Mile (the original 802.3ah group saw the network closest to the subscriber as the first mile, whereas many people, authors included, tend to think of this as the last mile—it depends on where you see the system starting). Besides the PON standard, 802.3ah defined P2P Ethernet to the home, either on fiber or twisted pair.

A while after 802.3ah was ratified, several other related activities sprung up. A working group was formed under the 802.3av name to consider increasing the speed to 10 Gb/s. This group has subsequently finished its work, and 10 Gb/s EPON (10G-EPON) has been incorporated into the 802.3 Ethernet standard. Another group, SIEPON, was formed to fill in some of the missing pieces of the EPON standard, in order to make it more robust for commercial applications. These missing pieces were built partially on the work of the Metro Ethernet Forum (MEF), which was formed from the old DSL Forum to promote Ethernet as more than an enterprise solution, by adding features to give Ethernet some ATM-like capabilities at a much lower cost.

The cable television industry in the US became interested in EPON as a way to compete with telephone companies installing GPON, and as the next architecture beyond the tried-and-true HFC. Some in the industry were concerned, though, about certain basic management philosophies and techniques that had gone into EPON, which were in conflict with the management of DOCSIS cable modem systems, which had captured the greatest part of the residential data business. Large cable operators had developed very complete management systems around the DOCSIS system, and they perceived that adapting EPON to use these management systems would make it easier to incrementally add EPON to their HFC systems. It is impossible, both physically and financially, to change out HFC systems for FTTH systems overnight. So the concept was to build new plant, possibly in greenfields and into business regions where cable was starting to penetrate, with FTTH, while continuing to operate existing

HFC plant for a number of years. Accordingly, Cable Television Laboratories (CableLabs) initiated the *DOCSIS provisioning of EPON* (DPoE—an acronym of acronyms) work, which as of this writing has produced two revisions defining how to adapt EPON to be managed by existing DOCSIS management systems.

Yet more activities were underway. Another perception of how to move HFC to FTTH was to build physical networks according to the FTTH concepts, as shown earlier in this chapter, but to retain the existing DOCSIS infrastructure at the ends. The Society of Cable Telecommunications Engineers (SCTE) undertook this standardization effort. Rather than terminate the network with OLTs at the hub (or headend) and conventional ONTs at the home, the network would be terminated at the headend with equipment identical to that used in HFC systems, with the possible exception that HFC uses a lot of 1310 nm downstream transmission, and in all FTTH systems this wavelength is reserved for upstream transmission. Downstream transmission would be on 1550 nm (a particularly convenient wavelength because fiber loss is extremely low, and economical optical amplifiers are practical). Two options were specified for the upstream wavelength: 1310 nm for people who wanted the most economical equipment and were not expecting to put PON data on the same fiber. The other option was for upstream transmission at 1610 nm, which would let the fiber network also accept PON transmissions. The first standard was ratified through SCTE then through ANSI, which is the top-level standards organization in the United States. This ratification was completed in 2010.

Not on the chart, there is yet another effort currently under consideration by the IEEE, which is intended to allow cable operators to adapt their existing HFC plant to PON gradually, by replacing nodes with a new device which would convert the PON optical signals to electrical format for transmission to the home on existing coax. This effort is known as *EPON Protocol over Coax* (EPoC). In turn, it is planning to use the physical layer of another CableLabs initiative, DOCSIS 3.1, an ambitious effort to provide much, much higher bandwidth over HFC networks by expanding the RF bandwidth used by DOCSIS by using more efficient modulation methods. This is one of the hazards of writing a book on such a contemporary topic; by the time you read it, there may have been some major shifts in direction of the industry that your authors were not smart enough to foresee.

CHAPTER 2

Deciding to Build an FTTx Network

INTRODUCTION

If you build an FTTx (a generic term for fiber-to-the-anywhere-you-want-to-take-it) network, you will have the most advanced network possible, with the ability to deliver all of the telecommunications services known today, to residential and small and medium business customers, with advances permitting you to move up the ladder to ever larger enterprises. However, building a new physical network is not an undertaking to be treated lightly. Installing physical plant is an expensive proposition for anyone, regardless of the technology used; just how expensive depends on who owns existing plant and rights-of-way, and local conditions. Many types of organizations are building fiber-to-the-home (FTTH) systems today, and each has different motivation and different financial expectations of that network. In any event, it behooves you to go into the venture with a full understanding of what you are getting into, and how you are going to deal with the pitfalls. We say this not to discourage you from undertaking construction, but rather to help you be successful when you get it built.

"If you build it they will come" is a euphemism, not an immutable law of the universe. We like to say that customers don't care how they get telecommunications services. If rats carrying little pieces of tape through the sewer system gives them the services they want, if those services are low in cost and simple to use, then that is what the subscribers will choose—technology for the sake of technology is just not that important to Joe Sixpack. Now, of course, rats carrying little pieces of tape will *not* give people what they want, but the point is, any technology that best does what the consumer wants is going to be what he chooses. Of course we believe that FTTH will let you provide subscribers with the best customer experience at the best price, but you will need to be able to take that message to the consumer in a way that he or she understands it. The first thing this means is to understand your competition (and you do have it). People high in your organization should be subscribing to satellite video services, telephone-based services, and cable services, whatever is in your area already. And you will need to get together to compare notes, so that you objectively evaluate your competition before you set your services and prices (and this in turn will drive your design).

FTTx Networks. http://dx.doi.org/10.1016/B978-0-12-420137-8.00002-0

We have seen municipal and utility companies build FTTH networks in competition with cable TV providers that had pretty good networks—not up to FTTH standards, but not bad. The FTTH provider offered 5 Mb/s data service, which of course is trivial or slower for any FTTH network. But the provider thought it plenty, and sized his Internet connection accordingly. The cable operator immediately upped his download speed to at least twice that (possible for a cable TV operator, though pushing closer to the limit than might be comfortable, depending on how the network is built—some hybrid fiber-coax (HFC) networks are now offering download speeds exceeding 100 Mb/s). So it looked like a 15-year-old HFC network was trumping a new FTTH network. Nothing was farther from the truth, but rather, the FTTH operator was losing the speed race as a result of his own short-sighted policy. To give you a concrete example, as we have been writing this, we have also had occasion to upload and download several large video files. Using our cable modem connection, we are consistently seeing downstream speeds of exceeding 60 Mb/s and upload speeds greater than 5 Mb/s to Internet locations not under the control of our cable operator. We just checked again, and on our local HFC network (not going over the Internet), we got 90 Mb/s downstream and 12 Mb/s upstream (experience has shown that we are unlikely to experience this over the Internet, but speeds are still fast). We are not even buying the provider's fastest package. Cable has a faster modem technology in the works (DOCSIS 3.1), though it may strain some operators to find the spectrum required to take full advantage of its speed. So let that set the bar for what you have to beat. You will beat HFC every time if you take full advantage of the technology you have, but if you get too conservative in how you deploy it, you may find yourself in second place in terms of speed.

TYPES OF ORGANIZATIONS BUILDING FTTH NETWORKS

Depending on the location, a number of different types of organizations may be building FTTH networks. Large telephone and cable TV companies have built them, but in North America, with a few notable exceptions, the majority of construction to-date has been done by smaller telephone companies, municipalities (often through owned utility operations), and independent for-profit utility companies. The cable TV industry is embracing FTTH, first for business application, then later for residential. Depending on what type of organization you are, you may have different payback time expectations for the investment, you may have access to capital under widely different conditions, and you may have different nonfinancial needs. For example, municipalities have built networks in order to attract new business and hence jobs to their communities, and we know of a number of cases in which this has been successful. So even if the FTTH system takes a long time to pay back, a municipality may be satisfied with the investment. But if you are a stockholder firm, you will not be all that impressed with the result if you don't get payback in a shorter time.

Without naming the systems, we shall describe several successful but different early systems built in different countries, with widely differing financial and technical models.[i]

System 1: US Municipal Electric System

As the state's oldest municipal electric system, and the first system in the state to receive power from the Tennessee Valley Authority, System 1 has a unique and unrivaled history of service. The municipality was voted an All-America City in 1993, with its industry-friendly environment and its beautiful country-side setting located near a major Interstate corridor. The Electric System currently serves nearly 15,000 customers and operates 1242 miles of line throughout the county.

In 2006 they decided to expand their service to include video, voice, and data. Initially they had planned to use the GPON standard, but their construction plans preceded the widespread availability of GPON equipment, so they decided to go with EPON, with a system that would allow them to change later if they needed to (they continue to operate the original EPON system).

The system is based on conventional broadcast video. Video is received on their own antenna farm and locally processed to both analog and digital broadcast video, which is modulated onto a 1550-nm optical carrier and amplified in Erbium Doped Fiber Amplifiers (EDFAs) as needed. Their contracted voice over internet protocol (VoIP) softswitch and peering to the public switched telephone network are located in a large metropolitan area about 220 miles to the southeast. Redundant dedicated circuits and core routers ensure reliable connection. Quality Internet connectivity was available locally.

System 2: Incumbent Local Exchange Carrier, Small European Country

As the official public telecommunications company of this small European country, this *local exchange carrier* (LEC) was formed as a public company for the management and exploitation of telecommunications and broadcasting networks for the people of that country. With a population of approximately 82,000, the country attributes its prosperity mainly to tourism, with 11 million tourists annually attracted by the many winter and ski resorts. The LEC currently serves nearly 47,000 customers and is the primary provider of POTS (plain old telephone service), data, video, mobile services, and full DVB-T (terrestrial broadcasting) radio and television broadcast.

Early in 2007, they decided to transition their existing voice, video, and data services from a traditional copper network with some dedicated fiber connectivity, to an FTTH architecture servicing each of its points of service (both business and residential). At the time, the LEC was managing a multitude of different network architectures and technologies, which had grown over the years as technologies changed and more bandwidth was required for the subscriber. With them being responsible for the national telecommunications infrastructure, universal services must be offered to 100% of the subscriber base in this rather mountainous region of Europe. As a result, they were faced with a rather extensive operational network, which was difficult to bring under a single management system.

Pressure to expand their video offerings, along with the complexity of their operational model, encouraged them to move to an all-fiber passive network to each of their wireline customers. As with the first example, they began the deployment of their network using EPON technology, choosing a system which will allow them to transition to other technologies with little impact to their overall operational or service models should they want to later (they continue to expand this system).

The network is based on a Next-Generation Network (NGN) architecture providing all services, POTS (serving existing analog telephones, based on VoIP within the network), voice (serving IP telephones), video, and data, over an all-IP-over-Ethernet implementation. Video is received from content providers at the LEC's facilities and encoded into MPEG-4 for high definition and MPEG-2 for standard definition, for transmission as internet protocol television (IPTV) over the FTTH network. Voice services are provided locally with a dedicated VoIP softswitch located in their central office, with peering to their public switched telephone network. Eventually, they will be transitioning all voice services, both POTS and cellular, to a single IMS voice platform, allowing for a complete integration of services between both technologies. The LEC provides redundant service interfaces to external service providers in two adjacent countries.

System 3: Northern European Municipal Power Utility

The city dates back to the early 13th century and has historically been a maritime region due to its ease of accessibility to the shipping channels throughout northern Europe and the Baltic States. It is also the headquarters of the subject major utility company which provides connectivity to a total of 30,000 electrical customers.

Early in 2005, the Board of Directors commissioned a separate entity to be managed by the Board, to roll out telecommunication services to their servicing community. The separate entity had a mission to provide voice, video, broadband, and mobile services to the community as an alternative to existing services. In the case of mobile services, they decided to make an agreement with a local leading mobile provider as a reseller, providing direct billing and customer support. With the remaining service options to be offered, the team made a decision to initially outsource voice and data services, allowing their team to focus on deploying the network infrastructure and building out an RF video headend. Additional video was provided by a third party. Initially a trap system was used to control the distribution of premium video. Later premium video was transitioned to IPTV using the data portion of the FTTH network. The IPTV content was provided by a third-party provider, and interfaced at their Internet point-of-presence.

They began with the installation of a core network utilizing their electrical sub-stations as the nodes on their network. From each of these nodes, the optical line terminal (OLT) equipment was installed with an all-passive architecture from each of these points to the customers. As an additional benefit of this architecture, they were able to actively monitor the health of each of the substations, allowing them better visibility into the possible failure of electrical services.

For the first 2 years of the deployment, they utilized a third-party service provider for both POTS and broadband services. These two areas of expertise were critical pieces of their service offering and they didn't want to take on more than they could support, as they were new to being a telecommunications provider. As the network began to grow and they were able to focus efforts on becoming a telecommunications provider, they chose to support all services directly, with the purchase of a Voice softswitch and media gateway, as well as providing redundant connections to local Internet service providers (ISPs) in their region.

System 4: US Municipality-Owned Utility

This system was a very early adopter of FTTH, preceding even the EPON standard—it used a prestandard system much like the EPON system that would be ready a few years later. As of this writing, the system has been in use for about a dozen years, and the utility is contemplating changing it out for a standards-based system so that they can offer advanced services not available that long ago.

The utility operated electric, water, and wastewater services in this town of some 20,000 residences, and at the time it decided to install FTTH, was being underserved by a large telephone company and a large cable MSO (Multiple System Operator—a large company owning a number of cable TV systems), neither of which expressed particular interest in providing updated telecommunication services. So the utility decided that since it owned the poles, and had a good bit of experience with their internal data network, it could build an FTTH system and take over much of the business of the incumbents. Now sometimes we have seen this attitude as a recipe for problems. But in this case, the utility invested sufficiently, and hired expertise from the telecommunications and cable TV industries, and they have been very successful.

Initially they ran into problems from a local ISP, who sued to stop the build. The ISP was dial-up-based at the time and was concerned that faster FTTH connections would decimate his business (a given, considering what has happened in the intervening years). The solution was to initially allow the ISP to be the

Internet and voice provider on the FTTH network, while the utility became the video provider. Later another third party was a data and voice provider for a short time, but was bought out by the utility, who then became the second data and voice provider on the network. This is about the only known case in North America of multiple service providers on the same network, though that model has become fairly common in parts of Europe and the Far East.

THE DECISION-MAKING PROCESS

The decision to build an FTTH network can lead to great success, but it can also lead to failure and disappointment (to say nothing of lost jobs) if not done properly. There are business, technology, and organizational factors to consider. A lot will depend on where you are now—what applicable resources you have available, what resources you will hire, and what resources you will contract. This section is written assuming that you are a new entrant into the triple play telecommunications area. If you are already a player, you may know much of this already.

Business Considerations

As we said earlier, the first thing is to understand the services that are available now from other providers, and your own service if you are already a provider. If you build a system, how will your competitors respond? We have seen competitors respond by cutting prices, and/or improving their service. We have also seen competitors respond by essentially conceding the race, closing local offices, and serving their declining subscriber base out of other offices. Whatever the response, it will affect you, either positively or negatively. If you are a smaller region and your potential competitors are large national telephone and cable operators, and if their local plant is old, they may not have that much interest in competing. On the other hand, if your area is attractive enough to them, they may decide to stand and fight, and they will have the resources to do it. Getting to know their local managers may give you some insight as to their likely response to you.

We know of one case currently in the early stages of planning, which expects to serve an underserved area. In parts of the proposed service area, there are a few very small cable TV systems with ancient plant, who have expressed interest in coming onto the FTTH network. They see that as more cost-effective than upgrading their old plant.

You must provide service to the subscribers that exceeds that of the competition, at a good price, and that price must provide you with the return on investment that you need. Since there are so many variables, we shall refrain from trying to provide a cookie-cutter approach to the service and financial model. However, if you can't do the models yourself, you absolutely need to hire a good consultant (and they are out there) who can help you with the model.

So the first decision is about services to be offered at what price point, in order to be competitive with other providers, even if they answer you by cutting their prices or improving their services. And, of course, you need a realistic assessment of your own costs to build the system, and your likely penetration. You may want to do customer surveys to get a better estimate of the number of subscribers likely to move to your service.

Of course you need valid estimates of equipment and construction costs, which can vary significantly from one location to another, and depending on how much plant will be underground versus aerial. For aerial plant, how much make-ready is needed before you can start construction? If you don't have this expertise in-house, it is available for hire. Don't forget the cost of drops to each subscriber. This can be a very significant expense in built-up areas. In *greenfields* (new subdivisions), you want to get in early while trenches are open, and then the installation cost of drops will be much lower.

Your operational expenses (op-ex) will be lower than those of your competition because fiber plant is much, much more economical to operate. But it will not be zero. People have been known to cut fibers when burying other cables ("backhoe fade") and vehicles still hit telephone poles and snap cables. Subscribers get confused about how to use their equipment and often expect free help from the service provider. There will be expenses for customer service representatives, whether in-house or contracted, and on-going expenses for Internet and telephone interconnect, and for video service. On rare occasions, equipment will break. A frequent source of service interruption is improperly cleaned fiber optic connections.

Technology Considerations

There are a number of technical decisions that must be made early in planning the network. Some can change later, but there must be decisions made early-on in order to reduce the inefficiencies that will develop later if they are not made. One decision is what services to carry. The three fundamental services, the so-called triple play, are video, voice, and data. Unless you have some very unusual circumstances, you should plan on carrying all three. Otherwise, you seriously risk being outperformed by someone with lesser technology. Experience has shown that the more services you sell to a particular subscriber, the "stickier" that subscriber tends to be. And keeping a subscriber is a lot less expensive than acquiring one.

We have seen some systems attempt to launch without, say, a video service. The rationale is that it is relatively hard to get a video service started if you are unfamiliar with it (those familiar with video will find it not hard at all), and the profit margin on video is not what it is for voice and data, depending on how you account for your network costs. So the thought has been to just let people use over-the-top (OTT) video services, video from the likes of Netflix, Hulu,

Amazon, and others. We certainly agree that there is a lot of interest in these services now, and that interest is likely to continue to build for a while. But the amount of conventional linear TV viewing is also growing, and accounts for many more hours of TV watching than does OTT. Video is a service that almost every subscriber understands and wants.

You will have a choice of either broadcast video as the cable companies do it now, using a 1550-nm overlay, or using IPTV. The choice in many cases will depend on what businesses you are in now and where your comfort point is. The nice thing about FTTH is that you have the widest range of options of any provider. You can start with a broadcast service and migrate some or all programming over to IPTV if it makes sense. Or you can provide premium service over IPTV, while operating a broadcast service for those not wanting premium service, and you will be able to service those people without any of your capital [in the form of set-top boxes (STBs)] in the subscribers' homes.

In the early days of discussions about delivering various digital services, there used to be a saying that "a bit is a bit is a bit," meaning that you could treat all services equally, operating one network for all of your services. Experience has shown this to be a very false and dangerous assumption, one which has gotten a number of people into serious trouble. Yes, you can operate all services on one network, but it is not easy, and you cannot do it with bargain-basement switching equipment. Nor can the equipment be configured by anyone other than an expert who knows the pitfalls and how to avoid them (he has probably learned that by falling into the pit more than once). We have seen many people who were "pretty good" voice and/or data operators get themselves into trouble by thinking that they were ready to provide triple play over an all-IP network. We have also seen people who did know what they were doing, and who were willing to make the requisite investment, be very successful with a single-network triple play.

Even people who can successfully set up their headend to provide reliable IP triple play have encountered unexpected expenses at the home. Most homes in North America and other places have been wired for coaxial cable (*coax*, the cable TV physical medium), which can be used by the FTTH operator if he is providing broadcast video service (under FCC rules, in most cases the coax belongs to the homeowner, even if a previous service provider installed it). But if you are providing IPTV service, you are going to have to get Ethernet from the ONT to the STB on the subscriber's TV. You can do this by installing cat. 5 cable, or you can add data-over-coax adaptors (MoCA or HPNA), or if you're feeling lucky, you can install wireless data (WiFi), but all of these solutions are going to cost you money in every home.

On the other hand, most video service beyond basic TV requires two-way communications between the STB and the headend. There are ways to accommodate this using a broadcast tier on FTTH, sometimes at a very economical cost, and sometimes at a less economical cost, depending on the STB system chosen and the FTTH vendor. Providing two-way communications using IPTV comes naturally, at no additional cost.

Those Hidden Extras

There are a couple of hidden extras that you will likely hit that are not that bad once you know about them and how to handle them, but at first they may cause you headaches if you are not prepared.

If you offer video, you will likely need an audio override system. This is required of cable TV systems, such that in an emergency, a government official can quickly take over the audio of all your channels, to broadcast emergency messages. Commercial equipment is available to make this happen. We got a reminder of this while writing this chapter, listening to cable-delivered music in the background. All of a sudden the music was interrupted for an Amber Alert for an abducted child in the area. (We are pleased to say that the child was found unharmed the next day.)

There is a Congressional Act known as *CALEA*, the *Communications Assistance for Law Enforcement Act*, also known as Lawful Intercept. Under judicial supervision, law enforcement personnel can get certain call records from you, and can also get specified internet traffic. In order to comply with the law, most smaller organizations contract with so-called *Trusted Third Parties* (TTPs), who can assist in properly configuring your switching equipment, and who will receive and process lawful demands for data. There are several TTPs from which to choose.

Organizational Considerations

We have previously alluded to doing an objective assessment of the organizational skills you have versus those you will need. We have seen a number of new players struggle because they misunderstood the match between the skills they had and those they needed. Since every situation is different, we cannot give you a list of skills you lack. Rather, we can maybe point out some issues we have seen in over 12 years of helping subscribers roll out FTTH systems, and a lot of years prior to that helping people roll out other technologies.

You may have the best engineer in the world for managing your SCADA network if you are doing that now. But does he know how to configure your entire data network so that it will pass voice with low latency and jitter? Can he evaluate your network for integrity of IPTV, during times when you have lots of channel surfing because the big game half your subscribers are watching just went to commercial? Remember that "a bit is not a bit is not a bit."

If you are the new entrant to the triple play service, you will be expected to meet a higher bar for good service than do the entrenched players. Understanding the economic difficulty faced by small entities, we strongly urge you to have a lab set-up identical to your deployed ("production") network. If this is impossible due to economics, at least you need an isolated PON in your lab that you can equip whenever you need to deploy new hardware or software. There are so many ways to configure networks, and so many ways that disparate pieces of equipment can interact, that it is imperative to test a new configuration before deploying it to subscribers.

If you have not served residential consumers previously, you will be surprised by what you find in homes. You will need installers who have good people skills as well as who understand all aspects of the services you are offering. Some operators do initial configuration of a consumer's data equipment as part of their service, others offer it as a revenue center for extra charge. You will want to think about how you will service your subscribers' equipment, and what the revenue model for that will be. And be sure to factor in customer service people.

INDUSTRY ORGANIZATION

You can never learn too much. One of your first moves should be to get involved with the FTTH industry by joining the FTTH Council.[ii] This is the industry's primary organization of all parties who are active in the field. They sponsor an annual conference, which offers training seminars, a chance to meet vendors, and a chance to meet and learn from those who have already put in systems. CDs from earlier conferences should be available for purchase, and more recent conference proceedings are online for members. Through the Council you will be able to access statistics related to FTTH installations, and you will have access to training, both Council-originated and through external commercial training resources. Many consulting engineers are members, as are equipment vendors.

While not strictly an FTTH organization, there is a commercial magazine and conference organizer, Broadband Communities,[iii] which offers additional information of interest to people installing FTTH.

There are many consulting engineering firms who can help with everything from preparing budgets to overseeing construction of the network. They tend to work best for you when you can give them as much information as possible regarding what you want to do, and your realistic estimates of penetration. They can help you do trade-offs such as deciding how to offer video, and they may be able to spare you grief in getting your VoIP system working. You can locate some of them through the FTTH Council.

Endnotes

i. Some of the examples are taken from James Farmer and Kevin Bourg, Practical deployment of passive optical networks. IEEE Communications Magazine 2008.

ii. http://www.ftthcouncil.org/.

iii. http://www.bbpmag.com/.

2

FTTx Technologies

CHAPTER 3

EPON

INTRODUCTION

In Chapter 1 we introduced the main types of FTTx networks in use or proposed for use in the near future. You may want to refer back to Fig. 1.3 of Chapter 1. In this chapter we shall talk about the most widely deployed technology, the IEEE's EPON standard, which gained an early lead in the Asia–Pacific region. EPON is also known as GE-PON (Gigabit Ethernet Passive Optical Network) and EFM (Ethernet in the First Mile). Some of us with cable TV backgrounds tend to think of the PON as being the last mile, because we draw networks with the headend on the left and the home on the right, and think of signals flowing left to right. On the other hand, telephone people tend to draw the home on the left and the central office on the right, and again think of signals flowing left to right. This makes the PON the first mile. There was debate within the IEEE about which way to look at it, and first mile won. So we won't quibble with the term *First Mile* rather than *Last Mile*.

Some people refer to the standard as GE-PON, but the IEEE 802.3 standard, which governs all of Ethernet including PONs, uses the terminology *EPON* and *EFM*. The 802.3av 10 Gb/s EPON standard (a newer and faster standard, described below) does use the terminology 1G-EPON and 10G-EPON to distinguish the older technology from the newer. We are seeing fewer people use the term EFM, so we are going to choose to refer to the technology as EPON (1 Gb/s standard or generic for both speeds) or 10G-EPON, as appropriate. We will use 1G-EPON if needed for clarity.

EPON is an integral part of the 802.3 Ethernet standard, and making it so caused a couple of interesting wrinkles during development of the standard.[i] EPON covers not only PON, the primary subject of this book, but also covers twisted pair and point-to-point systems (often called *active Ethernet*). We shall not cover twisted pair implementations, and shall pay scant attention to point-to-point, even though there have been such systems built.

The 1550-nm broadcast overlay, being essentially the same in both EPON and GPON, is not covered to any significant extent in this chapter, with one exception (a crosstalk issue introduced later). Some GPON advocates at one time advanced the hypothesis that EPON didn't allow for a broad-cast overlay because the standard does not explicitly say that 1550 nm is reserved for broadcast. But those who participated in the development of the EPON standard understood that 1550 nm was being reserved for this use, without excluding any other uses that may develop in the future. For example the 1550-nm overlay, using current cable TV digital modulation techniques, could be used as an auxiliary 6-Gb/s downstream data channel if desired. Many EPON systems using the 1550-nm band for broadcast are in use today.

From a user's standpoint, you may see very little difference between GPON and EPON, because there is usually an element management system (EMS) with which you will interact, and the EMS will hide most or all of the PON-specific variation from you. However, it is useful to understand some of the basic concepts of the systems in order to comprehend what you can and cannot do within the standards, and there may be times when understanding this material could help understand some unexpected behavior. So this chapter will attempt to summarize the important points regarding EPON that you might need to know in operating a system, though by no means will it make you an expert in EPON—if you want that expertise, see the end notes.

EPON AND VARIATIONS

So far we have described the physical implementation of the PON, but there are layers of implementation on top of the physical implementation. All of the technologies support optional RF broadcast on a 1550-nm optical carrier. Refer back to Fig. 1.3 as we go through this list.

- EPON: This is the original IEEE specification, which has found a lot of application in the Far East, its major market, and some application in the Americas and Europe. It became available after BPON and before GPON, and features a data rate of 1 Gb/s in each direction. As this is being written, the North American cable television industry is developing extended standards based on EPON. The EPON specification was done within the IEEE 802.3 Subcommittee, by the ad hoc 802.3ah Working Group. Sometimes you will see it referred to as 802.3ah, but officially it is just part of the 802.3 Ethernet standard.
- 2.5 EPON: this is not really a standard, but is offered by some manufacturers. It is EPON implemented at roughly GPON speeds, and uses GPON optics. Sometimes it is referred to as *Turbo EPON*.
- 10G-EPON: This is the newest of the IEEE standards, and offers downstream data at 10 Gb/s and upstream at either 1 or 10 Gb/s. In order to maintain backwards compatibility with the original EPON standard, it uses 1577 nm for downstream data and 1270 nm for

upstream data. We shall discuss wavelengths in Chapter 6. 10G-EPON was developed by the 802.3av Working Group, and is a part of the 802.3 Ethernet standard.

- SIEPON[ii] is not really a new version of EPON, but rather is a bridge to extend the abilities of EPON to meet the needs of commercial data carriers, as opposed to enterprise (institutional) use. We will say more about SIEPON below.
- There are several efforts within the cable TV community to bridge the gap between existing hybrid fiber-coax (HFC) technology and PON technology. The problem is that the industry would like to be moving toward PON, but as always there is no blank sheet of paper, and you need a practical, economical way of getting from here to there. At the risk of becoming prematurely obsolete, we list the efforts that are on-going as of this writing.
  - *Radio frequency over glass (RFoG)*: This is a very different PON implementation, but it uses the same fiber configuration, with different equipment on the ends. It is really not EPON, but we include it here because some see it leading toward cable TV-specific profiles of EPON currently being worked on. RFoG was standardized by the Society of Cable Telecommunications Engineers (SCTE).[iii] It is deployed. The downstream signal is the 1550-nm optical signal modulated with a complete complement of video as used in a cable TV system and DOCSIS data (including voice). The upstream signal originates from an analog laser at each home endpoint (called an *R-ONU*). The upstream laser turns on only when upstream RF, from a set top box or cable modem, is detected. The upstream laser wavelength may be either 1310 nm if the operator is not concerned about compatibility with other PON technology, or 1610 nm if compatibility with other PON technology is required. RFoG is usually seen as a bridge to EPON technology, enabling the operator to use existing termination equipment, while offering some of the advantages of fiber-to-the-home (FTTH) now, and more later with complete conversion to EPON. For example, if a cable operator has a new subdivision developing, he can put FTTH physical architecture in, and for now "light it" using RFoG, since that minimizes new equipment needed at the headend or home, and minimizes new training for the craft people. RFoG will be covered in Chapter 5.
  - *DOCSIS provisioning of EPON (DPoE)*: This is an effort by Cable Television Laboratories (CableLabs)[iv] to develop management of EPON such that existing DOCSIS management systems can be used to manage EPON systems too. It also seeks to implement many of the services defined in the IEEE SIEPON effort, maybe in a more

cost-effective manner. It uses either 1 or 10 Gb/s EPON systems with minor modification to the IEEE specification.

■ *EPON Protocol over Coax (EPoC)*: This is an IEEE effort (in liaison with Cable Television Laboratories) to run EPON over the fiber portion of an HFC network, and then convert to RF on coaxial cable. This allows a cable operator to begin offering the features of FTTH before he has updated his entire physical network to the newer technology.

EPON KEY FEATURES

EPON is promulgated by the Institute of Electrical and Electronics Engineers[v] (IEEE), headquartered in New Jersey, USA. It is a privately run professional organization consisting of individual members and their employers. Some years ago, its 802 (LAN/MAN Standards) Committee took on the task of maintaining and expanding the original Ethernet standard, which was first developed at the Xerox Palo Alto Research Center (PARC) in 1973–1974. The first 802 Ethernet standard was approved in December 1982, and owing to its continuing progress, wide acceptance, and economy (partly due to scale), Ethernet has become the most widely deployed data communications standard in the world. IEEE's approach has been to specify the minimum necessary to make things interoperate (keep it simple—KISS). The organization restricts itself generally to the two lowest layers of the ISO 7-layer model, which is widely used to categorize data communications systems. It is left to the marketplace to fill in the missing pieces, using or developing other standards as appropriate. With strong leadership of various working groups, it has been possible to produce new versions of the standard very quickly; hence the several-year lead enjoyed by 10G-EPON compared with the ITU standardization XG-PON effort. This KISS model has generally worked pretty well for the IEEE, but did result in some "holes" that had to be plugged in order to make the EPON system fully functional for commercial telecommunications. As a result, the IEEE formed the SIEPON (P1904.1) Working Group[vi] to address the issues.

This chapter is not intended to make you an expert in all aspects of EPON technology. Rather, it is intended to give you enough understanding of the characteristics that proper configuration of systems will make sense, and it should give you a better understanding of the reason something didn't work as you expected.

Speed

EPON operates at 1 Gb/s in both directions, though there is a private extension of the standard to let it work at approximately GPON speeds, which some manufacturers offer on some products. By contrast, maximum GPON speeds are 2.488 Gb/s downstream and 1.244 Gb/s upstream. The second generation of EPON (10G-EPON) operates at 10 Gb/s downstream and either 1 or 10 Gb/s upstream. This standard is complete, and equipment is on the market. As we shall see in the next chapter, GPON has also developed 10 Gb/s standards, under the name XG-PON.

DC Elimination and Clock Synchronization

Of necessity, there can be no dc component in the transmitted signal. That is, when measured over some time, the number of 0s and the number of 1s transmitted must be equal. If this criterion is not met, then the optical components on each end of the link get into trouble. Furthermore, it is imperative that a minimum number of transitions occur in the transmitted signal, in order to ensure synchronization of the data clock at the receiver. EPON employs a substitution method to ensure that this happens. For every 8 bits (1 byte), a 10-bit symbol is substituted, hence the name *8b/10b encoding*. The substituted 10-bit symbol is chosen to have very close to an equal number of 1s and 0s and three to eight transitions per symbol. The codes satisfy the requirement of no dc component in the signal, and the large number of transitions ensures clock synchronization. Furthermore, since a limited number of the available codes are used, the encoding provides another way to detect transmission errors. The penalty is that, since 10 bits must be transmitted to represent 8 bits, the bandwidth required is increased by 25%. For instance, in a gigabit Ethernet system, the payload plus protocol data are transmitted at 1 Gb/s, but because of 8b/10b encoding, the data rate on the fiber (the so-called *wire rate*) is 1.25 Gb/s.

Table 3.1 illustrates a few of the many valid code-groups used in Gigabit Ethernet systems. The two columns labeled *Current RD–* and *Current RD+* represent two so-called *running disparity* sets. The running disparity rules change the transmitted value from one column to the other based on certain conditions related to the number of 1s or 0s that have been transmitted in the previous code group. These rules ensure that there is no dc content and that there is not a long string of like binary digits, thus ensuring reliable clock recovery.[vii]

Table 3.1 Example 8b/10b Valid Data Code-Groups

Code Group Name	Octet Value	Octet Bits HGF EDCBA	Current RD– abcdei fghj	Current RD+ abcdei fghj
D0.0	00	000 00000	100111 0100	011000 1011
D1.0	01	000 00001	011101 0100	100010 1011
D2.0	02	000 00010	101101 0100	010010 1011
D3.0	03	000 00011	110001 1011	110001 0100

Ten Gb/s Ethernet systems, including 10G-EPON, use a more efficient 64b/66b encoding, in which 64 bits of data are replaced by a 66-bit transmitted data block, for a data rate overhead of just over 3% rather than 25%. This substitution still provides data and adequate control characters, with good error detection.[viii]

You don't get something for nothing, as we're sure you already know. The extra overhead caused by 64b/66b encoding, and much more so with 8b/10b encoding, requires the optical components to run faster than they would run otherwise. This tends to increase the signal-to-noise ratio (discussed in Chapter 6) required, and also tends to somewhat exacerbate the effects of dispersion in the fiber (also discussed in Chapter 6). But Ethernet and other systems have a long history of being able to live with this overhead, and it does permit simplifications elsewhere, in terms of automatic gain control (AGC) settling and clock synchronization time. GPON, by contrast, uses a scrambling method, which we'll explain in Chapter 4. It doesn't impose the speed overhead, but does cost in other areas such as AGC settling and clock synchronization.

Encryption

GPON specified the downstream encryption to be used, whereas EPON does not address that issue. However, EPON players are coalescing around standard encryption technologies. Commercial chips are being made with AES128 CFB and/or Triple Churning (CTC) downstream encryption built in. A general introduction to the subject of encryption is found in Appendix B.

Flow Control Versus Multipoint Control Protocol

While we think it is an important topic, we are not emphasizing the 7-layer ISO model in this book, because frequent reference to the model is not necessary for a practical book which seeks to show you how to efficiently operate a plant. However, some references to it are necessary in order to understand the technology, and to be conversant with others. When things don't work as expected, you need enough of the theory in order to figure out what is happening. In describing EPON, we now come to one of those moments when it is necessary. The second layer from the bottom of the ISO 7-layer model is the *data link layer*. For modern networks, the data link layer has been divided into two sublayers, the *logical link layer* and below it the *media access control* (MAC). It is at the MAC and in the lowest layer, the physical layer, that Ethernet is defined. The 802.3ah Working Group that developed 1 Gb/s EPON wanted the standard to remain part of Ethernet rather than to become something else, for a number of good reasons. However, this did present some interesting problems.

MAC itself has a control sublayer (yeah, maybe a control sublayer of a control sublayer). Prior to 802.3ah, the function of the MAC control sublayer was *flow control*. If the receiver filled up with data and could not take more, flow control sent a *PAUSE* signal to the transmitter, causing it to cease transmission until the receiver could accept more data. But for EPON, the MAC control sublayer has to do just the opposite: it has to enable transmission for a predetermined length of time, as shown in Appendix A. In order to do this, flow control was expanded to add the *multipoint control protocol* (MPCP). Traditional flow control and MPCP do the opposite; flow control stops a data flow if the receiver cannot accept it, and MPCP initiates data transmission for a predetermined time period. In order to do this, MPCP has to have a *bandwidth assignment mode* in which it grants bandwidth for each optical network terminal (ONT). It also has an *autodiscovery mode*, which allows discovery of newly activated ONTs.

Discovering the New Guy

A new ONT coming online is recognized by the OLT using an *MPCP handshake*. Periodically the OLT sends a *discovery GATE* message, asking any unregistered ONTs to announce themselves. When the OLT receives the *REGISTER REQ* message that the ONT sends in response to the GATE message, and the OLT approves the ONT, then the OLT sends a *REGISTER* message to the ONT. The ONT sends back a *REGISTER_ACK* message, which completes the registration process.

Part of the registration process described in the previous paragraph is to measure the round-trip delay to the new ONT. The propagation time of the signal through the fiber is not insignificant—a PON may be 20 km long, maybe longer, and the round-trip delay in a 20-km PON is about 220 μs, which at a data rate of 1 Gb/s, represents 220 kb of data, or about 18 maximum-length Ethernet frames. In order to get good efficiency in the upstream direction, the transmit time of each ONT must be advanced by an appropriate amount such that its signal arrives at the OLT at the appropriate time. The OLT measures this time and advances the transmit time it assigns to the ONT appropriately.

After Discovery

After the ONT is discovered, it sends *REPORT* messages telling the OLT how much data it needs to send upstream. The OLT gathers this information from all ONTs, takes into consideration how much bandwidth each ONT is allocated (by contract), and assigns upstream transmission times for each ONT. It sends *GATE* messages to the ONTs giving them their upstream transmission time assignments.

Logical Link Identifier

Now we come to a topic to which we will return later when we discuss cable TV extensions to EPON. It is a very important part of the EPON protocol for an operator to understand. We already have several ways that we might identify an individual ONT: a globally unique *MAC address* is assigned at the factory to everything Ethernet, and is carried with the equipment over its life (there frequently will be several MAC addresses in one piece of equipment). Then for most purposes today, a device receives an *IP address*, usually when it registers on a network, but sometimes it is assigned by the network operator in advance. But in EPON we deal with yet another address, the *logical link identifier* (LLID). At first, it seems strange that we would need yet another address, but there is actually a good reason for it. That reason stems from the fundamental difference between legacy Ethernet networks and PONs.

PtP Ethernet Versus PON

We assume you are familiar with at least the basics of the Ethernet protocol. There are fundamental differences in the operation of EPON and of normal Ethernet, which we should cover here. In order to retain EPON as part of the Ethernet standard, it was deemed necessary to NOT change any specification of the behavior of normal Ethernet systems. Yet there were a few things that PONs must do which other Ethernet systems do not have to do. This conundrum was resolved by adding a layer of protocol at the bottom of the data link layer to reconcile the two. The problem is that EPON systems have more than one device connected to the same physical port at the OLT, and there was no way to accommodate this within Ethernet as it was known before PONs. We shall eventually see the resolution of the conundrum was later extended to DPoE when the cable TV industry became interested in managing EPON as if it was DOCSIS. We are spending a good bit of space on this topic because it is important for people who understand Ethernet to understand the modifications needed to make it work in a PON.

Fig. 3.1 is a complex diagram showing the problems. At the top is a rather conventional Ethernet system, with three computers in each of two *access domains*. Computers in an access domain are connected by a switch, which can let any two computers in the access domain communicate with each other. The switch is a *point-to-point* (*P2P* or *PtP*) device, with a direct one-to-one connection with each computer. It receives a packet from one computer with an MAC *destination address* of another computer in the access domain, and the switch sends that packet to that destination computer. If the switch receives a packet with an MAC address it doesn't recognize, it sends the packet to all ports except the one from which it received that MAC address, and if and when it gets a response, then knows to which port that MAC address is attached, and the correspondence between port and MAC address is remembered for future use. In modern Ethernet systems with all P2P connections as shown in Fig. 3.1A, there is continuous data transmission in each direction, with short, repetitive null messages being sent when there are no data to be communicated. Continuous transmission in each direction is required so that receive clocks can all stay locked all the time, ready to receive data packets.

Typical enterprise networks are operated with multiple access domains interconnected by *bridges*, one of which is shown in the center. There are a number

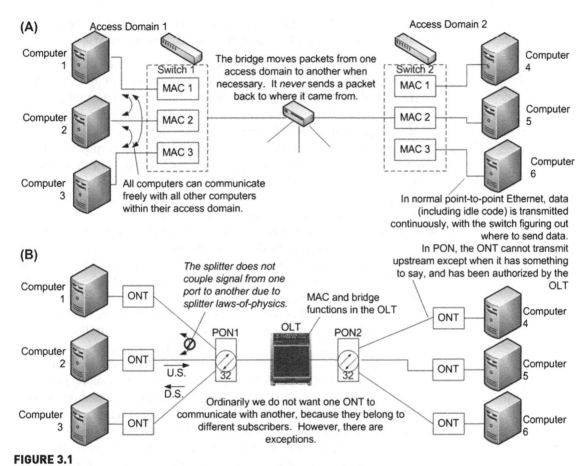

FIGURE 3.1
Comparison of conventional Ethernet and EPON functionality. (A) The way traditional P2P Ethernet is defined to work. (B) The way a PON needs to work.

of reasons as to why you might not want all computers in your network to be in the same access domain. Each department has its own access domain, potentially speeding up service, as one switch does not risk being a bottleneck. Also, there may be confidential information being exchanged in one department (maybe legal or finance), which for security reasons should not be available to other departments except on a need-to-know basis. A bridge is similar to a switch except that it can learn multiple MAC addresses on a port. But again, when it gets a packet in, it never sends a packet out on the port on which it was received. (In modern networks, the switch and bridge functions may be subsumed into one piece of equipment.)

Compare Fig. 3.1A with Fig. 3.1B, which shows corresponding PON components below those in Fig. 3.1A. We look at each PON here as being an access domain, since they are all connected to the same port on the OLT (which subsumes the functions of the switch and the bridge, among other functions). We find a number of differences between a PON and the Ethernet system above it.

- The communications medium between the OLT and the ONTs has vastly different characteristics than does the P2P medium of Fig. 3.1A. The only thing between the single central termination (the OLT) and the multiple edge terminations (ONTs) is passive optical fiber, including splitting. Downstream packets (from OLT to ONTs) are split and appear at the network interface of each ONT, which must reject all packets except those intended for it. Upstream signals (from the ONTs to the OLT) ONLY appear at the OLT interface. Except for a (usually) negligible amount of signal leakage, the upstream optical signal from one ONT does not appear at another ONT.
- It is impossible for upstream communications (from ONT to OLT) to take place continuously. In the upstream direction, only one ONT must talk at a time, managed by the OLT. This means that there must be some guard time between upstream transmissions (discussed elsewhere), and there must be synchronization time.
- In the downstream direction, each ONT on the PON "sees" all of the downstream data, not just the data intended for it. The ONT must reject the data not intended for it. However, in that downstream "pipe," there may be several data streams intended for one ONT. For instance, there may be email being delivered, while a voice call is taking place, while someone else is watching a TV show delivered over the Internet. Provision must be made for all of these and more to happen.
- While computers in an access domain of Fig. 3.1A are free to communicate with each other, we often do *not* want ONTs on the same PON to communicate directly with each other. The reason is that the ONTs are generally not part of the same enterprise, but rather are owned by independent subscribers, who do not want their neighbors prying on their network.
  - Having said that, though, there are a few exceptions. Among them is a voice-over-Internet-Protocol phone call (VoIP), where voice packets should be sent between ONTs over the most efficient path possible, up to the OLT and back down. Another case in which we may want two ONTs to talk to each other is if they are in two locations of the same enterprise, such as at two nearby commonly owned car dealers or two nearby locations of the same bank. So there must be some way to configure the OLT to either connect two or more ONTs in the same access domain, or to NOT connect them. (Usually, traffic that is to flow directly between two ONTs via the OLT is placed into a VLAN [a *virtual local area network*], which the system is configured to pass directly. Only the traffic placed in the VLAN is allowed to pass directly.)

- In the case of IPTV we would like to have the same program packet go to more than one ONT if the same program is being watched simultaneously in more than one home. This is called *multicasting*, and is key to distributing video efficiently on a data network.

In order to accommodate all of these requirements, which differ from the normal operation of Ethernet, the 802.3ah Working Group that developed the original EPON standard had to add to the Ethernet standard in a way that didn't require the Ethernet components to behave differently than previously. This was done by adding LLIDs between the layer where Ethernet performed its many useful duties, and the physical layer (in our case, an optical transport layer). Thus, after "conventional Ethernet" thinks a packet is ready to be transmitted, the LLID "takes over" and adapts that packet for the PON medium. Then on the receive end, the physical transport hands the packet to the LLID, which converts it into something that normal Ethernet processing can understand. This can be done without adding any extra bits to the packet, because Ethernet packets include 16 bits for clock synchronization, left over from days when half duplex transmission was used, but not needed in modern P2P Ethernet systems.[1] These bits were pressed into service as the LLID header, and turned back into the original (unused today) run-in sequence before presenting the packet to the Ethernet MAC.

LLID Downstream

Fig. 3.2 shows a view of the downstream functionality of the LLID feature of PONs, presented in a layered view. On the left is the OLT, sending downstream traffic to three ONTs, each of which is receiving a different mix of service. In "conventional" Ethernet, there would be an MAC instance for each ONT served by the OLT, and these are shown with numbers corresponding to the ONT. However, rather than hand-shaking directly (via the physical layer) with the MAC in the ONT, there is an added *reconciliation layer*. (Some people have referred to this layer as either the *point-to-point [PtP or P2P] emulation* or the *shared media emulation [SME]* layer depending on what it is doing. We happen to like this terminology, but we shall stick to what is in the 802.3 standard, which calls it the reconciliation layer.)

The reconciliation layer adds the LLID using an otherwise unused couple of words in the Ethernet header, based on the type of MAC address it sees. If a normal (unicast) destination MAC address is in the header, meaning the packet is intended for one and only one ONT, then the LLID assumes a value that was assigned for the target ONT when the ONT registered on the system

---

[1] There are more than 16 bits left over from the synchronization, or *run-in*, sequence, but 16 were coopted for this use. One is a status bit used to identify multicast LLIDs, and 15 are available for LLIDs.

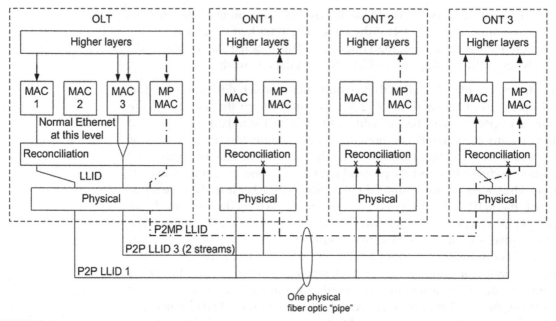

FIGURE 3.2

Downstream LLIDs (prior to 2012 Ethernet release).

(in this regard, the LLID is assigned somewhat analogously to an IP address, but it is by no means the same as an IP address).

The reconciliation layer addresses the packet to the particular ONT for which it is assigned. Any packet of any type (other than multicast, covered below) bound for a particular ONT carries that ONT's LLID. (As we'll see when we get to cable TV-specific modifications to EPON [DPoE] there can be multiple LLIDs assigned to one ONT, but for the purpose of the existing IEEE standard, there is one nonmulticast LLID per ONT.) Higher layers of the protocol stack decide what to do with the packet once received, using the normal Ethernet protocol. When an ONT sees an LLID other than its own, it drops the packet. Recall that the downstream transmission on a PON is continuous, as are transmissions on a normal Ethernet system. This transmission technique is called *TDM* (*time division multiplexing*).

Multicast packets are intended to be received by more than one ONT at the same time. Probably the most common type of multicast packet is IP television (IPTV), in which the IPTV packet is transmitted for the simultaneous benefit of multiple subscribers (as opposed to a *unicast* IPTV session, intended for one and only one subscriber). Multicast is analogous to conventional broadcast TV, in which every viewer tuned in gets the same picture at the same time. Multicast packets are identified by a range of IP addresses, but when we get to the reconciliation layer, there is one LLID reserved for all multicast packets regardless of what they are or to which ONT(s) they are destined. At the ONT, multicast traffic is always passed through the reconciliation layer to a higher layer of the protocol stack, which figures out what the packet is, and even if it is intended for that ONT. (Well, that's the way the multicast LLID originally worked, but in the 2012 edition of the 802.3 Ethernet standard, things were changed somewhat, and we'll cover that below.)

In Fig. 3.2 we show, somewhat unconventionally, packets being sent to each of three example ONTs. There is only one physical "pipe" between the OLT and the ONTs, and it has a splitter to connect all ONTs. What we are showing between the different pieces are logical conduits, all running over that one physical pipe (fiber optic cable), time division multiplexed.

ONT 1 is taking some sort of unicast traffic only, coming from MAC 1 in the OLT. Two streams of unicast traffic bound for ONT 3 are blocked at ONT 1's reconciliation layer, because they have ONT 3's LLID. There is a multicast LLID active, so the multicast packets are passed through the lower layers in ONT 1, but since it is not using the multicast, the multicast is stopped at higher layers (probably by IGMP snooping, which recognizes that this packet is not needed).

ONT 2 is only taking the multicast, perhaps a TV show, so the multicast packets pass all the way through the ONT, eventually to the port on which multicast output is designated to appear. Since there are no unicast packets for it, no packets have LLID = 2 in their header, so all unicast packets are stopped at the reconciliation layer.

ONT 3 is receiving two unicast streams—perhaps one family member is getting email and another is web surfing. So both of these unicast streams are being assigned the same LLID = 3 in the reconciliation layer at the OLT, and both pass through ONT 3's reconciliation layer, where the LLID is replaced by the traditional but today unused Ethernet run-in header, then separated into their respective streams at the MAC layer. There is also a P2P LLID for ONT 1 on the PON, but it is rejected at ONT 3's reconciliation layer, because it is the wrong LLID number for this ONT. ONT 3 is also receiving a multicast stream—it may be the same one that ONT 2 is receiving, or it may be a different stream. In either case, the streams get the single multicast LLID and pass through to higher layers of the protocol to be sent to the correct place (see the next section for modification of the way multicast LLIDs are used).

Then the Great Multicast Morph of 2012
What we described above was the way the downstream LLIDs worked according to the 2008 and earlier versions of the Ethernet specification. By the time the 2012 version of the specification was being debated, it was realized that expanded use of multicast LLIDs in the downstream direction would be a

good idea. Accordingly, the status bit footnoted a few pages back, which really had little justification for being, was pressed into service as what it had been intended to be, a flag indicating whether or not the following 15 bits represented a simple unicast LLID (indicating a packet bound for one and only one ONT), or a multicast packet potentially bound for more than one ONT.[ix]

For ONTs complying with the 2012 version, a different multicast LLID is supplied for every multicast stream being delivered on the PON, and is supplied to those ONTs receiving that stream. That previously underutilized status bit now indicates whether the packet is a multicast or a unicast packet.[2] Thus, each ONT can now reject multicast packets not destined for it, at the reconciliation layer, rather than processing the packet higher into the protocol stack before rejecting it.

However, the system must maintain backward compatibility for the millions of OLTs and ONTs that predate the 2012 version of the standard. Thus, use of the multicast LLIDs beyond the one specified originally must be optional.

LLID Upstream

Fig. 3.3 illustrates some upstream applications of LLIDs. The straightforward application is the packets coming from ONT 3, which are going upstream of the PON. The LLID is being used to implement the upstream time-shared communication in which each ONT transmits in its own timeslot, as managed by the OLT. This method of communication is called *time division multiple access (TDMA)*, as opposed to the *TDM* of the downstream direction. TDMA is not supported in Ethernet, so implementation of that function is assigned to the LLID.

Also shown in Fig. 3.3 is two-way packet flow between ONT 1 and ONT 2. Perhaps there is a VoIP phone call between the two parties. In VoIP, the *softswitch*,[3] which manages the call, sets up the call, and instructs the two ONTs where each is to send voice packets and from where it should receive them. Then the softswitch gets out of the picture until the call ends. The ONTs communicate directly with each other, over the shortest, most efficient path possible. When the two ends of the conversation are on the same PON, it is most efficient if the OLT turns the packets around, rather than sending them up to something else, which turns the packets around. However, Ethernet running alone in the OLT will not turn the packets around, because Ethernet never sends a packet out on the same port on which it came in, as would be required in the present case.

---

[2]Well, the status bit indicated whether a packet was multicast or unicast prior to 2012 too, but since there was but one predetermined multicast LLID, the status bit was really redundant.

[3]The softswitch is not part of the FTTH network, but exists somewhere in the operator's network.

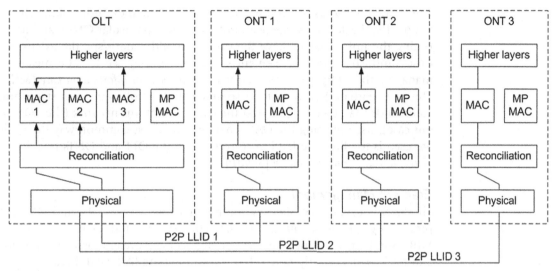

FIGURE 3.3
Upstream use of LLIDs.

So the reconciliation layer takes the incoming packet, replaces the LLID with the Ethernet run-in, and passes it to MAC 1 (for packets coming from ONT 1). The destination MAC added at ONT 1 is that of MAC 2, which creates the connection between MAC 1 and MAC 2 at the OLT. MAC 2 sends the packet to ONT 2, but so far as it is concerned, it is talking to a different port than that on which the packet came in. The reconciliation layer then adds LLID 2, sending the packet to ONT 2. The reverse happens with packets going the other way.[x] (The voice call will likely be in a VLAN that is configured to allow packet transmission between ONTs, but while important, introducing the VLAN is not necessary to explain what's going on.)

System Management
EPON uses an optional (but widely supported) *OAM* (*Operation, Administration, and Maintenance*) channel, which tends to be simpler than the OMCI used by GPON. OAM packets are transmitted over the PON with all other packets, but are limited to 10 packets per second, or about 123 kb/s for a 1 Gb/s data link. The OAM frames use what is called *Slow Protocol* frames (*OAM Protocol Data Units* or *OAMPDUs*), designed to limit the bandwidth consumed to only that necessary in order to provide management, while ensuring that those frames get through no matter what congestion may exist. The packets are transmitted using a reserved multicast MAC address, and ordinarily communicate with the ONTs, the OLT, an *EMS* provided by the PON vendor, and can be used for manual (bypassing the EMS) control and status indications when necessary. The OAMPDUs will not pass through a switch or bridger.

The defined purposes of OAM include remote failure indication (of the ONT), remote loopback (to test the health of a path to a particular ONT), and monitoring the link. Vendors have the option to add vendor-specific extensions to accomplish other management objectives as they see fit. The means of managing the equipment involved is the *management information base* (*MIB*). This is a (partially) manufacturer-specific data base of equipment status and commands that is exchanged over the communications network (the PON in our case), usually using the OAM channel. The most common way the MIBs are used is to allow the EMS to converse with the OLT and ONTs (via *Simple Network Management Protocol* [*SNMP*]).

Element Management

The EMS is usually supplied by the manufacturer of the OLT and ONTs. It presents a *graphical user interface* (*GUI*) to the operator, hiding the details of the MIBs. Sometimes a skilled operator or engineer will prefer to issue commands and read results directly rather than go through the EMS GUI, because if you are skilled enough on the particular equipment, you can get your job done faster that way than through the GUI. Also, there will be times when, for example, a new ONT is introduced for which the EMS has not been programmed to support all of its MIBs. Then someone with the requisite skill can interact directly at the MIB level to control the device.

The EMS, depending on the manufacturer, may be a very comprehensive tool for managing the PON system (other systems, such as video set top boxes and voice systems, may have their own EMSs). Among the features that may exist in the EMS are inventory, tracking what OLTs and ONTs are in the warehouse, on trucks for delivery to customers, and in operation at customer premises. The EMS will also have the ability to set up services for customers, such as setting their permitted data rate and their phone lines and phone numbers. If broadcast video is used, the EMS may be able to command video ON/OFF at a particular ONT. The EMS will also show a pictorial representation (*topology*) of the network and all of the network elements (OLTs and ONTs) on it. The status of the network elements will typically be displayed as pictures of each device, with reproductions of status lights. For higher-level views, the EMS may show that an alarm condition exists somewhere in the network, and graphically show you where the alarmed element is in the network. Multiple categories of alarms might be displayed, and the EMS may have the ability to automatically notify personnel of urgent alarms.

Typically the EMS will perform other duties too. These include software upgrades for the OLT and ONT, which can be managed in the background by the EMS. The EMS will also collect performance data, such as the number of packets received at each ONU and the number that were either errored or needed error correction. Such statistics can be invaluable for detecting problems in the network. Also, some operators are starting to count packets received by each subscriber, and charging an extra fee if the count per month exceeds some preset number. Usually the number is high enough that few subscribers are affected. But it is well-known that a few subscribers consume an inordinate amount of data, and that data do cost the operator. Because a few subscribers use so much data, data caps are being used today.

There are yet other data the EMS may collect from the ONTs. Received signal strength indication (RSSI) lets the operator know the optical strength of the received signal. A drop in signal strength can indicate a problem with the optical network.

Operational Support Systems

Larger installations will want a higher-level management system, called an *operational support system* (OSS), which integrates information from a number of EMSs from different subsystems (such as the subject PON subsystem), and can report overall status as well as accepting control commands from an operator. The EMS will have a *northbound interface* (NBI), which is used to exchange data with an OSS and also with a billing system. In larger installations, the primary operator interface is usually the billing system, and as customer changes are made there, the billing system informs the PON subsystem as well as other relevant systems. One and only one entry of the subscriber information is made, minimizing labor and the chance for errors. The manufacturer of each EMS specifies the NBI messages to be passed (usually using APIs in XML and HTTP), and the OSS and billing vendors adapt to it.

A word of caution is in order here. There are many variables between the many EMSs, OSSs, billing systems, and other support systems used in large installations, and they can interact in strange ways. Software updates can have unforeseen consequences when interacting with disparate systems—sometimes something as seemingly inconsequential as a change in the time one system takes to return a response to another system can cause problems. So just because your PON EMS software version and your billing software version are the same as what has been used elsewhere, you may not get the same results if your voice EMS, for example, takes a longer (or shorter) time to respond to some query. The moral of the story is to be very careful about integrating a new system or even an upgrade of existing software, because something unexpected may happen that no vendor will be able to reproduce. Large operators have independent lab systems that mimic their production system, and they can often find problems there before customers are affected.

EXTENSIONS TO EPON

If you are primarily providing residential service, the following will not necessarily be important, but they might be if you are providing certain business services. EPON followed the philosophies of the IEEE 802 Committee, which is responsible for the Ethernet standard and its extensions. IEEE 802 comes from an enterprise background—Ethernet was originally a data transmission standard for enterprises. The philosophy was to specify the minimum within the standard, and to rely on other existing standards as much as possible. Consequently, EPON by itself does an excellent job of transmitting data, but when you try to add on certain services demanded by modern telecommunications users, including businesses, there are some additional, supporting, standards needed.

In order to provide for those additional standards, the IEEE has undertaken some additional work, outlined below.

- *SIEPON* stands for *service interoperability in Ethernet passive optical networks.* The accepted pronunciation is to pronounce the letters S-I-E-P-O-N, rather than to try to pronounce the acronym as we usually tend to do. Recall that the original application of Ethernet was in an institutional (enterprise) setting, not in a public setting, where data from many entities were carried on the same path, with differing security and quality requirements. SIEPON is an IEEE initiative to extend EPON to make it more useful for business applications. SIEPON creates a system- and network-level standard for plug-and-play business solutions. It provides a number of services delivered over EPON, including:[xi]
  - Frame operations, such as VLAN modes, tunneling modes, and multicast distribution;
  - Bandwidth reporting and QoS enforcement;
  - Power savings;
  - Line and device protection and monitoring;
  - Alarms and warnings;
  - Authentication, privacy, and encryption;
  - Maintenance mechanisms, including software update, ONU discovery, and registration;
  - Extended management (eOAM).

Given sufficient computing power in the OLT and ONT, adding SIEPON should be a matter of software, not hardware. However, some early-generation equipment probably lacks enough processing power to make SIEPON practical to implement.

- IEEE 1588 is a key standard not developed specifically for PON, but it is needed if you are going to do backhaul (interconnect) for cellular towers. It maintains precision timing over an Ethernet network. Ethernet was not designed to maintain close timing. Very close timing from one cell tower to the next is needed in order to support handoff in 4G (fourth-generation) cellular networks and for certain other functions.

The 1588 standard works by defining a series of clocks and measuring the time delay from one to the next, ultimately estimating the end-to-end time delay that must be compensated in deriving consistent timing from one cell tower to another. High-precision oscillators at certain points in the network are a must, and additional hardware is required at certain points in the network to support 1588. So it is usually more than adding software to obtain the timing accuracy needed.

- *MEF, the Metro Ethernet Forum*, has established several standards that are being incorporated in EPON systems to provide functionality needed for certain business services. We shall cover MEF requirements in more detail below.

PON OPTICS

The optical interface at an OLT is normally handled by a plug-in optical module meeting certain standards. Several progressively smaller optical modules have been developed over the years, with the most common at this time being referred to as the *SFP* (*small form-factor pluggable*). You can get SFPs in several different power and sensitivity ranges, depending upon the length of the PON and how many times you are going to split it. Chapter 6 goes into much more detail concerning the optical issues in PONs.

Optics other than for the PON are also supplied in SFP packaging, but obviously will not work if you plug them into PON ports. You can get SFPs for short-distance multimode optics for use in a headend/CO, and you can get single mode 1 and 10 Gb/s Ethernet SFPs (typically a 10 Gb/s SFP is called an *SFP+*, or *XFP* in a different form factor). You can also get SFPs with electrical Ethernet interfaces rather than optical interfaces, as well as other types of SFPs.

Usually ONTs have integrated optics, the economics and the number of ONTs built resulting in greater efficiency if the ONT is designed that way. Frequently the ONT manufacturer will purchase the optics as a subunit, but to you as the user it will appear just as part of the ONT. You can also get an entire basic GPON or EPON ONT in an SFP; they are used in some ONT products, depending on the features needed.

EPON Optics Options

EPON is specified in terms of the optics required for two different distances, either 10 or 20 km, and three different split ratios. Table 3.2 shows the options defined as of this writing. Note that just because the standard provides for a particular distance and split combination does not necessarily mean that commercial products are available for that application, or if they are available, that they are priced such that you can make a business case for using them—the standards anticipate future advances in technology. Also, it may be possible to

Table 3.2 EPON Optics Designations

Optics Designation	Min. Distance (km)	Min. Split
1. 1 Gb/s symmetrical		
1000BASE-PX10	10	1:16
1000BASE-PX20	20	1:16
1000BASE-PX30	20	1:32
1000BASE-PX40	20	1:64
2. 10 Gb/s down, 1 Gb/s up		
10/1GBASE-PRX-D1	10	1:16
10/1GBASE-PRX-U1		
10/1GBASE-PRX-D2	20	1:16
10/1GBASE-PRX-U2		
10/1GBASE-PRX-D3	20	1:32
10/1GBASE-PRX-U3		
10/1GBASE-PRX-D4	20	1:64
10/1GBASE-PRX-U4		
3. 10 Gb/s down, 10 Gb/s up		
10GBASE-PR-D1	10	1:16
10GBASE-PR-U1		
10GBASE-PR-D2	20	1:16
10GBASE-PR-U1[a]		
10GBASE-PR-D3	20	1:32
10GBASE-PR-U3		
10GBASE-PR-D4	20	1:64
10GBASE-PR-U4		

[a]Not a typo; upstream designation is the same for 10 and 20 km reach; there is no U2.

operate other combinations of splits and distances, as shown in Chapter 6. But you should discuss your operating conditions with your equipment vendor.

Because the newer 10 Gb/s standards can operate with either 1 or 10 Gb/s upstream, there are more classes designated for it. 1G-EPON and 10G-EPON are specified to work compatibly on the same PON, allowing a graceful and gradual transition from 1 Gb/s EPON to 10 Gb/s EPON. However, mixing the two on the same fiber will require an OLT that works at both speeds. The 1 Gb/s ONTs and 10 Gb/s ONTs can exist on the same fiber (though an external filter may need to be placed in the input for the 1 Gb/s ONTs, depending on their design).

Fig. 3.4 provides the decoder for EPON optics. The term *PMD* stands for *physical medium dependent*, the term the IEEE uses to mean the interface between

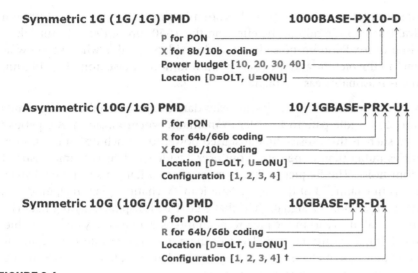

FIGURE 3.4
Decoder ring for EPON. *Courtesy Alan Brown, then of Aurora Networks, now with Commscope.*

the Ethernet system and the physical transport medium (in our case, limited to the optical fiber of a PON). Obviously the numbers preceding BASE represent the speed of the PON, in the downstream then in the upstream directions. The term *power budget* in 1G-EPON is effectively replaced by the *configuration* for 10 GE-PON, with either 1 or 10 Gb/s upstream.

In the 2008 and earlier EPON specifications, there were only two classes of optics, PX-10 and PX-20, defined for 10- and 20-km distances. The splits were assumed to be either 16:1 or maybe 32:1. A lot of this equipment is still being used.

SRS Effects

We shall go into more detail in Chapter 6, but we now introduce a concept that can be crucial to the success of a PON carrying broadcast video. There is a distortion mechanism in the fiber optic cable itself called *stimulated Raman scattering* (SRS). It has the effect of transferring power from a lower wavelength to a higher wavelength when both signals are traveling in the same direction on the fiber. The downstream data, which turn the optical signal ON for a logical 1 and OFF for a 0, are transmitted on a wavelength of 1490 nm, whereas RF-modulated broadcast signals are on 1550 nm. This wavelength separation is not optimum for transferring power, but it does cause significant power to be transferred from 1490 to 1550 nm due to SRS. Since the power at 1490 nm is on/off keyed, then sometimes power is transferred to the 1550-nm carrier, and sometimes it is not. This creates an undesired modulation component on the 1550-nm carrier. The transfer is worse at lower RF frequencies (as seen on the demodulated 1550-nm carrier). Normally, since the data on the 1490-nm optical carrier are random, the effect on the 1550-nm carrier is to introduce random noise. Random noise in an analog video signal is what we know as "snow" in the picture, and the effect of the additional noise from the 1490-nm carrier is reasonably easy to manage.

However, when there are no downstream data to transmit, Ethernet transmits a short 20-bit idle pattern in order to maintain synchronization. A repetitive pattern such as this causes the transferred power to "bunch up" at certain frequencies rather than to be spread out over a wide band, as is characteristic of random noise. The frequency that is most affected happens to be 62.5 MHz, which is in channel 3 of the North American TV channel plan. If channel 3 is carrying an analog TV signal, then that signal will display diagonal bars (RF engineers call it a *beat*) in the picture, at an intensity that is very objectionable. If the channel is carrying digital video, there is sufficient interference in the channel that potentially the signal may not be demodulated accurately, resulting in no picture or a very faulty and unusable picture.

Techniques have been developed to overcome the problem. When no downstream data are available to transmit, the idle code may be replaced by random data addressed to no ONT. For example, a VLAN might be created at the OLT, which does not terminate on any ONTs. Random bits put in that VLAN would not go anywhere, but they would preclude the power from bunching up in one channel. (Note that this solution is patented.)

SUMMARY

This chapter has served as an introduction to EPON, the IEEE standard for PONs. As with its counterpart, GPON, it operates on a network consisting largely of a central point with a single fiber radiating outward to a splitter, which serves 32 or, uncommonly, 64 endpoints (or it may serve 16 endpoints). The central termination is called an OLT, while the user endpoints are called either ONUs or ONTs.

In order to adapt the standard to contracted wide area telecommunications service with modern features, some newer standards complement the basic PON standard. SIEPON adds certain features to EPON needed for these applications. IEEE 1588 is a newer timing standard needed by any packet-based system to reproduce accurate enough timing to allow PONs to be used for fourth-generation cellular backhaul. The Metro Ethernet Forum has promulgated other standards needed to support business services.

The cable telecommunications (cable TV) industry is interested in applying EPON for certain applications, many involving business customers. There are several initiatives for aiding the industry in getting to FTTH from where it is now, in customer-friendly, economical ways. Among these are *RFoG*, a deployed technology that allows an operator to use the physical fiber architecture of PON while retaining existing endpoint equipment. *DPoE* is a technology that will allow a cable operator to offer full EPON services while retaining the familiar and integrated DOCSIS management system. *EPoC* allows the offering of services that have the look and feel of EPON, while retaining the current HFC physical architecture.

Endnotes

i. Kramer G. Ethernet passive optical networks. McGraw Hill; 2005.

ii. http://standards.ieee.org/develop/wg/SIEPON.html.

iii. http://www.scte.org/default.aspx.

iv. http://www.cablelabs.com/.

v. http://www.ieee.org/index.html.

vi. http://www.ieee1904.org/1/.

vii. Ciciora W, et al. Modern cable television technology. In: Kaufmann M, editor. 2nd ed. 2004. [chapter 19].

viii. IEEE 802.3, clause 49.

ix. Compare, for example, clauses 65.1.3.1 and 76.2.6.1.1 of the 2008 and 2012 editions of IEEE 802.3. These clauses are found in Section 5 of the standard.

x. William Diab W, Frazier H. Ethernet in the first mile: access for everyone. IEEE Press 2006.

xi. http://www.slideshare.net/ieeesa/siepon-3-1hajduczenia.

CHAPTER 4

GPON

INTRODUCTION

In Chapter 1 we introduced the main types of FTTx networks in use or proposed for use in the near future. You may want to refer back to Fig. 1.3 of that chapter. In this chapter we shall talk about a technology that recently has been widely deployed in the US and Europe, principally but not exclusively by the telephone industry. *GPON* (*Gigabit Passive Optical Network*), is a standard promulgated by the *International Telecommunications Union*, which is comprised of most of the major telephone carriers in the world. GPON is the third standard series in the ITU PON progression, the first being APON and the second BPON. Little if any APON is known to have been built beyond pilot projects, but BPON is rather widely deployed. GPON is codified in the ITU G.984 series of standards.[i] The follow-on standard for 10 Gb/s GPON, known as XG-PON, is codified as ITU G.987.[ii] This chapter will cover both GPON and XG-PON, but the other ITU PON standards are considered obsolete for new-build.

The 1550-nm broadcast overlay, being essentially the same in both EPON and GPON, is not covered to any significant extent in this chapter. Many GPON systems using the 1550-nm band for broadcast are in use today.

From a user's standpoint, you may see very little difference between GPON and EPON, because there is usually an *element management system* (EMS) in use, the EMS software being a graphical interface with which you interact in directly managing the system, and which will hide most or all of the PON-specific variation from you. However, it is useful to understand some of the basic concepts of the systems in order to comprehend what you can and cannot do within the standards, and there may be times when understanding this material could help understand some unexpected behavior. So this chapter will attempt to summarize the important points regarding GPON that you might need to know in operating a system, though by no means will it make you an expert in GPON—if you want that expertise, see the References.

FTTx Networks. http://dx.doi.org/10.1016/B978-0-12-420137-8.00004-4

GPON KEY FEATURES

GPON is promulgated by the *International Telecommunications Union*[iii] (ITU), headquartered in Geneva, Switzerland. It is a privately run organization consisting of large telephone companies worldwide. In the early 1990s, an ad hoc organization comprised of a subset of ITU members and other interested parties was formed to state the industry's vision of an all-fiber network. This organization was called FSAN, the *Full Service Access Network*.[iv] FSAN is not a standards organization itself, but rather it offers contributions to ITU-T SG15 Q2, based on completed FSAN work items that are intended to promote the development of global PON standards. The ITU then turns the contributions, after further deliberation among its members, into the GPON standards. ITU-T SG15 Q2 refers specifically to the organizational entity inside the ITU that is charged with generating and maintaining these standards.

Recently the Broadband Forum[v] has expanded on technical issues of the GPON implementation and interoperability. For example TR-156 defines several modes of VLANs, multicast traffic, and QoS in GPON access networks. TR-255 defines a GPON Interoperability Test Plan between OLT and ONU, which had been adopted by many operators as requirements for equipment vendors.

Speed

GPON operates at 2.48832 (often rounded to 2.5) Gb/s downstream, and 1.244 Gb/s upstream. The data rates derive from the ATM standards, the workhorse of the telephone industry. These are the so-called *wire speeds*, or actual data rates on the fiber. Slower rates are defined, but we are not aware of any applications for anything other than these fastest data rates. The 2.5 Gb/s speed versus EPON's 1 Gb/s speed, has been a major factor for the choice of GPON over EPON, particularly for operators who offer or are contemplating offering IPTV. The current situation with 10 Gb/s EPON running ahead of 10 Gb/s GPON clouds the issue for some potential providers.

XG-PON, the newer and faster version, has two variations. XG-PON1 operates at a nominal 10 Gb/s (the more precise speed being 9.95328 Gb/s) in at least the downstream direction. The specified upstream speed is 2.5 (more precisely 2.48832) Gb/s. This is the only variation defined as of this writing, but the intention is to define a faster variation in the future. That faster variation, XG-PON2, operates at 10 Gb/s in both downstream and upstream directions.

DC Elimination and Clock Synchronization

In Chapter 3 we noted the use of 8b/10b encoding for EPON, which increased the wire rate by 25% over the quoted data rate of 1 Gb/s, but which yielded some advantageous properties. GPON does not employ such encoding, so the quoted data rate and the wire rate are one in the same except for a small overhead component. One of the advantages of 8b/10b encoding is elimination of any dc component in the data. The same thing is accomplished in GPON by randomizing the data by exclusive OR-ing the data with a long pseudorandom bit stream known to both the transmitter and receiver. This is known as *scrambling* in data communication circles, not to be confused with the term as used in cable TV to mean rendering video unviewable to anyone who has not paid for the service. We can show that if any data stream is exclusive-OR'ed with a pseudorandom data pattern, that the resultant data pattern is also randomized, and by definition, a truly randomized data pattern has no dc component, a necessary requirement for the optical layer.

Since we now have a randomized transmitted data pattern, we can also assume that there are a number of transitions between 1 and 0, which are needed in order to synchronize the receiving clock. However, what this doesn't specify, and which EPON's 8b/10b encoding does cover, is a definition of how many data transitions you get in what time. There is no guarantee of the number of like bits in a row that you might get in GPON, whereas EPON guarantees at least three transitions per symbol. Another way of saying this is that EPON has a higher minimum frequency at which significant signal power is present, compared with GPON. Experience has led to a consensus that 72 like bits in a row in GPON is highly, highly unlikely. So if we design our ac coupling in the transmitter and receiver to deal with this, and if we design our clock recovery such that it can carry through 72 like bits without losing sync, then we are OK. It also means that, theoretically, EPON can be designed for less guard time between upstream transmissions, but we are not sure that anyone has taken advantage of this feature.

Encryption

GPON specifies the downstream encryption to be used, whereas EPON by itself does not address that issue. [However, EPON players are coalescing around standard encryption technologies. Commercial chips are being made with AES128 CFB and/or triple churning (CTC) downstream encryption built in.] GPON specifies a form of the AES encryption, but not the same one currently being employed by EPON. Only data, not management information, are encrypted. With GPON, the optical network terminal (ONT) selects the encryption key when it receives a request from the optical line terminal (OLT), and informs the OLT of its selection. By having the information flow from the ONT to the OLT, we have fairly decent protection against eavesdropping because it is very hard to intercept upstream communications in a fiber-to-the-home (FTTH) network; the amount of signal arriving at any port other than the one going to the OLT is so low as to be useless for data recovery. The encryption key is changed frequently, and once used, is not repeated. A general introduction to the subject of encryption is found in Appendix B.

Flow Control in GPON

While we think it is an important topic, we are not emphasizing the 7-layer ISO model in this book, because frequent reference to the model is not necessary for a practical book which seeks to show you how to efficiently operate a plant. However, some references to it are necessary in order to understand the technology, and to be conversant with others. When things don't work as expected, you need enough of the theory to figure out what is happening.

Since it is based on SONET, which in turn has its roots in earlier telecommunications protocols, GPON puts data into 125 µs quanta, sometimes referred to as *frames* (but caution, the word *frame* has many different usages in data communications). Initially GPON defined two *flows* (partitions) that might be in a frame, one containing asynchronous transfer mode (ATM) cells, and one containing Ethernet, encapsulated into *GEM frames*, where GEM stands for *GPON Encapsulation Method*. (There was also native T1/E1 transmission defined initially.) However, the multitude of types of flows made the standard unwieldy to implement, and people realized that Ethernet was the transport of choice, so the other options, ATM and T1/E1, were deprecated (removed) from the standard. Thus, today, transmission within GPON is Ethernet frames encapsulated into GEM frames of 125 µs length. At the downstream speed of 2.488 Gb/s, this is long enough to transmit up to about 25 maximum-length Ethernet frames (or about 12 frames upstream, since the data rate is half the downstream data rate). For the 10 Gb/s XG-PON, the GEM is called *XGEM*; the differences are not great. There can be multiple GEM frames bound for different ONTs inside one 125-µs frame (quanta).[1]

Each GEM frame starts with a *GEM header*, which contains, among other things, a 12-bit port identification (16 bits for XG-PON), used to define the ONT and a user port on that ONT for the following traffic. This means, of course, that the maximum number of ports capable of being addressed in GPON is 2^{12} or 4096 ports (often called *GEM ports*), with each ONT typically having multiple ports. With this limited addressing capability, obviously the GEM port ID is assigned when an ONT is discovered, not when it is built (as an MAC address would be assigned). While it should be pretty well hidden from you the user, the same port identification will be used many times in different PONs, though only once in a given PON.

The GEM header includes ranging information telling each ONT by how much it is to offset the beginning of its upstream transmission in order to compensate for fiber propagation delay. This is part of the *PLOAM* (*physical level operations and*

---

[1]We warned you that there are many different uses of the word *frame*. We have used it to mean at least three different things in this one paragraph.

maintenance) information used for activation of the ONU and for certain management information, as well as the ranging information. The GEM header also includes allocation information for the present downstream frame and the next upstream frame. It is possible for the OLT to communicate with more than one ONT during a GEM frame. Each communication is contained within a *T-CONT* (transmission container). The OLT establishes the mapping (assignment) of T-CONTs for all ONUs on the PON, using the *ALLOC-ID* (allocation ID). Thus a GEM frame may include a number of T-CONTs, with the data within each T-CONT destined to the same ONT. Different T-CONTs in the same GEM frame may be destined for the same ONT or to different ONTs, in any combination. One could perhaps see similarities between LLIDs in EPON and T-CONTs in GPON; it would not be appropriate to read too much similarity between the two.

A drawing will help here. Fig. 4.1 shows how the pieces of ONT identification fit together. Each ONT is identified by an ONU-ID (recall that we said in an earlier chapter that, while there was originally some difference in the terms ONU and ONT based on complexity, the two have become fairly synonymous). Each ONT can have one or more T-CONTS that carry a certain type of traffic, and each T-CONT can interface with one or more ports, the ports in turn interfacing with customer equipment. Of course, the customer equipment can itself be a switch, Internet Gateway, or whatever.

T-CONTS come in five different types that define different *classes of service* (CoS). A class of service is about the same thing as is often referred to as *quality of service* (QoS). CoS (or QoS) simply refers to how different packets are

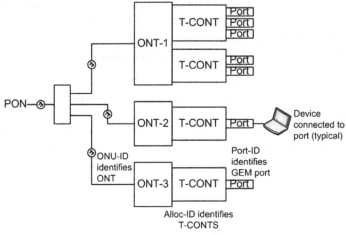

FIGURE 4.1
GPON ONT identification terminology.

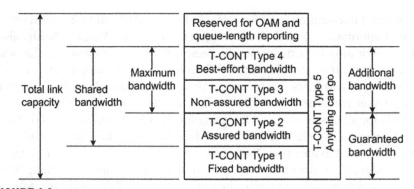

FIGURE 4.2
Types and function of T-CONTS.

treated when enough data traffic is being handled that not all packets can be forwarded as soon as received. This routinely happens to any shared network where different users can present traffic to the network at any time.

T-CONT Type 1 handles the most critical traffic, as shown in Fig. 4.2. It reserves bandwidth (usually in both directions) for the data traffic requiring reserved bandwidth—if the service which reserved T-CONT Type 1 is not sending information, the bandwidth remains reserved and not available to other users. Higher-numbered (lower-QoS) T-CONTS all deal with sharing data—if no traffic requires a given type of T-CONT, then traffic requiring higher-numbered T-CONTS (lower QoS) can use the bandwidth. Taking things a little out-of-order, the top T-CONT in Fig. 4.2 is reserved for the most critical communications, management of the system, as explained further in Appendix D. This information is carried in the GEM header, and always goes, no matter what—the GEM header *must* begin each GEM frame. The usage is based on rules that are outlined in the ITU standards, but the detailed implementation is left to the manufacturer.[vi] Appendix D covers the motivation for QoS.

T-CONT Type 5 is of mixed type, involving all bandwidth types 1 through 4. If an ONT is using T-CONT Type 5, it puts all traffic into that one T-CONT and sends it as it is granted bandwidth by the OLT. In this mode, the ONT prioritizes all of the traffic it has in the upstream direction, presumably putting higher-priority traffic first. Support for T-CONT Type 5 is not required, but can be useful for applications such as interactive games, where one is bundling video, voice, and the interactive elements of the game.

Discovering the New Guy

The process of discovering a new ONT is similar to that employed in EPON and covered in Chapter 3, but the terminology is a bit different. In order to let new ONTs be discovered, the OLT periodically transmits a *discovery grant*, which is a reserved timeslot for the purpose. No discovered ONTs transmit during this timeslot, but if there is an undiscovered ONT on the PON, it will transmit at this time. If its transmission gets through to the OLT, it will get back an acknowledgment message. It is possible that there is more than one undiscovered ONT on the network, so it is possible that more than one ONT will transmit during this time, in which case there will be a data collision at the OLT, with no one getting through. The solution to this is to use a variation of the technique developed for the original Aloha protocol way back when. If an ONT doesn't receive an acknowledgment of its registration request, then it waits a random time, and after that random time, when another discovery grant is announced, it again attempts to register. Since different random backoff times are chosen by different unregistered ONTs, then eventually there are no collisions, and all get registered. Usually there is little registration delay if the only issue is two newly installed ONTs coming online at the same time. But if there is a community-wide power failure and the ONTs are not battery-backed, then reregistration of all ONTs can take some time.

Part of the registration process described in the previous paragraph is to measure the round-trip delay to the new ONT. The propagation time of the signal through the fiber is not insignificant—a PON may be 20 km long, maybe longer, and the round-trip delay in a 20-km PON is about 220 μs, which at a data rate of 2.488 Gb/s, represents 547 kb of data, or about 45 maximum-length Ethernet frames. In order to get good efficiency in the upstream direction, the transmit time of each ONT must be advanced by an appropriate amount such that its signal arrives at the OLT at the appropriate time. The OLT measures the round-trip delay time to each ONT and tells each ONT how much to advance its transmit time from the nominal time the OLT calculates every frame. Upstream transmissions are timed to the 125-μs downstream frame boundaries, used as time ticks for upstream synchronization.

The more variation in length permitted in the PON, the longer the discovery grant must be, because there is more variability in the arrival time of a registration request back at the OLT. The longer the discovery grant, the more loss of upstream efficiency, since no payload upstream data can be transmitted during the discovery grant. GPON provides for PON lengths of up to 60 km, optics permitting (usually the optics don't permit). However, in order to keep the discovery grant time reasonable, the specification limits the *difference* in distance between the farthest and the closest ONT to 20 km.[vii]

After Discovery
After the ONT is discovered, it sends *REPORT* messages telling the OLT how much data it needs to send upstream. The OLT gathers this information from

all ONTs, takes into consideration how much bandwidth each ONT is allocated (by contract), and assigns upstream transmission times for each ONT. It sends *GATE* messages to the ONTs giving them their upstream transmission time assignments.

A number of housekeeping messages are exchanged between the OLT and ONTs during the PLOAM portion of each GEM header. A number of messages are related to fault management, though some serve other purposes, such as frequently updating ranging information. These include the signal degrade (SD) alarm, which indicates that the received signal bit error rate (BER) has exceeded a preselected threshold—communications can likely continue, but are degraded, so the problem needs attention. A related alarm is the signal fail (SF) alarm, which indicates a BER too low to reasonably continue communications. Other messages include *REI* (remote error indication), meaning that an errored block of data was detected in an incoming packet. An *RDI* (remote defect indication) is sent when the incoming signal is lost, or the beginning of a frame cannot be detected. If the ONT detects a problem within itself, it can send a rogue ONU detection signal, which may cause the OLT to start doing certain automatic detection and/or correction actions in an attempt to repair the problem. A *drift* problem occurs when the OLT and ONT clocks differ by a predetermined amount.

PON Protection

GPON specifies two methods of providing protection for the PON, called *duplex PON systems*. The idea of protection is to provide redundant signal paths and equipment interfaces in order to protect the integrity of data transmission in the event of a fiber cut or some equipment failures. Of course, protection costs money in the form of providing redundant fiber paths to one or a group of customers, and perhaps more termination resources. But for a business sufficiently concerned about telecommunications reliability, the extra cost may well be worth it. Here we shall show the duplex systems described in the GPON standard. Initially four types of protection were written into the standard, Types A through D. Types A and D have been deprecated (removed) from the standard, leaving only Types B and C. We shall describe those protection standards here. EPON does not prescribe protection, though some manufacturers have implemented their own.

Type B Protection

Fig. 4.3A illustrates the first duplex system, Type B. It uses a 2 by *n* (where *n* is the number of ONTs supported by the PON) splitter, which first combines two signals before splitting the signal into *n* paths. Two fibers from the OLT are driven by two different OLT ports. One OLT port and fiber are active, the other is in standby. The OLT monitors the network for a fiber

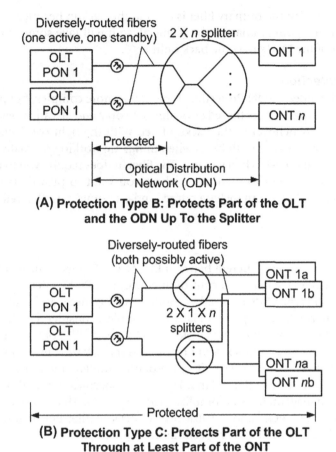

**(A) Protection Type B: Protects Part of the OLT
and the ODN Up To the Splitter**

**(B) Protection Type C: Protects Part of the OLT
Through at Least Part of the ONT**

FIGURE 4.3
Duplex GPON protection systems.

breakage (or certain OLT port faults might be determined too, depending on implementation). If a fault is detected, then the OLT switches over to the other port/fiber combination and resumes communication on the standby path until the fault is repaired. All of the ONTs on the PON benefit from the protection.

The PON is protected up to the splitter but not beyond. Typically the fiber run from the OLT to the splitter encompasses most of the distance of the PON, so the majority of the distance is covered. In order to make the redundancy of the second fiber path real protection, the two fibers must not run together; rather, they must take different routes from the OLT to the splitter. If they were in the same cable bundle, then cutting that cable would take out both paths. Since the two fibers run in different paths, then they will almost never be of the same length. Thus, when the primary fiber is cut and the backup becomes active, all of the ONTs are going to have to be reranged, so it will take some amount of time for all of the ONTs to come back online.

Type C Protection
Fig. 4.3B illustrates GPON Protection Type C. It is more complex, but provides protection all the way to the edge of the network, and it can provide near instantaneous switchover to the backup fiber. With the right configuration, it might be possible to use both fibers when things are working normally, and to simply loose data speed when you lose one fiber. It does require you to run two route-diversified PONs to each place where you want to provide redundant service. But both PONs can include nonredundant points as well as redundant.

OMCI

One feature that is very different between EPON and GPON is the inclusion of *OMCI* (ONT management and control interface) in GPON. There is no direct equivalent in EPON. OMCI is a rather complex management and control interface—as evidence that the protocol is rather complex, consider that the current OMCI standard document, ITU-T G.988, has 594 pages![viii] Some say the standard is unnecessarily complex, and not all vendors may have implemented all of OMCI. However, if you have OMCI properly implemented, it does a lot. OMCI has evolved from the original ITU APON specification, and defines in detail how management is accomplished in the PON. This latest version of OMCI applies to GPON and the 10 Mb/s XG-PON. Earlier PONs in the series (BPON and APON) had earlier specifications for OMCI.

We have talked about the GEM header, which among other things carries PLOAM messages. PLOAM might be considered the lower-level or housekeeping messages that must be passed frequently in order to keep the system working and synchronized. By contrast, OMCI messages control other features of the operation of the network. PLOAM messages generally were addressed to more than one ONT on the PON, whereas OMCI messages are directed specifically to individual ONTs. OMCI is used to manage PON services and ONU equipment. It may be used to manage voice-over-Internet-Protocol (VoIP) services, or VoIP may be managed by means external to the OMCI (OMCI sets up management via IP in this latter case). OMCI is carried in a GEM frame, as are T-CONTS bound for one or more ONTs.[2]

---

[2]While data in a T-CONT are normally sent to one and only one ONT, an exception is *multicast*, in which the contents of a T-CONT may be sent to all of the ONTs receiving that multicast message. The most familiar application for multicast is to distribute a TV program simultaneously to multiple subscribers.

OMCI is used by the OLT to manage the ONU in the following areas:

1. Configuration management;
2. Fault management;
3. Performance management;
4. Security management.

This interface allows the OLT to:

1. Establish and release connections across the ONU;
2. Manage the ONT user ports [called *UNIs* (user network interfaces) in the specifications];
3. Request configuration information and performance statistics.

The OMCI also allows the ONT to inform the OLT autonomously of alarms, performance threshold crossings, and changes to the values of many of the *MIB* (management information base) attributes.

The OMCI protocol is asymmetric: the controller in the OLT is the master, while the ONT is the slave. A single OLT controller using multiple instances of the protocol over separate control channels typically controls multiple ONTs.[viii] There are some service configurations not defined in OMCI, and equipment vendors have to resort to other methods (such as SNMP), for example in the area of VoIP and POTS functionalities.

ELEMENT MANAGEMENT

The EMS is usually supplied by the manufacturer of the OLT and ONTs. It presents a *graphical user interface* (GUI) to the operator, hiding the details of the MIBs. Sometimes a skilled operator or engineer will prefer to issue commands and read results directly rather than to go through the EMS GUI, because if you are skilled enough on the particular equipment, you can get your job done faster that way than through the GUI. Also, there will be times when, for example, a new ONT is introduced for which the EMS has not been programmed to support all of its MIBs. Then someone with the requisite skill can interact directly at the MIB level to control the device.

The EMS, depending on the manufacturer, may be a very comprehensive tool for managing the PON system (other systems, such as video set top boxes and voice systems, may have their own EMSs). Among the features that may exist in the EMS are inventory, tracking what OLTs and ONTs are in the warehouse, on trucks for delivery to customers, and in operation at customer premises. The EMS will also have the ability to set up services for customers, such as setting their permitted data rate and their phone numbers. If broadcast video is used, the EMS may be able to command video ON/OFF at each ONT. The EMS will also show a pictorial representation (*topology*) of the network and all of the network elements (OLTs and ONTs) on it. The status of the network elements will typically be displayed as pictures of each device, with reproductions of status lights. For higher-level views, the EMS may show that an alarm condition exists somewhere in the network, and graphically show you where the alarmed element is in the network. Multiple categories of alarms might be displayed, and the EMS may have the ability to automatically notify personnel of urgent alarms (e.g., via email or SMS). Many times one fault can generate many alarms, which can overwhelm an operator. The EMS may be able to filter the alarms, displaying only the one or a few alarms that are the root cause of a problem, and hiding the other alarms that were generated secondarily by the root cause failure.

Typically the EMS will perform other duties too. These include software upgrades for the OLT and ONT, which can be managed in the background by the EMS. The EMS will also collect performance data, such as the number of packets received at each ONU and the number that were either errored or needed error correction. Such statistics can be invaluable for detecting problems in the network. Also, some operators are starting to count packets received by each subscriber, and charging an extra fee if the count per month exceeds some preset number. Usually the number is high enough that few subscribers are affected. But it is well-known that a few subscribers consume an inordinate amount of data, and that data do have a cost to the operator.

There are yet other data the EMS may collect. For example, received signal strength indication (RSSI) lets the operator know the optical strength of the received signal at the OLT. A drop in signal strength can indicate a problem with the optical network. *Digital diagnostic monitoring* (DDM) reports on a number of parameters at the ONT, allowing the operator to assess the health of the network and the ONT.

OPERATIONAL SUPPORT SYSTEMS

Larger installations will want a higher-level management system, called an *operational support system* (OSS), which integrates information from a number of EMSs from different subsystems (such as the subject PON subsystem), and can report overall status as well as accepting control commands from an operator. The PON EMS will have a *northbound interface* (NBI), which is used to exchange data with an OSS and also with a billing system. In larger installations, the primary operator interface is usually the billing system, and as customer changes are made there, the billing system informs the PON subsystem as well as other relevant systems. One and only one entry of the subscriber information is made, minimizing labor and the chance for errors. The manufacturer of each EMS specifies the NBI messages to be passed (usually using *APIs* in *XML* and *HTP*), and the OSS and billing vendors adapt to it.

A word of caution is in order here. There are many variables between the many EMSs, OSSs, billing systems, and other support systems used in large installations, and they can interact in strange ways. Software updates can have unforeseen consequences when interacting with disparate systems—sometimes something as seemingly inconsequential as a change in the time one system takes to return a response to another system can cause problems. So just because your PON EMS software version and your billing software version are the same as what has been used elsewhere, you may not get the same results if your voice EMS, for example, takes a longer (or shorter) time to respond to some query. The moral of the story is to be very careful about integrating a new system or even an upgrade of existing software, because something unexpected may happen that no vendor will be able to reproduce. Large operators have independent lab systems that mimic their production system, and they can often find problems there before customers are affected.

PON OPTICS

The optical interface at an OLT is normally handled by a plug-in optical module meeting certain standards. Several progressively smaller optical modules have been developed over the years, with the most common at this time being referred to as the *SFP* (small form-factor pluggable). You can get SFPs in several different power and sensitivity ranges, depending upon the length of the PON and how many times you are going to split it. Chapter 6 goes into much more detail concerning the optical issues in PONs.

Optics other than for the PON are also supplied in SFP packaging, but obviously will not work if you plug them into PON ports. You can get SFPs for short-distance multimode optics for use in a headend/CO, and you can get single-mode 1 Gb/s and 10 Gb/s Ethernet SFPs (typically a 10 Gb/s SFP is called an SFP+, or XFP in a different form factor). You can also get SFPs with electrical Ethernet interfaces rather than optical interfaces, as well as other types of SFPs.

Usually ONTs have integrated optics (commonly called 2 × 5 SFF without the DDM function or 2 × 10 SFF with DDM), the economics and the number of ONTs built resulting in greater efficiency if the ONT is designed that way. Frequently the ONT manufacturer will purchase the optics as a subunit, but to you as the user it will appear just as part of the ONT. You can also get an entire basic GPON or EPON ONT in an SFP (sometimes called EPON or GPON sticks); they are used in some ONT products, depending on the features needed.

GPON Optics Options

GPON is specified in terms of the optics required for two different distances, either 10 or 20 km, and three different split ratios. Split ratios up to 128:1 are specified, though that is not likely to be practical given current optical components. A number of data rates are specified for GPON, but the only one of practical interest is 2.488 Gb/s downstream and 1.244 Gb/s upstream. In order to complement the data rates originally specified, the ITU originally specified three optical classes, Class A, Class B, and Class C. However, none proved optimum for the data rates of interest, so another class, Class B+, was adopted for most GPON systems (not XG-PON). Later, another set of optical specifications for higher loss budget were specified, Class C+.

In order to meet the requisite ONT receive sensitivity of –27 dBm, two options were specified. We shall cover the optical components in more detail in Chapter 6. There are two receive diode technologies that can be used: *PIN photodiodes* are simpler and less costly, but don't have the requisite sensitivity. They may be used at the ONT, but in order to meet the sensitivity requirements, *forward error correction* (FEC) encoding must be used in order to correct errors introduced by marginal receive level. An intuitive introduction to FEC is presented in Appendix C. In order to use this option, the OLT must support FEC in the downstream path. It is likely that most on the market do support FEC, but some early equipment may not support FEC.

The other type of receiver diode that can be used is the *avalanche photodiode* (APD). It exhibits better sensitivity than does the PIN photodiode, but requires a higher supply voltage, as well as certain other accommodations. And it is somewhat more expensive.

Table 4.1 summarizes the two most common optical classes for GPON systems. The downstream launch power is that launched from the OLT, and if a broadcast video overlay is used, it would be considered to be measured at the output of the wave division multiplexer (WDM) that combines the 1550-nm broadcast wavelength. The downstream received power is measured at the ONT, and for Class B+ may either be interpreted as with or without FEC, and with the appropriate optical detector as described above. Similarly, the upstream optical power is measured at the ONT and the received power at the OLT.

The overload optical power in the received power column refers to the maximum optical signal level at the optical receiver; signal levels above this may

Table 4.1 GPON Optical Classes

Class/Direction (Nom. λ, nm)	Optical Launch Power (Min/Max, dBm)	Optical Receive Power (Min/Overload, dBm)	Optical Penalty (dB)	Loss Budget (dB)
B+ downstream (1490)	+1.5/+5	–27/–8	0.5	28
B+ upstream (1310)	+0.5/+5	–28/–8	0.5	28
C+ downstream (1490)	+3/+7	–30/–8	1	32
C+ upstream (1310)	+0.5/+5	–32/–12	0.5	32

cause malfunction of the receiver, and in the worst case, may actually cause hardware failure of the receive diode. Generally, you would not expect to see these values in practice, but if for some reason you build a short PON with few splits, you may see it. This could happen in a lab system, too, where you may be tempted to reduce the number of ONTs in order to save money and effort. We do not recommend doing so, as not only might you damage your equipment, you may miss issues that only show up when you load a system to near full capacity.

The range of launch powers reflects normal anticipated production and lifetime and temperature variation in output power. It is normal for a laser diode to lose power output over its lifetime. Usually a feedback circuit is employed around the laser to keep the power constant as the diode ages. However, after a number of years, it is expected that the power output will drop to the point that the minimum power will not be met, and the device will have to be replaced.

The optical penalty is a factor included to compensate for certain optical fiber issues (the most significant in PONs is *dispersion*, covered in Chapter 6). It is a crude but practical way to allow increased power to compensate for the effectively reduced signal-to-noise ratio caused (primarily) by dispersion.

The loss budget is the difference between the minimum output power from the transmitter and the minimum received power needed at the receiver, reduced by the optical penalty. Note that, just because a Class B+ system says you *can* build a network with 28 dB of loss, this does not mean that you *should* build a network with this much loss. Remember that there are things that may cause the loss to go up in the future. Connectors that start out pristinely clean (and that is the exception, not the rule, even for new builds) may be unplugged and plugged back in with a little dirt in the future. Optical cables above ground get pulled down when a truck with a too-high load passed under them or a car hits a pole. Underground cables get cut when someone tries to bury another cable or pipe in the same place (and despite everyone's best efforts to mark cables, such "backhoe fades" do happen). Repairs sometimes have to be made hurriedly and under very bad environmental conditions, and so do not always get made to new-build standards. Yet the system must work anyway, and you need some loss margin to make sure that happens.

XG-PON Optics Options

What could be more straightforward than repeating the same tabular parameters for XG-PON (10 Gb/s down, 2.5 Gb/s up) systems? Unfortunately, things are expressed somewhat differently in XG-PON, with systems being divided into classes called *Nominal1* (N1), *Nominal2* (N2), *Extended1* (E1), and *Extended2* (E2) classes. In order to complicate matters, N2 and E2 are each

Table 4.2 XG-PON Optical Classes

Class/Direction (Nom. λ, nm)	Optical Launch Power (Min/Max, dBm)	Optical Receive Power (Min/ Overload, dBm)	Optical Penalty (dB)	Loss Budget (dB)
N1 downstream (1577)	2/6	−28/−8	1	29
N1 upstream (1270)	2/7	−27.5/−7	0.5	29
N2a downstream (1577)	4/8	−28/−8	1	31
N2a upstream (1270)	2/7	−29.5/−9	0.5	31
N2b downstream (1577)	10.5/12.5	−21.5/−3.5	1	31
N2b upstream (1270)	Same as N2a	Same as N2a	0.5	31
E1 downstream (1577)	6/10	−28/−8	1	33
E1 upstream (1270)	2/7	−31.5/−11	0.5	33
E2a downstream (1577)	8/12	−28/−8	1	35
E2a upstream (1270)	2/7	−33.5/−13	0.5	35
E2b downstream (1577)	14.5/16.5	−21.5/−3.5	1	35
E2b upstream (1270)	Same as E2a	Same as E2a	0.5	35

divided into subclasses, called *a* and *b* respectively. The differential distance[3] allowed in GPON is 20 km. In XG-PON, two differential distances are defined, DD20 and DD40 for, respectively, differential distances of 20 and 40 km.

You can see from Table 4.2 that XG-PON provides for different loss budgets. Classes N1 and E1 provide, respectively, for 29 and 33 dB loss budgets. N2 and E2 provide, respectively, for 31 and 35 dB loss budgets, and within each of those two classes, you have a trade-off of launch power and receive sensitivity in order to achieve the loss budget. Presumably the solution used will change with time, advances in the state-of-the-art, and cost models.

SRS Effects

We shall go into more detail in Chapter 6, but we now introduce a concept that can be crucial to the success of a PON carrying broadcast video. There is a distortion mechanism in the fiber optic cable itself called *stimulated Raman scattering* (SRS). It has the effect of transferring power from a lower wavelength to a higher wavelength when both signals are traveling in the same direction on the fiber. The downstream data, which turns the optical signal ON for a logical 1 and OFF for a 0, is transmitted on a wavelength of 1490 nm, whereas

---

[3]The fiber distance between the farthest and closest ONTs on the PON, as measured from the OLT.

RF-modulated broadcast signals are on 1550 nm. This wavelength separation is not optimum for transferring power, but it does cause significant power to be transferred from 1490 nm to 1550 nm due to SRS. Since the power at 1490 nm is on/off keyed, then sometimes power is transferred to the 1550-nm carrier, and sometimes it is not. This creates an undesired modulation component on the 1550-nm carrier. The transfer is worse at lower RF frequencies (as seen on the demodulated 1550-nm carrier). Normally, since the data on the 1490-nm optical carrier are random, the effect on the 1550-nm carrier is to introduce random noise. Random noise in an analog video signal is what we know as "snow" in the picture, and the effect of the additional noise from the 1490-nm carrier is reasonably easy to manage.

However, when there are no downstream data to transmit, GPON transmits a short 40-bit idle pattern in order to maintain synchronization. A repetitive pattern such as this causes the transferred power to "bunch up" at certain frequencies rather than to be spread out over a wide band, as is characteristic of random noise. The frequency that is most affected happens to be 62.2 MHz, which is in channel 3 of the North American TV channel plan. If channel 3 is carrying an analog TV signal, then that signal will display diagonal bars (RF engineers call it a *beat*) in the picture, at an intensity that can be very objectionable. If the channel is carrying digital video, there is sufficient interference in the channel that potentially the signal may not be demodulated accurately, resulting in no picture or a very faulty and unstable picture.

Techniques have been developed to overcome the problem. When no downstream data are available to transmit, the idle code may be replaced by random data addressed to no ONT. For example, a VLAN might be created at the OLT, which does not terminate on any ONTs. Random bits put in that VLAN would not go anywhere, but they would preclude the power from bunching up in one channel. (Note that this solution is patented.) In addition, GPON can scramble the idle sequence as part of its dc elimination and clock synchronization process described above, and this can effectively remove the "bunching up" of the interference power.

SUMMARY

This chapter has served as an introduction to GPON, the ITU standard for PONs. As with its counterpart, EPON, it operates on a network consisting largely of a central point with a single fiber radiating outward to a splitter, which serves 32 or, uncommonly, 64 endpoints (or it may serve 16 endpoints). The central termination is called an OLT, while the user endpoints are called either ONUs or ONTs.

Endnotes

i.   http://www.itu.int/rec/T-REC-G/en. Go to the G.984 series of standards.

ii.   http://www.itu.int/rec/T-REC-G/en. Go to the G.987 series of standards.

iii. http://www.itu.int/en/Pages/default.aspx.

iv.   http://www.fsan.org/.

v.   http://www.broadband-forum.org/.

vi.   http://www.slideshare.net/mansoor_gr8/gpon-fundamentals.

vii. Hood D, Trojer E. Gigabit-capable passive optical networks. John Wiley & Sons; 2012.

viii. ITU-T G.988, Available at: http://www.itu.int/rec/T-REC-G.988-201210-I/en.

CHAPTER 5

Other Network Standards

INTRODUCTION

Besides the EPON and GPON standards, there are other fiber-to-the-home (FTTH) standards that we should mention. Some are standalone standards in their own right, others are really supplementary standards intended to enhance other standards, or to be bridge standards, where the end game is GPON or EPON, but for various reasons, the operator is not prepared to make that leap yet. We present them so that you will understand what people are talking about when they mention them, and so that you can make a decision regarding incorporating them into your plant.

POINT-TO-POINT SYSTEMS

Point-to-point (P2P), or *Active Ethernet* (AE), is an alternative to EPON and GPON, installed by some operators. A single *home-run* fiber is installed from the headend to each customer. Because there are no splitting losses to account for, optical signal levels can be quite low. Standards to support P2P were codified in the original IEEE 802.3ah standard, now part of the 802.3 Ethernet standard. In a P2P system, each subscriber has a dedicated Ethernet port in the headend, a dedicated fiber to his home or business, and a dedicated optical network terminal (ONT) at the home (as always). As shown below, it is not really feasible to carry broadcast video on a P2P network: most operators carry IPTV if they carry a video service, though we have seen a very few operators actually build a parallel HFC or PON network to deliver video.

P2P Architecture

Fig. 5.1 illustrates a P2P architecture (as distinguished from a PON architecture). One or (usually) more P2P switches, which include the fiber interfaces on the subscriber side, connect to individual subscribers, using a 1550-nm downstream data carrier and a 1310-nm upstream data carrier (as we shall show shortly, it is not really feasible to use broadcast video with a P2P system, so using 1550 nm for data is not a problem).

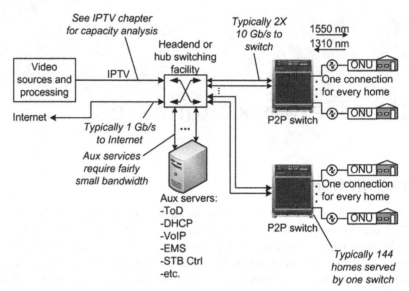

FIGURE 5.1
P2P architecture.

The P2P switches are connected to the headend (or hub) primary data switch, typically using multiple 1 Gb/s or 10 Gb/s (preferred) Ethernet links, which may be either electrical or optical. The primary data switch connects to all of the auxiliary servers needed, to the Internet, and to the IPTV headend. There may be other servers used that are not shown. For example, some of the IP video service providers [they are called *over-the-top* (*OTT*) providers, because they provide video outside of the operator's video service] may place servers in the headend of a large system. The reason is so that popular OTT programs can be buffered locally, relieving the data burden (and cost) of the Internet connection, and providing better service because you don't have to worry about Internet congestion.

Data Concentration in P2P Networks

An advantage often cited for P2P networks over PONs is that you don't have the shared data path you do in PONs, so you can get a full Gb/s (or whatever) data speed to each subscriber. Well, yes and no, but mainly no. Fig. 5.1 shows why. Suppose I have a small system with just the two P2P switches shown. A typical number of subscribers served from one switch chassis might be 144 subscribers. If each were to get 1 Gb/s, then the total data bandwidth required by the chassis is 144 Gb/s. While it is possible, we have rarely if ever seen a chassis connected to the headend switch by more than two 10 Gb/s data links. If the two links could each be utilized to 100% capacity (impractical in the real world), then the maximum average data rate you have to provide to each subscriber at this point, is really 20 Gb/s divided by 144 subscribers, or 140 Mb/s, a far cry from the 1 Gb/s assumed.

But it gets worse! Now figure in the two chasses, serving a total of 288 subscribers (not really a big enough system to be practical). OK, so each subscriber really uses an average of 140 Mb/s to the headend switch. But for economic reasons, you are not too likely in a small system to have more than 1 Gb/s to the Internet, and even this is likely to be cost-prohibitive for a small system. But if I have 288 subscribers sharing a 1 Gb/s link to the Internet, then I really have 1 Gb/s divided by 288 subscribers, or just under 3.5 Mb/s on the average for each subscriber, not the 1 Gb/s assumed.

Case in Which P2P May Have an Advantage Over PON

There may be some advantage in a P2P network over a PON if you do find you need more speed for a few subscribers. With P2P networks, you can change out terminal equipment for one customer needing more speed. Both the GPON and EPON standards claim seamless upgrade to the next generation, though doing so may require a larger investment for the first customer who wants more speed. Also, if you were to design for a certain speed in the PON and later found you needed more, you would need to change the entire PON termination equipment (but not the fiber). With P2P, you could simply add more data capacity on the network side of the P2P switch.

Case in Which P2P May Have a Disadvantage Over PON

It is hard to imagine a P2P system being installed for the same cost as a PON. And while the operational expense (op ex) is definitely going to be less than for copper or coax plant, it is hard to imagine P2P op ex being as low as is that for PON. There is a good bit more fiber needed for P2P than for PON, and while the cost of the fiber itself is not that great, and the installation cost is arguably similar in both cases, there will be a much higher splicing cost with P2P; typically you leave the headend with a few large bundles (cables) of fiber strands. Along the way, the fibers diverge, and when they do, you will need to splice each fiber strand to one in a smaller cable. This can result in a larger, much larger, number of fiber splices with P2P, each splice being rather labor-intensive.

Finally, the larger numbers of fibers leaving the headend can produce quite a headache in the case of a backhoe fade (any cable break). If the cable break occurs in most of the plant, you will have about 32 times the number of splices to make with P2P. Cable breaks seem to have a tendency to occur in the most difficult locations, at the most difficult times, increasing the cost and delay of service restoration.

Oversubscription

For residential service, this is not nearly as bad as it seems, and now we shall see why the Internet works at all, the magic being oversubscription. First, we have not taken into account that some people are using some of their data bandwidth for video, and this does not take away from the Internet bandwidth as we have defined it (but see the Chapter 12 on IPTV for a lot of "gotchas" with IPTV service). Also, no residential subscriber is using his Internet bandwidth continuously, and when one subscriber is NOT using it, the protocols used make that bandwidth available to other subscribers. This bandwidth sharing is what makes the Internet so efficient. A subscriber may pull down a web page, and he is using his bandwidth in the process. But then he may spend 5 minutes on that web page, during which time he is not using any bandwidth.

We can illustrate the power of statistics very nicely with a totally unrealistic picture of an unrealistic situation depicted in Fig. 5.2. What we have done is to assume that each subscriber in the system of Fig. 5.1 is using either 100% or none of his allowed bandwidth during any arbitrary time period. We have further assumed that the probability of any one subscriber using his bandwidth during any one time period is 10%—unrealistically high except maybe for some video applications. We have let a random number generator go through a lot of cases and we have totaled up the bandwidth used as a percentage of the bandwidth that would be available if we added up everyone's allowed bandwidth.

If we do this experiment with only one user, we see that he is using all of his bandwidth, but for only about 10% of the time, not surprising since these are the parameters we programmed into the simulation. So if we are going to give this subscriber the bandwidth we promised, we have to provide the capability of that bandwidth. Seems logical.

But now let's look at the situation in which we have 25 subscribers sharing the total bandwidth we promised them. Do we really need to provide 25 times the bandwidth in order for each subscriber to get what we promised? No, not

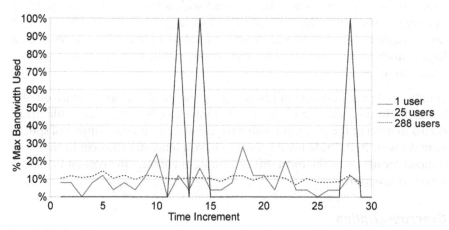

FIGURE 5.2

A very unreal example of the power of statistics.

according to this simulation. We never even used 30% of the bandwidth—that's the power of statistics. Not everyone is going to be using all of their bandwidth at the same time, so sharing works well. Keep the logic going, and let's total up all 288 subscribers doing the same unrealistic thing, each using 100% of his bandwidth but only 10% of the time. We can satisfy this need while providing only 15% of the promised bandwidth—statistics are working really well in our favor!

Now remember that this is hardly a real-world simulation. Not every subscriber is going to demand 100% of his bandwidth 10% of the time. The real-world is infinitely more complicated than this, with one subscriber pulling significant bandwidth while another reads a book, another grabs a snack, and another works on his car. ISPs like to keep such statistics to themselves, but some casual conversations in the past have indicated that you could oversubscribe about 30 times without anyone complaining. That is, if you have 30 Mb/s total bandwidth available (not an FTTH number, but we got this from cable TV a while ago), you can sell subscribers bandwidth totaling 30 times this, or 900 Mb/s without subscribers noticing any problems. Of course, you cannot sell any one subscriber more than 30 Mb/s, since that would hit the maximum available.

These numbers may be changing, though, as subscribers pull more OTT video, which may not conform to the old norms. Those old norms involved mostly pulling down web pages and email. So we can't guarantee the same numbers in the future. The bottom line is that you may not be able to oversubscribe as much in the future, but only time and monitoring bandwidth usage will tell you for sure.

Business Services
So far we've talked about residential service. Business services, now that's another matter. You may well have *service-level agreements* (SLAs), with businesses, which *do* require you to provide constant connectivity for the business, and you will be tested to see that you are delivering. This bandwidth can be shared with residential so long as you have enough residential bandwidth after you deduct that which you are selling to business customers under SLAs. Then you will need a mechanism to prioritize bandwidth, so that businesses get what they contract for before you start doling out the remaining bandwidth to residential customers, who can share. Fortunately the protocols needed to get this done exist, and we'll get around to them in later chapters.

RF OVER GLASS (RFoG)
The cable TV industry has defined and is installing in some places, an FTTH architecture with the most fun acronym we have ever encountered: or *RF over glass* (RFoG). RFoG uses an identical physical architecture to EPON or GPON,

and many people see it as an interim step in moving to one of those standards. Rather than use downstream binary data at 1490 nm and upstream binary data at 1310 nm, with a 1550-nm broadcast overlay, as do other PON standards, RFoG places a downstream carrier modulated with many radio frequency (RF) carriers, on 1550 nm. It places upstream data, modulated onto RF carriers which are then modulated onto either 1310 nm or 1610 nm. The reason for two upstream wavelengths is that some operators want to keep cost down by using more common 1310-nm lasers, at the expense of compatibility with EPON or GPON. Other operators, anticipating eventual conversion to EPON or GPON, elect to put the upstream signals on 1610 nm, which is not used by the other standards.

The advantage of RFoG for a cable operator is that it allows using termination equipment which is already being used, and with which the employees are familiar. The video service comprises a large number of RF carriers, each either modulated with one analog video channel, or more commonly, modulated with several digital signals. Downstream data use some of those RF channels, with the modulation being produced by a DOCSIS CMTS [DOCSIS defines a series of standards for transmission of data on cable TV systems, and a CMTS (cable modem termination system) is the headend equipment supporting DOCSIS modems]. The upstream data come from each home, and are generated either by a DOCSIS modem or by a set top box, which must have an RF transmitter in order to transmit control data back to the headend.

RFoG System Block Diagram

Fig. 5.3 illustrates the block diagram of the RFoG system.[i] To the left is the optical hub or the headend, depending on the physical architecture of the system. It includes one or more downstream optical transmitters putting out a signal at approximately 1550 nm. It is amplified in an optical amplifier and split according to the number of PONs needed. In some cases there may be more than one downstream optical transmitter. Each output of the splitter is supplied to a wave division multiplexer (WDM), which separates the 1550-nm downstream from either the 1310- or 1610-nm upstream transmissions, depending upon which wavelength the system is using. The upstream wavelength goes to an upstream optical receiver, whose output is the RF signal as it entered each R-ONU, as shown below. The output of the receiver will go to the CMTS and likely also to a set top control system.

The optical distribution network (ODN) is identical to that of an EPON or GPON system, including the 32-way or 64-way splitter. As always, the splitter may be located in one place as in the diagram, or splitting may be distributed in any way the operator sees fit, so long as the total loss budget is respected. The standard recommends a loss budget of 25 dB if analog signals are present,

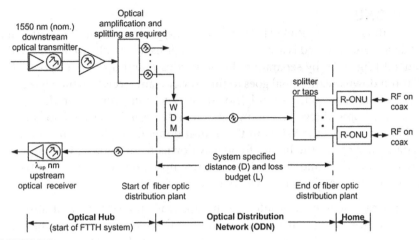

FIGURE 5.3

RFoG system block diagram.

with more loss being tolerable if all digital signals are being transmitted. The standard also refers to other situations in which you might be able to operate with a little more loss. However, the EPON standard is written around a 25-dB loss budget (though more loss is usually practical), so if one contemplates upgrading to EPON in the future, this specification limitation must be taken into account.

The subscriber-facing side of the R-ONU (*RFoG ONU*, so named to distinguish it from an EPON or GPON ONT) looks just like a normal cable TV system terminating on coax at the subscriber's home. The downstream signals appear every 6 MHz starting at 54 MHz (North American standard—different frequencies are used elsewhere). The maximum frequency usually specified today is 1 GHz, though not all systems may be using frequencies that high; even higher frequencies may be used in the future. Any signal may be modulated with one analog TV channel, multiple digital TV channels, or data (including voice data). Control signals sent with the digital TV channels or on a separate RF carrier tell the set top what frequency to tune and what channel to display. For digital TV, additional information tells the set top where to find data packets for each of the several TV signals in the channel to which it is to tune. The old paradigm of a one-to-one correspondence between channel number and frequency is still used internally to describe the frequency plan, but is of little to no relevance today for the subscriber, as the set top may be told to display any channel number for any frequency.

Upstream signals injected into the subscriber-side port (labeled "RF on coax") comprise upstream signals from cable modems and set top boxes. Different frequencies are used for the two types of signals.

The R-ONU

Fig. 5.4 illustrates the R-ONU. At the fiber side, coming from the splitter, the first device encountered is a WDM which functions identically to the one at the headend (Fig. 5.3), by separating the downstream and upstream signals. The 1550-nm downstream signal goes to the downstream receiver, which has some form of automatic gain control (not shown) to compensate for changes in the received optical level. Its output goes to a diplexer, which functions in the RF domain as does the WDM in the optical domain. By that we mean that it separates and routes the higher-frequency downstream signals (54–1000 MHz in North America) and the lower-frequency upstream signals (5–42 MHz in North America) sending them where they should go.

The upstream signals are routed to the upstream transmitter, and also to a signal detector circuit. The purpose of the signal detector is to determine when an upstream signal is present at the RF port on this R-ONU, and to turn on the transmitter. This is necessary because each R-ONU has its own upstream optical transmitter, and if all were on at the same time, a lot of interference would result.

The upstream transmitter is an analog transmitter, required because a digital transmitter would introduce unacceptable distortion to the RF input signal, and cause out-of-channel splatter, which could prevent other subscribers from communicating upstream.

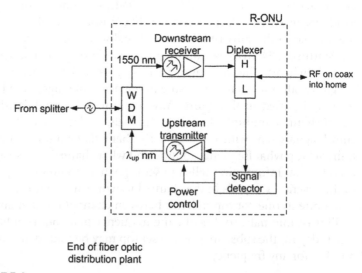

FIGURE 5.4
The R-ONU.

DOCSIS PROVISIONING OVER EPON (DPoE)

In the late 1990s, the cable TV industry began the deployment of broadband services using a standards-based architecture called DOCSIS, as mentioned in the previous section. The DOCSIS architecture defined two network elements beginning with the cable modem termination system (CMTS) at the headend and the cable modem (CM) located within the subscribers' premises. This standard was developed by CableLabs then sent to the Society of Cable Telecommunications Engineers (SCTE) to provide the formal development of the standard. Over the following decades CableLabs continued the development of the DOCSIS standards to include QoS, Voice, and high-bandwidth services.

As DOCSIS gained in popularity, becoming the primary technology for the deployment of voice and high-speed data services in North America and elsewhere, CableLabs continued to expand the operational aspects of the protocol to include operation, administration, and maintenance (OAM) features, security, operational support system extensions, and other features. Eventually, the cable TV industry found itself managing millions of cable modems globally, supported by a complete industry of hardware and software vendors.

As the cable TV industry began considerations for FTTH technologies beyond RFoG, CableLabs commenced the development of a new standards-based architecture. With participation from the vendor and operator communities, CableLabs defined the DPoE specifications.

CableLabs made the selection of EPON based on feedback from the participating operators leaning toward 1G-EPON and 10G-EPON technology. During the initial drafts of the DPoE specifications, 10G-EPON had already been standardized, supporting symmetrical 10G services while being backward compatible with 1G-EPON technology. The vendor community was in the infant stages of producing 10G-EPON equipment, making EPON the logical approach for the cable TV industry to standardize. As this is written, there is talk about doing the same for GPON.

Common Provisioning, Management, and Services

A network supporting DPoE service models such as IP HSD (high-speed data) or MEF (business-related standards promulgated by the Metro Ethernet Forum) operate correspondingly to a similar DOCSIS network. Within the DPoE architecture the OLT is analogous to a CMTS and the DPoE optical network unit (ONU) operates like a DOCSIS cable modem. The same back office servers should be capable of managing both the DOCSIS and DPoE system concurrently using the same standards-based cable modem configuration files. Fig. 5.5 illustrates DPoE and cable modems under a common management umbrella.

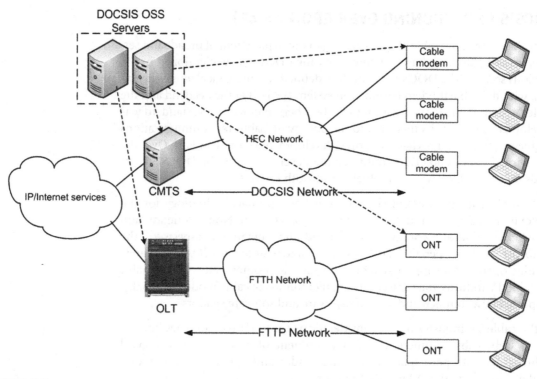

FIGURE 5.5
DPoE overlaid on an EPON system.

The initial specifications for the DPoE v1.0 standard process consisted of seven different specifications. These specifications defined the complete operational and management interfaces. Fig. 5.6 provides an overview of each specification.

OLT/ONT Interoperability

In addition to defining a cable TV operational model within an EPON environment, CableLabs took on another challenge to ensure the interoperability between OLT and ONT devices from different suppliers. Historically, when defining the initial 802.3ah specification (the original EPON specification), the IEEE did not provide an OAM&P (operations, administration, maintenance, and provisioning) context to support end-to-end service provisioning between the UNI of the ONT and the NNI of the OLT.

Up to this point, the cable TV industry was not constrained by such lack of interoperability within the vendor community. Operators were free to choose CableLabs qualified equipment, guaranteeing complete interoperability and integration within their DOCSIS network. In order for the deployment of

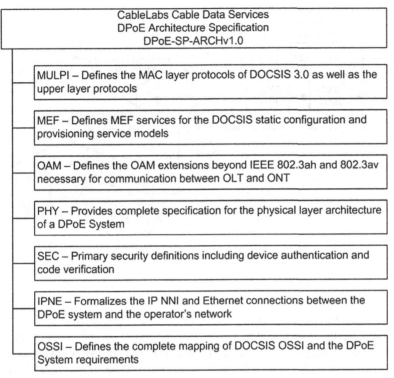

FIGURE 5.6
DPoE architecture specification.

EPON technology using DPoE to be successful, CableLabs had to address this deficiency of EPON (the deficiency being lack of a defined OAM&P), not only defining the necessary interfaces but also a process to qualify vendors.

Using similar processes in place to guarantee CMTS and CM interoperability, CableLabs has established a complete interoperability program for vendor community participation. CableLabs hosts multiple "certification waves" throughout the year where vendor OLT and ONT equipment are qualified. The cert waves (as they are called) are handled independently by CableLabs without vendor participation.

EPON PROTOCOL OVER COAX (EPoC)

In 2011 a group of operators in China, joined by North American operators, saw a market requirement for the development of a standard to extend the IEEE 802.3ah point-to-multipoint architecture to operate over a coax-based PHY (physical) layer. The goal of this community was to deliver the same scheduling, management and quality of service (QoS) models to operate the same way

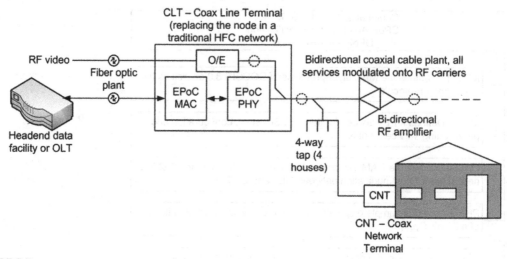

FIGURE 5.7

EPoC system.

regardless of an optical or coax connection to the subscriber. A call for interest (CFI) was initiated during this period with interest from all areas of the cable industry including global operators, chipset vendors, and system vendors, with Broadcom taking the lead role. The formation of the EPoC Task Force was chartered by the IEEE 802.3 Working Group as the IEEE 802.3bn Task Force.

Fig. 5.7 shows the concept of EPoC. Where the node goes in a traditional HFC plant, we substitute the CLT. The CLT accepts the same inputs as would be supplied to an OLT in a conventional FTTH system, or an output of an OLT may drive the CLT. The CLT converts all signals to RF modulation, required in the coaxial cable plant, and modifies the EPON protocol to work in this environment. Signals are coupled to homes via in-place coax plant, and terminate in a CNT at each home.

The high-level architecture of an EPoC network is consistent with its big brother, EPON. In an EPON network, the MAC and PHY layer located in the hub site is termed an optical line terminal (OLT). Within an EPoC network the node is exchanged with a *coax line terminal* (CLT). Similarly, the MAC and PHY layer located at the residence or subscriber location is termed a *coax network terminal* (CNT) rather than an *optical network terminal* (ONT). The term coax network unit may be substituted for coax network terminal. In a PON, the communication channel between the OLT and ONT is an optical network allowing for multiple ONTs to be connected to a single PON interface on the OLT, while in an EPoC network the coax portion of the communication channel allows multiple CNTs to be connected to a single interface on the CLT.

The physical layer in the coax network conforms as much as possible to the physical layer in DOCSIS 3.1. DOCSIS 3.1 adds OFDM (orthogonal frequency division multiplexing) to the QAM modes used in earlier versions of DOCSIS. It also has the ability to bond many channels in order to achieve higher overall data rates. At the same time, it provides the ability to vacate channels when there are conflicts with off-air use of those channels.

Current Status

The standardization work is being done by the IEEE 802.3bn task force. Their result of the PHY standard will allow for multiple deployment models as well as an objective for a migration path toward 10 Gbit/s. The deployment models could be characterized as a single deployment model of a standalone EPoC system or an EPoC system operating as an extension to an EPON network with a single deployment and services model in place.

As this is written, EPoC is in the early stages of balloting in the IEEE process, with the intent that it will become an amendment to the 802.3 Ethernet standard. After that, the market will take over and determine how EPoC fits into the solutions available to the operator.

SERVICE INTEROPERABILITY IN ETHERNET PASSIVE OPTICAL NETWORKS (SIEPON)

In 2009 a group of industry vendors focused on extending the capabilities of the IEEE 802.3ah EPoN specifications formed a working group under the sponsorship of the IEEE. The objective of the working group was the development of a standard to allow for service-level interoperability among EPON and future 10G EPON vendors. Prior to the working group focus, the EPON and 10G EPON standards focus was on the interoperability at the physical layer and data link layer between the OLT and ONT. This was great if you just needed two pieces of network equipment to communicate with each other. Not so good if someone is trying to access the Internet, make a phone call, or even watch TV. Communication at higher service and QoS/CoS levels was more-or-less the wild wild west. Every vendor had their unique "theory of operation," making interoperability at the service level a challenge at best.

Hence, the SIEPON working group was formed, entitling their efforts the Service Interoperability in Ethernet Passive Optical Networks (SIEPON). Rather than pronounce the acronym, it is usually spelled out in speech. The working group focused on the development of a standards-based architecture for EPON devices to follow with two purposes: (1) open competition of suppliers of OLT and ONT equipment and (2) drive innovation and price reductions within the EPON community through direct competition. The SIEPON organization was not intended to become a certification authority, but rather would define the

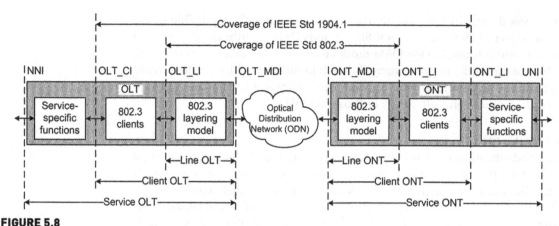

FIGURE 5.8
SIEPON coverage model.

specifications by which the vendor community may abide, with other possible organizations to certify compliance.

The IEEE SIEPON working group drafted a standard in September 2011, with the first official standard published in September 2013 as IEEE Standard 1904.1-2013. The standard defined an operational and management architecture layered above IEEE 802.3 and 802.1 without impacting higher-level service protocols necessary for end-to-end communications. Fig. 5.8 shows the level of coverage the IEEE 1904.1-2013 standard supports.

One of the primary strengths of SIEPON was allowing for coexistence of existing and upcoming networking models within the access community. Existing DSL/G.PON-driven standards from the Broadband Forum and ITU-T, namely TR-200 and SG15/Q2, were still able to coexist in an environment with SIEPON. Furthermore, the development of the DPoE specification by CableLabs allowed for the DPoE Service OAM Specification (DPoE-SP-SOAM) to extend SIEPON as the basis for its development.

Current Status

Within the SIEPON specifications a series of three packages were defined based on different deployment models. Package A was assigned to those services associated with North American operators. Package B was assigned to those services associated with Japanese operators and Package C was assigned to Chinese operators. Currently the SIEPON working group is focused on the definition of conformance test procedures for each package.

Once the Annexes are completed, under the direction of the IEEE Conformity Assessment Program, the SIEPON Conformity Assessment Steering Group will develop a "testing and certification program" to be executed by independent and authorized test facilities.

Endnote

i. Information and diagrams in this section are from the RFoG standard, ANSI/SCTE 174 2010, Radio Frequency over Glass Fiber-to-the-Home Specification. It is available from the standards section at http://www.scte.org/default.aspx.

CHAPTER 6

Optical Layer Issues

INTRODUCTION

One of the key enabling fiber-to-the-home (FTTH) technologies is, not surprisingly, the optics needed to make it all work. This includes cable, passive devices (splitters, wave division multiplexer [WDMs], connectors, splices, etc.), optical sources, and optical detectors. We shall describe key components needed and how they interact in the network, and we'll provide some very important information as to how to use them successfully. With that last topic, we get into the problems that we have seen more than any other types of problems in FTTH networks: improper network design, and improper fiber handling (connector cleaning, fiber bending, etc.) cause more problems in FTTH networks than do any other issues. And with a little personnel training and a lot of diligence these problems can largely be avoided.

We shall concentrate on so-called *single-mode* fiber here, because it is suitable for longer-distance transmission as we do in FTTH. Single-mode is contrasted to *multimode* fiber, which is larger and operates on shorter wavelengths and at shorter distances. You may use multimode fiber in a data center, where its low-cost terminations, ruggedness, and ease of termination are more important than is low loss. But for the distances and splits we are talking about with FTTH, it is only single-mode fiber.

Be sure to also read Chapter 9 on Outside Plant Design. It has further practical information on the care of fiber optic plants.

FIBER OPTIC TRANSMISSION

Light exhibits properties of both particles and waves, as you may recall from physics courses. It is an electromagnetic wave, as are the radio waves that bring us radio, television, and cell phone communications, and as are microwaves that deliver satellite broadcasts and heat our food. The difference is that the electromagnetic light waves we're talking about now are at a much higher frequency than are the others we mentioned. Your WiFi signals that wirelessly couple your computer to the Internet operate on one of two bands: most

85

FTTx Networks. http://dx.doi.org/10.1016/B978-0-12-420137-8.00006-8

commonly about 2.4 GHz, and another band at about 5 GHz. Microwave ovens operate at about 2.5 GHz. In single-mode fiber optic systems, the frequencies run to about 230,000 GHz.

Frequencies and Wavelength

If you're an engineer familiar with frequency and wavelength, feel free to skip the next couple of paragraphs. Waves have two properties related by the propagation speed of the wave. *Frequency* describes the number of times a second that the wave alternates between its opposite states (e.g., peaks—maximum values as in Fig. 6.1—or valleys, minimum values), seen as if we were standing in one place and observing the number of peaks of the wave going past us in 1 second. *Wavelength* describes the distance between consecutive like places on the wave (e.g., the distance between peaks), seen as if we were observing the wave stopped in a moment of time.

For audio waves traveling through air, the alternate states are compression and rarefaction of the air (pressure). For electromagnetic waves, including radio and light, the waves are electromagnetic waves propagating through free space, or whatever medium will support transportation (including glass, the subject of the present discussion). Electromagnetic waves propagate as alternating regions of electrostatic charge (positive and negative) and also as the direction of a magnetic field (i.e., north pole to south pole), the two inextricably bound by the intrinsic impedance of the medium (about which we need say little here), as defined by Maxwell's equations (about which we shall, mercifully, say nothing). As the wave moves past a point in space (or in a guided medium such as a fiber optic strand), an observer at that point will see a series of alternations, which we can diagram as positive and negative peaks, with intermediate levels usually describing a sinusoidal function (the sinusoidal function coming from mathematics from which we shall spare you).

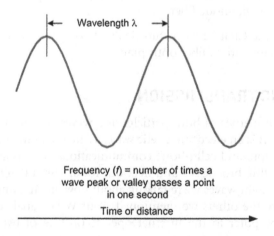

FIGURE 6.1
Frequency and wavelength.

Fig. 6.1 illustrates the concept. Let this represent, say, the electric component of the electromagnetic wave as it moves from left to right. The *wavelength*, represented by λ, is the distance between consecutive peaks as the wave moves, or *propagates*. If you are standing at one point and counting the troughs or peaks of the wave passing in 1 second, the number you count would be the *frequency* of the wave. For audio, we measure frequency in cycles per second, a unit of measure called the *hertz*, after Heinrich Hertz, a pioneer in radio experimentation. The abbreviation is Hz. For radio, frequencies are higher, and thus are measured in kHz ($1\,kHz = 1000\,Hz$) megahertz ($1\,MHz = 1000\,kHz$), or gigahertz ($1\,GHz = 1000\,MHz$). For light we measure frequency in terahertz ($1\,THz = 1000\,GHz$).[1]

Wavelength and frequency are related by the *velocity of propagation* of the wave, the speed at which it moves. For sound in air the speed is about 343 meters per second (m/s). Radio waves and light waves do not need a medium through which to propagate, free space being fine with them. The velocity of propagation in free space is about $3 \times 10^8\,m/s$ (more closely 299,792,458 m/s). So for light propagating in free space, the relation between frequency and wavelength is

$$f = \frac{c}{\lambda}$$

where f = frequency in Hz; c = speed of light in a vacuum = $2.99792458 \times 10^8\,m/s$ (through you might want to take 2.998×10^8 or 3×10^8 as close enough); λ = wavelength in meters.

Customarily, when we talk about a sound or radio wave, we specify it in terms of frequency, though in the early days of radio, it was more common to specify the wavelength. In fiber optic work it is more common to specify the wavelength of the light. The International Telecommunications Union (ITU) has specified standard wavelengths for optical communications, a sample of which is reproduced in Table 6.1. Note that both the frequency and wavelength are designated. The ITU has specified both *coarse* and *dense* wavelength plans. Generally, you can take the odd channel numbers in the table as being the coarse wavelength plan, and if you put one more wavelength between these, you get the generally accepted dense wavelength plan. Fig. 6.2 is based on frequency separations of 100 THz, so you can take standard coarse wavelengths as every 200 THz, and the standard dense wavelengths as being half again the

---

[1]Note capitalization here: we are using the accepted convention. The H in Hz is always capitalized, it being the first letter of a proper name; but when "hertz" is written out as a unit of measure, it is not capitalized. "k" in kHz is lower case. "M" in MHz must be capitalized because lower case would indicate millihertz (thousandths of a hertz). By the time people got to GHz and THz, the convention of capitalizing the first letter was sufficiently established that it stuck.

Table 6.1 Sample ITU 100-THz Grid

ITU Channel	Frequency (THz)	Wavelength (nm)
1	190.1	1577.03
2	190.2	1576.20
3	190.3	1575.37
...	...	...
57	195.7	1531.90
58	195.8	1531.12
59	195.9	1530.33

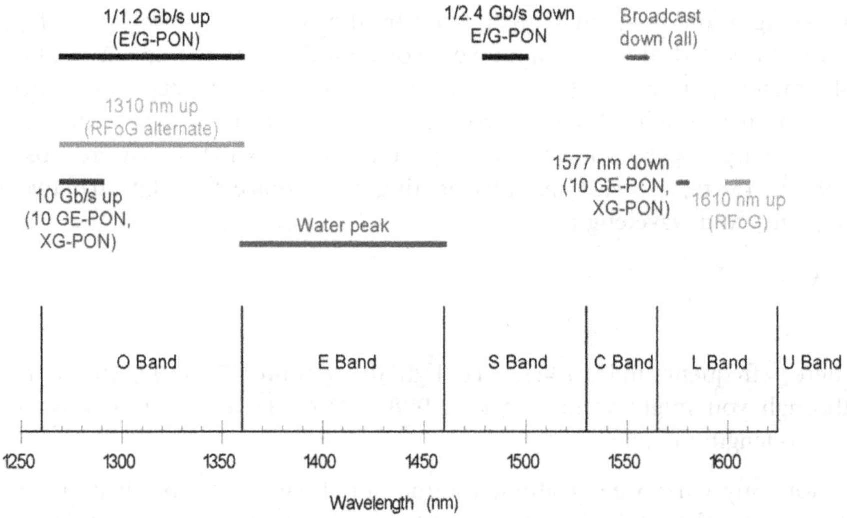

FIGURE 6.2

Wavelengths of significance in PONs.

frequency spacing in this table, a spacing of 50 THz.[2] Yes, we know we just said that we customarily specify light by the wavelength, and then we immediately showed you a table that is defined in terms of frequency. All we can say is that, yes, this is the way it is; most of the time you talk about wavelength, but the ITU specification is driven by frequency. Remember the equation just above, and use the speed of light in a vacuum to convert.

To add a little complication, light slows down when you put it in a medium such as glass—in fact, it is the change in the velocity of propagation that makes refraction (discussed below) possible. It also means that light moves more

---

[2]Some people are even going to dense wavelength plans separated by only 25 THz, putting four other wavelengths between the ones we show.

slowly in a fiber than it does in free space. In a single-mode fiber, the speed might be as low as 60% of the speed of light. That's still fast, but there are times when it makes a difference.

THE GRAND WAVELENGTH PLANS

Fig. 6.2 illustrates the wavelengths of interest in passive optical network (PON) technologies, putting all of the significant wavelengths for all systems on one chart. The ITU has divided the relevant optical wavelength span into multiple bands, called the O, E, S, C, L, and U bands, corresponding to the wavelengths shown. The O band is what is also known sometimes as the *second window*, because it is a window in the spectrum in which telecommunications is practical (there is a lower-wavelength first window used with multimode fiber but not used with single-mode fiber, the only type used to implement FTTH networks). Because this band exhibits the lowest *dispersion* (defined below), it is particularly useful for upstream communications, where we have the most optical transmitters (at the optical network terminals [ONTs]), and where the optical transmitters in some cases are subject to the widest temperature swings. These conditions make it desirable to use the lowest-cost transmitters for upstream, and this in turn means that we want the most forgiving communications path for upstream communications. When all is taken into account, the O band meets these requirements. Both EPON and GPON use this band for upstream communications. The entire 100 nm bandwidth is reserved for this purpose, though higher-performance optical sources don't necessarily use the entire band. We shall return in a few moments to discuss the 10 Gb/s upstream band shown.

The next band up is the E band. Traditional fibers exhibited a peak in adsorption (signal loss) in this band due to a hydroxyl radical that adsorbs energy in this band (with a peak adsorption at 1383 nm). While modern fiber has overcome this problem, this band is still the last to be considered for data transmission because older fiber is still out there, and one piece of old fiber in a plant can cause communications failure in this band.

Next is the S band, which includes the downstream wavelength (1490 ± 10 nm), used by both first-generation EPON and GPON for downstream data transmission. This band, though operating at the same or higher speeds than the upstream in the O band, uses a spectrum slice only 20 nm wide. This is possible because we can assume that the relatively expensive, higher-performance optical transmitters needed to stay in this band are used in the optical line terminal (OLT), where one transmitter can be used for up to 32 subscribers, reducing its cost sensitivity somewhat (at least until you ask the purchasing manager).

The C band is where we put the downstream RF broadcast optical carrier. The broadcast band is specified as being from 1550 nm to 1560 nm for FTTH applications. We can build very cost-effective optical amplifiers in this band, using a technology called *erbium-doped fiber amplifier (EDFA)*. It is possible to build optical amplifiers for a wider bandwidth, and indeed the cable TV industry uses a wider band for RF transmission applications. However, the traditional cable TV industry does not deal with a carrier transmitting in the same direction at 1490 nm, and it does not deal with the higher-wavelength carriers (which were added after the original specifications were written). The FTTH specifications state that the band to be used is 1550–1560 nm. We cannot guarantee that filters in FTTH equipment will support wider bandwidths, so we don't recommend going outside of the 1550–1560 nm band.

Use of the L band is relatively new, older fibers not supporting it. Only in the last few years have people started putting subscriber signals up here (*order wire*, or craft person communications circuits, have been placed in the U band for a while). Contemporaneously with IEEE work on the 10 GE-PON standard, the SCTE was working on the *RFoG (radio frequency over glass*—described in Chapter 5) standard. RFoG needed a wavelength it could use for upstream RF-modulated signals, which would not interfere with anything existing on the PONs, because the RFoG Task Force was charged with design of a system that was compatible with EPON and GPON. One upstream wavelength selected was the O band, seen as a possibly lower-cost alternative for cable operators who wanted RFoG and who did not care about E/GPON compatibility. But the RFoG Working Group needed a wavelength that would be compatible with E/GPON. The candidates were 1590 ± 10 nm and 1610 ± 10 nm. While the RFoG working group was considering this, IEEE was working on 10 GE-PON and needed a downstream wavelength that would coexist with first-generation EPON, since they assumed that there would be a market for putting both 1 and 10 Gb/s on the same PON. They settled on $1577 + 3/-2$ nm (a tight band, but with few viable options, this was the decision). The ITU has also accepted this for the XG-PON 10 Gb/s downstream. Since this specified wavelength would let the IEEE and ITU 10 Gb/s EPON operate up to 1580 nm, it seemed imprudent of the RFoG people to choose 1590 nm for their upstream, as it could go as low as 1580 nm, yielding zero transition region for filtering. Thus, 1610 ± 10 nm became the RFoG upstream standard. Most cable TV fiber has been installed since this band became part of the passband handled by the fiber, so it didn't seem to be unreasonable to use it.

We need to return to the O band for a moment. The IEEE needed an upstream band for 10 Gb/s transmission that would be compatible with 1 Gb/s. But suitable wavelengths were in very short supply. Officially, the O band, 1310 ± 50 nm was completely taken by the 1 Gb/s upstream signals, extending down to 1260 nm. But this wide a band was only needed for *Fabry–Perot* (F-P) lasers (which we shall describe below), and the industry was transitioning to *distributed feedback* (DFB) lasers (also described below), which could maintain a tighter (better) wavelength tolerance. We knew that in order to support 10 Gb/s we would need DFB lasers, which can with some effort hold within a ±10 nm wavelength tolerance. But the entire band was reserved for F-P upstream lasers, and we could not assume that no first-generation upstream signals would be used on the same PON as 10 Gb/s upstream. So the solution was to specify the lowest part of the O band, 1260–1280 nm for 10 Gb/s upstream, with an acknowledged overlap with the older 1 Gb/s technology, which might occupy those same wavelengths. The specification says that even though in most cases there will be no problem because 1 Gb/s will be using DFB lasers closer to 1310 nm, the OLT handling 10 and 1 Gb/s upstream will have to "use TDM techniques" to separate the two. In other words, an OLT supporting 10 Gb/s upstream will have to be able to use its a priori knowledge of what types of ONTs are out there, and will have to manage the upstream as if the same wavelength was used by both 1 and 10 Gb/s upstream equipment. It does appear that this is possible.

Guiding Light

Fiber optics is a fairly simple technology on the surface. Guiding of light by *refraction*, the principle that makes fiber optics possible, was first demonstrated by Daniel Colladon and Jacques Babinet in Paris in the early 1840s. John Tyndall included a demonstration of it in his public lectures in London 12 years later. Tyndall also wrote about the property of *total internal reflection* in an introductory book about the nature of light in 1870. *Refraction* refers to the bending of light when it obliquely encounters a smooth boundary between two media of different *refraction coefficients*, or density. An example is a prism, used to separate white light into its constituent components, or wavelengths. Other familiar examples are eyeglasses and refracting telescopes, which use a big lens where the light enters the telescope.

Contrast *refraction*, with *reflection*. Refraction refers to a bending of light when it transitions from one medium to another, whereas reflection refers to the throwing back of light (or other radiation) when it encounters a suitable surface. Mirrors are the most common example of something designed to reflect light.[i]

Propagation in Fiber Optics

Fig. 6.3 illustrates the principle of propagation in a strand of fiber optic cable. In Fig. 6.3A we show the textbook principle of light reflection and refraction at a boundary of two materials of different density (equating to a different *index of refraction*, $n1$ or $n2$). In general, some of the light is reflected; that is, it bounces off the boundary and continues in the first medium, with the classical "angle of

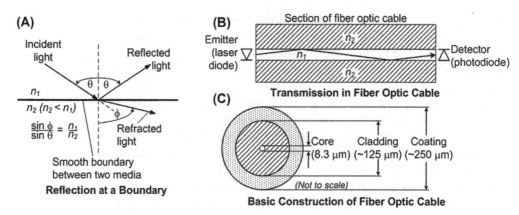

FIGURE 6.3
Propagation in a fiber optic strand.

reflection equal to the angle of incidence," designated by θ in Fig. 6.3A. (A plane is always defined by a line perpendicular to it, represented by the dashed line in Fig. 6.3A.) Other light passes from one medium to the other, the two media being characterized by their indices of refraction, $n1$ and $n2$. The refracted light in Fig. 6.3A shows that the direction of travel of the light is changed as it moves from one medium to the other, with the angle of the reflected light being ϕ. We show the classic equation for the relation between the angle of incidence, θ, and the angle of refraction, ϕ, as a function of the ratio of the two indices of refraction. A little reflection (pun intended) on the equation will show that if the incident light is nearly parallel with the boundary (θ almost 90 degree) and the ratio $n1/n2 > 1$, that there will be no refracted light ($\sin \phi > 1$, an impossible condition). This is called *total internal reflection*, and the principle behind fiber optic cable.

Fig. 6.3B and C illustrate this principle applied to a strand of fiber optic cable. The cable is built with a very small internal glass *core* having index of refraction $n1$. It is surrounded by a much larger *cladding* having index of refraction $n2$, where $n2 < n1$. The *coating* over the cladding is a plastic, usually colored, material for strength and identification. (The coating is shown in the end view of Fig. 6.3C, but not in the lateral view of Fig. 6.3B.) Light from a laser diode is launched into one end of the fiber with a geometry that ensures that the light strikes the boundary of the two glasses at such an angle that it is all internally reflected. It propagates down the fiber by total reflection from the boundary (the mechanism of reflection actually involves penetration into the cladding). At the far end of the fiber, the light exits the fiber and strikes a *photodiode*, which turns the optical energy back into electrical energy.

Advantages of Fiber Optic Transmission

A major advantage to fiber optic transmission is the extremely low *attenuation* (reduction of power) of the signal, 0.25–0.38 dB/km at the wavelengths of interest, compared with hundreds of times this (depending on RF frequency) for coaxial cable, and even worse attenuation for twisted pair. This means that the signal can go long distances without amplification. The lack of need for amplification means the network can be, within limits, all-passive. That is, intermediate amplification need not be provided. This creates a host of advantages: no electronic equipment in the network that will need servicing and which is a point of potential failure, and no tapping into the power distribution grid to power amplifiers, coupled with no need to provide expensive and maintenance-intensive backup power. The low loss of fiber is often cited as a reason for FTTH being an excellent solution for low-density installations.

Since the fiber is made of glass, a very stable nonconductor (a *dielectric*), several more advantages and maybe one disadvantage accrue. Fiber tends to be impervious to corrosive elements such as a salt environment. While we do not recommend it, we have heard cases of customers who have found fiber splices immersed in floodwater but still working. Also, there is no danger of the fiber inadvertently carrying electrical current it is not intended to carry. This can happen with both twisted copper pair (telephone) cable and coaxial (cable TV) cable, as a result of electrical storms or ground faults in the electrical distribution system. Cable television engineers call this *sheath current*, which has been known to wreak havoc with both the operator's and subscribers' equipment.

The one disadvantage, if it can be called that, is the same as the last advantage, and that is the fact that fiber optic cable does not conduct electricity. This means that, as opposed to twisted pair copper and coaxial cable, the fiber cannot intrinsically carry power (efforts to transport useful amounts of power as optical power over the fiber have consistently run into messy real-world laws-of-physics problems). Thus, in order to power customer termination equipment, you are forced to either parallel the fiber with copper wire or, much more common today, have the subscriber provide power, with or without battery backup. Generally, if voice service is provided, backup battery power is provided, either as a part of the service or as an optional extra-cost feature. Or the consumer may provide his or her own uninterruptible power source (UPS).

REAL FIBER OPTIC CABLES

There are several windows of favorable transmission in single-mode fiber optic cable. The first window is around 850 nm, and is used for short-distance transmission, but still has too much loss for long-distance transmission. The second window is around 1310 ± 50 nm. Above this is a peak of attenuation centered at 1383 nm, cause by adsorption of light by hydroxyl ions in the fiber. This is called the *water peak*. Much modern cable is free of hydroxyl ions, and so this wavelength may be coming into use, though it is usually the last place where people put signals. The third window is around 1550 nm, which is also a wavelength for which we have good, economical optical amplifiers, put to good use when you want to carry broadcast signals on an FTTH system.

While we have accurately described the construction of single-mode fiber above, there is a lot more to it than implied. The doping profile may be varied throughout both the core and cladding to achieve certain desirable characteristics.

As we looked through the section below, we realized that it may scare some from building fiber optics networks of any type. So let us say before you read it, that fiber systems work very, very well when done right. Do not fear when you read of issues in the fiber, because fiber optics have been used for well over a quarter of a century for transmission of both RF-modulated signals and digital signals. Good countermeasures for each of the issues we mention have been developed. Our purpose in presenting this information is to make you aware of some of the things that can happen if you don't exercise sufficient care and engineering due diligence in designing, constructing, and operating your network. Indeed, that same thing can be said of earlier technologies.

This is not an exhaustive list of fiber issues, but does summarize the ones we have found to be most significant in today's FTTH networks.

Dispersion

Dispersion is a phenomenon in fiber optic cable which can limit the data speed you can achieve, and can add noise in RF transmission. Dispersion refers to the fact that not all light traveling through a cable will travel at the same speed. Thus, some light gets to its destination before other light does. This can cause smearing of pulses when you are transmitting using binary (on/off) keying, as is common today for data.

There are several mechanisms that cause dispersion, and the David Large reference in the References goes into a lot more detail. *Chromatic* (wavelength) *dispersion* is probably the one of most significance in FTTH networks. It is composed or two factors: *material dispersion*, a measure of the change in refractive index of the glass with wavelength, and *waveguide dispersion*. The latter dispersion component is due to the fact that the light travels partially in the core and partially in the cladding, and the percentages are a function of wavelength.

With normal fiber, the minimum dispersion occurs around 1310 nm, sometimes allowing the use of lower-cost optical transmitters at this wavelength. It is possible to build *dispersion shifted* fiber, with the minimum dispersion at other wavelengths, such as 1550 nm, but it is uncommon in FTTH applications to use such fiber. We shall discuss optical sources later, but for now suffice it to say that all optical sources transmit their signal over some band of wavelengths, and the larger the tolerated wavelength range the cheaper the transmitter and the more chromatic dispersion you get.

Another source of dispersion is *polarization mode dispersion*, referring to the fact that the light has its electric field (and associated magnetic field, though we usually refer to the electric field in this case) lines extending in two different directions at right angles to the direction of propagation in the fiber.[3] For several reasons, fiber exhibits different propagation speeds for the two polarizations.

Bending Loss

Bending loss is a big one, especially when you are doing inside fiber wiring. As you bend a fiber sharply, more of the signal power will strike the cladding at less than the critical angle, and will NOT be reflected. Sometimes we use this characteristic to our advantage, in test situations or in intentionally added attenuation. But usually bending loss is bad. Longer wavelengths are more affected by bending loss than are shorter wavelengths. A typical loss for a single turn of fiber around a 32 mm (1.26 inch) diameter mandrel is 0.5 dB at 1550 nm, less at shorter wavelengths.

Bending loss is a serious problem where you are doing inside wiring using fiber. You might do this in an apartment building, known in the trade as an *MDU (multiple dwelling unit)*. Furthermore, even for single-family dwellings, inside installation of the ONT is common, requiring fiber to be brought inside the structure. There are special *bend-insensitive* fibers you can get to address these needs. They are highly recommended for inside wiring.

Stimulated Brillouin Scattering

Stimulated Brillouin scattering (SBS) is of significant concern to FTTH operators, particularly those using the broadcast overlay on 1550 nm. SBS occurs because the glass is electrostrictive—that is, an electric field causes mechanical stress on the material. You will recall that we mentioned the electric field component of the light wave above. When that field reaches a certain amplitude, only some of the energy from the excited electrons is returned as forward-transmitted waves. The remaining energy is translated into an acoustical wave (vibration) that is transmitted through the material, in turn modulating the index of refraction of the glass, which causes several problems for the transmitted signal. The end result is that, at low light levels the output power at the end of the fiber is proportional to the input power as you'd expect. But as the input level increases, the output level stops increasing and noise and distortion increase rapidly. The phenomenon is worse for longer fibers.

---

[3]For those of you who, like the writer, get puzzled by the concept of the electric field extending in two orthogonal (right angle) directions at the same time, the explanation is as follows. Usually the field is at some angle other than horizontal or vertical, so we break it into two components for convenience in analyzing the situation.

Lacking SBS countermeasures, the SBS threshold can be as low as about +7 dBm at 1550 nm and with long fibers. But countermeasures against this low threshold are well-known. Lasers that have to launch at higher optical levels (and that is pretty much any laser carrying broadcast signals on an FTTH system, as well as on cable TV HFC networks), use additional modulation on the laser to spread the transmitted spectrum. The SBS threshold is a very narrow-band phenomenon, and if you spread the power over some wavelength range, you can launch at +18 dBm or more without encountering the SBS threshold. Some transmitters can be adjusted to be optimized for a given length. If the fiber is shorter, then you can launch at higher levels, and this is usually the case with FTTH networks. Fig. 6.4 illustrates the calculated SBS threshold for a transmitter rated at +16 dBm launch power at infinite fiber length. Note that the length with which we are concerned is the length to the first place where the fiber is split. Since a split reduces the power by more than 3 dB, then after that first split, the optical power level is almost certainly too low to get you into SBS issues.

We have not seen it needed, but if the worst happens, you could always use two optical transmitters in the 1550–1560 nm region, each with half the video channels. It is hard to conceive of a practical system where this is needed, though we have seen some corner designs that, had they been built, might have benefitted from this technique.

Stimulated Raman Scattering

Stimulated Raman scattering (SRS) is a crosstalk phenomenon in which a lower-wavelength optical signal on the same fiber acts as a pump laser to transfer power to a higher-wavelength signal traveling in the same direction on the fiber. It is sensitive to the power level of the lower-wavelength signal, the separation between the two wavelengths, and the fiber length. The effect is on the lower RF frequencies carried at the longer wavelength (victim) optical carrier.

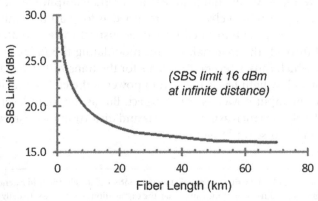

(SBS limit 16 dBm at infinite distance)

FIGURE 6.4
SBS threshold versus fiber length.

The primary way it manifests itself in FTTH systems is interference from the 1490 nm downstream data signal crosstalking and causing interference into the 1550 nm broadcast signal.[4] When real data are being transmitted, the data pattern is random enough to spread the spectrum of the 1490 nm data so that the SRS crosstalk manifests as random noise imposed on the broadcast signals. This can be controlled if need be by controlling the level of the 1490 nm signal, by care in where the 1490 and 1550 nm wavelengths are combined, and possibly by increasing the OMI (*optical modulation index*) on the lower-frequency RF signals.

When no data are being transmitted on the 1490 nm downstream optical carrier, both GPON and EPON transmit idle codes in order to keep the downstream data receivers in the ONTs synchronized. The idle code is a short, repetitive data sequence. The repetition of the sequence causes a peak in the spectrum of the modulation on the 1490 nm carrier, which spectral peak is transferred to the 1550 nm broadcast carrier. This causes a concentration of signal power at one frequency. The worst frequency is 63.5 MHz for EPON and 63.2 MHz for GPON. These fall in TV channel 3 in North America. The power concentration is sufficient to potentially cause digital detection to fail, particularly if 256-QAM or higher modulation is being used. If an analog signal is on channel 3, the result can be a classic "beat" pattern in the video—diagonal bars in the picture. This problem can be mitigated by substituting a random data pattern for the idle code of the specifications. Not all vendors have mitigation in early generation equipment, so be careful to test this if you are using broadcast video. Note that there may be patents on the mitigation technique.

OPTICAL SOURCES IN FTTH NETWORKS

There are a number of optical sources (transmitters) found in every PON. At the OLT there is a downstream digital (binary) transmitter for each PON and a binary receiver for the PON. Similarly, the ONT must receive downstream data and must transmit upstream data. If you are using a broadcast overlay on 1550 nm, there will be at least one and maybe more transmitters at the headend, and an additional receiver at each ONU. We shall cover transmitters in this section, and receivers in the next.

Broadcast Transmitters (1550 nm)

The broadcast optical transmitter (Fig. 6.5) has an output between 1550 and 1560 nm for FTTH use. For cable television systems a wider wavelength range is

[4]In some cases, the power taken from the lower-wavelength signal and transferred to the higher-wavelength signal can be a problem for the lower-wavelength signal, though we have not seen this be a limitation in FTTH networks.

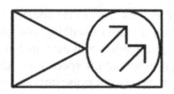

FIGURE 6.5
Block diagram symbol, broadcast optical transmitter.

used, but because of the other wavelengths used in FTTH, the standards restrict the output to this range for FTTH. So be careful when you order a transmitter, because some very good manufacturers have default outputs on wavelengths outside this range. However, they can easily supply the transmitter with output between 1550 and 1560 nm, on one of ITU channels 31 (1552.52 nm), 29 (1554.13 nm), 27 (1555.75 nm), 25 (1557.36 nm), or 23 (1558.98 nm).

Broadcast transmitters fall into two classifications: internally modulated and externally modulated transmitters. In internally modulated transmitters, the modulating signals (typically in the 54–1002 MHz or even higher frequency spectrum) are applied directly to the laser diode. This yields a relatively economical transmitter, but with a drawback: as the laser diode is modulated, its output not only changes in amplitude, but to an extent, also changes in wavelength. Dispersion (described above) in the fiber converts this to distortion. In FTTH, as opposed to HFC, we typically drive the laser transmitter about as hard as we can, because we want to be able to reach the ONTs with the lowest possible signal level consistent with good noise performance. The motivation is to achieve a lower overall network cost. So we need to start out with the strongest optically modulated signal possible.[5] While there may be smaller networks that can get by with internally modulated transmitters, the best practice is an externally modulated transmitter.

An externally modulated linear transmitter uses a transmitter diode biased with direct current and usually a spectrum-spreading signal designed to improve the SBS threshold described above. The light output of the diode goes to an external Mach–Zenhder modulator. The Mach–Zehnder modulator works by passing light in two different paths in a suitable material such as lithium niobate, which exhibits an electro-optic effect such that the propagation speed of the light is a function of the electrical potential across a capacitor with the light channel between the capacitor plates. A beamsplitter divides the laser light

---

[5]Cable TV systems which will follow the optical receiver with several amplifiers must limit the modulation of the optical transmitter in order to improve distortion in the optical portion of the network, to reserve some budget for distortion in the RF portion. Since there is no RF portion of an FTTH network, then we can trade off higher modulation of the RF carriers onto the optical carrier (resulting in better carrier-to-noise ratio) for more distortion of the signal.

into two paths, one of which has a phase modulator as described above. The beams are then recombined. Changing the electric field on the phase-modulating path will then determine whether the two beams interfere constructively or destructively at the output, and thereby control the amplitude or intensity of the exiting light. This yields an extremely linear output with well-controlled SBS threshold characteristics. Thus, an externally modulated transmitter is recommended for nearly all FTTH broadcast applications.

Erbium-Doped Fiber Amplifiers

One of the reasons for using 1550 nm for broadcast video is the ability to amplify the optical signals very economically at this wavelength. This is done using *erbium-doped fiber amplifiers* (EDFAs). We'll have more to say about EDFAs in Chapter 11, broadcast video, but for now we'll just say that they work by putting the input 1550 nm optical signal through a piece of fiber doped with erbium atoms, along with power from one or more pump lasers operating at specific wavelengths that can raise the energy level of the electrons in the outer shell of the erbium atoms. When the input 1550 nm light passes the erbium atoms, the electrons fall back to a lower energy level. This releases another photon of light at 1550 nm traveling in the same direction as the input photon. Thus, an EDFA can directly amplify the light entering it.

Data Transmitters

All FTTH systems will have data transmitters (Fig. 6.6) at the OLT to transmit downstream data, and at the ONTs for upstream data. Obviously the downstream transmitter cost is not as critical for a PON, because one transmitter serves a number of subscribers. The same cannot be said for the upstream transmitter at the home, since there must be one transmitter for every subscriber.

Fabry–Perot Laser Diodes

Two technologies are in widespread use for data transmitters. The older and lower-cost technology is the F-P laser. It is a simple PIN (*positive-intrinsic-negative*, a diode with a non-polarized layer of silicon at the junction) diode cavity with mirrors on each end. One mirror may be nearly completely reflecting, and the other

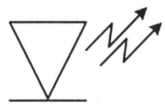

FIGURE 6.6
Block diagram symbol, data transmitter.

partially reflecting, in order to let some of the light escape the diode to enter the fiber. The cell length is fabricated to a multiple of the wavelength of the desired output, so that light at the cavity will be resonate at the correct wavelength. This produces a rather wide output spectrum as the output *mode-hops*, or jumps from one resonant wavelength to another very quickly. This obviously creates chromatic dispersion in the fiber as described above, limiting the use of F-P laser to 1310 nm, where the dispersion is lowest. This is the driver for using 1310 nm as the upstream transmitter: since we must build more upstream transmitters than downstream transmitters, we want the lowest-cost technology in the upstream transmitter. Thus, we need minimum fiber dispersion at the upstream wavelength.

Distributed Feedback Laser Diodes

The other technology used is the DFB laser. It resembles the F-P laser, with the exception that a grating is inserted in the cavity to restrict the lasing to a single wavelength. The output of the DFB laser is more temperature-stable than is the output of the F-P laser and the energy is concentrated on one wavelength—there is no mode-hopping. Consequently, the output of the DFB laser is "cleaner," and will not cause nearly as much interaction with the chromatic dispersion of the fiber. Thus, we can use DFB lasers at 1490 and 1550 nm (and other wavelengths), where dispersion is greater in the fiber. With volume and competition, the cost of DFB lasers has come down, and today they tend to be used extensively. Table 6.2 summarizes the two laser technologies commonly used in FTTH systems.

Laser Operational Characteristics

Fig. 6.7 illustrates appropriate operational characteristics for both analog lasers used for the 1550 nm broadcast application (Fig. 6.7A) and for digital transmitters (Fig. 6.7B). In both cases, we plot the drive current to the laser against the output power from the laser. In both cases, the laser is biased to the *average* output power, and this is how we define *laser optical power*, by that average value.

Table 6.2 Comparison of Laser Transmitter Technologies Used in FTTH

Laser Technology	Advantages	Disadvantages
Fabry–Perot (F-P)	Low cost	Wide optical spectrum makes them unusable except at 1310 nm, the nominal zero dispersion wavelength in most fiber. High wavelength drift with temperature
Distributed feedback (DFB)	Much narrower optical spectrum makes them usable at any practical wavelength. Lower wavelength drift with temperature	Higher cost

At very low currents, we get some noncoherent light out of the laser, but this light is not useful to us (see the heavy line beginning at the origin in both Fig. 6.7A and B). It is only after we reach a threshold at which the laser goes into its *lasing* mode, that we get useful coherent light. This point is shown in Fig. 6.7A as the *onset of lasing*. For the analog laser, we cannot let the drive current drop below this point, as we will get severe clipping of the laser if we do. We also cannot let the drive current get so high that the laser starts losing the linear relation between input current and light power out (the point at which the laser begins to saturate). For the binary laser, we can maybe go a little into the saturation region, but we cannot go too far without risking pulse distortion. Even when the laser is turned off (which the upstream laser is most of the time), we must bias it so that it stays barely into the lasing region, because it takes a relatively long time (too long) to start the lasing process.

A significant figure of merit used to describe how the analog laser is operating is the *optical modulation index* (OMI), which is expressed as a percent. We can talk about the *composite OMI*, which is shown in Fig. 6.7A. Fig. 6.7A shows a sinusoidal waveform, but in real life the waveform is comprised of maybe over 100 modulated sinusoids. This composite waveform is not at all sinusoidal, but rather is very "peaky," with a peak level much higher than the average level. Frequently we talk about the OMI per channel, since the input is really composed of many, many RF carriers, and not the one carrier shown. A typical

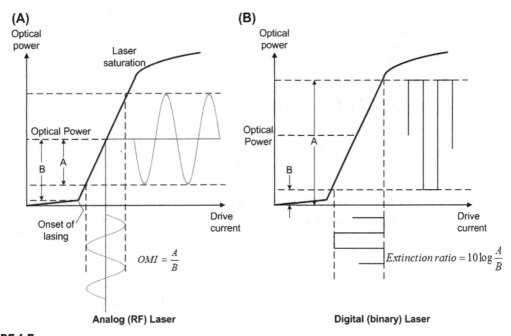

FIGURE 6.7
Laser operational characteristics.

maximum OMI per channel for the 6 MHz channel spacing we use in North America is about 3.5% per channel, more or less. Beyond this, we start getting into trouble with clipping, when the laser either drops below the onset of lasing, or enters saturation. The exact drive current at which this happens is a little hard to predict, because the actual waveform is far from the nice sine wave shown; it tends to have occasional very high peaks, depending on the relative phases of the carriers and the instantaneous modulation on them. Lacking a better metric, we usually work to maintain a consistent power per carrier into the transmitter as the number of carriers (channels) varies. Indeed, some transmitters have automatic gain control (AGC), which holds the power to the laser constant regardless of the number of carriers or their individual average power. (Though there are those who disagree, we prefer to NOT use AGC in this case, because it makes it difficult to obtain correlation between application and test signals, which are either not modulated or are synchronously modulated, hardly real-world conditions. Testing is best done without AGC.)

For the binary optical transmitter of Fig. 6.7B, the laser cannot be turned off all the way when the low-power state is transmitted, because doing so will delay turn-on. Thus, it is standard practice to turn the laser power down as much as possible without risking it dropping below the lasing threshold under all conditions of temperature, power, data patterns, and aging. The figure of merit is the *extinction ratio*, the ratio of the high-power to the low-power state, usually expressed in decibels.[ii] The higher the extinction ratio the more difference in signal level between the ON and OFF states the receiver has to work with (assuming, of course, that the level of the OFF state is not buried in noise). We have seen situations in which the extinction ratio played a major part in the length of PON that could be supported.

OPTICAL DETECTORS

At the receiving end of a link, the optical detector plays a vital role in recovering the signal (an obvious statement, we realize). Block diagrams of RF broadcast and data receivers are shown in Fig. 6.8.

Conventional Photodiodes

Conventional *photodiodes* are common for both linear and data (binary) receivers. The photodiode is optimized to receive light and to release electrons in proportion to the light power received. As commonly used in our applications, the photodiode is reverse biased by a few volts. The output is coupled to a *trans-impedance amplifier* (TIA; not shown in Fig. 6.8) in data (binary) receivers. The TIA is often integrated very closely with the photodiode (in the same package) because any capacitance between the two can have a very deleterious effect on frequency response and hence pulse shape. The output impedance of the photodiode is high, and the TIA converts the impedance to something that can

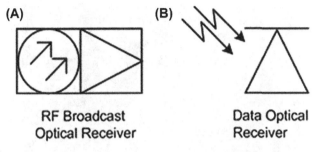

FIGURE 6.8
Block diagram symbols, optical receivers.

Table 6.3 Comparison of Receiver Diode Technologies Used in FTTH		
Receiver Diode Technology	**Advantages**	**Disadvantages**
Common photodiode	Lower cost, lower noise with no input signal	Not as sensitive as APD
Avalanche photodiode	High output, high sensitivity	Higher cost, requires higher bias voltage, more noise with no received signal

be handled in the real world. The TIA is a reasonably linear amplifier which accepts current in and outputs signals at a controlled impedance (often $100\,\Omega$ differential). For broadcast (linear) detectors a similar arrangement is used, but due to the power needed and the higher component count required in the amplifier (in order to make it sufficiently linear while providing sufficient output power), a TIA is usually not integrated with the diode, but rather is placed as close to the diode output as practical.

Avalanche Photodiodes

The other type of diode used is an *avalanche photodiode* (APD, as opposed to the conventional photodiode described above). It has a similar structure to a normal photodiode, but is designed to be operated at higher reverse voltage. The high reverse voltage creates an avalanche effect, in which every electron–hole pair generated by a photon causes the release of several other electron–hole pairs after having been accelerated by the electric field produced by the bias voltage. APDs can increase the sensitivity of a detector a good bit, but under no-signal conditions can be noisier than regular photodiodes. Table 6.3 provides a brief comparison of the two photodiode technologies in common use.

TRANSCEIVERS FOR THE OLT

An important component is the interface between the electronics of the OLT and the optics. Usually this is accomplished with a plug-in component called an *SFP (small form-factor pluggable)*. These modules, shown in Fig. 6.9, are often

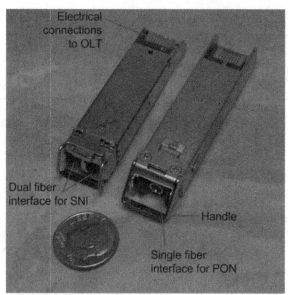

FIGURE 6.9
SFP interfaces used on OLTs and other places.

used as interfaces between the OLT and the FTTH network. When used for this purpose, they may be obtained with any of the standard performance criteria outlined in Chapters 3 and 4.

SFPs are also used between the OLT and the SNI (*service network interface*) interfacing the OLT to the headend switching network. SFPs with Ethernet electrical interfaces are also available for this purpose. They have other uses too, in switch and router interfaces, and some minimally functional ONTs are actually being built into SFPs. Typically you purchase the SFPs separately from the OLT, though you may purchase them from the OLT vendor. They are available from third parties also. Some OLT vendors may require you to use only their SFPs, and others may allow any compliant SFP to be used (though you may be on your own if a problem develops). For 10 Gb/s interfaces, two similar plug-in devices have been used, SFP+ modules being the most recent. *XFP* modules, which are similar but not interchangeable with SFP+, have also been used.

OPTICAL PASSIVES

Passive optical components (*passives*) are very important to the operation of FTTH systems, and we have seen many problems caused by improper application of passives. There are many types of optical components available, of which we shall show only those most important to FTTH systems.

Optical Connectors

The most basic and most misused optical passive is the connector. It is here that we have probably seen more system problems than due to any one other fault. The problems are preventable, but often are not prevented—more below on this issue. A number of optical connectors are available for different applications.

SC Connectors

Fig. 6.10 illustrates the most commonly encountered connector in FTTH networks, the *SC* (variously said to stand for *simplex connector*, *subscriber connector*, *square connector*, or *standard connector*). It is a simple plug-in connector with a latching mechanism to hold it in place, and a guide pin (key) to make sure you insert it in the correct orientation, especially important for APC styles, which we shall describe next.

As with other types of connectors, the SC comes in two configurations for single-mode fiber (and more for multimode fiber, which we are not covering). The *UPC* (*ultrapolished connector*) version has a blue shell and the *APC* (*angle-polished connector*) version has a green shell. Both are pictured in Fig. 6.11A. Fig. 6.11B illustrates the end of the fiber for the UPC version. The fiber is cut and polished at right angles to the fiber direction. In the connector, this fiber butts up firmly against the connected fiber, and light passes smoothly from one fiber to the other.

In the APC version, shown in Fig. 6.10C, the end of the fiber is cut and polished at an angle of 8 to maybe 12 degree. This can be seen in Fig. 6.10A, where we have drawn the angle; one line is at a right angle to the fiber and the other parallel to the cut angle. The lines indicating the angle have been moved back from the end of the connector so that you can see the angled surface on the photograph. When two APC connectors are mated, the two angled facets complement each other such that there is an essentially continuous fiber, just that the two fiber ends are at a slight angle with respect to the fiber.

Under perfect conditions of connector cleanliness, the UPC makes a slightly better connection in terms of through loss (the amount of the signal that makes it from one side of the connection to the other). Arguably modern APC connectors are close in performance, though. The real difference in the connectors comes under two real-world conditions: unmated connectors and dirty connectors. The problem is that, when a light wave (or a radio wave, or a ripple in a pond, or any other wave) meets any *discontinuity* in the medium, some of the signal is reflected. You can easily see this if you have water in a bucket and you drop a small rock in the middle, causing waves to radiate outward. When the wave hits the side of the bucket, it causes a wave to be reflected back into the water. Similarly, a light wave encountering the junction of two fibers should see nothing, because the two fibers should butt up against each other with no air in between. But the real

(A)

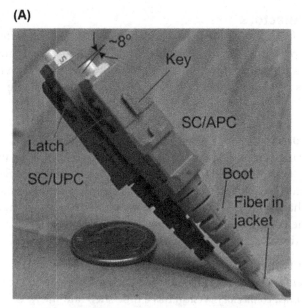

SC/UPC and SC/APC connectors

(B)

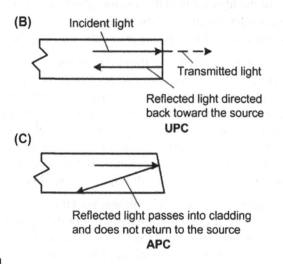

FIGURE 6.10
SC connectors.

world is not this nice; there will always be some very slight gap between the two fibers, even if the air is just a few molecules thick. Worse, much worse, is any dirt in the connector—we'll have more to say about cleaning connectors just below. Any particle of dirt, no matter how small, can seem as a boulder to the light wave. Remember, we are talking about an 8.3 μm (about 0.0003 inch) diameter core which transports most of the light. And the dirt will reflect and scatter light.

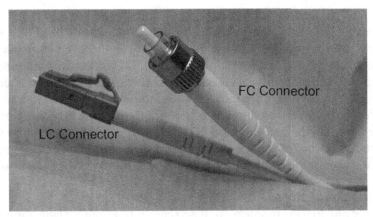

FIGURE 6.11
LC and FC connectors.

Figs. 6.10B and C compare what happens when light is reflected from the end of the UPC and APC connectors. With the UPC connector, light is reflected back up the fiber. If it reaches the light source, it can interfere with the lasing action of the source and cause problems. This is especially true for broadcast video signals; they can be damaged badly if light is reflected back to the source. And a UPC connector will send reflected light back to that source. An APC connector, on the other hand, will reflect the light into the cladding, where it is dissipated and does no harm. If the mating connectors are perfectly clean, either UPC or APC connectors will do a fine job of coupling signals with little reflection. But when you let just a little dirt in the connector, the APC is much, much more forgiving than is the UPC connector. That is why we say that we recommend APC connectors as the standard connector in any FTTH system. If the system is carrying broadcast video, then APC connectors MUST be the only connector used where the 1550-nm signal is present. It is not unusual to see UPC connectors used on OLT interfaces, but any fiber that carries broadcast video *must* have APC connectors.

But you say that you carefully clean your connectors. You do well. But do you clean them adequately? We have been in laboratory environments where every connector was cleaned using recognized cleaning systems, then everything was carefully connected. When we inspected the connections using an inspection microscope, we were shocked at how much dirt we had left. And we saw how much better things worked after we had gone through and cleaned connectors until microscopic inspection had shown the connectors to be really clean. You'd also be surprised at the number of jumpers we have taken out of bags that came straight from the factory that were not really clean. More information on connector cleaning is below.

Other Optical Connector Types

There are at least two other series of connectors that you will find in FTTH networks, mostly at the OLT. They are shown in Fig. 6.11. The *LC connector* is often used on the SNI, or network side of the OLT, where two connectors are plugged into the SFP (in headend or data center applications, two fibers are often used, one for each direction). *LC* is said to stand for *lucent connector, little connector,* or *local connector*. Among other applications, the FC connector may also be found on the network (non FTTH) side SFPs in the OLT. *FC* may stand for *ferrule connector*, or for *fiber channel*. Sometimes multimode fibers may be used for these data networking applications, depending on the SFPs chosen.

Cleaning Connectors

If there is one biggest problem we have seen in fiber optic plants (and there is), it is cleaning connectors. There are several effective cleaning systems on the market, both dry and wet (using pure alcohol, *not* the drug store variety, which is guaranteed to make matters worse, not better). It is imperative that you clean connectors every time you mate them, with inspection of your cleaning job. Even the best cleaning may not yield a well-cleaned connector every time, and the only way to verify cleanliness is to use an inspection microscope. There are several good presentations available regarding cleaning and inspection. A particularly good presentation is available from BICSI.[iii]

Fig. 6.12 shows clean and dirty optical connectors taken with a JDSU (a manufacturer of test equipment, more recently known as Viavi and Lumentum)

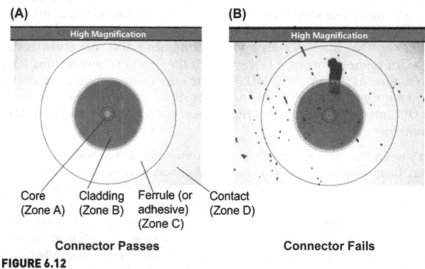

(A)

High Magnification

Core
(Zone A)   Cladding   Ferrule (or   Contact
(Zone B)   adhesive)   (Zone D)
(Zone C)

Connector Passes

(B)

High Magnification

Connector Fails

FIGURE 6.12

Clean and dirty optical connectors.
Courtesy, Aurora Networks, an ARRIS Company

digital probe microscope connected to a computer running their viewing software. Fig. 6.12A shows a very clean connector, which had just been cleaned with a laboratory automatic cleaning system. It identifies the parts of the fiber, the core, cladding, and the ferrule (sometimes called the adhesive zone), the portion of the connector that encloses the fiber. Also shown is the contact zone, not really active in the process of transferring optical power. (The coating shown in Fig. 6.3 is removed before the connector is put on.) International Electrotechnical Commission Standard IEC 61300-3-35[iv] defines the zones A, B, C, and D for the purpose of defining tolerable amounts of contaminants in each. The standard gives the amount of contaminant acceptable in each zone, and an automatic inspection scope such as the one used to obtain these pictures will measure the defects and give you a pass/fail result. Fig. 6.12B illustrates a failed cleaning effort.

Such automatic test stations as used here may not be practical for field use, but there are simpler manual inspection microscopes that can and should be used in the field to ascertain the cleanliness of a connector pair before mating. These should be used before mating connectors in the field, as field conditions are hardly conducive to properly cleaning connectors. A word of caution is in order: *do not look at a live fiber through a direct-view microscope, as the optical power being transmitted may cause permanent damage to the eye*. Always make sure that a fiber is not active before inspecting it with a direct-view microscope. Since the wavelengths of light we use are not visible to the eye, there is no way to tell by looking at the fiber if it is active or not; the first indication of activity may be permanent eye damage. The electronic microscopes such as the one we used to take the above pictures are not a problem for eye damage, since you are viewing a computer screen.

Sometimes you are going to do proper cleaning of a connection time after time, and the microscope still says it is not clean. After perhaps three unsuccessful cleanings, it may be time to cut your losses and replace the connector. Sometimes a connection can be damaged by physical abuse, or in some cases a piece of dirt may become fused into the end of the fiber. Even though we are dealing with milliwatt power levels, the small cross-sectional area in which that power exists means that the power density is very high. It is not unheard of for a piece of dust to be fused into the fiber, rendering the connector incapable of being cleaned. When that happens the usual recourse is to replace the connector. If you are lucky, the connector is part of a jumper that is easily removed and replaced with a new one, the old jumper being repurposed to the trash can. If the other end is not easily replaced, then you are going to have to cut the connector off and fusion splice a new pigtail (installation of connectors on fiber is still not recommended in the field). There are repolishing machines that, if you have one, you can try repolishing the end of the connector with and see if that makes the connector pass.

Optical Splitters

Optical splitters divide the signal into different optical paths. They are symmetrical devices, meaning that they will also combine signal in the opposite direction. Each time a signal is split into two equal parts, each output experiences a power loss of just over 3 dB. This comes from a basic "law of physics," which says that if I divide power into two equal parts, then half the power goes each way. Half power is a loss of 3 dB. As a practical matter, the loss is slightly higher due to unavoidable losses in the manufacturing process and to unavoidable variations in the loss from one port to another.

Fig. 6.13 illustrates optical splitting. In Fig. 6.13A are shown several of the many symbols we've seen used for optical splitters. Everyone seems to have his or her own idea for a symbol. One of the few attempts we've seen to standardize symbols is by the Society of Cable Telecommunications Engineers,[v] and they have several symbols they recommend for different applications. Frequently inside the circle common to many symbols, you will see two arrows, indicating an optical device rather than an electrical device (unless someone has chosen to use arrows in an electrical device symbol—this is not an accepted practice but we have seen it done). Frequently, but not always, the arrows will be pointing in different directions, indicating that the device is bidirectional (we are not

(A)

Some of the Symbols Used for Splitters

(B)

Loss in 2-way splitter:	Loss in n-way splitter:

$$L = -10 \log(0.5) = 3 \ dB$$
Adding 0.5 dB for splitter loss and port-to-port variation, total loss is 3.5 dB

$$L = 3.5 \frac{\log(n)}{\log(2)}$$

Loss Formulas

(C)

Fused Biconical Taper: Fibers are twisted and fused at high temperature to form the splitter

(D)

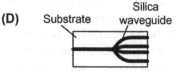

Planer Lightwave Component: Silica waveguide lithographed onto silicon substrate

FIGURE 6.13
Optical splitting.

aware of any passive devices that are *not* bidirectional). Since splitters can split more than two ways, the number of outputs, n, is sometimes given, or the loss at each port may be given either as a percent or in decibels.

Fig. 6.13B shows a couple of useful formulas relating to loss in the splitter. The left formula shows where the nominal 3.5 dB loss of a two-way splitter comes from. The laws of physics dictate that if you divide the power evenly, you will have a 3 dB loss at each output port. There is always some excess loss and manufacturing variation; 0.5 dB per two-way split is pretty conservative to account for that extra loss.

The right-most formula lets you estimate loss for more splits. The ratio of logarithms calculates the equivalent number of two-way splitting stages, and the 3.5 dB is as just described for a two-way splitter. Note that with optical splitters, it is not necessary for the split ratio to be a power-of-two (2, 4, 8, 16, 32, 64, etc.), though most of the time you will see these ratios. The formula should work even if the loss ratio is not a power of two.

You can buy splitters with other than nominally equal output on each leg. Typically, when splitters have unequal output, the relative outputs will be expressed as a percentage of the total output optical power. The percentages must, of course, add to 100%. In order to convert to decibels of loss at the output, convert the percentage to a decimal and take 10 times the logarithm of the decimal value. For instance, if you have a 95%/5% splitter, the first output will be something lower than

$$Output = 10 \log (0.95) = -0.22 \text{ dB}.$$

The lower level output will be a little lower than

$$Output = 10 \log (0.05) = -13 \text{ dB}.$$

Each is with respect to the input level, with the minus sign indicating that the output is lower than the input. You will have to add something for the loss and manufacturing variation of the asymmetrical splitter. How much depends, so the best bet it to check the vendor's literature.

Splitters are always bidirectional: what they do in one direction, they do in the other. So a splitter having, say, 17 dB loss is the same identical part that, when used in the opposite direction, operates as a combiner with 17 dB loss from each port to the common output. A splitter used in a PON divides the downstream power so that each subscriber gets (nominally) the same optical downstream power (with variation due to production variations and to the differing loss in different fiber lengths). Upstream optical signals are combined in the same splitter, and encounter the same loss as in the downstream direction.

At least two technologies are used to produce optical splitters. Probably the most common as of this writing is the *fused biconical taper* (FBT) of Fig. 6.13C. This splitter is made by twisting together several strands of fiber and melting them into a fused mass. By controlling the twist length, tension, and temperature, various split ratios can be attained. The resulting splitter is contained within a splice, stiffening material used to protect the splice against damage. The splitter may then be placed in a module, such as the LGX modules described below.

The other technology used to manufacture splitters is the *planar lightwave component* (PLC) illustrated in Fig. 6.13D. It consists of a small slab of silicon, much like that on which an integrated circuit might be built. The silicon is infused with impurities to form transparent silica—making a fiber optic cable except it is planar, embedded in a piece of silicon. Channels can be added for as many outputs as desired. The incoming and outgoing fibers are terminated at the edges of the silicon, usually in a small V groove etched in the silicon.

By the nature of their construction, both types of splitters may have two inputs, so you will sometimes see reference to, say, 2×32 (2 by 32) splitters, and not just 1×32 splitters.

Optical Filters

Optical filters are supplied analogously to RF filters. You can get high pass, bandpass, bandstop, or low pass filters using any of several technologies. The bandwidth of the filters can be adjusted as needed for the application. The loss varies with filter characteristics and with technology.

Wave Division Multiplexers

WDMs are three-port (or maybe higher port count) filters used to combine or separate wavelengths of light. Essentially they are wavelength-sensitive combiner/splitters. Being wavelength-sensitive, they don't extract the same loss penalty that a broadband splitter would extract—there is some loss, but not as much. The most familiar application for WDMs in FTTH systems is for combining the 1490 nm downstream and 1310 nm upstream wavelengths with the 1550 nm broadcast wavelength. A WDM is also used to combine the 1310 nm and 1490 nm wavelengths, but this is usually contained internal to equipment and not obvious to the operator. WDMs can be packaged in LGX housings the same as splitters, as in Fig. 6.16 below.

Optical Attenuators

Optical attenuators are obviously used where you have too much optical signal level and need to attenuate it. This happens commonly during test, where you seek to understand how much reserve optical level you have before things stop working correctly. It may be that you have a PON with characteristics such that the downstream data wavelength (1490 nm in first-generation systems) is too high in amplitude, so you need to insert attenuation into it at the output of the OLT.

Optical attenuators come in many styles and technologies too numerous to describe here. A common technology for making fixed attenuators is to intentionally offset a splice in the fiber, such that the splice exhibits excess loss. This yields a small, stable, wavelength-insensitive attenuator. Two fixed optical attenuators are shown in Fig. 6.14. They are oriented opposite to each other to show the male and female ends. Fixed attenuators are ordered by the number of decibels of attenuation.

A simple variable attenuator may be made by wrapping the fiber around a mandrel of an appropriate size—in order to achieve more attenuation at 1550 nm we have used a pencil or the pen in our shirt pocket in an emergency. We have held the turns in place with office tape for short-term test use. Such attenuators are very wavelength-sensitive, unstable, and run the risk of damaging the fiber. But they work when you need to run a short-term experiment.

Better variable attenuators can be made using variable neutral-density filters; they are common for laboratory use. They can be very stable, wavelength-insensitive, highly accurate, and, of course, rather high in cost. Some are electrically actuated to allow for computer control of repetitive measurements.

FIGURE 6.14
Fixed optical attenuators.

The LGX Module

The LGX module (usually referred to as a *cartridge*) is not really a fiber optic component, but rather is a standard housing for a lot of passive optical components. Fig. 6.15 shows a typical cartridge with two WDMs installed (other components could have been installed, but the one we happened to pick up to make the picture had two WDMs in splice enclosures). The module cover was removed for the picture. The second WDM is at the bottom of the cartridge, hidden by the cartridge wall.

LGX cartridges form a standardized way to package fiber optic components. They slide into a rack-mount chassis designed to accommodate cartridges such as the one shown. The fasteners are used to hold the module in the chassis. Modules come in various widths and depths, depending on the application. They are available to fit in rack-mount chasses of either 3U or 4U height.[6] Sometimes the rear of the cartridge (the end away from the connectors) will be tapered to a narrower height.

Fig. 6.15 shows one of the splice enclosures referred to above, a metal tube that provides physical protection for a fiber splice, a WDM, or a splitter. The splice enclosure is held in place using either hot-melt glue or a clip. There is another splice enclosure that is not visible in this picture. Note that there is a lot of seemingly excess room in the cartridge. There is a good reason for this space: you cannot bend a fiber too tightly. If you do, then you will introduce

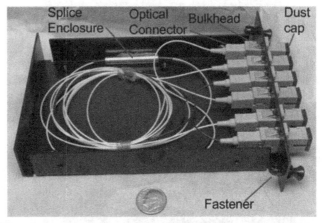

FIGURE 6.15
LGX module with two WDMs.

[6]A rack unit (RU) is a height of 1.75 inches, applied to something mounted in either a 19- or 23-inch wide rack. Thus, a 3 RU chassis is 5.25 inches high, and a 4 RU chassis is 7 inches high. The height applies to the chassis, so individual modules, such as the LGX modules, will be somewhat shorter.

wavelength-dependent loss into the fiber. So the LGX enclosure is big enough to permit adequate turn radius to prevent this loss.

Included in Fig. 6.15 is the front panel with about as many connectors as you can get on a 3 RU high narrow front panel (LGX cartridges also come in wider dimensions). Note that there really are no male and female connectors in fiber optics; rather, there are two like connectors which are mated using the *bulkhead* connector mounted in the front panel. Note also the dust cap installed on the outside connections. As we've discussed above, the one biggest mistake we've seen people make with fiber optic systems is failure to keep optical connections clean. In order to keep dust out of the connection, dust caps such as this *must* be installed on all unused connections at all times. In addition, the connections must be cleaned when mated.

Bulkheads make for an interesting problem in cleaning connectors before mating. As you can see from Fig. 6.15, the bulkhead has a connector on the inside of the module, and that connector has an equal chance of being dirty as does the connector you are about to plug in. Yet it is hard to get in to clean the internal connector. There are cleaning systems designed for this purpose, though, and you should use them; else you will clean the external connector possibly for naught, as dirt on the internal connector is equally damaging as is dirt on the external connector. And inspection is more difficult for the internal side. (Of course you can take the cover off the LGX module as we did for the picture, and you can clean the internal connections, but in the pressure of getting things assembled, that is rarely done. Doing so on active equipment is particularly problematical, and might even void a warranty.)

HEADEND FIBER MANAGEMENT

Of considerable importance is getting from the output of the OLT to outside of the headend. For each PON you have a fiber from the OLT. If you are carrying broadcast video, this fiber will go to a WDM (usually in an LGX module as described above), which has as another input, an output of an EDFA, which carries the broadcast signal. Then you have to get the output of the WDM to the outside fiber. This is usually done by routing the output of the WDM (or the output of the OLT if no broadcast tier is supplied), to a *fiber distribution panel*, where the inside fiber is connected to the outside fiber. Fig. 6.16 assumes PON splitters in the field. In some cases, you may want to put your PON splitters in the headend, or you may be doing point-to-point (active Ethernet) architecture, which has a fiber running from the headend to each subscriber. In those cases, you are really handling a lot of fibers in the headend!

There are any number of fiber distribution panel systems on the market; your job is to determine which one fits your needs best. Fig. 6.16 illustrates

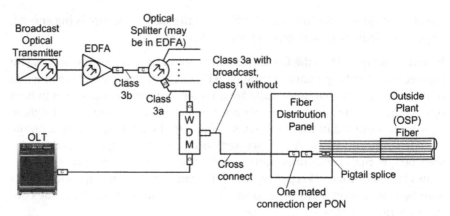

FIGURE 6.16
Minimal headend fiber management system.

what might be a minimal headend fiber management system with RF video. Coming out of the OLT per *PON* is a fiber jumper which goes to a wave division multiplexer (one per PON), used to combine the data signals to and from the OLT, with the video wavelength from the *EDFA*. Another fiber cross-connects the WDM with the fiber termination patch panel, used to connect internal fibers to the outside plant (OSP) fiber. The OSP fiber has been brought inside the headend, where it is spliced to a pigtail having a suitable connector on it. This pigtail is brought to the fiber distribution panel, where it is connected to the inside cross-connect jumper. Of course, in systems not carrying broadcast video, the WDM and all components above and to the left of it are not used. Note, though, the several connections and splices in the headend; they have loss that needs to be accounted for in the loss budget of the system.

Of great importance is the labeling of fibers, both in the headend and in the field. Unless you have some way to know what each fiber is doing, troubleshooting, and modifying the network later is going to be a nightmare. While standalone network elements have individual names, there is a convention for identifying OLT ports and ONTs:

- OLT name (your choosing);
  - Blade number in the OLT (follows manufacturer's numbering convention, usually left-to-right, PON blades only);
    - PON port number on the blade;
    - ONT number on the PON (might be assigned sequentially as ONTs are added, must be cross-referenced somewhere with the subscriber).[vi]

LASER SAFETY—AGAIN

You need to be aware of potential safety issues with the laser light. The light wavelengths used for FTTH are not visible to the naked eye, so you may look at the end of a fiber and not know laser energy is entering your eye. (Of course, just looking at a length of fiber is not a problem because no light escapes along the length of the fiber—only at the end.) Above certain power levels the energy may damage your eye. Several standards for laser safety exist, but probably the most recognized standard is IEC 60825.[vii] It incorporates the US standard, ANSI Z136.1 and .2. This standard was formerly known as IEC 825. Above certain power levels, IEC 60825 requires certain precautions. If you are not operating broadcast video, you are not likely to deal with levels exceeding Class 1, +9.4 dBm at 1310 nm or +10 dBm at 1550 nm. This class of laser is considered inherently safe. The only thing required is a protective housing to prevent higher emissions and a safety interlock in the housing to prevent access to higher levels, along with caution labels and safety information. What this boils down to in practice is not much of anything except labels—the device manufacturer should take care of it.

At higher emission levels, up to +14 dBm at 1310 nm or +17 dBm at 1550 nm, you are in Class 3a (now Class 1M), safe if a viewing aid such as a microscope is used. The output of a 1550-nm broadcast transmitter is usually in Class 1, but the output of an EDFA is likely to be at least in Class 3a, and may be in Class 3b (below). In Class 3a, there must be key control, so that someone working on the fiber can turn off the source, and put the key in his or her pocket while working on the fiber, thus being confident that the source will not be turned back on, probably by a well-meaning person who doesn't realize that work is going on. There must also be a beam stop (often in the form of a shutter on the optical connector), and a visual or aural "laser on" warning.

At emission levels up to +27 dBm at either wavelength, you are in Class 3b, which adds the requirement of a remote control switch to allow disabling the laser by a door circuit, and an aperture label to indicate the location of the radiation output.[viii] If you encounter this class, it will be at the output of the EDFA. In Fig. 6.16 we showed an optical splitter separate from the EDFA. In practice, the splitter is usually located in the EDFA, and the outputs you need for FTTH work usually are at or just over the border between Classes 3a and 3b. Most if not all 1550 nm optical transmitters and EDFAs we've seen have shutters on the optical connectors that might possibly be handling signal levels falling into Classes 3a or 3b. The active units have key switches on the front panel for satisfying the requirement to disable the output.

IN SUMMARY: IF YOU'RE GOING TO MAKE A MISTAKE, MAKE IT A BIG ONE

We said in the introduction to this chapter, that some of the biggest mistakes you can make in an FTTH network will be at the optical level. We mentioned them as we came to them, but let's recap.

Mistake #1: Don't Design in Margin

There are things that happen to FTTH networks that cost you, and which are hard to recover from later. You can design networks with 64-way splits with today's technology, but don't try to cut it too close on optical margin. We have seen designs that work on paper. And they work in practice most of the time. But when they don't work, there is not much to be done about it. Things happen in the real world. Connectors are dirty, reflections are a bit high, fiber splices are a bit high in loss, you need to extend the network "just a little farther, because we can pick up two more customers out here." Cars hit poles and take out cable in the middle of a holiday weekend night, in a blowing snowstorm, and some poor technician has to put it back before he can get back to his holiday—sure he is going to do his best, but will his best be as good as it is on a warm spring day with no pressure on him? Now don't you wish you'd been a bit more conservative in your design of the system?

Mistake #2: Dirty the Connectors

Oh boy, if there was ever a universal mistake, this is it. Fiber optic systems work really well when the connectors are clean (all else being done right). But you would not believe the number of problems we've seen over the years due to connectors not being cleaned correctly. Even in laboratories and head-ends, the easiest environments to control, we've seen problems. If you are carrying analog video on a broadcast tier, you will see problems here first, but even if you are not, dirty connectors will grab you when you least expect it. Absent broadcast analog video, it is harder to trouble-shoot dirty connectors, because all you know is that the system sometimes doesn't work. At least the analog video degrades slowly so you can see that you have a problem before things just quit.

There are several good connector cleaning systems on the market today, so we're not going to endorse our favorite (alcohol cleaning followed by an air spray). But you need to choose one, and drive home to your technicians the importance of cleaning connectors. Train them to do it right—don't just assume they know how. Then retrain them. Schedule another training session in 6 months.

The job is not done when the connector has been cleaned; it has to be inspected, because sometimes cleaning doesn't get all of the dirt. Sometimes the connector is damaged, and you think it is clean, but it is not clean and cannot be cleaned. Make sure your people have inspection microscopes and that they know how to use them. A huge caution is worth repeating here: you cannot see the light coming out of a fiber, but if it is intense enough it can damage your eye. The optical levels we encounter in FTTH systems are frequently below what is considered the safe threshold for exposure, but better safe than sorry. NEVER look at the end of a fiber unless you know that no light is being transmitted through it. Indirect inspection microscopes, such as the one through which we took the inspection pictures above (Fig. 6.12) are safe, but others will not necessarily protect your eye.

Mistake #3: Bend the Fiber Too Sharply

You are most likely to have the opportunity to make this mistake when you are putting fiber inside a building. If you bend the fiber too sharply then the photons that are supposed to be completely reflected back into the core of the fiber can escape, increasing insertion loss. This problem is more prevalent at longer wavelengths. Fiber manufacturers make bend-insensitive fibers for use in situations where you may have to bend a fiber sharply around a corner.

Oh, there is another opportunity to bend fiber too sharply beside inside or outside buildings. Many ONTs have fiber management built in, with the fiber wrapped around fingers designed to hold it in place. But the fiber is held loosely, and we have seen it pulled tightly enough to put a bend in it at one of the fingers. Or else it is pulled tightly where it disappears from the fiber management, going into the packaged optical unit in the ONT. Often this connection is where it cannot be seen with just the cover of the ONT open. We have seen ONTs, especially outdoor ONTs, returned for troubleshooting, with the only problem being that the installer put a nice finishing tug on the internal fiber strand, thereby bending or even breaking it.[7]

Mistake #4: Not Enough Labels

You are going to need to troubleshoot your network at some point. You are going to need to add to your original network. There are hundreds to thousands of fiber optic connectors in the headend. How do you know which one goes where? You don't unless you have taken time to label all of the fibers. And tracing them through fiber trays is somewhere between extremely difficult and impossible. So label things from day one.

---

[7]The break is a shattering of the internal structure of the fiber—it does not always cause the fiber to visibly separate into two pieces.

CONCLUSION

Well, as you can see, there are a lot of important defining characteristics of the fiber optic cable and associated passives. The passive part of the plant deserves as much thought as does the active part. There are a number of fine fiber and passive vendors who will be happy to help you make good choices in these areas.

Endnotes

i. This material is largely taken from David Large, et al., Broadband Cable Access Networks, Morgan Kaufmann, 2009. A more detailed explanation of fiber optic propagation may be found therein. That reference is highly recommended for a better understanding of fiber optics physics.

ii. http://www.its.bldrdoc.gov/fs-1037/fs-1037c.htm.

iii. https://www.bicsi.org/uploadedFiles/BICSI_Website/Global_Community/Presentations/Middle_East_and_Africa/JDSU%20FIT%20workshop_final.pdf.

iv. http://webstore.iec.ch/preview/info_iec61300-3-35%7Bed1.0%7Den.pdf.

v. ANSI/SCTE 87-1 2008. Available at: http://www.scte.org/default.aspx.

vi. Hood D, Troier E. Gigabit-capable passive optical networks. Wiley; 2012.

vii. http://webstore.iec.ch/preview/info_iec60825-2%7Bed3.0%7Den.pdf.

viii. Green P. Fiber to the home: the new empowerment. Wiley; 2006.

CHAPTER 7

Choosing an FTTx Technology

INTRODUCTION

As with many decisions one makes throughout life, choosing an FTTx technology should not be taken lightly. There are many contributing factors which over time will determine the success of the deployment, including but not limited to, customer churn, long-time customer penetration, growth and technology upgrades. Many times a community will deploy an FTTx technology or network architecture because of decisions by a neighboring community or competitor. Be careful! Business cases and network goals for every network are different, especially in a competitive environment. This chapter provides guidance on choosing an FTTx technology.

THE GREAT DEBATE: PON VERSUS ACTIVE ETHERNET

The debate between passive optical network (PON) and active Ethernet technologies has been going on since day one in the world of FTTx networks. Both technologies have their merits and places. At the end of the day, a single large-scale multiservice FTTx network may find opportunities where both active Ethernet and PON may be deployed together (Table 7.1).

Historically, fiber-fed commercial services were delivered over point-to-point (P2P, also referred to as active Ethernet) connections. This was typically mandated by the commercial subscriber due to services required such as Synchronous Ethernet, MEF (Metro Ethernet Forum) transport, and services requiring large packet size and high bandwidth such as storage area networks (SANs). Furthermore, in the residential market place primarily in Europe, P2P services were popular due to the relative ease of extending existing enterprise-based network designs into a full-scale access network. With the competitive open-access models in this region, a new entrant into the market, such as a power utility company, may extend existing fiber networks in a region with carrier-grade switches overnight, becoming a competitive player in the residential services market.

As technologies have progressed over the years in the FTTx industry, the historical debates for PON versus P2P have faded for large-scale network rollouts. We

121

FTTx Networks. http://dx.doi.org/10.1016/B978-0-12-420137-8.00007-X

Table 7.1 Active Ethernet, PON Network Characteristics

	Active Ethernet	PON
Penetration	Dense serving area such as an MDU or office park	Lower penetration among more residential services
	Predictable growth and penetration	High level of customer churn
Services: video	RF video services are not available over an AE deployment	Supports both IPTV and RF video services
Services: commercial business	Cell-tower backhaul services traditionally demand AE solutions	Small to medium-sized business services requiring traditional service models
	Solutions requiring higher amounts of jumbo frames such as storage area networks	
Headend/Central office infrastructure	A full-scale rollout traditionally requires higher equipment costs and space requirements	A PON deployment at the central office/headend requires only a single interface to support between 32 and 64 subscribers. This results in a smaller footprint and lower thermal load than does an AE solution

are now left with decisions focused on the design of the outside plant to ensure that a flexible network architecture is in place. Key attributes of the architecture include long-term subscriber penetration, availability of fiber within a serving region and accommodation of services to be made available.

Penetration

Within the business case of an FTTx deployment the one decision which continues to pop up within the dialog is expected penetration. When deciding upon an FTTx technology, the expected penetration plays a major role in identifying which technologies may not be acceptable.

Consider the case where a service area expected penetration could range from 25% to 45% throughout the lifecycle of the network build. The difficulty comes when the network is being architected; the outside plant should provide for 100% of the passing since y ou are not sure where your customer base may reside—even if you are right on the penetration numbers, you have no idea in advance where those subscribers will be in your network. In order to ensure acceptable time between when a customer requests services and the service is activated, the fiber plant should be deployed well into the network, avoiding the high-cost civil works required in building out such a network later in piece-meal fashion. If active Ethernet (AE; Fig. 7.1), is chosen, a large amount of fiber must be deployed from the head end to cabinets within the field, allowing for potential future subscriber activation. This could lead to additional splices and infrastructure, resulting in significant additional costs. Furthermore, when a fiber cut does occur within the network, service availability will be impacted due to the number of splices required.

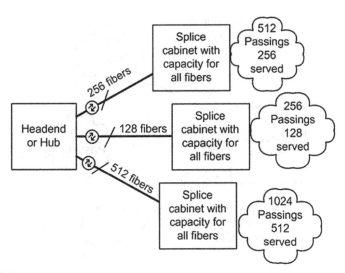

FIGURE 7.1

Active Ethernet Architecture.

As shown in Fig. 7.1, if you design for 50% maximum penetration, you would be limited to 50% penetration, because you don't have any more fiber from the headend to the area served. If you were successful and got 51% penetration, then you would be faced with the expense of putting in a new fiber to the cabinet, and fiber installation is one of your biggest expenses. The solution, of course, is to put in enough fiber to satisfy 100% penetration. Despite the additional costs for splicing and infrastructure, the incremental cost of using higher strand-count fiber to satisfy 100% penetration is very reasonable, and the construction cost per foot for deploying a larger-count fiber cable either aerially or underground (splicing excluded) is typically the same as for the lesser-count fiber used in Fig. 7.1. The overall incremental cost provides reasonable insurance in the event that penetration exceeds projections, or an adjacent new area is built which may be served from the extra fibers strands. Therefore, while installing active Ethernet, as you can see, plant design should allow for greater penetration success or expansion of the area to be served.

Now consider the same deployment area using PON technology (Fig. 7.2). Penetration uncertainties may be overcome with the deployment of trunk fibers into the network, with each trunk fiber capable of extending to 32 or more subscribers via a field-mounted splitter. This allows for an FTTx deployment where penetration numbers are not well understood, with the capacity of serving close to 100% of the subscriber base. By grouping several splitters in the same small cabinet, you can minimize the hub cost. You do so by connecting the first 32 subscribers to the first PON, the second 32 subscribers to the second PON and so on. Typical optical line terminal (OLT) blades in the hub have between four

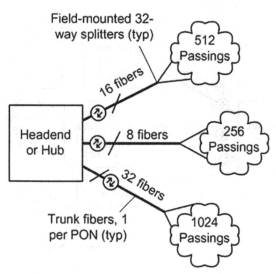

FIGURE 7.2

Passive optical network (PON).

and 12 PON ports per blade, so there is no need to buy a second blade until you have almost finished filling the first, and so on.

Looking just at the costs at the headend or hub location, in an AE deployment, fiber termination and routing must be put into place for each of the deployed fibers within the field—since you don't know where your subscribers will reside, you must provide for serving all possible subscribers, even if half of the connections will never be used. With a distributed passive splitting architecture, a PON environment could provide up to 75% less passive infrastructure termination, requiring only termination for those deployed PON fibers.

Video Impacts on Network Architecture

If all of your video is to be delivered over IP, then you can use either a PON or AE architecture. However, if you contemplate using broadcast video for at least some channels, which can be more cost-efficient and simpler, then you should think of ruling out AE. The problem is the cost of wave division multiplexing the broadcast wavelength onto each fiber needing it. This creates a significant cost burden, as well as creating a more complex fiber cabling infrastructure at the headend. We know of a few early FTTH designs that put one fiber in using PON architecture for video, and a second P2P fiber for data. This was a very expensive solution!

Fiber Availability

In many markets around the world, an operator may not be given the opportunity to dig up the civil environment for the deployment of an FTTx solution. The operator is forced to lease fiber from either a municipal authority or private enterprise, to a specific point in the network where the final drop fibers to the subscriber may be put into place. In these situations, the deployment of an active Ethernet solution may incur additional costs based on expected penetration of subscribers within a serving area. With PON technologies today capable of serving 32 or 64 subscribers on a single distribution fiber and PON technologies bandwidth up to 10 Gbps symmetrical, the costs of deployment for a PON solution will be far less than an active Ethernet solution.

WHAT ABOUT A NOT-SO-PON ARCHITECTURE?

More recently operators have been considering the deployment of a distributed PON model whereby the OLT is deployed deep into the field. Within the distributed network model, an operator may provide FTTH connectivity to a serving area of maybe 1000 ONTs within a facility no larger than a cable TV node housing, which is designed to hang in strand in overhead plant, or to mount in a small cabinet for underground installations.

As the growth of broadband networks continues to expand, putting pressures on copper-based technologies, a distributed architecture allows an operator to push deep into a targeted area using a single fiber to service that area. This may be done in response to a competitive market place, a new greenfield housing area, or possibly a commercial park expansion. A single fiber can reach a lot of subscribers by being extended from the headend to a wave division multiplexer in the field. It has, in Fig. 7.3, three sets of wavelengths, λ1, λ2,

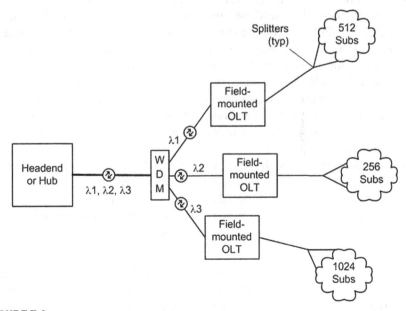

FIGURE 7.3

Field-mounted OLT in a PON.

and λ3, with each λ representing two wavelengths, one for downstream and one for upstream data for each field-mounted OLT. Of course, it is possible to also route a common broadcast wavelength to all field-mounted nodes for broadcast video.

TECHNOLOGIES EVOLVE AND NEW STANDARDS ARE WRITTEN

As with most things, the one constant in life is change. In the world of FTTx technology, changes are felt by an operator on multiple fronts. One of those areas of change is the PON technology chosen. At any given time, the standards are pushing the envelope of technology, the goal being to increase the number of supported subscribers while increasing bandwidth provided to each subscriber. As an operator, the proverbial fork in the road for a PON deployment is making the decision between the various standards bodies. The two primary standards bodies are the ITU-T/FSAN (GPON) and the IEEE (EPON). For many, the decision comes down to something as simple as the group with which you feel more closely aligned. For others, the decision is based on existing surrounding technologies used. Regardless of the path the decision follows, the following are questions every operator should consider:

- Has the standards organization under consideration provided a backward-compatible upgrade path to the "next" evolution of the standard?
- What are the costs in the future to add a single subscriber to the network using the "next" evolution? Do you have to replace all ONTs within the PON to move to the next upgrade? (Note that this question is more about equipment that will be stranded in an upgrade, than it is about the actual cost of next-generation equipment. That equipment cost may not be known when you are making your decision.)
- Based on projected bandwidth considerations (which should include subscriber growth and new service introductions), how many years of service will the selected technology provide before upgrades may be required?
- Does the technology chosen fit well within the current operational and service models in place within the network today?
- How closely does the proposed standard come to providing all of the features you will want to sell during its lifetime, and are ancillary standards in place and supported by the manufacturers if you need them?

The answers to these questions only provide guidance on selecting a path down the stated fork in the road today. It is important to understand that more often than not, the evolution of a standard takes much longer than expected.

This may be due to political influences within the standards body or possibly the industry waiting for specific technical advances to catch up. Even after the standard is ratified there is still a major step by the technology suppliers to develop a cost-effective solution. This may take another 18–24 months before the building blocks necessary to build an end-to-end system are available.

A Short Aside on Standards Organizations

The goal of this chapter is not to provide an in-depth understanding of the ITU-T and IEEE standards bodies; however, a bit of background on how the organizations approach their standards development may be in order.

Both organizations have been engaged in the definition of communications standards for decades, providing us the users with technologies such as Ethernet communications, Wi-Fi connectivity, DSL broadband, and Integrated Services Digital Network (ISDN) to name a few. Although each organization has a different approach to standards development, neither provides a significant advantage over the other.

In the world of PON standards definition, the ITU-T standards body works together with the Full Service Access Network (FSAN) organization on the development of PON-based standards. FSAN is made up of major public telephone and telegraph (PTT) operators around the world along with equipment vendors and testing facilities. A focus of FSAN is the definition of PON-based standards to operate within similar telco-based network architectures and management solutions. Many times this requires the development of a complete solution as in the definition of the standard ITU-T G.984, more commonly referred to as GPON. This standards definition took on not only the definition of the physical and MAC layer definitions but also extended the standard to include management, security, and encryption unique to the implementation.

As a contrast, the IEEE standards body, those responsible for the GE-PON (EPON) based standards, take the approach of defining the basic physical and MAC layer for PON-based environments using existing higher-level standards to accommodate techniques such as management and security. The IEEE 802.3ah (GE-PON) and IEEE 802.3av (10G E-PON) standards can be thought of as a chapter in an overarching book (called IEEE 802), whereby similar management and security techniques used in Wi-Fi and standard Ethernet are re-used and not redefined.

Neither of the standards bodies could be thought of as being better than the other, just a different approach to accomplish the same outcome. In many cases competition can be thought of as a good thing and in this case we firmly believe this has enabled the industry to progress the development of next-generation PON architectures, allowing both organizations to better their standards, while cooperating in some areas such as wavelength definition. The good news is the decision an operator makes will be supported by a large-scale base of operators and vendors, all improving the respective standard, hoping to drive down costs and ease the challenges to deploy an FTTH solution.

NETWORK OPERATIONS AND SERVICE ACTIVATION

Another key in choosing the right PON technology is making sure the end-to-end operational models are capable of being supported by the systems and service models already in use in your network (if any). A hidden piece of a new large-scale FTTx deployment is underestimating the costs required to integrate a new operational support system (OSS) platform while training customer service employees and the various technicians. Regardless of feeds and speeds provided by the platform, standards are evolving on a regular basis. Making sure existing operational systems are not interrupted is critical to a successful production launch and service migration across multiple technologies. In other words, OSS integration should be considered as important, if not more so, than the specific FTTx architecture under consideration.

A good example occurred when CableLabs commenced the development of a standard applying those operational models deployed within a DOCSIS environment to those of an IEEE EPON environment. The goal of the CableLabs organization was to develop a standard such that an FTTx network operating within a qualified CableLabs' *DOCSIS Provisioning over EPON* (DPoE) environment could slide right into an existing operator's DOCSIS CMTS environment. For the most part, all existing back-office systems operating within a CMTS deployment would just point over to the EPON deployment no differently than adding a new CMTS within the system. CableLabs took this effort a step further by defining a complete interoperability program whereby qualified OLT and ONT suppliers are capable of working together. This extension within the EPON market place has provided cable operators a strong case for the deployment of FTTx technology.

CHOOSING THE RIGHT TECHNOLOGY(IES) FOR SERVICES GOALS

Another technology change within the FTTx industry is advances in service capabilities available to an operator. For many years, services such as cell tower backhaul (CTBH) were delivered over a traditional active Ethernet. This decision within the industry was made due to advances within the active Ethernet industry in providing a higher level of redundancy and perceived stability as compared to that of a PON-based network.

With recent advances in PON technology supporting features such as timing resources needed to support Synchronous Ethernet, new levels of services may be deployed alongside other commercial and residential services within a PON deployment. This provides operator deployment options for the delivery of CTBH services alongside those services provided for small–medium business and residential services.

Although the advances within the PON industry have broadened deployments within the industry, PON does not have the answer to all service models. Take for instance a *service area network* (SAN)-based network service model. Within an SAN network, the traditional service delivery consists of super jumbo frames allowing for large capacities of traffic to be delivered with little overhead and fragmentation. As the upstream of a PON environment is a shared medium delivered over time division multiplexing, when one ONT is transmitting other ONTs must remain silent. If an ONT providing SAN-based services is located within a highly dense PON, additional latency and jitter may be experienced by the other ONTs. Therefore, if such services are required to be delivered, an active Ethernet solution should be considered in parallel by a physically separate and isolated network, or possibly as an overlay.

CONCLUSION

In this chapter we have looked at several physical architectures which all fall under the banner of fiber-to-the-home. These include active Ethernet and passive optical networks, along with the PON variation of field-mounting the OLT equipment. We have also provided some discussion regarding considerations that might drive you toward one higher-layer technology or the other. The good news is that there is no one right answer to the question of which technology to use: you can be very successful with any standards-based choice.

PART

3

FTTx Network Implementation

CHAPTER 8

Planning to Implement the Network

INTRODUCTION

With the decision to proceed with the creation of the FTTx network affirmed through careful business analysis; the review, assessment, and comparison of the competing passive optical network (PON) technologies completed; and the placement of independent oversight to ensure the success of the network project; it is time to begin the planning process for the design and implementation of the network.

During this process the myriad of details and decision points concerning the requirements, design, and implementation stages of the project will be considered and addressed. It is here in the planning process that the success of the network will be both understood and assured. In many cases, the core team of executives and technical staff tasked with the design and implementation planning will supplement their knowledge and execution capabilities with the selection of key technology and business consultants to aid in their work.

With the extended planning team identified and in-place, the following chapter presents a roadmap to the development of a successful network implementation blueprint.

THE PLANNING REQUIREMENTS: WHAT MUST THE NETWORK DO?

The starting point of any network build is defining the requirements of the network. Foremost, what must the network do? In particular, what services and benefits must it provide to the customers of the network? The topmost level of requirements analysis begins with this deceptively simple question. Some potential answers which are identified for many network projects are captured here in broad categories. From the high-level requirements, the next and subsequent levels of technical requirements are identified, through the thought process that follows.

FTTx Networks. http://dx.doi.org/10.1016/B978-0-12-420137-8.00008-1

Technical Goals

- Allow for high-bandwidth connectivity to provide services (such as telemedicine) and products which are not possible with existing access network technologies;
- Deploy new types of services made possible with FTTx and the telecommunications technologies it can support.

Business Goals

- Replace aging telecommunications infrastructure with newer fiber-based facilities, or allow the migration from leased facilities to owned facilities;
- Provide state-of-the-art and future-proofed telecommunications infrastructure which will serve customers for years to come;
- Improve competitive position relative to other telecommunications providers which are using legacy access network technologies;
- Reduce operating expenses compared to existing nonoptical fiber plants;
- Integrate the new network's operation into the organization's existing business structure and leverage the network for the organization's core utility services, if applicable.

Access Goals

- Provide wider residential telecommunications connectivity for underserved constituents of the community;
- Allow network operators to introduce future-proofed technologies into the telecommunications market in the local served community or serving area which will increase end customer awareness and support rising demands for bandwidth.

Mapping Top-Level Requirements to Technical Requirements

These high-level requirements are valuable for articulating the goals of the network and are the guiding principles under which the network realization will be undertaken. In the next step of analysis, the network design and implementation teams refine the compiled top-level goals and requirements to a further level of detail, mapping these requirements to the set of technical requirements. During this step in the requirements analysis, additional concerns regarding technical details and operational criteria which are not covered in the top-level requirements will be identified and included as part of the network design and implementation planning. This full set of combined requirements fall into the following broad technical categories relevant to all FTTx network implementations:

- Inside plant—inside plant requirements are those related to the logical design, supporting equipment which realizes the data transmission and management systems of the network.
- General networking—general networking requirements are those which specify the networking equipment which supports the FTTx access

network; later we will explore the network partitions in depth and the purpose of each.

- Services deployment—services deployment requirements are those related to the equipment which is required to implement the services over the network end-to-end.
- Management systems—management systems requirements guide the development of control systems for the network for configuration, provisioning, performance management, and security.
- Outside plant—outside plant requirements are those related to the physical design, and implementing equipment which realize the optical distribution network (ODN).

Maintaining a Network Requirements Repository

As the network requirements: business, technical, and operational, are being developed and refined, a repository of these requirements must be created, and should be maintained over the life of the network. The as-built final construction of the network will be compared against these requirements, but more importantly these requirements will drive all the design and implementation work that is required to realize the network. This is true whether the network design and build is a standard multilevel waterfall project established and completed by a single team, or is the result of a number of rounds of proposal development, vendor proposal receipt, assessment, and selection handled with a number of outside consulting firms for both products and services, or is a hybrid approach combining some internal team functions with a mix of vendor and consultant input for varying parts of the network's inside and outside plant systems. Depending on the type of organization engaging in the FTTx project and their skill sets, these requirements and project organization may take any of several forms, but ultimately must be used as the benchmark during the entire implementation process to ensure that the components of the final system perform their intended function in providing the services envisioned at the beginning of the project.

FTTx Network Build Project Organization

The likely project team organization for the network requirements, design, and engineering consists of the network operator executive and technical staff. These individuals, depending on their combined skill sets, will often round out their team with additional members, bringing requisite skills and knowledge which may not be found on the network operator's team:

- Engineering and business consultants skilled in network planning, requirements, design, and implementation as well as network operations;
- Consultants or vendors acting as consultants for very specific technologies to be deployed in the network;

- Technical implementation teams which will be responsible for network build and integration activities, ultimately turning the resulting network over to the operator for long-term operations (using a build–operate–transfer model, for example);
- Network operations organizations who are engaged during the build and integration process and upon network operations go-live, maintain, and service the network long term for the network operator;
- The types of project organization and network build models are detailed in the discussion of Production Operations in Chapter 16.

TECHNICAL REQUIREMENTS OVERVIEW

Inside Plant Requirements

The organization of the inside plant requirements typically breaks down into the following large subcategories of implementation equipment.

FTTx Equipment

In this category, capture requirements for all aspects of the FTTx access portion of the network, to support services which will be provided to subscribers of the network. This will include the optical line terminal (OLT) and optical network terminal (ONT) device requirements, including the form factors and placement of the equipment based on deployment requirements for indoor or outdoor operation and scaling, based on the number of subscribers in the network and the types of services deployed. Depending on the implementation of service deployment this will also include ancillary customer premises equipment (CPE) devices which connect to the ONT for:

- Data services—home routers with potential numerous data features including wireless networking capability (these may also be embedded in the ONT), subscriber computers and servers.
- Video services—set-top boxes (either radio frequency [RF] or IPTV).
- Voice-over-Internet-Protocol (VoIP) services—the voice capability may be embedded in the ONT device or it may in an attached *analog telephone adaptor* (ATA).

Also included are headend devices which are critical for providing services, which reside in the inside plant because they support all the subscribers in the network:

- VoIP services—VoIP switches (soft switches), border session controllers for VoIP integration and security, and voice gateway devices (as necessary) which provide interconnect and send VoIP traffic into the general upstream VoIP provider network.

- Data services—edge routers and gateways which connect to and send data into the general upstream data provider networks, devices for securing these data services and in many cases (again depending on services design) provide for rate limiting, rate shaping, metering, security, and authentication of the data subscribers on the network.
- Video services—content descrambling and scrambling, middleware and content management, advertising insertion, video service on-demand implementation and management, and electronic program guide.

General Networking Requirements

In the general packet network category, capture requirements driving the design and implementation of the packet network into which the FTTx access network components at the edge (the OLT) will connect (or "up-link") to receive connectivity in the upstream network direction, including the partitioning of the network into transport, core, edge, and access.

Network Partitioning

The equipment in this area will likely take the form of multilayer switching and routing devices with high capability for packet processing, and a large amount of connected equipment. The upstream network partitions which support the FTTx access network's requirements of providing services to the subscriber, take on specific functionality based upon their location in the overall network end-to-end. Fig. 8.1 identifies the partitions of the overall network implementation which are present in all networks, but may have different scale based upon the size of the network and protocol support based upon the logical design chosen by the implementation team.

- Upstream network interface partition—The upstream network interface partition implements resilient and typically high-bandwidth connectivity to the wider network world accessed through large general connectivity service providers. The connectivity on which the entire operator services network depends is represented by the capability and logical design of this partition. At the edge of the network the operator is concerned with overall bandwidth usage and resilient, fault-tolerant operation. Therefore, the backhaul circuit represented by the upstream network interface partition must be designed and established with sufficient sizing and redundancy to provide uninterrupted connectivity at the oversubscription levels designed by the operator. Typically this partition is providing its resources at layer 2 and layer 3 so route redundancy, link aggregation and fail-over, and flexibility in increasing bandwidth quickly by the addition of physical interfaces or the increase in speed of interfaces are all requirements. Due to the critical nature of this partition, the redundant upstream connections will likely follow

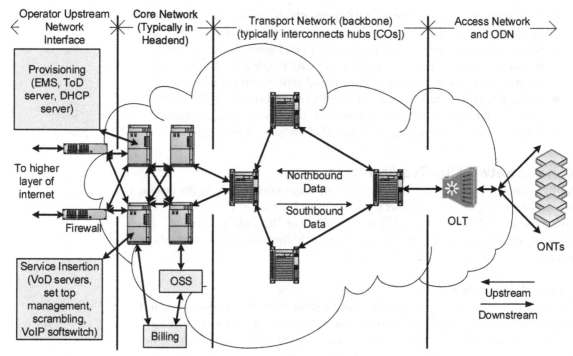

FIGURE 8.1
Operator network partitions.

different physical paths, allowing for a physical failure to affect only a single link. Note the term "oversubscription" above. It is unnecessary and unaffordable to add the bandwidth of all subscribers, then attempt to provide for this much provider edge bandwidth. Since residential subscribers don't use the bandwidth all of the time, it can be shared. Oversubscription ratios, the amount of oversubscription possible before subscribers notice a reduction in bandwidth, are figures that most operators keep to themselves. The best rule-of-thumb we can offer as a starting point is a 50:1 oversubscription ratio for residential service. Add to this the contractual edge interface bandwidth you are obligated to provide for business clients. Then watch your actual utilization. When it reaches 70–80%, it is time to provide more north-facing bandwidth. (While we think 50:1 is a good starting point oversubscription ratio, as more over-the-top [OTT] video is consumed, you may find that a lower ratio is needed—this will be a dynamic ratio for at least several years.)

- Core network partition—In the core of the network, powerful multilayer switch routers with multiple physical connections forming a mesh between all devices are utilized to provide the backbone over which service traffic is inserted into the operator network, connectivity to the upstream network interface(s) is introduced into the operator's domain, and service traffic is provided to and from each of the transport network pick-off points. The power, scalability, and resilience of this partition are driven by the requirement to switch, route, and prioritize the entire aggregated set of operator, customer, and services traffic. Typically the devices in this partition reside in either centralized or geographically limited locations due to the expense and criticality of the equipment needed to provide the core networking function.

- Transport network partition—The transport of combined services and management traffic to distinct geographic locations and over distance to where the traffic is destined, is the domain of the transport network nodes. Its job is to resiliently provide services traffic to the access network partition to which those services are bound. The devices need to be reasonably powered and provide resilient operation, but they do not need to take the load of the entire network, only the specific access portions they are designed to serve. This partition of the network may be providing layer 2 and layer 3 connectivity, depending on the physical and logical design of each of the transport nodes. The transport network may also be called a network backbone. Where the transport network interfaces into a direct connection to the access network, it may be referred to as the provider edge portion of the network.

- Access network partition—The access network partition—implemented by the OLT, and its connectivity to subscribers (via the ONT) and to the transport network, via the OLT uplink—provides the direct interface to the subscribers in the network consuming services. The access network is concerned with ensuring resilient delivery to and from the individual subscribers in the network. The amount of resilience and network resources provided to each subscriber depends on the type of services they are consuming and the criticality of those services. Over time, as more types of subscribers are served by this partition and the types of services become more mission critical, the resilience of the physical and logical design becomes paramount.

The exact number of devices required for each partition is implementation-specific. Based on the sizing of the network, the number of locations or geographic area, layout of the subscriber base which must be served, number of transport nodes, and potentially other factors such as planned scaling schedules will determine how this implementation will start and change over time. Of course for smaller networks, some of the partitions may collapse into each other or be combined together, but the functions represented by the partitions will still be present.

Sizing, Scaling, Resiliency, and Quality of Service in the Network

All the partitions represented in the operator network have requirements for *sizing and scalability, resilience,* and *quality of service.* Each of the partitions must be sized by designing for the necessary loading when the network is initially commissioned and implemented, with scalability in mind. As the number of subscribers and the services deployed change over time, the ability to adjust the network in a proactive fashion is required, sometimes at a speed unforeseen when the network is initially brought into service. Resiliency ensures the network continues to operate in the event of a failure of an element, while quality of service guarantees that the services and resulting customer experience are maintained at acceptable levels when multiple subscribers and services are competing for shared, finite network resources, in a dynamic fashion, by differentiating the services.

Sizing of the network is defined as supplying the resources required to serve the expected number of subscribers, and thus deployed services, on the network. Sizing requirements should be assessed anywhere in the network an identified finite resource can affect system operation—for example, based on aggregation over the entire network, a portion of the network, or a single network device. In all these cases the resource will likely be simultaneously serving groups of subscribers and multiple services, but may in some cases be specific to a single subscriber. Consider an example such as interface capacity. When loaded by data traffic, a percentage of port utilization provides a measure of the resource. When interfaces serve aggregated traffic for a number of subscribers or where traffic combines from multiple network partitions through a single interface, the resource is shared. Contrast this to a single device, serving a single subscriber but with an internal table of MAC addresses where the size of the table represents a capacity resource. Some devices which serve the network and are aggregated over a number of subscribers may be scaled at first and when a certain threshold of service level has been reached, may be supplemented by allocating additional resources or equipment to that point in the network. Table 8.1 describes the types of resources which are typically sized in a network deployment with examples and notes for how to size them. Sometimes the resource cannot be scaled so the network must be sized to take it into consideration, and work within the constraint.

As an example, consider the first resource in Table 8.1, utilization of a physical interface or shared medium. For a PON port which feeds a certain number of subscribers, the loading of that port (ingress towards the OLT, for example, and egress toward the subscribers on the PON) can be sized by using the following steps to define the number and type of subscriber devices per subscriber premises along with the bandwidth requirements per device/service:

- The upstream and downstream data service packages sold to each subscriber provide the measure of the individual data service loading per subscriber (in this case the subscriber is limited to the data services they have purchased, regardless of the number of data devices which are utilizing the data service). Multiplying by the number of subscribers on the PON provides a measure of the utilization for data services for all subscribers on the shared medium.

- The number of anticipated set-top boxes per subscriber and the number of IPTV streams which are anticipated, along with the anticipated channel encoding per stream, provides the loading for broadcast IPTV. Also to be considered is the amount of data expected due to individual on-demand IPTV viewing. Note that in both cases, this is an asymmetric service, such that the downstream data flow is much larger than the upstream data flows. The aggregate of the subscribers provides a loading of the sustained IPTV service on the PON.
- Next consider the loading of voice traffic. While small, this traffic will be differentiated and prioritized highly within the set of aggregated traffic.
- Finally consider other loading such as management traffic required by the network operations functions.
- The full sizing of the number of subscribers which can comfortably coexist within the shared PON medium is a total of all the traffic types and their sum, balanced against the capacity of the PON link (including Ethernet overhead).

Scalability describes how easily the network can be changed to accommodate larger capacity as this capacity is required. The network has the requirement to support the addition of capacity without significant redesign by deploying readily available resources or making changes in the logical design of the network (i.e., changing from a layer 2 to a layer 3 approach). Scalable resources must either be added quickly through planned design changes or designed in from the beginning and brought online at the appropriate time. Examples are:

- Bandwidth capacity represented by the number of interfaces allocated to a network partition such as the FTTx SNI;
- Many of the resources described above in the discussion on sizing, such as resource pools within DHCP or authentication servers which support service deployment on the network, may require additional configuration;
- Some resources which are bound by the internal capacity of a certain inside plant component may require an upgrade of either software or hardware to expand capacity or capabilities;
- Scaling the interconnects of the various network partitions based upon the types of traffic exchanged between partitions and the number of subscribers in each partition should be a planned-for expansion as part of the requirements analysis.

Resiliency requirements are strategies that provide for redundant elements that ensure continued operation in the event of a network element failure. The services affected by a failure should be automatically restored by the operation of the redundant network element and allow a replacement

Table 8.1 Network Resource Sizing

Resource Classes for Sizing	Description	Examples	Scaling Considerations
Points of resource contention	Points in the network where a number of subscribers or individual subscriber services aggregate. These scale by adding additional equipment resources	Utilization or amount of bandwidth used at physical network interfaces or in the shared PON medium	Utilization is assessed by the number of subscribers aggregated and the amount of bandwidth each is using and/or guaranteed
Internal finite resources scaled by the design or implementation of equipment	These need to be allocated by partitioning, and if possible scaled by additional resources (i.e., at some point partitioning will run out)	MAC tables (note that MAC addresses are learned for all Ethernet devices in the L2 segment)—the size of such expected MAC tables versus the expected number "seen" by all devices on the segment must be addressed	This resource is likely constrained for the device when deployed, so the number of devices which are subtended to a device with a MAC table constraint should be an engineered requirement
		Routing tables, number of routes to be defined and shared amongst layer 3 (L3) devices. Note also that providing L3 partitions can help to scale large L2 segments (behind the L3 interface)	These resources can be difficult to size, but the number of subscribers and IP address utilization by the number of devices allocated to a subscriber can be sized
		Virtual local area network (VLAN) allocations (tables of available VLANs). The number of VLANs intended to be used per segment based on the services type should be considered	This resource is similar to MAC tables in that it is likely an attribute of the device which is likely to not be changed. However, modern switch devices tend to be well resourced when it comes to numbers of VLANs or VLAN combinations (i.e., ability to stack VLANs)
		Internal bus speed or aggregated bus capacity	This resource can be considered in both customer premise devices such as ONTs or in the larger multiuser devices such as OLTs. In the design consider requirements such as the amount of aggregated service traffic which must flow from one input of the OLT across the backplane and to the upstream network interface. In this way the amount of traffic capacity available to the system will be sized, and also therefore the number of subscribers available to each PON port and interface card
		Internal memory resources	This resource is unlikely to change for any specific device. The equipment vendor should provide conditions under which the memory may be taxed

System parameter or attribute		
For a given equipment type, such as a management system, provisioning system, or FTTx or networking component, there will be operational resource constraints which must be considered as sized and scaled requirements or as resource constraints	Database sizes	These resources come into play when considering the overall number of subscribers for which provisioning or configuration information must be stored. The vendor of the specific equipment should have a recommendation for hardware requirements to support a certain numbers of devices or subscribers
	Logical network resources such as available network addresses (DHCP lease pool sizes)	These important resources controlled by the network operator should be considered based upon the number of subscribers and devices per subscriber which must receive IP addresses. This may drive a move to IPv6, and will also inform the network operator where they can use public or private addressing for particular services

element to be entered into service and operated until the failure has been resolved, and then either manually or automatically moved back into a standby configuration. Resiliency requirements should be considered for all critical links between network partitions, supporting network servers, and device powering.

Quality of service (QoS) ensures end-to-end service delivery in the presence of multiple and differing service types vying for shared network resources. Requirements for QoS are created on a per-service basis and combined to create an overall QoS plan. Assess each of the service types for the following.

- Relative prioritization of all network traffic types;
- Where there are shared resources in the network, planning for the appropriate marking of traffic types to ensure end-to-end delivery through all parts of the network;
- The methodologies used to mark and differentiate traffic through the various network partitions—either at L2 or L3;
- The decision to trust or untrust traffic as it enters the operator's network. (Typically traffic is untrusted and remarked by the operator upon ingress to their network. This concept is discussed in significant detail in Chapter 10.)

Services Deployment Requirements

In the services deployment category, capture requirements are related to the insertion, network support, and premise distribution of individual service types. Every FTTx network implementation will break down into the deployment of data, video and voice services—the triple-play. Depending on the goals of the network, only one, two or all three service types may be deployed initially. This decision might be reached if the operating organization has decided to deploy initial services they are comfortable with or wish to prove success with—and then deploy other services they feel are more challenging in the future. Furthermore, the services may not be deployed at the same time, with the implementation of one or two services first and other services later. For example, a network may provide video and data to customers first. Voice services (while planned for in the original requirements and design) might not be deployed until after the first two services are working well. This phased roll-out approach must be planned for carefully since the logical design, equipment, and processes deployed in the first phases, must be flexible enough to allow the deployment of the additional services at a later time.

Closely related to the definitions of the service requirements are important ancillary requirements which help fill out the design of the inside plant portion of the network. This important category of requirements is those general networking requirements related to upstream connectivity to the wider networked world, network resiliency, availability, and scalability—within the boundaries of the original intent of the network but with some margin for unforeseen growth in services or technology.

A discussion following each of the service types here, from a requirements perspective, will set the stage for a deeper treatment of each service from a design and implementation standpoint in subsequent chapters.

Data Services

The broad category of data services includes a number of data products provided to a wide range of customer types. The highest level break down of the data service category is residential versus commercial (also known as business) services.

Residential Data Service

Residential data services are those which are typically provided to individual private residences, with the expectation that those residential subscribers are interacting with the FTTx network and its upstream connections to the wider Internet, in a direct interactive fashion—i.e., they are not interacting with their neighboring subscribers in a direct network connection. While they may, for example, be sending email to their neighbor, they are doing so through a mail server with which they are interacting, and similarly their neighbor will be interacting with their mail service to retrieve their messages. Furthermore, in the PON standards the direct communication with peer neighbors typically is forbidden as a security risk.

Two attributes of this type of service are the amount bandwidth (sometimes also called the size of the data pipe) provided to each subscriber and the priority or relative importance to other traffic on the network assigned to the residential service. Usually, garden variety residential service traffic is provided a "best effort" priority. Typically high degrees of oversubscription can be tolerated (thus saving money) because all subscribers do not use the network's available bandwidth at the same time. Current acceptable levels of oversubscription may be as high as 50 to 1, meaning that if the cumulative amount of bandwidth subscription levels among all subscribers is 50 Gigabits, then a 1 Gigabit data link would be sufficient to ensure acceptable data transport performance. Having said that, and with video streaming now dominating traffic, some of the old oversubscription models may be changing. Priority and bandwidth are two of the universe of attributes within the discussion of QoS, the engineering of which is critical to the success of any network. Residential data service may also provide a "tiered" rate, where for an increased price, a premium service or services with higher bandwidth and perhaps even higher prioritization (which mean high-priority data packets are transmitted before lower-priority packets) may be purchased. (Appendix D provides a brief introduction to prioritization.)

The residential data services mentioned here are usually designed to interface to any number of expected devices which are subtended to the PON ONT, whether these are supplied by the network operator or the subscriber. In the majority of cases, these will be subscriber-supplied devices, such as personal computers, laptops, tablets, and increasingly home broadband routers with any number of network interface ports, wireless access, and residential gateway functions. The ability of such sophisticated subscriber-owned devices to affect the network service will be addressed later.

Commercial Data Services

The other broad category of data services, for commercial or business applications, may be similar to the residential services described above. Typically for a commercial subscriber, depending on the application, their bandwidth and prioritization may be greater than for a typical residential service. In some cases, the commercial service may dynamically change over the time of the day, for example, increased bandwidth during nonpeak hours for large file transfers.

Metro Ethernet Services. Another class of commercial service which is being rapidly deployed is Metro Ethernet service. The standards supporting Metro Ethernet services are produced by the Metro Ethernet Forum, and collectively are known by its initials, MEF.[i] In this case, a business which maintains multiple locations may identify a requirement to link those sites together from a networking perspective. This may be accomplished in a number of ways. With Metro Ethernet services, the two sites' local area networks (LANs) are able to view each other as being on the same Ethernet network—and yet the two networks are separated by perhaps great distances and a number of networks in between. Ethernet networks are typically designed to directly attach endpoints in a local area network in a collocated area (within Ethernet standard distances). However the usage of MEF standard technology allows for networks in disparate locations to function as if at the same location. The MEF standards define various architectures, implementations, and tests for the equipment which are used to deploy these types of extended Ethernet networks. We shall outline the most significant standards below.

Circuit Emulation Services. Commercial data services also covers a number of applications for special IP-packetized services with a data payload mimicking a point-to-point or circuit connection by creating an IP-stream with critical requirements for low latency (a low value of time delay between the generation of the packet at its origin and delivery of the packet to its endpoint), jitter (variation in delay of received packets), and failure recovery (ability of the system to recover from failure events in an automated and systematic fashion). Some examples of these are the following:

- T1/E1 circuit replacement (to allow legacy TDM systems to exist on the FTTx network);
- Mobile telephony backhaul (special IP circuit emulation);
- Wireless network hotspot backhaul.

In general these types of services require a dedicated IP packet stream which must always be present, whether or not there is a signal generated by the endpoint circuit emulation equipment. Thus the "circuit" is always available even when idle from a signaling perspective. Such circuit emulation equipment can detect failures and send alarms and warnings that the circuit is compromised or not available. The types of conditions detailed above (latency, jitter, and data failure) are all symptomatic of an IP path which is experiencing issues with timely packet delivery. While the FTTx network equipment may not include the devices generating such data packet streams, the FTTx network must be capable of delivering these services with the required quality of service in order to avoid these types of issues.

Data Service Requirements Considerations

The following are generic questions to be applied to each of the deployed services from a requirements perspective (and later these same questions will have a network design and implementation component):

- How will subscribers be billed for their service? Will this be in the form of a flat fee for a certain data rate, regardless of the amount of service used? Will there be a metering of the service such that if a certain threshold amount of service is used, a higher rate will ensue?
- What integration needs to happen to ensure the service end-to-end? The data service must be protected, and yet subscribers must be able to attach to the network with a minimum of effort. The FTTx system, as well as other components of the network must work together to ensure the data service is available, easy to use, and yet secure.
- How do subscribers buy the service/sign up for the service and make changes to their data service over time? There are many methodologies available, such as direct interaction with a customer service representative (CSR), or the walled garden (do-it-yourself) approach, where the network operator provides an interface which allows the subscriber to make an initial purchase or change an existing data service.

Video Services

After data services, video services are perhaps the most important because access networks have generally been known for providing video since the initial deployments of cable networks. The ability to broadcast high-quality video is very well known and FTTx networks have a number of options which may be used seamlessly to deploy video services. These include the well-known legacy approach of using an RF video overlay in conjunction with the typical FTTx standard data path on the PON—of which there are several variants, including the case where satellite video reception (modulated onto an optical carrier) is used to create an RF video service.

RF Video

RF video is a special and well-known method for providing broadcast television services. In this case, the RF video content is provided as an overlay "on-top" of the standard data content. This is accomplished using a different wavelength for video than for the data service, which is then added to the PON plant via passive wave division multiplexing. RF broadcast video is an excellent choice for the ability to relieve the bandwidth requirements in the system data path for IPTV. It can be thought of as "buying back" the bandwidth utilized by the entire multicast plant which would be required for supplying broadcast video over the PON network (and the other network partitions for that matter). RF video also enables the operator to utilize the existing coax wiring inside the subscriber's home to serve all of the television outlets, rather than rewiring the home with a new category 5 (Cat5) outlet at each television location as required for IPTV. (It is also possible to put data over coax using either the MoCA or HPNA standards, but these carry a cost which may be similar to that of installing Cat5 cable, depending on your cost models.)

IPTV Broadcast

Broadcast television services utilizing IP protocols are increasingly becoming popular with FTTx network projects due to the high bandwidth capability of the PON network. Also, the benefit of sending video as encoded IP packet streams allows the operator to optimize the network for the delivery of datagrams. In this case, the datagrams are transported over *multicast streams*, which are Ethernet/IP frames optimized for sending and receiving to multiple IP hosts simultaneously. The fact that there are a number of simultaneous recipients of the multicast data means that network resources can be reused in specific methodologies which preserve those resources. It also presents additional requirements for the services integration, transport, and provider edge partitions of the network to ensure the end-to-end efficacy of the IPTV services.

In the packet world, *multicast* refers to what is called *broadcast* in the RF/traditional radio-TV world. It refers to sending the same program at the same time to as many people as want to receive it. In the IPv4 world, *broadcast* had a slightly different meaning, but in the IPv6 world, this term was dropped. By way of contrast, *unicast* refers to sending packets to one and only one receiver.

Video on Demand

Video on demand (VoD) services may be implemented either in the RF or packet domains, respectively using the RF overlay or packet approach. The primary difference for the packet approach from the IPTV broadcast deployment of video services is the datagrams are unicast IP packets instead of multicast IP packets, since they are to be delivered to a specific IP set-top box. With this type of high-priority service, the VoD packets are prioritized over the best effort data services, such that they are guaranteed to be received by the end-user IP set-top box in the event of network congestion.

Video Services Requirements Considerations

When considering requirements generation for video services, the choice of the video delivery method will drive the necessary components for implementation and the resulting technical requirements. For either method once the content is received into a central location for processing it needs to be inserted into the network for the particular delivery style used.

For IPTV systems, consider the following attributes related to IP stream generation, network delivery, and content and customer management.

- The received video content must be encoded into IP multicast packet streams at frame rates which are supported by the content and the network available bandwidth;
- The supporting network from the content insertion in the core network and the distribution through the transport and access networks must support the end-to-end delivery of the multicast streams through multicast protocol support at both switching and routing layers;
- Supporting software services for the management of network admittance, IP space, and specific configuration for set-top boxes, as well as insertion of specific content;
- Middleware supporting the content selection, customer management, and set-top box content configuration;
- For VoD systems, the location of cached content for delivery of unicast streams in an efficient manner which does not affect overall network bandwidth requirements.

For RF video systems consider the following attributes related to either analog or digital video delivery over an RF overlay.

- Modulation of the video into an RF plant with analog and/or digital channels;
- Conversion of the RF content via externally modulated transmitters onto the optical (FTTx) plant;
- Distribution of the optical content from transmitter to EDFAs (optical amplifiers) where the content may be combined with the PON data services distribution (typically on a per-PON basis);
- RF return services for the transmission, capture, and actions related to customer-generated requests for special services and content.

Voice Services

Voice services requirements in an FTTx network, usually implemented as voice-over-Internet-Protocol (VoIP) service, include two primary sets of components for which service requirements and equipment design must be assessed. These are broken down into central office (CO, telephone terminology) or headend (cable TV terminology) equipment requirements and customer premise requirements. For the two sets of requirements, design and equipment implementation must be coupled closely together for the operation of the VoIP system. If the network operator intends to deliver the voice service directly from his own equipment, a very significant investment in equipment and telephony experience is required and must be considered very seriously. Alternatively, if the network operator intends to use an approach where voice services are provided by an outside voice service operator and transported over the FTTH network, there still exists a significant amount of technical requirement generation for the secure and high-quality delivery of voice over the network. The network operator's approach to providing voice services should consider the following:

- Will the network operator provide the voice service as part of the on-going network operations?
    - If the network operator is providing VoIP services, what will their CO gear vendor selection be based upon? Will it be based upon what legacy devices are available, or will there be an investment in a new soft switch device?
    - Which protocol does the operator wish to deploy (MGCP versus SIP)?
    - CO gear and CPE gear protocol and feature support interoperability;
    - Will the operator be providing both commercial and residential service offerings? How will those offerings be different and what special services support may be required?
- On the other hand, will the network operator provide access for outside service provider(s) to sell and provide voice services to the FTTx network subscribers?
- Will the network operator engage a wholesale VoIP provider to provide a "white label" telephone service that the operator can brand and market as its own service, or will it be sold by, and branded by, the wholesale provider?
    - Is the wholesale provider's service compatible with the network operator's network equipment?
    - Does the wholesale provider offer the level of services and features desired by the operator?
- CPE gear telephony support: analog interface support for interfacing to telephony devices in the premise, especially in the case where the network operator is providing the voice endpoint as part of their FTTx CPE gear and must ensure interoperability with both the voice service provider's soft switch equipment and also their subscriber's telephony handsets and in-home or business equipment and wiring;
    - ONT analog telephony interface to subtended device signaling support (far end disconnect supervision, DTMF support, caller ID support, ringing voltage, etc.);
    - Interface to legacy systems such as fax, modem, PBX call-out side, etc.

VoIP Special Circuits

In addition to standard residential and business telephony requirements, there may also be legacy special circuits which must be replaced with the FTTx system. The best case is for these devices to have an adapter which takes them from their analog output to an IP stream which can be transported over a standard data service across the IP network of the FTTx access and upstream networks. There must be a peer network interface adapter in the central office which converts these circuits back to an analog signal which may be interpreted by the local voice switch.

Management Systems Requirements

Development of sets of requirements for network management reside in three broad categories: provisioning systems, business support systems, and operational support systems. The FTTx network is a complex set of components providing a wide range of functions operating together to fulfill the goals of the network, and it requires a complete set of management functionality to ensure the operations team can operate and maintain the network at a high level. At the next level of detail, these requirements drive the development of the control systems for the managers and operators of the network.

Provisioning systems control the application of services configuration to various points of the network. A central repository of provisioning information for the various equipment in the network is required to realize the end-to-end service. Additionally, each set of equipment in the network which requires configuration to deploy services to the subscribers, requires a provisioning interface. In the best case, the provisioning interfaces are programmatically configured by a centralized provisioning system—known as *flow-through provisioning*. The situation where multiple provisioning systems are required to be used to provision a service end-to-end, is known as *swivel-chair provisioning* due to its manual nature.

Operational support systems (OSSs) ensure the day-to-day overall management of the network through the collection of information from the network to provide a window into the current state of network health using performance management and fault information. For more details in this area, see Chapter 15, Performance Management.

Business support systems (BSSs) ensure that subscribers of the network can be serviced efficiently through customer interaction, and that the system can be financed through the gathering of appropriate billing information.

Provisioning Management Systems

Provisioning is the application and maintenance of configuration information pertaining to service assignment to subscribers using the network, and management activities related to the gathering and usage of the provisioning data.

Consider requirements of the following types for provisioning systems which receive and apply provisioning information, and mediation systems which share provisioning information between peer provisioning systems. Examples are:

- Requirements for systems to receive sets of services configuration related to ONT devices as services are required to be applied to a subscriber, based on network events: as devices are added to or removed from the network or moved within the network, as services are required to be added, changed, or removed from a subscriber, as network audits occur and services are reapplied in a controlled manner;
- Requirements for the interfacing of provisioning and mediation systems to any number of equipment-specific, vendor-supplied management systems created specifically for the management of individual solution components (for example, the specific element management system (EMS) for a VoIP soft switch);
- Requirements for billing systems to receive provisioning information for the assessment of usage fees for network services, linked to individual subscribers through provisioning, interface statistic gathering, reporting, and other performance management telemetry;
- Requirements for the retrieval of provisioning information from the network elements to be transferred to higher-layer systems for issue resolution, report generation, and network audits.

Business Support Systems

Business support systems fill the requirements for allowing nontechnical and management staff to interface with the technical aspects of the network effectively. Consider requirements of the following types:

- Requirements for systems to allow nontechnical service representatives to apply provisioning information to technical elements of the system for the assurance of services to the subscriber, typically through a system-to-system interface or mediation system;
- Requirements which allow nontechnical service representatives to retrieve, verify, and change provisioning information for subscribers;
- Requirements for systems to initiate and manage the billing of services to subscribers;
- Requirements for inventory systems to record the receipt and removal of network assets, the current status and use of those assets as they enter deployment into the network and are removed from the network. Note that when assets enter the network is a critical time, as they are associated with (attached to) certain locations in the network, since this is how they will receive their services provisioning information. This is how you will physically keep track of your assets, too;

- Requirements for lawful intercept via network management equipment activities related to the collection, compilation, and transfer of services-related data for law enforcement activities (see Chapter 13).

Operational Support Systems

Operational support system (OSS) requirements are related to the on-going maintenance and caretaking of the network and its supporting resources. All except the smallest systems should have an OSS, available from several vendors. Consider requirements of the following types.

- Performance management requirements related to the collection of network telemetry for the on-going assessment, maintenance, and long-term realization of the network including logs, management traps, and alarms associated with individual network devices;
- Requirements for gathering and receiving performance data related to the throughput of traffic through device interfaces; gathering of device-specific service provisioning and system health information all geared toward creating a snapshot of network health and integrity;
- Requirements related to the security and secure management access of the network and supporting equipment;
- Requirements for performance management, including fault management, statistical gathering for network assessment, upgrades and scalability, configuration management of the network, inventory of devices, and health assessments of supporting network equipment.

The collection and maintenance of performance management data will often fall into the purview of the individual element management systems which are responsible for each solution element. However, oftentimes operators will rely on higher-level or integrated management systems whose job it is to create an "integrated" or "rolled-up" management view of the network by combining these sets of device or service-specific telemetry.

Outside Plant Requirements

Outside plant (OSP) requirements are those related to the creation of a well-designed and maintainable optical distribution network. The outside plant represents one of the most important investments the network operator will make, and therefore these sets of requirements are critical to the deployment success. Whether the optical plant will be buried, aerially deployed, the locations of fiber cabinets, passive splitters and test points, will drive which skills are required: fiber trenching, fiber cable and duct burial, aerial fiber rigging, optical enclosure and cabinet deployment, and fiber splicing. Typically, the outside plant is implemented by a contracting agency skilled at these methodologies used for ODN implementation. Additionally, the OSP contracting agency can help with the choices available to the operator and current best practices in ODN deployment.

OPEN ACCESS NETWORKS

The special case of open access networks is an option to be considered by many network operators currently developing or envisioning an FTTx network. An open access network is one where there are a number of service providers which sell retail services over the same access network infrastructure simultaneously, allowing the subscribers to decide from which service provider they will purchase their services. In practice, this allows competition for subscribers and service providers to engage in markets to provide and purchase services, while the network provider is paid a fee by the service providers for the privilege of using the network. Open access networks are becoming increasingly popular in many regions of the world where the network operator is an entity charged with providing access for subscribers, but not necessarily with a mandate for providing competitive service offerings.

There are special requirements for the FTTx network to provide an open access model and these must be taken into account as the network is being planned and designed. In these cases, the network operator task may seem to be simplified because they are only providing the "pipe" for the delivery of the services to the subscribers. However, the operation of an open access network has just as many requirements to be considered as does a closed network run by the network operator. The open access model can apply to all services (data, voice, and video), but is primarily known for data and voice. For an open access model, video services will almost always be provided by IPTV, and this also presents special requirements for all parts of the network including the FTTx component.

One of the primary challenges for the network operator is the task of integrating with disparate service providers. In the case of the voice, data, and IPTV services, much agreement must be made in the network engineering for the end-to-end service delivery from the introduction of the service to the upstream network connection partition to the subscriber CPE equipment. In the case of an open access network, almost all of the service's data are transferred to and from outside the network operator's domain. In the case of management systems, for example, provisioning data cannot be shared across service providers, so mechanisms to allow each individual service provider to gain access to only their customer's information is required. Usually the responsibility for this falls to the FTTH network equipment provider. Additionally, since the network operator has full access to the subscribers, many times they are required to gather and provide specific data to the service provider. If multiple service providers require disparate data, multiple types of integration projects may need to be initiated.

For the case of subscriber CPE equipment, each service provider may need to supply critical equipment based on the individual service requirements. Since this will impact the network operators' installation and maintenance practices, such important integration requirements will need to be considered as the service providers for the open access network are being engaged.

CONCLUSION

The network planning process, completed by the creation of a rich set of requirements to guide the design and implementation stages of the network realization process, cannot be avoided if the network is to be implemented successfully. Starting at the top level, the requirements which represent the goals of the network will naturally flow to the categories of technical requirements that allow the design and implementation team to complete the engineering analysis, technology and vendor assessments and selections, implementation team choices, and network build methodology choice to bring the network to production launch. The breadth and complexity of the network requirements demand that they are treated with great importance, requiring a skilled team to develop them and a repository to maintain them for the long term, as they represent the guiding requirements specification for the end product.

Endnote

i.   https://www.mef.net/.

CHAPTER 9

Outside Plant

INTRODUCTION

Now we are going to talk about the outside plant (OSP), the part of your network between the headend and the optical network terminal (ONT) on or in the subscribers' homes. We're not going to get into a lot of detailed design because there are plenty of sources of that information, and each system is different. You're going to go in one of three directions in designing and building your OSP:

- You're going to hire design and construction firms who have a lot of experience with fiber-to-the-home (FTTH) design and construction, and they are going to handle it for you (best bet for almost everyone).
- You are a big company and you have qualified people in-house (a few cases).
- You are going to read a book on the subject and learn as you go, using inexperienced personnel. (You are in trouble and about to lose a lot of money.)

What we will do is talk about a number of considerations you need to be aware of even if you are smart and use qualified outside contractors. We'll try to suggest things of which you need to be aware, and hopefully suggest some things that will keep you out of too much trouble. Hopefully we can help you avoid some grief. And as you may have already gathered, we may be able to have some fun with it along the way.

WHAT SKILLS DO YOU NEED?

Before undertaking operation of an FTTH project, you need several skills in-house. There are certain pieces of essential test equipment mentioned below, such as optical power meters. They won't do you any good if your craftspeople don't know how to use them. You will also need your people to know how to properly clean connectors, and how to ensure that they are, indeed, clean. This takes training, followed by retraining, followed by reminders to do it right. And more training.

FTTx Networks. http://dx.doi.org/10.1016/B978-0-12-420137-8.00009-3

You will need people trained in proper splicing of fibers, especially under adverse conditions. You can probably call in contractors for big jobs, such as initial system construction and turn-up, but for everyday needs, you will need someone on staff. You will also need trained installers to put in the drops. You might contract the initial design of the system, but you will need someone inside to understand the design so that you will be able to maintain and add to it later. You may have similar skills available from operating hybrid fiber-coax (HFC) or twisted pair networks, and these people might be capable of being retrained on fiber. But do not assume that they know how to deal with a fiber install just because they have done coax installs, for example.

Training is available through several organizations—take advantage of what they know.

HOW FAR CAN YOU GO?

This might be a good point to discuss the limitations in distance from the head-end, also referred to as the central office (CO) or network operations center (NOC), to the farthest home on a passive optical network (PON). Generally, two things set the maximum distance. The first and more obvious is signal loss; while the signal loss in fiber is small, it is nonetheless present, and ultimately causes the signals to drop too low to allow more distance. Related, in any real fiber optic system, there is some *dispersion* in the fiber. Dispersion means that some of the optical energy will move faster through the fiber than will other optical energy. There are several reasons for this, but probably the dominant type of dispersion in FTTH systems is *chromatic dispersion*; light is launched into the fiber at slightly different wavelengths, depending on several factors. Each wavelength propagates (travels) through the fiber at a different speed. This causes light pulses, which may start out at the transmitter as nice, square-shaped pulses, to become smeared as they propagate further. The result is a pulse that is hard to recognize at the receiver when combined with the noise present when a weak signal is received (the noise is analogous to "snow" in an analog TV picture). Thus, we must have a stronger signal at the receiver in order to reduce the "snow" to the point that the pulse can be received.

The other limiting factor in distance is the round-trip propagation time of a signal in the fiber—propagation speed in fiber may be 60% of the speed of light in free space. Now it is easy enough to measure the round-trip of a packet from the OLT to the ONT and back, then tell the ONT how much in advance of its normal transmit time it should start transmitting a packet in order for it to wind up back at the OLT at the correct time. The problem, though, is how do you get a new ONT started: you must measure its round-trip time without having its transmission step on any packets arriving from other ONTs, given that the new guy does not yet know its time advance. So you periodically set aside a long time period in which no registered ONT transmits. Then the OLT sends a downstream packet that says, "OK, if you are not registered and don't have your time offset, send a short packet now and let me measure the round trip." When the OLT gets the packet from the new ONT, it knows the new guy's address, and it knows its round trip time. So on the next transmission to it, the OLT says, "OK, Joe (not the real identification, obviously), I have you, and you need to advance your transmissions by 120 ns (a number grabbed from thin air) in order for your occupied timeslot to be right when your packet gets back to me." If two or more new ONTs respond at the same time, the OLT has techniques to get them to retransmit one at a time, but this takes time, and when you are recovering from a major power failure it can take a fairly large amount of time (tens of minutes) to get everyone back on.

So now Joe knows what to do. But suppose we had not allowed that really long *acquisition timeslot*, so that Joe's transmission overlapped someone else's transmission. In that case, we would miss data from an already-registered ONT, and that is bad. Think about it some, and you realize that the longer you allow the PON to be, the longer *ranging time* you have to deal with, and the more upstream dead time you have to allow. You don't know if the new ONT is next to the OLT or if it is at the end of the system. This dead time comes off your upstream data rate, so obviously you don't want to allow too much dead time. But if you allow too little, then you are going to have missed data when an ONT is farther away. So the designers of the systems had to work out a compromise.

That compromise was 20 km initially. The GPON folks decided to go a little farther, and to allow for several sets of round-trip distances (translated, of course, into round-trip times), and defined that the distance from the nearest to the farthest ONT could be between 0 and 20 km, or 20 and 40 km, or 40 and 60 km, anticipating that future optics would support those distances. The standard will not allow a range of distances of 0–40 km though, because that would make for too long a ranging time. Other more advanced PON standards can be expected to do this same kind of thing. We have known some operators to "stretch" the 20 km maximum a little and get away with it, but we cannot recommend it, as a chip manufacturer can set his timing close to this limit and your "stretched" ONT may not work. The chip guy would be within his rights to do this, so long as he met 20 km, even if he didn't meet 20.1 km.

It should also be noted that the size of the network's coverage area is not necessarily limited to the maximum distance of the PON from the headend. A remote hub site(s) containing additional OLTs interconnected to the headend by fiber links can be strategically located beyond the headend's PON reach to serve more distant areas within the operator's service area. From the hub site(s), a new PON service area can be established. Some access equipment manufacturers may make hardened chasses and OLT equipment that can be located in outdoor cabinets mounted on poles or at ground level.

SPLITTING PHILOSOPHY

There are different ways we can architect fiber coming out of the headend. The three most commonly discussed are homerun (point-to-point, or P2P, or active Ethernet), distributed splitting, and centralized splitting.

Homerun Fibers

In a homerun configuration, each home is served with its own fiber all the way from the headend. Homerun fiber is also known as point-to-point, P2P, and active Ethernet (AE). We regard this as the most expensive way to build fiber systems for several reasons.

- It is difficult to use broadcast video with homerun architectures due to the headend cost of wave division multiplexing (WDM-ing) the broadcast wavelength to individual homes.
- It costs a little more for the fiber, since you are running potentially 32 times as much fiber from the headend as you would otherwise, though we have argued that this is a relatively minor cost.
- While the headend interfaces may be relatively low cost in this case, consisting essentially of a switch port and a fiber optic transmitter and receiver, that are still a lot of fiber optic transmitters and receivers in the headend, and a lot of fibers to be managed.
- The biggest cost penalty may be the cost of splicing all of those fibers, both initially and after a cable break: you have up to 32 times as many fibers to splice as you do with other architectures.

Some proponents argue that homerun fibers offer the highest ultimate bandwidth, since no fiber shares bandwidth between any two users. But this argument loses validity when you get back to the headend and realize that you must of necessity combine signals there, resulting in shared bandwidth (nowhere do we find a bigger shared bandwidth system than the Internet itself). The other argument for homerun fibers is security: you can't possibly see what's on your neighbor's fiber if his data are not on your fiber. But in shared systems, data are encrypted on the fiber using the most practical advanced encryption systems, so the chance of your neighbor spying on your cat videos is very, very remote.

Distributed Splitting

Distributed splitting is used identically with EPON and GPON systems, so we can be talking about either here. When we first developed an FTTH system in about the

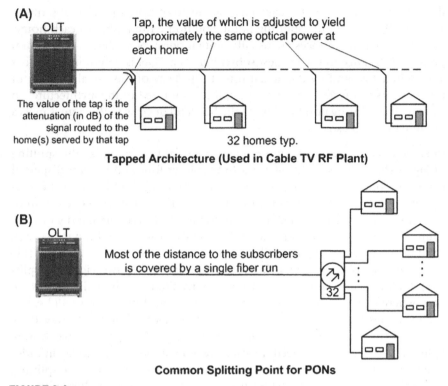

(A)

OLT

Tap, the value of which is adjusted to yield approximately the same optical power at each home

The value of the tap is the attenuation (in dB) of the signal routed to the home(s) served by that tap

32 homes typ.

Tapped Architecture (Used in Cable TV RF Plant)

(B)

OLT

Most of the distance to the subscribers is covered by a single fiber run

32

Common Splitting Point for PONs

FIGURE 9.1
Tapped and centralized splitting for PONs.

year 2000, we thought people would flock to a distributed splitting architecture of the type cable TV's HFC plant uses (see Fig. 9.1A). You run a fiber down a street, and you provide optical taps where you have homes, each tap removing some of the signal and feeding it to the home(s) at that location. This architecture has been used some, especially in rural areas, where you may have long roads with few side roads, and a few homes per mile on the road. FTTH is quite nice in this case, because the loss per km in fiber is very low, meaning you can go a long way without amplifying the signals, a distinct improvement over HFC.

However, with the possible exception of rural situations, this architecture didn't prove popular with system builders. Rather, a centralized splitting architecture emerged as the more popular approach.

Centralized Splitting

Fig. 9.1B shows the centralized splitting architecture that is very popular today. Since most of the distance from the headend to any one cluster of subscribers (e.g., part of a subdivision) is bypassed by a PON, it makes more sense to run a single fiber out to a point close to the "clump" of subscribers to be served by that one PON, then split the signal at a single point close to those subscribers, as in Fig. 9.1B. From the splitting point, you home run a fiber to each home, but the homerun distances are usually quite modest. Note that the maximum permitted distance to the farthest subscriber on a PON is determined by fiber and splitter loss and by the actual round-trip delay of the signal. Neither of these factors is affected by where the splitter is located in the architecture. So whether the splitting point is close to the headend or close to the homes makes no difference whatsoever.

In some cases, it may make more sense to partially decentralize the splitting of Fig. 9.1B, perhaps by using a four-way splitter followed by four dispersed eight-way splitters. This cascading of splitters may also build in some flexibility for the future, allowing you to reduce your PON size, for example, from 32 homes to 16 homes (thus doubling the pool of available bandwidth) by simply replacing the one four-way splitter on the front end with two two-way splitters, each fed by separate fibers connected to a separate OLT port. This will create two 16-home PONs (a two-way splitter feeding two eight-way splitters). It all depends on the geometry of the installation; where the homes are now, where they may be in the future, and what your future needs will be. Fig. 9.2 illustrates a couple of scenarios. The main figure shows a 32-way PON (the most common split today), with provision for splitting it into two 16-way PONs in the future if you need the capacity. All you need to do today in order to allow for this eventuality is to provide an extra fiber strand to the splitting cabinet, and this comes almost for free. Fig. 9.2 also shows an alternative to a 16-way split, in which you cascade a single four-way splitter with four four-way splitters. Obviously you could use two-way splitters too, if it made sense.

An Even More Practical Centralized Splitting Architecture

With Fig. 9.2 we get to the most practical splitting architecture for most FTTH installations. This is very important in new subdivisions, and can even be useful in existing neighborhoods. There are slightly different considerations for new-build (greenfield) and existing neighborhoods (brownfield), but they both usually come back to this architecture. The big problem we are solving, or at least mitigating, is that you are not going to get all of the homes in the area, and you don't know which ones you will and will not get. Furthermore, for greenfields, it may be 5 years or more before all of the homes are built, and you really don't want to make any more investment than necessary until you are close to getting revenue from that investment.

As shown in Fig. 9.3, you locate a large splitting cabinet with room to serve many homes at a convenient place in the subdivision. Then you bring drops from each home to that splitter cabinet. The first 32 subscribers you get, regardless of where they are in the development, go on the first splitter (PON 2 in Fig. 9.2). Only when you fill that splitter do you put in a second splitter and start putting

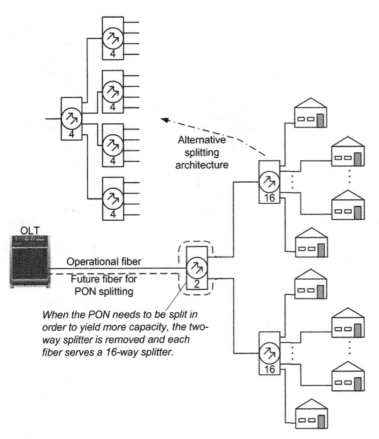

FIGURE 9.2
Allowing for future PON splitting.

subscribers on it. How does this save you money? Well, in the first place you don't buy splitters to go in the cabinet until you need them, so you put off that cost until you are ready to start getting revenue from the investment.

The other saving is back at the headend and in somewhat larger blocks. The subscriber cards in the OLT are relatively expensive, so you would like to NOT buy them until you have subscribers to support that cost. Depending, a subscriber card in an OLT will have four to 12 PON ports on it. With the architecture of Fig. 9.3, you don't need to invest in a second PON card until the first is almost filled. You are adding subscribers in a number of neighborhoods at the same time, so you dedicate one PON port of a subscriber card to one neighborhood and another PON port to another neighborhood, and so on. The point is that you want to fill up the first PON card as fast as you can, to maximize the revenue you are getting from it before you buy and start filling the second PON card. This architecture helps you do that.

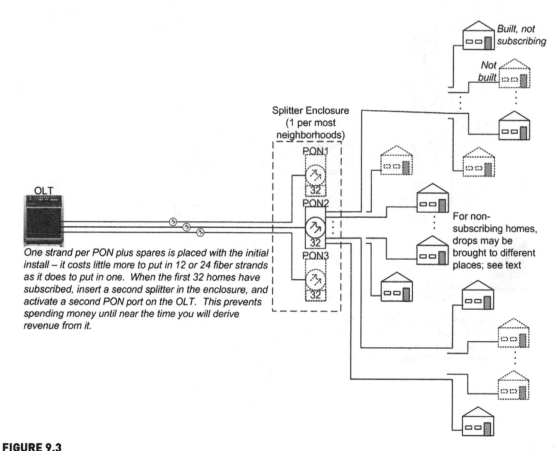

Built, not subscribing

Not built

Splitter Enclosure
(1 per most
neighborhoods)

PON1

32

OLT

PON2

32

PON3

32

For non-
subscribing homes,
drops may be
brought to different
places; see text

One strand per PON plus spares is placed with the initial install – it costs little more to put in 12 or 24 fiber strands as it does to put in one. When the first 32 homes have subscribed, insert a second splitter in the enclosure, and activate a second PON port on the OLT. This prevents spending money until near the time you will derive revenue from it.

FIGURE 9.3
The most common fiber architecture today.

Greenfields

Greenfields are by far the easiest place to put in FTTH. If you can get into the common trenches when they are open, it is an easy matter to put in the fiber you need for the planned build-out of the neighborhood. Bringing a drop from every home back to the splitting cabinet is (pardon the pun) dirt cheap, and prevents you having to do it later. No need to terminate the drops until you get a subscriber, though labeling the drops will make it easier to locate the one you want later.

If you don't label the drops, you can always locate the one you're trying to connect later: first put a connector on the ONT end. Then connect it to your red (visible) light fiber tracer. Go to the splitter end of the fiber and start looking for the one glowing red. Remember, this visible light is not going to hurt you to look at it; it is only the invisible communications light that will be on the fiber later that has the potential to hurt you. See Chapter 6 for what to do about it.

Brownfields

Things are a bit more complex when going into existing neighborhoods. You don't have any choice but to run fiber from the headend to the splitter cabinet, using overhead and buried cable as required. Once you get to the splitter cabinet, what do you do? You may want to run fiber along the streets in front of homes while you have the installation folks and equipment on-site. But usually one doesn't run drops to the side of homes until one gets a subscriber; the expense of running drops to each house in an existing neighborhood is pretty steep, considering how many homes we're talking about and how many hazards we may encounter in the yard, assuming buried fiber (overhead is easier, but again, no use bearing the cost until you get a customer). Buried fiber issues include, but are not limited to, having to go through prize flower beds, utilities, and PVC underground sprinklers (which may be hard to get marked), and going under driveways, cobblestone sidewalks, and digging up grass, which may not be put back to the owner's satisfaction. Best to postpone the actual drop until you have a customer to go with it.

CABLE COLOR CODES

Fiber strands usually are placed into buffer tubes inside cables that contain multiple buffer tubes for more efficient handling. The total strand count of a cable will depend on the application; for example, a 96-count fiber will contain eight buffer tubes with 12 loose fiber strands inside each tube. In order to identify the fiber strands within the buffer tube, a color coding system is used with the protective sheath surrounding each fiber. Each buffer tube then also conforms to the same color-coding standard. For example, the first buffer tube of four tubes in a 48-count fiber cable is blue, just as the first fiber strand inside the buffer tube is blue. The colors are defined in TIA-598.[i] This standard defines the recommended identification system for individual fibers, fiber buffer tubes/units, and groups of fiber buffer tubes/units within a cable structure. The identification methods may be used to locate specific fibers for connection, termination, or testing.

Table 9.1 provides as an example the first 4 of the 48 fibers whose colors are defined in the standard. Above 12 fibers, the individual protective covering

Table 9.1 Example Fiber Color Code

Fiber #	Color	Printed
1	Blue	1 or BL or 1-BL
2	Orange	1 or OR or 2-OR
3	Green	3 or GR or 3-GR
4	Brown	4 or BR or 4-BR

colors repeat, with the distinction being provided by a tracer(s) in the fiber bundle, or by some other means such as a number for the subunits or bundles of fibers.

A third column in the table shows abbreviations that can be used for print legends in documents. By these means, you are able to identify one individual fiber in a large bundle of fibers. For example, you may have a splitter cabinet where you house all of the splitters for a large subdivision of 1000 homes. Serving it will require at least 32 fibers (plus spares) to service all homes. If those fibers are brought together at one place, how do you know which fiber you need to use to connect a particular home? You use the color code and your excellent documentation, of course.

AERIAL OR UNDERGROUND: A DECISION MADE FOR YOU

Will your plant be aerial (on poles) or buried. In many cases that question will already have been answered for you based on local practice. The power company, the phone company, the cable company, and maybe some wholesale data carriers are already there, and looking at where their plant is will answer this question very quickly. Most newer residential areas have underground utilities, and in some countries underground is required.

Aerial Plant

Usually aerial installation is lower in cost for several reasons, though there are a lot of variables. Unless you are an incumbent provider with your attachment space on the poles already assigned, your fiber cable attachments may be relegated to the lowest cable position on the pole, or some other position between the lowest existing cable and the highest attached facilities (such as the electric power lines). Generally, when telephone, cable television, and electric lines share the same pole, the telephone company occupies the highest position (below the power company wires), followed by other communication companies like long-distance fiber carriers (Level3, Windstream, etc.) or cable television companies. Power always occupies the highest part of the pole for safety reasons. The owner of the pole will assign your position during the attachment application process. Your cable will have to be a minimum distance from the ground (if the lowest position) in order to not be a hazard to (and victim of) high vehicles, and your cable must maintain minimum safety clearances from the other cable attachments. If there is not room on a pole for you to meet spacing rules, then you have the dreaded *make-ready*: you will have to pay for rearrangement of other cables on the pole before you can start putting your cable up. In some cases, it may be necessary for the pole owner to replace the current pole with a taller pole in order to achieve the necessary safety clearances for all attachments. The general rule is that the last company to attach bears the make-ready cost of achieving proper clearance for any affected cables, if necessary. You pretty much have to inspect all poles in the build area to determine which ones will need make-ready and which ones have adequate room for you now. During the design process, you and your construction contractor will want to *walk out* the plant and catalog all of the issues you need to overcome during construction.

Of course if you don't own the pole, you are going to have to pay rent to the owner. At one time this was a very contentious issue between pole owners and others who needed space. In most places the issue is not as widely argued today, with accepted practices and regulations taking the place of fights.

If you are also the power company you may have some options not available to others in terms of installing the fiber. By using an all-dielectric cable (as opposed to one having a metallic strength member), you may be able to install your fibers in your power space on the pole. (Power space is allocated at the top of the pole, with communications space below, and specified minimum distances between the two.) This can eliminate your make-ready expense, but the craftspeople you have do the installation and maintenance on the plant must be qualified to work safely in the power space.

Optical Ground Wire
An interesting option for power companies is the use of *optical ground wire* (*OPGW*), also known by the name used in the IEEE specification, *optical fiber composite overhead ground wire*. Power transmission systems include a ground wire above the current-carrying conductors on the pole. This provides for a common ground potential at each pole, and also provides lightning protection for the current-carrying conductors. Because fiber optic cable is all-dielectric, it can go in the hollow center of the ground conductor (frequently conductors are woven over the fiber optic cable to make the OPGW). Quite a few optical fibers can be accommodated in the OPGW, enough for your own uses and enough to lease to others, either as *dark fibers* (the lessee provides terminating equipment at each end of the fiber) or as *lighted fibers* (you provide the terminating equipment, and maybe use the same fiber strand for several customers). Of course, because of where the OPGW is located, you will need to use craftspersons certified for power work.

Snowshoes in the Summer
As you drive through a town looking at the aerial plant (and if you don't do this now, you will be in the habit soon), you may see something attached to fiber optic aerial plant, that resembles a snowshoe. Usually you will see them in pairs near where a fiber optic cable crosses a roadway, or wherever there is a chance that the cable could be broken by an errant car or truck, or anywhere you may need to splice the cable later. Very creatively, these things are called

snowshoes. They are used to wrap extra fiber slack in a figure-of-8 pattern. The extra fiber is stored on the snowshoes, just waiting for the day that a section of the cable is damaged by a rogue vehicle. Then rather than having to cut out the damaged section of cable and splicing an extra piece between the two good ends, you simply pull the needed amount of cable from the figure-of-8 wrap, and only have to make half the number of splices you would otherwise. Splices are bad in that they cost money, they keep the network out of service while splices are being made, and they contribute some small amount of extra loss even if they are done right. Snowshoes are also found near splice enclosures, providing enough slack fiber to be able to detach a splice enclosure from the cable strand and bring it to ground level, or perhaps in a fiber splice trailer, for easier and cleaner working conditions for splicing.

Underground Plant

Most newer areas and some older areas require utilities to be underground for esthetic reasons. While initial construction may be (even) more expensive than aerial construction, we like underground construction for its usually superior reliability—dirt and paving help protect the plant from many human-induced problems as well as nature-induced problems. The only aboveground elements you are likely to have are splitter cabinets, and there will be few of them. You may have *hand-holds* (small underground vaults) at grade level to hold splices and maybe connectorized terminations for drop cables. But compared with aerial construction, there are few targets for damage.

The reliability of underground plant may exceed that of aerial because in aerial plant you have thousands of targets for errant vehicles to aim for, called poles. In fact, some vehicles don't even have to hit the target; if they are high enough, they can snag your cable when they go under it—remember that in many cases, you are the lowest cable on the pole, and while there are rules for minimum height of cables and maximum height of vehicles, Murphy's law is just as valid here as it is anywhere. The cable itself is a target for falling trees and other natural occurrences. In underground plant you have only a few targets, called splice cabinets. (However, there are a few target opportunities, as we shall describe at the end of the chapter.)

New Developments

New developments are a dream for underground construction. If you can get into the common utility trench when an area is first developed, your costs are going to be much lower than if you have to construct underground plant in a developed area. You don't have to worry about getting other utilities marked, you don't have to bear the entire cost of trenching, and, probably most importantly, you don't have to go under driveways or streets. Of course, you may put down some fiber to homes that will never subscribe, but that cost should be minimal compared with the savings. One end of the drop terminates in a hand-hold and the other end at the side of a future home. You will come back and connectorize the drop when you get a customer; no use spending the labor to connectorize a drop fiber that is not going to provide revenue soon.

Existing Developments

Existing developments are where you are going to spend the most money for underground construction. A lot of work has gone into making the process more economical, but you still have to worry about passing under driveways, sidewalks, and roads. And don't underestimate the problems of having to dig up finished lawns and flower beds. Bodies of water can also be expensive to cross, so make sure you have a bridge handy.

Several techniques have been developed to improve your lot in life here. *Horizontal boring* may get you under sidewalks and driveways, and maybe some streets. One construction technique popular where the author lives is called *stitch-and-bore*, also called *stitch boring*. Every 20–50 feet a slit trench is hand-dug, just big enough to accommodate the horizontal boring machine. Then a horizontal boring machine connects one hole to the next with fiber and/or conduit. Digging the slit trenches is a manual process in finished areas, because you have to be careful to put the grass back in place, and not leave any dirt on top—when a good crew walks away from a slit trench, you have a hard time telling where it was.

Where you have to go under longer stretches of pavement, there are techniques for making a very narrow slit and pushing in a small fiber cable. The slit is then filled with a suitable liquid material that will harden into something almost as strong as what you cut through. And it can be hard to see. This beats trenching through pavement, burying your cable, and repaving. But of course if you are crossing a parking lot, you have to do it when the lot is empty (i.e., late at night), and if you are crossing a roadway, you are probably going to do it not only late at night, but with police support, for which you will pay. Thus, the faster you can get in and out, the better.

Probably the worst scenario is more prevalent in Europe than in North America and Asia. That is the dreaded cobblestone sidewalk or street. There is no cutting through the cobblestone; you have to remove the stones, keeping track of which stone went where. Then you bury your cable and replace the stones. Obviously you don't want to do this too often!

Repurposing coax is becoming popular where an operator is moving from HFC (cable TV's hybrid fiber-coax) plant to FTTH. There are now techniques that can strip the center conductor and dielectric out of installed hardline coax, leaving the aluminum shield, which becomes a conduit through which you can pull or blow fiber.

To Conduit or Not to Conduit

In any underground construction, there is the question of whether to use direct burial fiber or to bury conduit. The conduit may be supplied with fiber already installed, or you might bury empty conduit then pull or blow fiber later. There are plusses and minuses to every approach, so we will not recommend one over the other—direct fiber burial is cheaper initially, but can be very expensive in the long run. The choice is going to depend to an extent on local conditions.

The one precaution we would interject at this point concerns the number of fibers installed. We are not sure we have ever heard anyone complain that when the system was installed too much fiber was put in. No matter how much fiber you put in, sooner or later you (or your successor) are likely to regret not putting in more initially. Yet even though the actual cost of the fibers is a small component of the cost of installing the system, it can be difficult to sell the money people on putting in more fiber than you can show that you need now. This speaks to installing conduit that is larger than what you need right now— it will be easier and cheaper in 5 or 10 years to blow in more fiber through conduit than it will be to bury more. Plus, you may later have the opportunity to lease surplus conduit space to other operators and help recover your own installation costs.

Trace Your Cable

We have many times extolled the virtues of the all-dielectric nature of fiber optic cable, and those virtues are real. But when we talk about underground cable, we need to modify that just a bit. The fiber is still dielectric, but you need to run a conductor with the fiber. The reason is that later you are going to have to locate your cable, either so that you can dig it up and work on it, or more likely, so that someone else will not cut your cable when they are digging. In most cases you will want a *tracer*, a wire installed with the fiber optic cable, or maybe embedded within the conduit. When you need to locate the cable underground, you will connect a special-purpose transmitter to the tracer, and then you will use a portable receiver that looks a bit like a first or second cousin to a metal detector. You sweep the receiver and it tells you when you are over the activated tracer with your cable. There are a few locators that don't need a metallic tracer, such as a ground-penetrating radar system, but for the most part, you are probably going to want to include a metallic tracer in underground cables. And you will need a locator so that you can mark your cable before someone wants to dig.

CONNECTING FIBERS

At many places in your plant, you are going to need to connect one fiber to another. This will happen when you have a big cable with many fiber strands which needs to diverge in more than one direction. It may also happen as you go along a route, dropping some fibers off at splitter cabinets or other places. And it will happen when you split the signal to go to a number of subscribers. There are two ways to connect fibers, fusion splicing and connectors. And among connectors, there are a number of different connectors used.

Fusion Splicing

Fusion splicing is recommended where it is unlikely that you will ever have to disconnect the fibers. It has the lowest potential forward and best return signal loss of any method of connecting two fibers, but it does require a specialized machine to make the splice, and operating the machine requires skill. In fusion splicing, the two fibers to be joined are cut at right angles, the protective coatings are removed, and the two ends aligned in a very precise butt joint. Then the fibers are heated until they become fluid and fuse together. The splice is protected by a metal sleeve installed over the splice after the splice is completed.

The fusion splicing machine and its accessories are normally housed in a small trailer, which provides the splicing technician with a clean, dry, air-conditioned, and well-lit place in which to work. The trailer will need to be parked close enough to the pole line so that there is enough slack in the cable to bring it down into the trailer for splicing—another reason for the extra fiber wrapped in a figure-of-8 around snowshoes.

Connectorization

Where it is likely that a connection will have to be changed during the life of the system, optical connectors are often used. Making a change is only a little more involved than is connecting an RF cable. We say it is a little more involved because cleaning the connection before mating the fibers is essential. The subject of connectors and cleaning is covered in Chapter 6, where connectors are used extensively, and we strongly recommend reviewing that information.

There are several different series of connectors in use, as detailed in Chapter 6. All of them work by enforcing a good joint between the fibers, as with a fusion splice except not physically connected. Within many connector types there are two variations in how the fiber is cut, either at right angles (often referred to as an *ultrapolished connector*, UPC) or with a small angle at the fiber end (referred to as an *angle-polished connector*, APC). UPC connectors are acceptable for fibers not transporting (RF-modulated) broadcast video, though APC connectors also work fine in such applications. APC connectors are mandatory if you are carrying broadcast video on the fiber. When either a UPC or APC connector is cleaned to laboratory standards (which admittedly doesn't always happen in a laboratory), then either type of connector works, and the performance may favor the UPC by an exceedingly small margin. The problem is when connectors are not cleaned to perfection, and that means pretty much every connection made in the field (and often in the lab). UPC connectors are very unforgiving of improper cleaning, whereas APC connectors will often yield acceptable performance anyway, assuming they are not too dirty. The explanation is given in Chapter 6. It involves the angle on the end of the fiber, which reflects optical power into the cladding rather than back toward the source. The reflection is due to the incomplete cleaning of the connection.

Though people are working on the problem, there remains no good way to install a connector on the fiber in the field; it is a factory operation. Thus, you buy jumpers with the correct connector, cut the jumper in two, and fusion splice the ends onto the fibers you need to connectorize. Using a jumper is better than using a single connector on a pigtail, because you can test the jumper before you cut it, then you know that both connectors are good.

Preterminated Drop Cable

Some installers like to use preterminated drop cable. You buy the drop cable in certain increments of length, and when you install a drop, you grab the correct length preterminated cable. Extra length is stored usually out-of-doors, in a box on the side of the home, maybe behind the ONT if an outside ONT is used. Preterminated drops can save the significant cost of field termination, especially if you don't have qualified fiber splicers available. The downside to using preterminated drops is inventory management. You may only have drops in stock that are too short to reach the customer's premise, or ones that are too long, resulting in unnecessary cost and unsightly slack storage.

INSIDE CABLING

Running fiber inside a building can be a particular challenge, but fortunately manufacturers have been working on the problems and have come up with some excellent solutions.

Bend Radius

If you bend a conventional fiber too tightly, you will cause some photons to enter the cladding at too great an angle, meaning that they will not get reflected back into the center of the fiber. Thus, they will be lost, and your fiber loss increases. Bend the fiber even more and you will cause small breaks in the fiber itself, rendering the fiber permanently damaged. There are actually several bend radii that must be respected at different times during installation and use of the cable. The largest bend radius is the *dynamic bend radius*, and this defines how tightly you can bend the fiber during installation, when you are likely pulling the fiber while it is moving around a bend. Then you may see a *long-term, or static, bend radius,* which defines how tightly the cable may be bent long-term, after it has been pulled. These will be applied usually to outside plant cable, and will be given in terms of so many times the cable diameter.

The bend radius of individual strands of fiber optic cable, which you might be connecting to an ONT, is less than that above, and depends to an extent on the maximum wavelength being transmitted on the fiber—1550 or 1610 nm wavelengths require a larger bend radius than do fibers carrying only 1310 and 1490 nm wavelengths. For example, typical loss for a single turn of fiber around a 32 mm (1.26-inch) diameter mandrel is 0.5 dB at 1550 nm, less at shorter wavelengths. For this reason, it is important to take care installing the fiber to make sure you don't violate the bend radius restriction.

Of great importance is to make sure you don't violate the bend radius when connecting an ONT. Many ONTs include a fiber management tray in the ONT housing, typically wrapping a few turns around a race with a diameter larger than two inches or so. We have seen ONTs "fail" and be returned for repair for no reason other than that the installer made sure the fiber was pulled tight in the fiber tray. Sometimes the fiber is routed through a hole in the inner ONT housing to the optical receiver, and we have seen times when the installer gave the fiber a tug where it went through the housing. This can put a bend in the fiber, causing the ONT to lose sensitivity.

On the other hand, we have used the bend loss of a fiber strand to confirm a suspected case of too much signal level. We have loosely wrapped a few turns around our ink pen in order to introduce some temporary and uncalibrated loss, to see if that would cure a problem we had.

Fiber for Indoor Installation
In recent years, a lot of work has gone into manufacturing fibers with much smaller bend radii, so that they can be mounted unobtrusively inside apartments and the like. The result has been individual fiber strands that can practically be bent around a wall corner. Fiber intended for surface installation in finished areas might include adhesive and a special installation tool, making installation very fast. The fiber is so small it is almost impossible to see after installation. Again, consult your vendor for specifics. But if you need to install fiber in buildings, you will want to look into this type of fiber very carefully.

Ribbon Fibers
In certain cases, it will be advantageous to use ribbon fibers: fiber cables with the fibers lying parallel to each other. Machines are available to mass terminate ribbon fibers, greatly improving the efficiency of splicing or connectorization. Errors are reduced in the splicing process; conventional fibers can be accidently cross-spliced in any number of ways. With ribbon fiber, if the operator lines

up the two fibers with the colors in the same sequence, all of the splices will then be correct. There are only two ways to align the ribbons for splicing: the right way and the wrong way. You don't have all of the possibilities for errors you have with other cables, and the machine can do all of the splicing at once.

OPTICAL PERFORMANCE OF THE FTTx NETWORK

We've covered the optical components of the FTTx network, but it remains to cover the end-to-end performance and reach of optical networks. This section primarily addresses the limitations in the data portion of the FTTH network, not the broadcast RF portion, if used; that is covered in Chapter 11. There are several ways we can approach the performance issue, and all have some ambiguities built in. We must include some safety margin because optical components can age and suffer some component degradation.[1] Also, there will be some cable breaks with time, as trucks snag overhead cables, cars take out poles, and as underground cables get cut ("backhoe fades"). This means more loss at splices to be added at a later date, at unknown places in the fiber. In fact, breakages tend to happen at odd times and in bad weather, resulting in temporary repairs that are made at night in a storm, with the intention of coming back later and making permanent repairs. Such repairs may have more loss, but the system must work anyway. Also, as we mentioned above, reality is that not all mechanical connections are as clean as they should be, and this costs safety margin. So it is prudent to allow margin in the design to allow for these and other "Murphy's law" issues that plague the real world.

DESIGN METHODOLOGIES

The most common methodology used in designing FTTH systems is to look at the lowest transmitter output optical signal level allowed by the appropriate standard, and to look at the minimum acceptable received signal level, again specified by the standard. The difference between the two defines the maximum loss (the "loss budget") we can tolerate in the fiber optic network. The calculation must be done for both the downstream and upstream directions, and it is our experience that the upstream direction tends to be the limiting direction by a slim margin in many cases.

The loss budget is then reduced by a factor specified by the manufacturer or by generally accepted practice, to account for other distortion factors such as dispersion, discussed earlier in this chapter. This is called a *penalty*, and is usually

---

[1]However, as this is written, we know of pre-EPON equipment that has been in continuous operation for more than a dozen years and is still working to its original specifications.

expressed for both 10- and 20-km distances. It typically runs on the order of 0.5 dB for 10 km and 1 dB for 20 km, but this depends on the type of source and the characteristics of the fiber. The available loss budget is reduced by the penalty, and the remaining loss budget can be spread among splitting loss, fiber loss, and connection loss.

We shall use a different methodology here to explain the reach, one that relies on computer models for real optical fiber and assumed characteristics of sources and receivers.[ii] This methodology will show in more detail the effect of dispersion on performance of the system. We'll show examples from both EPON and GPON, though the two are similar in performance. We are just showing the data transmission portion of the PONs in this section. RF transmission is covered in a later chapter. The effect of RF overlay on the data transmission is that you will lose a little signal level (on the order of 0.5 dB) due to the WDM used at the headend, so you will equivalently lose 2–3 km of reach, no other changes being made.

EPON Optics

We introduced EPON in Chapter 3. Originally, there were two classes of optics defined for EPON: PX-10 (nominally 10 km reach) and PX-20 (nominally 20 km reach). To these were added more classes when 10 Gb/s PONs were introduced. But the principals involved are the same in any case. We shall look at two reach cases using the analysis methodology outlined earlier.

PX20 Optics at OLT and at ONT

For this example, we looked at the vendor-specified minimum transmit level of the transmitter (which should take into account *end-of-life* (EOL) degradation) then subtracted the vendor-specified minimum sensitivity of the receiver. The difference is the maximum loss budget we have to work with, in this example 28.7 dB in the downstream direction, and 28.2 dB upstream. Maybe we should have used the optical values from the IEEE specification, but we found early-on that they are quite conservative, and not consistent with what is being provided. So, while there can be variations from one product to another, you are probably OK using manufacturers' specifications so long as they are guaranteed worst-case. The specification numbers tend to be cast in concrete once and for all when the standard is written, but the state-of-the-art progresses, yielding better components as time goes by.

The link budgets calculated from our optical model appear as nearly horizontal lines near the top of the graph (Fig. 9.4). They represent the total loss that the system can have at a given distance. The lines would be exactly horizontal if it were not for the dispersion characteristic of the fiber, which interacts with the spectrum occupied by the laser transmitter to reduce the loss budget as you go to longer paths. In this case the lines are very nearly horizontal (there

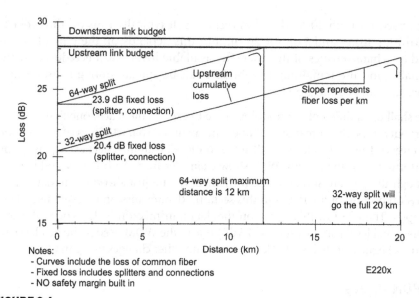

FIGURE 9.4
EPON reach, PX20 optics at OLT and ONT.

is a downward tilt for the downstream line, but it is hard to see), but below we shall show a much different case, and we'll explain more fully what is going on when we get to that case. (Dispersion means that light travels at different speeds in the fiber, based on several variables. The most important variable in this case is probably the wavelength of the light, and this form of dispersion is called *chromatic dispersion*. While the light is nominally of one wavelength coming out of the laser, there is a small spread of wavelengths, and each wavelength travels at a slightly different speed in the fiber. The result is pulse *smearing* at the receiver. This has the effect of requiring slightly more light level in order to overcome the effective noise caused by the smearing. Put another way, we have a slightly smaller loss budget due to the dispersion.)

Note that there is a greater link budget in the downstream direction than in the upstream direction. We have seen this to be generally the case using specifications published by all the optical subsystem vendors. This combined with the greater loss per kilometer of the fiber in the upstream direction[2] tends to make the upstream the most common limiting factor in reach. However, there are a few cases in which we have observed the downstream to be a limiting factor.

So the top lines of Fig. 9.3 start at a loss budget of 28.2 and 28.7 dB for upstream and downstream directions, respectively. This loss budget is almost

---

[2]Downstream transmission is at 1490 nm for this example, where fiber exhibits a loss of about 0.27 dB/km. Upstream transmission is done at 1310 nm, where the loss is about 0.38 dB/km.

constant over the length of the fiber. We now put in the lines representing the total loss of the network. We have shown both 32-way and 64-way splits. Our assumed losses are pretty high, 20.4 dB for the 32-way split, and 23.9 dB for a 64-way split. Of these losses, respectively, 15 dB and 18 dB represent the laws-of-physics loss of the splitting process—if you split a signal equally, half the signal power goes in each direction, so you will have half as much signal power in each leg (3 dB loss). Then we add the loss for variation in signal splitting amplitude and loss in the splitter, which adds another 2.5 and 3 dB, respectively, so you are starting with 17.5- and 21-dB loss. The remainder of the loss is a provision for connectorization and splicing loss, plus that all-important safety factor for system degradation. These losses are conservative, and you may be able to do better—by the time this was written, we were already seeing some splitters with tighter tolerance on splitting loss than what we assumed, but they were not universal.

The diagonal lines labeled "64-way split" and "32-way split" start at the left side (zero PON length) with the fixed loss of the network. The fixed loss includes splitter, splice, and connector loss, as shown above. Only the upstream graphs are shown, as we are limited by the upstream, not the downstream characteristics. The slope of the lines is equal to the loss per kilometer of the fiber. When the sloped lines, representing the cumulative loss of the network, intersect the link budget, we have reached the maximum length network that we can build, under the assumptions we made.

Note in this case, that you can easily reach 20 km with a 32-way split, and you can reach 12 km with a 64-way split. Remember, though, that while these graphs assume worst-case end-of-life passive component specifications, they do NOT include any other safety margin, other than that we were conservative in the fixed loss we assumed. We limit the distance to 20 km, even though the optics would support greater distance. The reason is that the optics is only one element in determining total distance. The protocols include provision for the maximum propagation delay of the optical signal in 20 km, and except where they state further distances, don't guarantee operation over 20 km. Longer distances may work (we have seen longer networks built), but we cannot guarantee that every device will work when you go outside of the distance specifications. We explained this earlier in this chapter, in the section entitled, "How Far Can You Go?"

PX20 OLT, PX10 ONT

Many PONs can work well with PX10 optics at the ONT, and PX10 optics are lower in price than are PX20 optics, though the difference is quickly diminishing. Thus, it makes sense to do the modeling with PX20 optics at the OLT and PX10 at the ONT. This will dramatically demonstrate the effects of fiber dispersion on the performance of the network.

Fig. 9.4 illustrates this situation, and may be compared directly with Fig. 9.3, which uses PX20 optics at both ends of the network. There is no difference in the downstream loss budget, because the ONT receiver sensitivity is specified the same as for the PX20.

Note something different here that we have not seen this dramatically before: the *upstream* curve bends downward as distance increases. The reason for this is that we are seeing the effects of a Fabry–Perot (F-P) laser for the first time. All PX20 lasers are distributed feedback (DFB) lasers, which have much narrower spectral width (and somewhat higher prices). Narrower spectral width prevents the curve from bending noticeably downward. The reason for the downward bend is that the F-P laser output, due to laser design, occupies a relatively wide spectrum. A characteristic of the fiber is *chromatic dispersion*, meaning that light at different wavelengths propagates through the fiber at different speeds (dispersion was described earlier in this chapter). Thus, light at different wavelengths that leaves the ONT laser at the same time, arrives at the OLT at different times, resulting in a "smearing" of data pulses. The longer the fiber, the worse the effect becomes, hence the downward bending of the *upstream* curve in Fig. 9.5. The effect of dispersion and the smearing of the data pulses is that we need a higher signal-to-noise ratio (which in this case implies higher signal level, and hence less system loss) in order to recover the signal.

Strange point here: the zero dispersion wavelength of the fiber is about 1310 nm, and yet with PX-10 optics, we are most severely limited in performance at this wavelength (the upstream wavelength). Why? Well, that

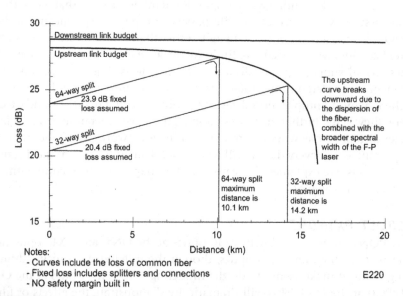

FIGURE 9.5
EPON reach, PX20 at OLT, PX10 at ONT (compare with Fig. 9.4).

is because with PX-10 optics, the standard permits an upstream F-P laser, which exhibits much mode hopping, over a wide wavelength range—almost all wavelength ranges are ±10 nm wide except for the 1310 nm upstream wavelength, which is ±50 nm wide (see Fig. 6.2 of Chapter 6). The reason for this width is to accommodate the F-P lasers with their vice of mode-hopping (but virtue of lower cost). With this wide a possible bandwidth; even putting the zero dispersion point in the middle of the band cannot make up for the dispersion.

From Fig. 9.5, we see that the 64-way split distance is about 10.1 km, while the 32-way split distance is about 14.2 km. We don't get much extra distance by reducing the split ratio because the *upstream* slope has gotten steep by this point. Due to the steepness of the slope, one should add more safety margin than one would if the *upstream* slope was lower.

More on the Penalty
We mentioned above a more common methodology used in fiber optic network design, wherein the curves shown are not used, but rather the system gain is used, and a penalty is introduced to compensate for the dispersion in the fiber. From what we have just discussed, you can see that the penalty is actually a measure of the downward departure of the link budget curve, as dramatically illustrated in Fig. 9.5. So introducing the penalty can get you in trouble if you are working at such a length that the link budget curve is breaking downward significantly. But the penalty concept is simple, and as long as you stay out of this region, it yields reasonably good results. At 10 km, a 1 dB dispersion penalty would be adequate for the system of Fig. 9.5. But if you want to push the network a little farther, you need a more accurate method of design.

GPON Optics
GPON optics are designated by class, where the class letter tells you little about how the optics will perform. This was discussed in Chapter 4. About the only thing the class letter tells you is that as the letters get deeper into the alphabet, the loss budget gets larger. Originally Class A, B, and C optics were defined, but early experience indicated that none were optimal for many practical situations. Thus, Class B+ was born, based on that early experience.

Class B+ Optics at the OLT and ONT
The link budget calculated from our optical model appears as nearly horizontal lines near the top of the graph (Fig. 9.6). The lines would be exactly horizontal if it were not for the dispersion characteristics of the fiber, which interact with the spectrum occupied by the laser transmitter to reduce the loss budget as you go to longer fiber routes. In this case, the lines are very nearly horizontal, as with the above EPON PX-20 example.

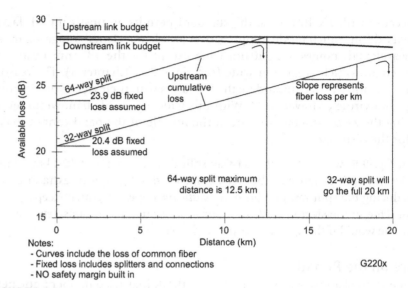

FIGURE 9.6
GPON reach, Class B+ optics at OLT and ONT.

Note that there is slightly more link budget in the upstream direction than in the downstream direction, particularly for longer PONs. Due to the greater loss per kilometer of the fiber in the upstream direction, the upstream direction is usually the limiting factor in reach. However, there are a few cases such as this one, in which we have observed the downstream to be the limiting factor.

The diagonal lines labeled "64-way split" and "32-way split" start at the left side (zero PON length) with the fixed loss of the network. The fixed loss includes splitter, splice, and connector loss. We show the losses assumed, which are fairly conservative—you may be able to do better.

Note in this case, that you can easily reach 20 km with a 32-way split, and you can reach 12.5 km with a 64-way split. Remember, though, that while these graphs assume fairly high connection loss and worst-case end-of-life component specifications (from the data sheets of the optics manufacturers), they do NOT include any other safety margin.

TESTING OPTICAL NETWORKS

No matter how good a job you do building your network, there is going to come a time when something goes wrong with the fiber. Either there will be a bad splice or connector, or the fiber will be cut somewhere that you cannot easily identify the location of the break, or something else will go wrong. There are a few instruments you can use to help you identify the problems.

Visible Light Source

Used only for test, you can get visible (usually red) test light sources into which you can plug fibers. These are safe to look at, and will visibly make the fiber slightly red when test light is going through it. This makes it relatively easy to trace one fiber in a bundle of possibly several hundred fibers: you will see light at the end of the proper fiber, and you can see a reddish tint to the light along the fiber.

Optical Level Meter

You need an optical level meter which will allow you to measure the optical power at all relevant wavelengths in your system. If you are using a first-generation FTTH system with no broadcast carrier, you need a meter that can read 1310-nm and 1490-nm light. If you have broadcast carriers, you will want to add 1550-nm measurement capability, not a hard thing to do at all. You can get handheld meters that you insert in active systems, which will measure downstream and upstream light levels. Of course, there will be a service interruption when you put the meter in the PON if you already have subscribers on it.

Measuring upstream light levels can be a little tricky because you are not dealing with one source, but rather are dealing with multiple sources, each at different amplitude, with one transmitting right after the other. So unless your meter has some special magic in it, it will likely read an average upstream signal level, which is limited in its usefulness. Some meters may have peak detection so that you can read the highest upstream level. This can be useful in some circumstances, particularly when you can put just one ONT on the PON and measure its upstream level at some convenient point. Fortunately, when troubleshooting a level problem, the downstream and upstream levels are usually affected about equally, so you may be able to troubleshoot using the downstream light, which is constant, coming from only the one source that is on continuously.

Optical Time Domain Reflectometer

A particularly useful instrument is the optical time domain reflectometer (OTDR). It transmits a light pulse down a fiber, then measures returns from that light as it travels down the fiber. You will see a graph of the loss in the fiber, and you will be able to see discontinuities at splices, connectors, etc. You will be able to see the loss through a splitter. Perhaps most importantly, you will be able to see a break in the fiber. Because the OTDR knows the speed of light in the fiber, it can tell you the distance from where you are to the problem, with excellent accuracy even if the fiber is buried. So you know where to start digging. An OTDR can be an extremely useful tool for testing fiber plant as it is being built; a bad splice or a break in the cable is a lot cheaper to fix while the contractor is on-site doing fiber installation than it is a few months down the road, when you try to hook up customers and something is not working.

THE DUMB, SIMPLE, STUPID STUFF

When problems occur with any network, it is usually not problems with the nuances of the technology (though it can be). Rather, it is often what we like to call the dumb, simple, stupid stuff that gets you: errors and omissions that creep into a system and seem harmless enough initially, but which can come up later to cause great problems and cost. We take the opportunity to repeat some of our favorites here in order to introduce a little levity into the book, but more importantly, to remind you of how easy it can be to get into trouble when you think you are doing everything right. Some of these are from personal experience, some we have read about in the newspaper (you DON'T want someone to read about your system like this), and some have been supplied by others.

Fiber cable properly installed is much, much more reliable than is any other cable technology, but while manufacturers try hard to make it foolproof, we don't seem to have run out of fools yet.

Mixing Green and Blue

We got a call one day from a sales engineer who was working with Third World Cable TV, which was converting portions of its plant to FTTH. The broadcast pictures were terrible, even at the headend. The sales engineer had gotten more than a little suspicious when he saw jumpers with blue optical connectors plugged into the green connectors coming out of an EDFA. All of the jumpers in the headend fiber management system had blue connectors, though the other network components had green connectors. All of the connectors were of the SC type commonly used in FTTH. The headend engineer was sure that there was no difference between the connectors except that they were made by different manufacturers, who used different colors for their connector shells. Nope, not anywhere close to correct. As we discussed in Chapter 6, green shells mean the connector is angle-polished (an SC/APC connector in this case), and blue shells are reserved for ultrapolished connectors (SC/UPC). We also showed in Chapter 6 why you should not ever use UPC connectors with broadcast video—reflections from insufficiently cleaned connections (and almost all connections are insufficiently cleaned) can play havoc with the signals. The SC/UPC jumpers were replaced with SC/APC jumpers, and the pictures got a lot better!

Lesson Learned

Don't mix green and blue, at least where fiber optic connectors are concerned. Make sure you use the right color for the intended use.

Fiber is Fiber is Fiber

We later found that the fiber loss in certain parts of the same operator's plant was a little high. Turns out that they had some odd pieces of fiber cable left over from other jobs, so they were spliced together to make the outside plant. What type of fiber was each piece? Well, it had the right number of fibers in it. How long had it been in the warehouse? Don't know. What were the specifications on the fiber? Don't know. (Between 1984 and 2009 the ITU published eight revisions of its G.652 specification for single-mode fiber of the type normally used in outside plant.[iii] Several of those versions came out after the subject operator had been in the business. Most versions of the specification reflected improvement in the performance of the fiber. The operator had no idea what revision of the spec applied to the fibers he spliced together.) Had he swept the fiber to test its performance? Even better, had he tested it with an OTDR? What do you think?

Lesson Learned
It can be very expensive to save a few dollars on fiber.

What, Mark My Cable Route Accurately?
This actually happened where the author lives a few years ago. We are close to a major limited-access highway that has the ubiquitous traffic cameras to let people monitor traffic along the route. All was well until one day the pictures in the DOT (Department of Transportation) monitoring center went dark. It took the engineers quite a while to decide that the problem was not in the monitoring center. Then someone decided that it was time to get in a car and drive out to see what was happening along the roadway.

Turns out that a contractor for a utility was digging a trench into which he was going to install more fiber optic cable. Per proper procedure, he had contacted the center he was to notify to get existing cables marked. Per proper procedure, they had contacted all interests having buried facilities along the route. Per proper procedure, the DOT had gone out and marked their fiber route. NOT per proper procedure, they had marked it incorrectly—just a few feet off. Per Murphy's law, the contractor digging the new trench had successfully found where the DOT fiber SHOULD have been marked. Before the DOT engineers had gotten the car out to see what was happening, about 7 miles of fiber optic cable had been turned into little glass pins a few centimeters long! Now per Dr. Murphy ("if anything can go wrong, it will, at the worst possible moment") this occurred during a time of massive fiber construction and the resulting fiber shortage, so it was a number of months before the DOT was able to get new fiber and get it trenched in. And we bet that everyone was really, really careful to mark their cables correctly that time.

Lesson Learned
Make sure you can trace your fiber later. Make sure your people know how do to it in perpetuity.

What Can Possibly Go Wrong?

I had a boss who would ask that whenever I brought him an estimate for a job we were bidding, when he thought I was bidding too high. I always hated it when he asked what could possibly go wrong, because if we got the job, inevitably I found out what could go wrong. These next few stories are from Joe Byrne of m2fx[iv] in the United Kingdom—he reminded me that things can go wrong on both sides of the pond (used with permission). There is nothing here that cannot go wrong in North America too—in fact, some of these WERE from North America.

Animals—You Can't Hide From Them

From squirrels to rats and rabbits, rodents like to chew whatever they can find. Squirrels seem to show a particular liking for fiber cables—in 2011, Time Warner Cable had to replace 87 miles of cable in Western New York, due to squirrel chews. Across the Atlantic, rats knocked out internet access for Virgin Media customers in parts of Scotland after attacking cables twice in 2 days.

Meanwhile in the Rockies, bears can be a problem if cables are small enough to fit between their jaws. More exotically, Indian engineers complain about monkeys eating fiber—a particular issue around temples dedicated to the animals. Why can't they just stick to peanuts and bananas?

Lesson Learned

Ummm, fiber encased in reinforced concrete? Some sheathing is pretty good, but better ask how it is against the varmints in your area. Proper conduit may help, too.

Vehicle Damage

You'd think that drivers of tall vehicles or heavy plant would look up as well as forward, but often they seem to completely lack spatial awareness. Damage ranges from the mundane—such as truckers running into poles and bringing down lines—to the ridiculous.

A dump truck in Kentucky tipping salt took down 300 feet of fiber by driving along with its dump bed up, while a trucker misdirected down a residential street in Pennsylvania plowed on, collecting cables as he went. Not every cable is strong enough to survive this—though some cable has coped with a 32,000-pound military vehicle parking on it...

Lesson Learned

Uhhhh, Continue the search for intelligent life?

Vandals

Sometimes it seems that the world is full of idiots who think it is fun to destroy property—even though it is likely to cut Internet access to their own homes or communities.

According to the Federal Communications Commission (FCC) there were more than a thousand malicious attacks that led to severe outages between 2007 and 2014 in the United States. And that only counts incidents that affect at least 900,000 minutes of user calls or 911 services.

From people who dig up fiber thinking it can be resold, to those who use cables for target practice, a large proportion of avoidable network damage comes from the very people that would be on the phone complaining of a lack of service. Or they would, if they hadn't just trashed the network they rely on...

Lesson Learned
Sometimes you just can't fix stupid.

Mother Nature
There's not much you can do to prevent natural disasters, but networks need to be reliable and protected enough to deal with normal weather conditions, such as ice, snow, and wind. No matter how well you build a network, freak weather and natural disasters, such as hurricanes or earthquakes, can undo all your good work. This has a knock-on effect as cable damage hits wired and wireless communications, leaving communities isolated exactly when they need access to information.

On the plus side, the devastation caused by Hurricane Sandy led Verizon to significantly upgrade its network, replacing copper with fiber cables in affected areas.

Lesson Learned
Fiber is much, much more reliable than copper. But don't sell your ham radio set; only the sun can destroy its communications medium, and that for only short, rare times.

Hard to Foresee
Some things you simply can't plan for. A boat's anchor cut through not one, but two, Egyptian undersea cables in 2008, cutting connectivity to the Middle East and South East Asia and forcing traffic to go along different routes.

On land (just barely), level 3 communications had to replace aerial cables after a small plane clipped them while trying to touch down at Burbank International Airport in California.

Lesson Learned
Sometimes you just have to shrug, and get on with fixing the damage. Well, I guess that if you buried things under 300 m of ocean or dirt, you might resolve a few problems. Until you found the new problems you created.

My Favorite

And the most dangerous fiber foe is... a little old lady.

Back in 2011, an unnamed 75-year-old Georgian woman cut fiber access to the whole of the neighboring country of Armenia. While scavenging for copper her spade went through the main fiber link between the countries, blacking out the internet for 3.2 million Armenians for 5 hours. The cable was normally more securely buried, but landslides or heavy rain may have exposed it. If she could cut through the sheath with a shovel, we have to wonder about the quality of the sheath on the fiber cable.

Obviously cables get cut by contractors (or even homeowners) all the time, but not normally causing damage on this sort of scale. Let's hope the police reminded her that bits of fiber don't have any resale value...

Lesson Learned

I'm drawing a blank. Redundant paths? Harder sheaths on the fiber?

Endnotes

i. https://global.ihs.com/.

ii. The computer model used was developed by Wave7 Optics, now owned by Arris Interactive.

iii. https://www.itu.int/rec/T-REC-G.652-200911-I/en.

iv. http://blog.m2fx.com/.

CHAPTER 10

Data Services Architecture

INTRODUCTION

For the PON access network, the data services architecture represents the basic underpinning transportation mechanism of the overall system. In large part, all the information flows over the network as data services in some form (including digital video within a radio frequency (RF) overlay, though here we are concerned with what is traditionally considered narrowcast data). Besides the services such as voice, data, and Internet protocol TV (IPTV), additional information such as network management, provisioning, performance management, monitoring, and network control traffic all travel across the network within the data services architecture. Thus the engineering, design, and implementation of the data services architecture are critical to the success of the network deployment.

NETWORK ENGINEERING FOR ACCESS NETWORKS

The network design team must concern themselves with the following important attributes of the data services architecture:

- Service model architectures—providing both a logical and physical model for each aspect of the network, from the integration point of services and the access network uplink, down to each type of device deployed in the customer premise, largely based upon a clear understanding of the applicable engineering standards in this area—this provides the clear blueprint for implementation.
- Transport models—using the well-known and practical constructs of switching, routing, and higher layer protocols to implement the best solutions for the types of services deployed in the network and the expected scale of the network are the foundation for building the network.
- Network services support—for each of the service types, the data services architecture must provide specific utility support within the transport models to each of the device types found in the network, whether

FTTx Networks. http://dx.doi.org/10.1016/B978-0-12-420137-8.00010-X

individual customer premise devices or shared resource devices, in order to allow the deployment of secure and efficient services. A good example of such utility is the ability for networking devices to support Internet group management protocol (IGMP) snooping for the smooth deployment of IPTV.

- Data service integration—whether the data services architecture supports integration of other services into the network (indirect integration) or is integrated itself (direct integration), as well as the upstream network interface into the wider network world. (As discussed in Chapter 8, depending on the size of the network, this upstream edge may be part of the transport or core networks maintained by the network operator.) Planning for the required resiliency and capacity of each of the network integration points is key.

- Network scalability—the data services architecture must be designed with the ultimate scale of the network in mind. It may not be clear at the time of initial implementation which parts of the network will need to scale first or at what rate, so building in the capability to add scale in the least disruptive fashion is important, even if difficult to identify and predict the actual order and rate of scaling. At the same time, in order to support scalability, the specific scaling attributes and their variability or degrees of freedom driving the network sizing will need to be determined.

- Network resiliency—with the requirement of implementing the primary transport mechanism of the passive optical network (PON)/access network system, the data services must also provide the appropriate level of network resiliency to ensure operation in the event of failures to both hardware and software. This is particularly important for business services and mission-critical services that demand high network availability.

- Management integration—within all aspects of the management system integration, data services must be considered, especially in the production phase of the network, since they give the most compelling and complete picture of the operational state, health, and current load of the network.

- Assessment of vendor systems—each vendor system to be selected for data services implementation will require specific assessment criteria, both in hardware, software, and integration interfaces, based on the selected architectures for the implementation phase. The key factors in assessing the equipment are providing the necessary scaling, supporting controls and utilities, and integration capability to implement the services properly.

Although many of the familiar data services requirements, design concepts, and implementing protocols are similar or identical to the same attributes of core, upstream interface, or edge and transport network designs, there are others germane specifically to access networks and to PON networks, which will be specified and covered here in detail. To ensure the consideration of special access-related requirements and design, in the implementation stage, protocols developed for other networking scenarios, adapted for access networking, with resulting security flaws or weaknesses, will be highlighted so they can be avoided along with the resulting headaches for the network management team.

ASSESSMENT OF VENDOR SYSTEMS

The network design and operation teams must ensure that the protocol and feature support in the products today work as expected, and also must anticipate what it will take to add functionality later—both with respect to new features which are future-looking and for features which are lacking but will be added by the equipment vendor (Table 10.1). It is difficult to add features and

Table 10.1 System Assessment Checklist

Assessment Area	PON Assessment Criteria
Networking support—Switching	Standard switching throughput capability, PON specific switching requirements including VLAN tagging capabilities, sizes and functionality of media access control (MAC) address tables, standard Internet Engineering Task Force (IETF) switching test results
Networking support—Routing	Standard L3 forwarding throughput capability, routing protocol support for IPv4/IPv6, routing protocol interoperability testing
QoS support—Data path	QoS support for queueing, rate limiting, packet inspection and ACLs (access control lists; the number of items in the list and how the system acts on the rules). Does the ACL system protect the system CPU and the data path? How is the PON point-to-multipoint link implemented in the hardware and what are the control points available to the provisioning system?
QoS support—Controls	What controls are provided for the QoS functions and how are they accessed? Special consideration should be given to the PON link to characterize the functionality of the management and control of optical network terminal (ONT) endpoints within the PON link
QoS support—Provisioning	What provisioning mechanisms and interfaces are supported for the QoS subsystem? Are the provisioning interfaces standards-based? Is the provisioning integration available through the PON vendor's software systems for third-party applications allowing flow-through provisioning?
Resiliency	For the upstream interfaces to the access system, what resiliency functionality is supported? Does it require interaction or interoperability with the operator's other data equipment?
Scalability	What are the points of scalability upgrade for the access system, such as service network interface (SNI) utilization or optical line terminal (OLT) backplane utilization? How are they assessed? What degree of reconfiguration or bringing new resources into production is required in order to apply additional scale to the system?
Management system integration	Does the management system packaged with the hardware include shelf management for the OLT, element management for the combined OLT/ONT system, and performance management and provisioning integration? What are the programming interfaces to the management system and are they standards-based?

Continued

Table 10.1 System Assessment Checklist *Continued*

Assessment Area	PON Assessment Criteria
Provisioning system integration	Do the hardware and management system support integration into flow-through provisioning in order to avoid swivel chair provisioning of numerous systems? The driver here is that for the PON access system almost all the other service-supporting systems will need to configure or request configuration of not only the OLT and ONT, but other supporting subsystems—for large network scalability the level of integration between numerous vendor systems is critical
ONT integrated service end point—integration	For services hosted within the ONT, ensure that requirements for other supporting subsystems are clearly defined and that those systems when selected can be maintained and are scalable to the size of network ultimately required
ONT integrated service end point—provisioning	For services hosted within the ONT, provisioning interfaces should be standards-based in order to ensure the highest level of integration with other northbound provisioning systems. An example is supporting TR-069 for ONT services configurable by an Auto Configuration Servers (ACS). Proprietary interfaces typically are more difficult to support long term and can be prone to error when modified over a number of system iterations

functionality after the network has been deployed. For features that require additional hardware support, the only option is for hardware replacement, which is undesirable. Similarly, features which require additional software functionality should be examined carefully: is the code to be developed proprietary to the vendor? Is the vendor using freeware code packages which must be integrated? Are they obtaining the additional functionality from third-party design and implementation shops? Operators should be critical in their assessment of the vendor organization's ability to provide such functionalities and support for years after the sale. Typically the best methodology is to ensure the networking design is fully supported by the system as purchased, with additional functionality added later to either assist in simplifying the network design, adding scalability, or enhancing the system from the basic configuration, through software feature development and deployment. In other words, get all of the customer features you anticipate needing now, and only count on the vendor to deliver future software features that aid in operating the network.

The best practice recommendation for operators is to purchase dedicated support packages for the initial year of the system design, build, and production deployment for each of the critical devices that implement each data service type. The decision to move to a lower-tiered support or service package should only be made once the full services have been in production and proven to be working as expected. Another best practice is to provide checkpoints within the network ramp-up to production to assess the performance management of the network. Is it falling within the scale that both the operator network design/implementation team and the vendor anticipated? Only if the data indicate the operation of the network is in compliance with expectations and documented benchmarks should the operator consider a service-level adjustment.

DATA SERVICES ORGANIZATION AND PON-SPECIFIC ATTRIBUTES

High-speed data services in FTTx networks are defined as the transport of multiclass, differentiated (e.g., residential or business) packet-based network resources for any number of varying functions—typically enabling subscribers to reach and interact with general-purpose higher-level networks and/or specific private networks throughout the world—sometimes simultaneously utilizing a single ONT device. The following sections describe the organization and attributes of data services as they are applied to PON access networks. The subsequent detailed treatments of the multilayer networking capabilities and services of the PON network and its supporting equipment will allow the detailed design of both types of services.

Residential Services

Residential class data services are those providing networking access to the Internet through the operator's network and up to higher-level northbound network providers—this class of service may have differing levels of service premium based upon the network resources provided (or allocated) to the subscriber for their particular class of service (implemented by quality of service attributes). The resulting services could include for example a silver standard and a gold premium data service, both with specific bandwidth capabilities (e.g., more bandwidth for the higher-tiered premium service). Then these differing bandwidth capabilities are ensured by the operator via prioritization marking, queuing, and rate-limiting resources at the ONT (and perhaps at other elements in the network).

The residential data service may be for a single residence (with one subscriber mapped to a single ONT) or a multidwelling residence with multiple subscribers mapped to a single ONT device. In either of these cases, the ONT must provide sufficient resources for providing bandwidth, prioritization, and queuing to provide the services at the capability sold by the operator.

Commercial Services

Business class data services provide access to the Internet—also through the operator's network and up to higher-level northbound network providers in the same way as residential services—but also simultaneously implement customer-specific networks, taking various forms and uses, with the following attributes:

- Architecturally, the commercial services network may take several forms, encompassing point-to-point communications between two dedicated corporate locations, or point-to-multipoint connectivity for multisite businesses or other private entities. These architectures are best described by the standards bodies which deal in this type of secure, private connectivity. As an example, commercial layer 2 Ethernet network services are described by the Metro Ethernet Forum (MEF) with their MEF and Carrier Ethernet (CE) sets of standards.

- The commercial services network provides private, secure communications: while the data for the commercial services network are traversing the same transport infrastructure as the residential services, they are not available or seen by other subscribers in the network—thus they are being transported over a *virtual network*.
- For the operator maintaining the premium service levels of the commercial services network, ensuring data security, maintaining availability, and limiting downtime to ensure service-level agreement (SLA) contracts is primary.
- The use of quality of service (QoS) mechanisms within the FTTH network components is required for the commercial services data to receive special, differentiated handling, justifying the higher premium charged over typical residential services for the performance delivered.
- The commercial services network provides special services and connectivity: examples are businesses that require outside communications to go through a central location while maintaining secure communication between locations; or for neighborhoods or private organizations which provide secure or special access to network resources which are allocated to only those ONTs participating in that private service group.
- For the commercial services virtual private network (VPN) function, the secure end-point device may be provided either by devices subtended to the ONT or by the ONT itself. The VPN function may include layer 2 and/or layer 3 attributes depending on the implementation—with the overall access network providing transport security across the OLT.

PON Standards for Data Networking

Both the most well-known and widely implemented PON standards for access networking, Ethernet passive optical network (EPON) (IEEE 802.3ah Ethernet in the first mile) and Gigabit passive optical network (GPON) (ITU 984 GPON), provide specific criteria for data networking architectures, and in particular a standard nomenclature for indicating the various interfaces within the PON network.

Both standards for the PON link provide Ethernet interfaces upstream of the OLT and downstream of the ONT for data networking. Whether these interfaces are fast Ethernet, Gigabit Ethernet, or higher standards such as 10 Gigabit Ethernet, depends primarily on both vendor implementation and what networking speeds are commercially available and cost-effective for network operators. However, within the PON link of the access system, that is the shared communication link between the OLT and ONT stations, the two standards differ in both design and implementation. The differences in the two standards in their PON link implementation are described in Chapters 3 and 4.

It is instructive to consider the overall architectural design of the PON system as specified in each of the standards in order to have common points for this treatment of the data services architecture. Fig. 10.1 details the reference configuration for the OLT and ONT access network, in particular interfaces for data networking for the ITU 984.1 GPON standard are shown. Note that the upstream integration interface at the edge of the OLT is the service node interface (SNI), while the downstream integration interface in the customer premise is the user network interface (UNI). These will be key interfaces in our description of the data services architecture. Note also the interface between the OLT and ONT. For GPON this is defined as the IF_{PON} and it occurs within the optical distribution network between the OLT and ONT (the PON link). This is the shared PON medium as implemented by the set of splitters, optical fibers, splices, and connectors.

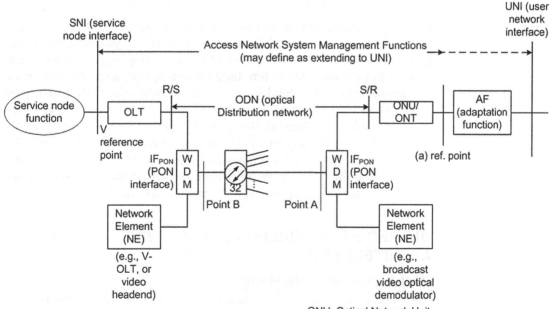

OLT: Optical Line Termination
R: Point on the network facing either the OLT or ONU
S: Point on the network facing the termination equipment

ONU: Optical Network Unit
ONT: Optical Network Terminal
Points A and B: Not necessary if WDM is not used.
(a) ref. point is not needed if AF is included in ONU

FIGURE 10.1

GPON reference model.

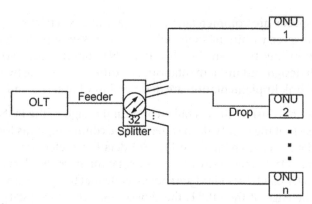

FIGURE 10.2
EPON reference model.

The IEEE 802.3 view of the PON network is (typical of this standard) less specific in enumerating the overall PON system interfaces. Fig. 10.2 provides the IEEE 802.3 view of the PON network reference architecture. Here the PON system is represented in simplified fashion as an OLT with a number of ONT devices subtended to the OLT.

While both standards present reference architectures, we will now develop a unified view which (especially in the case of the IEEE standard) is much more practical in creating a useful methodology to develop and document service models. In addition to the architectural references, both standards also provide operational criteria for the data service flows within the PON system (both upstream and downstream). Once again, the standards are vague as to how these should be implemented. However, PON system designers have been able to provide solutions to these operational requirements. Part of the development of the unified model for PON service model architectures will expand on these items as they relate to the treatments in the standards, but more importantly how they relate to practical working PON systems.

UNIFIED MODEL FOR PON DATA SERVICE ARCHITECTURES

PON Access Network Model

After considering each of the standard architectures, next we synthesize a unified PON system model which will be used to describe the service models moving forward. Fig. 10.3 represents this model and provides the system interfaces and model components we will use going forward to describe the PON system data services architectures. This model can be applied to either GPON or EPON operating at any speed.

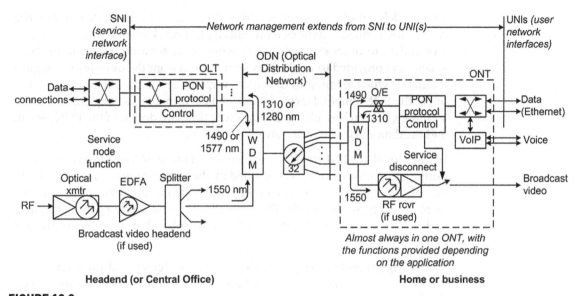

FIGURE 10.3
Unified view of PON as used in this book.

The SNI is the connection between the OLT device and upstream or northbound network cloud. Packet-based services, management, and provisioning data all flow over this interface down to the PON system.

The optical distribution network (ODN) is the shared medium connection between the OLT and the set of ONT stations on any particular PON. There is one optical distribution network per PON, with multiple PONs controlled by one OLT, accessed individually (i.e., per PON port). On any of the PON interfaces of the OLT, there are individually accessible ONTs, one per port of the optical splitter in use on the PON. Each of the ONTs on a given PON has its upstream WAN (Wide Area Network) interface to the ODN and a single or multiple UNI ports facing the subscriber to present user services.

For each PON/ODN combination, the model shows the addition of a broadcast video input available from an optical transmitter and erbium-doped fiber amplifier (EDFA), which after being split to allow transmission to a number of individual PONs, is added via wave division multiplexing (WDM) to the PON upstream and downstream signals. At the ONT reception side of the PON system, another WDM is used to remove the RF video signal from the PON-specific wavelengths and present the video feed separate from the data and voice interfaces of the ONT. In this case, the data information is in the form of the packets that originated at the OLT, while the voice, which was previously in the form of data packets, is converted to an analog voice signal.

This model is useful to describe physical interfaces of the PON system since each of the defined interfaces represents a physical element of the system or is a boundary to other external devices where data are accepted from the PON system and provided to the PON system (to and from the outside) and logical interfaces which are used to define the way that services are mapped into and out of the PON system. Having established these interfaces, they can be used in a number of exercises related to the description and design of the PON system and the data services architecture.

In this model, the SNI and UNI are considered secure service ingress and egress ports, whose provisioning is controlled by the network operator only and hidden or not available to outside entities connected to the network. This provisioning will typically identify the subscriber or some aspect of the subscriber, such that a service may be deployed to that subscriber unambiguously and securely.

Service ingress and egress points are also where elements of the service attributes are removed or remapped when leaving the transport network device (in the case of an FTTH network, the ONT). Service traffic arriving at the subscriber's premise equipment and the converse, elements of the service provided by the subscriber's premise equipment in the upstream direction, are either modified in some fashion or maintained as they are received. Later, when we consider the SNI and UNI in detail, we will identify the service traffic attributes maintained or modified at the point of being provided to the subtended network equipment, and which attributes of the service traffic are maintained or modified by the OLT and ONT upon entry to the access network from the subscriber's (ONT/UNI) or the operator's (OLT/SNI) viewpoint.

This ability of the SNI and UNI to either *trust* (accept) or *untrust* (overwrite what is received) the attributes of a service associated within an interface (e.g., a VLAN), or the interface itself (for all services associated with that interface) is a key function to assure services within the FTTx equipment.

In addition to the PON system handling of services traffic at the external interfaces, internally the PON system will implement functionality which impacts services architectures by either modifying traffic or handling traffic flows in a well-defined manner. The internal traffic handling is primarily concerned with elements of QoS because the PON system internal elements provide shared resource constraints either through the traffic busses, switching fabrics, or PON ASIC devices. These resource constraints must be resolved by enforcing QoS rules designed to identify and differentiate the treatment of traffic classes through queuing and rate limiting. The intent of the QoS subsystems within the PON system is to protect critical traffic while providing sufficient resources (queuing and bandwidth) for other less critical traffic classes. Using our unified model, we can identify three locations within the PON system where this internal handling must be understood by the PON system designer, implementer, and network operator:

- Internal to the OLT, the ability to provide queuing and rate limiting based on priority marking of services traffic at L2 or L3. The internal architecture of the OLT will be largely vendor-specific. However, the expectation is that there are physical components, typically multilayer switches, within the system to protect and ensure the integrity of the shared resources.
- Internal to the ONT system, the ability to provide queuing and rate limiting based on priority marking of services traffic at L2 or L3. Note that the ONT will necessarily provide fewer QoS resources since it is concerned with only a single subscriber's traffic, while the OLT, for example, is concerned with the aggregate of many subscribers' traffic and is a much more expensive and capable networking device than is an ONT.
- Internal to the PON link between the OLT and ONT—in the case of both EPON and GPON, the PON specifications provide detailed functionality for the handling of this shared medium resource, and the PON system equipment designers and implementers will typically have followed the specifications very carefully to ensure compliance of their equipment to the PON standard. The uniqueness of an individual system implementer/vendor for this well-specified part of the PON system is typically in how the system is presented to the operator, including how much control over the individual attributes of the QoS subsystem the operator is provided.

PON Access System Integration

Direct integration is to subtended devices directly connected to the SNI and UNI interfaces. The OLT and ONT must integrate at the physical and data link layers with the devices physically subtended to them. Since the devices are standard Ethernet on both sides of the interface, the physical layer connectivity, whether copper or optical, is well understood. From a data link layer perspective, the service model definition will define the virtual local area network (VLAN) tagging modes, 802.1p prioritization marking, aggregated physical interface groups, resiliency model, and other pertinent layer 2 transport attributes.

Indirect integration of the OLT and ONT to other nonsubtended devices providing networking services (for higher networking layers, typically at layer 2 and above) is required for subscriber equipment to gain access to those networking services supporting the service models. The OLT and ONT work as secure interfaces, meaning they are operator-controlled devices which accept provisioning only from the network provisioning systems, and they provide logical data elements which allow other devices to authenticate requests for network services from subscriber devices. Depending on the type of service model and subscriber device or whether the service interface is actually embedded in the ONT, these secure data attributes supplied by the interface can vary, and will be explored in more detail.

Forced Forwarding Upstream

The purpose of forced forwarding is to protect each subscriber's data from inadvertently getting to his neighbor. Forced forwarding accomplishes this by not letting data cross from one user to another in the PON system. To ensure the secure transmission of subscriber data from the ingress at the UNI port—through the access system and out through the egress at the SNI—the subscriber traffic is directed via L2 forced-forwarding through each part of the PON system, disallowing the ability to switch locally or peer-to-peer in a hairpin along its forwarding path. Upstream from the UNI ingress point no local switching is allowed internal to the ONT UNI ports (assuming that there are multiple ports in the ONT device). This is often called *switching isolation*. This may be disabled by the operator, but in practice it is typically a default setting. In the multidwelling or multibusiness case, where several subscribers may be using the same ONT device for services, this is a critical function to isolate the traffic of each subscriber using the MDU (*multidwelling unit*—an ONT serving multiple apartments or businesses). When the subscriber traffic is in the shared medium PON link, it is protected within either a GEM (*GPON encapsulation method*) port in the GPON case or an LLID (*link layer identification*) in the EPON system. (Both a GEM port and an LLID are packet encapsulations that ensure that the packet is delivered only to the port for which it is intended.) In the PON link, this is typically implemented through the restricting switching between ONT stations, or peer-to-peer switching. When the data reach the OLT, and are switched upstream through the OLT system to the SNI egress point out of the PON system, the data are protected by their VLAN partitioning and the use of either MAC forced forwarding or switching protection available in the switching fabrics which make up the Ethernet switching implementation of the OLT system. In this case, the Ethernet frames are forced to proceed out certain ports in the direct path to the SNI ports and internally prohibited to either switch to another part of the OLT or back to the port on which they entered the switch. This is also sometimes referred to as *split horizon*. However, this is, strictly speaking, a routing term.

These switching constructs are alluded to in the GPON standard. Page 20 of ITU-T G.984.1 (03/2008),[i] in the description of the data functions, mentions that there are "several mainstream arrangements of VLANs; these are specified in [b-DSL TR-101] ."[ii] The handling of traffic in a split horizon methodology (i.e., traffic forced upstream—not allowed to switch on the ONT or OLT, but rather forced to be forwarded from the UNI to the SNI) is covered for GPON in

TR-156.[iii] TR-156 specifies the usage of GPON access in the context of TR-101 (which defines Ethernet access networking architectures and guidelines), and TR-200,[iv] which specifies the usage of EPON access in the context of TR-101.

The protection of subscriber data via the separation of L2 data flows in this way is an important aspect of access systems and PON systems in particular. The VLAN architecture determines how many subscribers and devices (or alternatively L2 endpoints or MAC addresses) are included in each VLAN. In the event that the OLT is architected as a multibladed, distributed Ethernet switch, the VLANs can cross Ethernet switch ports and be allocated across switching domains. For example, one VLAN may contain only a single ONT or even UNI—or one VLAN may contain a number of ONTs or UNIs—either way the enforced separation of those data flows is key to subscriber security. Whether the VLAN is allocated across the entire OLT, on a single OLT line card, or a single PON port within the OLT, the network operator needs to understand and sometimes force how the frames will be switched—based on the equipment vendor implementation and the control points that the solution provides.

The VLAN allocation will determine the number of included MAC address endpoints and the resulting size of the broadcast domain. Since all the devices in an individual broadcast domain "see" each other, i.e., will receive broadcast messages originated in that broadcast domain, in general the number of devices should be limited in size to reduce the number of endpoints which generate and receive broadcast traffic together. Lastly, in an access system the best practice is to prohibit Ethernet frames from egress on the same port on which they are received (i.e., the port on which their MAC address is learned). In summary the primary operational aspects of L2 forced forwarding are:

- ONT UNI port isolation;
- Prohibiting peer-to-peer local switching between ONT stations on the PON link. A notable exception to this rule is sometimes allowing ONT stations to receive peer-to-peer VoIP traffic on the voice service VLAN. Another exception is to support business connection between ONTs on the same PON.
- The usage of switching protection or isolation based upon logical or physical interfaces; or MAC forced forwarding in the upstream internal to the OLT system.

Security of the Shared Medium

Among PON system operators, a common fear is that the PON link presents a special security hazard. Due to the nature of the shared medium, all ONT stations sharing the PON link "see" (that is, receive) the downstream data for all the other ONT stations. On the PON link, the question is not will the ONT receive its data, but more importantly, where and how will the data received, but not destined for a particular ONT station, be discarded? In the upstream direction, one ONT does not typically "see" data from other ONTs due to the way the optical path is constructed. Thus, this discussion applies to downstream data.

ITU-T G.984.1 on page 11, in Section 15 Security, mentions that "Due to the multicast nature of the PON, GPON needs a security mechanism adapting the following requirements: (1) to prevent other users from easily decoding the downstream data. (2) To prevent other users from masquerading as another ONU/ONT or user. (3) To allow cost-effective implementation." In order to meet the intent of the specification, several methods are utilized in the practical implementation of PON systems.

- OLT MAC learning—normal Ethernet switching gets the frames through the OLT implementation to the correct PON port;
- PON link standard containers (EPON and GPON)—implementation-specific traffic holders of the PON link which secure the subscriber traffic; For example, 802.3 EPON encodes the LLID in the Ethernet frame preamble and the ONT PON Soc will discard downstream traffic not destined its assigned LLID;
- PON link encryption—the ONT station and the OLT utilize shared key encryption to allow secured reception of the standard data containers for each ONT station. Each ONT uses a different encryption key to receive data from the OLT. It is not possible for one OLT–ONT link to learn the encryption key of another link;
- ONT-specific implementation of downstream data services (include handling of unlearned unicast/multicast, etc.) treat the ONT as an access system device—not a general purpose switch.

Fig. 10.4 shows the interaction of these methods for securing the shared link. The OLT MAC learning gets the data switched to the correct PON port. The PON link standard data containers are the constructs used by the PON link to package and send the data to the correct ONT station. The PON link encryption ensures only data received by the ONT station for which the information is destined will be received, all other data will be dropped. Once the data bound for the ONT station are decrypted, the ONT functionality of MAC learning (i.e., forwarding frames only on ports for which the destination MAC address has been learned) are followed. Additionally, security measures, such as discarding frames, which are not bound for any learned MAC address on the ONT, dropping non-IPTV multicast control frame traffic (unless the ONT has been configured to flood those frames as part of the specific data service applied to the ONT), and limiting broadcast frames are typically provided in the ONT basic functionality.

ESSENTIAL TRANSPORT MODELS

Data services in the access network are typically transported by the OLT via layer 2 VLANs, with the allocation of VLANs to data service defined by a tagging

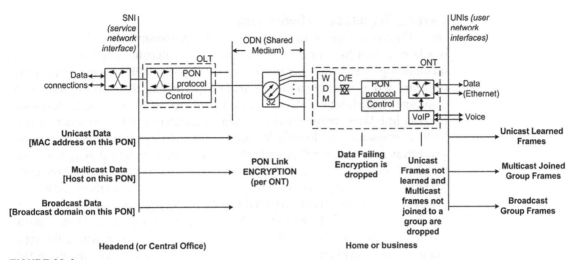

FIGURE 10.4

Shared medium data path.

mode or tagging model paired with a logical to physical mapping of the VLAN to a subscriber or group of subscribers. There are a number of potential tagging modes (i.e., single tagged, double tagged), which fit different service model application types and two VLAN mapping topology models, as well as the additional L2 networking support functions of prioritization and L2 switching.

The OLT may also provide L3 or routing functionality as part of its data path processing and protocol support, with the ability to forward frames at both L2 and L3. The addition of L3 functionality at the OLT provides potential scaling and functionality capabilities, but at the cost of potential increased complexity in the implementation of the data service model. The OLT may also provide what is considered layer 2.5 support which is implemented by protocols such as MPLS (Multi-Protocol Label Switching). The inclusion and specific implementation of these types of L3 and L2.5 capabilities are driven by the upstream core and transport networks, where higher layer network capabilities may certainly be employed and therefore desired in the OLT access network.

The ONT also includes layer 2 and potentially layer 3 interfaces. In general, the ONT is providing support for the two transport mechanisms via: (1) a bridge mode or switching function implemented as Ethernet or Wi-Fi service interfaces, (2) a residential gateway or routing function with an IP interface as a services endpoint, and (3) additional service interfaces such as a voice interface. The data service model for these interfaces also includes specific networking capabilities to allow the ONT to identify and request services from the networking support functions such as DHCP (Dynamic Host Configuration Protocol) servers further upstream in the core network.

Layer 2 Transport—Switching

For FTTH access systems, the basic transport mechanism over which data move is a layer 2 switched, or alternately bridged, architecture. The basic transport methodology is switched, because in practice modern PON systems are typically implemented as directly connected arrays of switching elements, resulting in a distributed switching architecture. Directly connected networking devices over the data link layer are the purview of layer 2 protocol practice, so this falls naturally in the switching domain. Within the OLT/ONT system and at the ingress and egress points of the OLT and ONT to the upstream and downstream networks (into or out of the UNI and SNI), as previously defined in our basic PON data model, the transport of data frames is via the ubiquitous Ethernet data link protocol. The exception within the OLT/ONT system is the shared PON medium, which in the case of EPON and GPON have their distinct point-to-multipoint handling of the OLT to ONT data link. The use of Ethernet switching throughout the PON system allows the utilization of key services of Ethernet networks: VLAN tagging, Ethernet priority marking, and Ethernet switching—allowing careful management of the data link layer throughout the PON access system.

- VLAN tagging models ensure the logical service grouping and identification of service flows through the OLT/ONT system. Next, defining appropriate VLAN models, associating the VLAN over physical partitions of the OLT/ONT system, and placing the subscriber services into the appropriate VLAN topologies for those service types, is the key L2 design point of the PON access network, with the selection of the VLAN topology enabling the correct scaling and security of the service.
- Ethernet priority marking ensures the correct handling of Ethernet frames for various service types in relation to each other, when the frames are competing for shared resources amongst themselves in queues at L2 ingress and egress points through the system. Note that prioritization can also occur at L3.
- Ethernet switching based on MAC learning, but also utilizing security features such as forced forwarding, logical or physical switching protections, frame filtering (also known as access control lists), and broadcast domains allow the scaling and security of the layer 2 component of the PON system.

VLAN Architectures

PON access system VLAN architecture consists of a VLAN tagging mode, a VLAN distribution or topology model, and a priority marking.

VLAN Tagging in Networking Standards

Designing appropriate VLAN architectures utilized in PON access systems using the defined tagging modes is a topic addressed in several standards which seek to cover the PON access space, or in standards specific to other existing types of access networks, which have since been applied to PON access networks.

A quick overview of what these standards address will allow us to create a unified treatment which will allow the PON network operator to design their VLAN tagging models appropriately based upon the service type, how that service is VLAN tagged and transported within the PON access system, and how that service is received and delivered to the networks upstream and downstream of the PON access system. Additionally, the network operator will be able to fashion a set of service models based upon the capabilities of their particular vendor solution and its capabilities with respect to the standard tagging models.

VLAN tagging modes are identified in a number of standards, initially for general networking, and ultimately for application in access networks. As the number of separate PON standards for access networks has been defined and more standards bodies have widened their scope of definition to include PON access networking, the number of available standards which provide VLAN tagging mode guidance for PON networks has increased. Table 10.2 provides a mapping of the applicable VLAN tagging mode standards guidance and the relevance of each for the individual PON access network types. Essentially, the access standards and PON-specific standards take advantage of the original networking VLAN tagging mode definition. These standards are useful for further study, and to allow the tagging modes to be put into context for service implementation, allowing us to create a unified definition for service models practical for modern PON systems.

Note that these standards may or may not be supported in particular manufacturers' equipment, so ensure what is required to supply the services for the network and that the requisite standards support is included.

VLAN Tagging Modes

The IEEE 802.1Q standard defines the basics of single VLAN tagging operations, including the contents of the VLAN tag and how it is to be setup and utilized in switching operations. Furthering the functionality of the basic VLAN tagging operation, the IEEE 802.1ad standard addresses the concept of double VLAN tagging—allowing two VLAN tags to be added to the Ethernet frame. For the purpose of the PON access system, both tagging types are important and used in designing the layer 2 architecture. These basic VLAN tagging capabilities are used for both commercial and residential data services.

In addition to the basic Ethernet standards which define the attributes of the VLAN tag, other standards bodies provide directly applicable guidance for utilizing these tags at a system level for both commercial and residential services. Table 10.3

Table 10.2 Ethernet Standards for VLAN Tagging and Service Architectures

Standards Area	Standard	FTTx Applicability
IEEE Ethernet	IEEE 802.1Q	Basic Ethernet standard describing the mechanism and format for VLAN tagging
	IEEE 802.1P	Basic Ethernet standard describing the mechanism and format for VLAN prioritization
	IEEE 802.1ad(S/C)	Ethernet standard describing the methodology of using VLAN tagging to transport subscriber data across extended carrier Ethernet networks
IEEE EPON/EFM	BBF TR-200	Broadband Forum standard which expands on basic VLAN standard theory into a practical set of implementations for service architectures in broadband networks—based upon the important TR-101 standard, but focused here on EPON networks
	IEEE 1904 SIEPON	Extensive treatment of services models for EPON networks, providing practical guidance for implementation
	CableLabs DPoE	CableLabs set of specifications for the usage of DOCSIS as a provisioning methodology for EPON systems. Provides not only guidance for provisioning but service model implementation guidance based upon relevant DOCSIS methodologies
ITU GPON	ITU G.984.4	ITU standard for GPON which provides guidance for the implementation of GPON equipment to support a full set of attributes enabling the deployment of services using the overall FTTx system
	BBF TR-156	Broadband Forum standard which expands on basic VLAN standard theory into a practical set of implementations for service architectures in broadband networks based upon seminal TR-101—but here focused on GPON networks
Metro Ethernet Forum (MEF)	MEF standards	Complete set of standards covering the theory and implementation of extended Ethernet LAN services (across LAN boundaries of geography and equipment vendors to the multisite WAN). The set of standards is often used by other standards in describing such services for commercial networks of various types—at the subscriber level.
	Carrier Ethernet (CE)	Expansion of multisite Ethernet networking theory and practice to multiregion networks for services with well-defined levels of performance. Useful for mapping FTTx network services for operators planning to use the PON network for implementation of parts of the CE network
IETF		Specific Internet standards which are important to switching, routing, performance management, and networking support protocols

defines the VLAN tagging modes which are typically used in PON access systems. For each tagging mode in the table, the following attributes are defined:

- VLAN tagging mode—Introduces the common syntax or nomenclature for the VLAN tagging mode.
- Definition—Supplies a common definition for the VLAN tagging mode. Other definitions may be used, but the ones presented here are typical in practice for a PON access system.
- Description—Provides a description of the tagging operation.
- VLAN model type—Provides the potential VLAN model for the tagging mode. VLAN models are typically applicable to both commercial or business services and residential services. However, some of the modes may be more typically used for one class of services or another.

Table 10.3 VLAN Q-Tagging Modes

VLAN Tagging Mode	Definition	Description	VLAN Model Type	Service Type	Tagging Rule
Q-U	Stack VLAN	Add a single VLAN tag to incoming untagged frame	Typically 1:N	Residential data, residential IPTV	Add tag on ingress to port, remove tag on egress from port, tagged frames received at the port are not allowed to ingress (an exception being downstream IPTV)
QQ-U	Double stack VLAN	Add two VLAN tags to incoming untagged frames	Typically 1:N for the outer tag and 1:1 for the inner tag	Residential data	Add tags on ingress to port, remove tags on egress from port, tagged frames received at the port are not allowed to ingress. Note that if the first tag is added to the frame in the ONT, the second tag may be added in the OLT
Q-Q	Pass-through or transparent VLAN	Receive frames with a specific defined tag and forward	Typically 1:1	Commercial data service (where the VLAN is being transported)	Maintain the received tag, untagged frames, and frames with other tags are not allowed to ingress
QQ-Q	Stacked pass-through	Add a single outside VLAN tag to incoming tagged frame and forward based on that outside tag	Typically 1:1	Commercial data service (where the received VLAN is being tunneled through)	Add tag on ingress to the port for tagged frames with the correct VLAN ID, untagged frames and frames with other VLAN tags are dropped
QQ-Q or Q-U	Always add a tag	Add a single VLAN tag to any incoming frame (tagged or untagged) and forward	Typically 1:N	Commercial data service (where all frames received on the port are being tunneled through)	Add a tag on ingress to any frames, tagged with any VLAN ID or untagged. Remove the tag on egress.

- Service type—Identifies the service types, commercial (business) or residential, which typically utilize the VLAN tagging mode.
- Tagging rule—Specifies the rule defining the conditions under which the tag will be applied, removed, or modified as the frame is incoming or outgoing from the Ethernet port at the boundary of the PON access system, either the UNI or SNI. For most cases, the tagging model is symmetric such that the rule is applied both at the UNI and the SNI. In some cases this may not be the case, such as with IPTV where the tag may be applied at the UNI port for the ONT side of the tagging rule, but the tag may be applied higher in the network than the SNI. These special cases are addressed as the end-to-end service models are detailed later.

In Table 10.3 the VLAN tagging mode designator "Q" defines a single VLAN tag. The VLAN tagging mode designator "U" defines an untagged frame. The mode definitions, where Q is used to define a single VLAN tag, and QQ is used to define a double VLAN tag, are based upon the IEEE 802.1Q standard. In these cases, the TPID field of the added VLAN tagging header is 0x8100 [the *TPID (Tag Protocol Identifier)* is the Protocol Identifier field of the VLAN tag header, where 0x8100 indicates an 802.1Q VLAN tag]. In Table 10.4, where the VLAN mode is described with an S-tag or C-tag model, the relevant standard is IEEE 802.1ad, with the expectation that the OLT/ONT devices will be able to manipulate and switch accordingly, the TPID field with values other than 0x8100, which is the methodology that standard uses to differentiate the VLAN tagged fields. In Table 10.4, the VLAN tagging modes are extended to include the Q-tagging cases in Table 10.3 with the updated syntax.

The tag application rule, on the ingress of the Ethernet frame into the PON system, is activated based upon attributes which help to identify the frames as belonging

Table 10.4 VLAN S/C-Tagging Modes (S-tag Is the Service Identifier, C-tag Is the Subscriber Identifier)

Tagging Mode	Description	Mapping to Q-Q Modes	Tagging Rule
S-U	Add a service VLAN tag to untagged data arriving at the UNI port	Q-U (add a Q-tag or a stack PVID)	All untagged data will be tagged. Arriving tagged data will be dropped
SX-X	Always add a tag to either tagged or untagged incoming data	Q-U AND QQ-Q (always add a tag, or stack PVID and nested)	All arriving data, either tagged or untagged, will receive a tag
SQ-Q	Add a service tag to specific incoming tagged frames	QQ-Q (double tagged, mapped)	Arriving frames with a different Q-tag than the expected, will be dropped
S-Q	Translate an incoming tagged frame to a service tag	Q-Q (transport tagged, where S=Q or transparent) (note that QQ-QQ is double transparent)	Arriving frames with a different Q-tag than the expected will be dropped. Frames with the expected tag will be accepted and Q-tag translated
SC-U	Add subscriber and service provider tag (S-VLAN and C-VLAN tags)	QQ-U (add double tag or double stack PVID (Port VLAN ID)	Arriving untagged frames will be accepted and double tagged. Arriving tagged frames will be dropped
SC-Q	Translate C-Tag, subscriber identifier tag and add service provider tag	QQ-Q (add double tag, translated also known as nested)	Arriving tagged frames with the expected Q-tag will be accepted and double tagged (or inner tag translated and double tagged). Arriving untagged frames or frames with an unexpected Q-tag will be dropped
	Add single service identifier S-VLAN tag to VoIP traffic	Q-Q (S-Q)	The Ethernet service frames to be tagged are originated internal to the ONT at the VoIP interface
	Add double S-VLAN and C-VLAN tag to VoIP traffic	QQ-Q (SC-Q)	VoIP traffic is typically only single tagged

to the service to be tagged. Other frames not matching the required attributes and therefore not applicable to the service are dropped at that interface. By design, they are not allowed to enter the PON system. As noted in Tables 10.3 and 10.4, the most basic matching rule is whether the incoming frame is tagged or untagged, and if tagged, whether the incoming tag matches the expected required tag.

Some of the additional attributes used to decide whether a tag or tags should be added are defined in the following list, with the first rule as the aforementioned tagged/untagged definition. Note that these attributes are in general more advanced networking attributes than those typically used in most PON implementations.

- UNI port on which the frame is received;
- Received 802.1p priority mark;
- VLAN ID;
- Source MAC;
- Source MAC OUI;
- Source Ethernet type;
- Source/destination IP;
- Destination MAC;
- Protocol type;
- Source/destination TCP/UDP ports;
- DSCP (differentiated services code point) (layer 3 prioritization marking).

Tags are typically added and removed at the ingress and egress points of the access system, i.e., at the UNI and SNI interfaces to the system. However, there are some service models where a tag may be added internally within the PON system. In these cases, the tagging operation still happens at an Ethernet port interface. Even though the UNI port of the ONT is part of a less sophisticated device than the typical OLT SNI interface, typically there are extensive VLAN operations available on current ONT devices as these devices need to handle a number of sophisticated residential and commercial service types. One area where the SNI may surpass the UNI in capability is the number of VLAN operations that can be performed simultaneously. Since the SNI supports all the service flows in a single OLT/ONT system, it handles many more VLAN operations than a typical UNI, where the typical UNI is handling a single VLAN operation.

A case where the VLAN tag may not be removed, but maintained when the frame is passed to the next directly connected device, is the case of VLAN trunking. Typically the VLAN trunking cases occur when an L2 data flow must be maintained between one networking device and another to create a secure conduit or circuit across device types and ultimately across a network. This service attribute will usually be implemented for commercial services to meet Metro Ethernet Forum (MEF) or carrier Ethernet capabilities and requirements. Essentially these are service models where an Ethernet circuit must be projected across multiple L2 connections, creating an "extended" Ethernet service. In many PON deployments these service types will be implemented and the key points to consider are the capabilities of the next directly connected device to either the UNI or the SNI interfaces and the direct integration of the PON system with that next directly connected device. VLAN tags should be maintained and prioritization marking should be maintained. If the tagging and prioritization attributes are to be changed as they are transported out of the PON system, then the next directly connected device will need to support VLAN translation and priority marking translation operations—and in fact, the PON system may need to also support these operations as well. MEF CE2.0 certification has recently become a mandatory requirement for operator to select FTTx system equipment. Typically at least CE2.0 E-Line and E-LAN services must be supported, and support of E-Access service is desirable.

VLAN Model Topology

Applying the VLAN tagging mode to a single individual ONT within the PON system provides a 1:1 VLAN architecture—for example, the specific VLAN is configured to provide a single VLAN tag on a single UNI port on a specific ONT within the PON access system (regardless of the PON on which the ONT resides). Applying the VLAN tagging mode to a set of ONTs within the PON access system provides a 1:N tagging mode. The number of physical interfaces and ONTs that the 1:N VLAN encompasses depends on whether the VLAN must cross PON boundaries to include ONTs on different PONs within the OLT. These two basic modes are defined further in Table 10.5.

L2 Quality of Service (QoS)—Prioritization Marking and Handling

The services traversing the PON access system ultimately arrive at a point within the architecture where they are competing for shared network resources not plentiful enough to supply the demand of all the services simultaneously. In typical PON access systems, these points are at the interfaces into and out of the system

Table 10.5 VLAN Topology Descriptions

VLAN Model	Description	Typically Associated VLAN Tagging Mode	Applicability of the VLAN Model
1:1	VLAN or combination of VLAN tags contains a single participant	Can be single or double tagged. If double tagged then the service is usually trunked to the upstream network	This tagging model is used to transport a unique data service for a single VLAN participant across the access network. Used for residential and business data services
1:N	VLAN contains numerous participants	Will typically be single tagged	This tagging model is used to transport a shared VLAN data service for multiple participants across the access network. Used to transport telephony or IPTV data services. If used for data services, then the number of participants in the VLAN may be restricted to only those on a single PON or subset of PONs within the OLT

(e.g., ports of various types—PON ports, UNI and SNI ports), across interfaces or busses that aggregate traffic from a number of sources together (e.g., across backplanes or between chips in the design) or through switching fabrics which must switch traffic for all services in one element of the design (e.g., in a single card of a multibladed system). In order for the system to operate properly with the data services all receiving the appropriate amount of resources a QoS strategy must be implemented. The QoS strategy contains the following elements:

- Relative prioritization amongst the service packets;
- A methodology for marking the services indicating the relative prioritization placed on them;
- OLT and ONT mechanisms capable of enforcing the allocation of resources, based upon the priority marking.

To accomplish the strategy, a network engineering plan for relative priority must be established for each data service. Table 10.6 shows a typical priority mapping for the L2 services in a PON access system. For each data service in the table a relative priority is selected based upon the requirements of the service for delivery (best effort or guaranteed, for example), network resources (required bandwidth), network performance attributes (latency or delay and jitter or variation in delay as examples). As the criticality of the data service increases in the table, the resulting resources required for the service increase as well. To indicate the relative priority, each VLAN, or combination of VLANs in the double-tagging case, representing an instance of a service, is marked using the 802.1p L2 VLAN priority indicator of the previously defined Ethernet frame's header. These markings are indicated in the table using a numeric value from zero to seven. Finally, in the implementation of the switching fabric, each of the priority levels is assigned to a queue in the switching infrastructure. In the example here, the eight levels of L2 prioritization are assigned each to a single queue, since there are eight available queues in the system. However, each system implementation may be different in the number of queues and, therefore, the priority levels could be assigned differently, i.e. if there were only four queues in this part of the system, priority levels could be assigned as follows: 0 and 1 assigned to queue 0, 2 and 3 assigned to queue 1, 4 and 5 assigned to queue 2, and 6 and 7 assigned to queue 3. In fact, a full system implementation from UNI to SNI (and SNI to UNI) may include different switching infrastructures that differ in the number of queues available. In such cases, the assigned levels may differ based on where the QoS model is implemented. Note also that the system queues are the attribute of the QoS system that is examined closely, there may be other resource mechanisms in the QoS system, and they may have other considerations beyond the queue mapping enumerated here.

In implementation, the PON system will typically enforce the prioritization marks as defined here by default, since L2 prioritization is so well-known and widely implemented within switched networks. However, if there are special

Table 10.6 Example Relative Priority Plan for PON Access System

Data Service	Description	Relative Priority	Typical Marking (L2 With 0–7 Level Marking)	802.1p Queue (Example Only, Number of Queues Depends on Implementation)
Best effort data service	Residential level Internet data services	Lowest priority traffic which is best effort delivery, not guaranteed delivery	0	0
Business service data tier	Higher-priority data services for businesses	Business traffic which is to ensure delivery, carries higher relative priority than standard residential services data	1	1
IPTV	Broadcast IP-based video service, which can also include on-demand video services	Video requires dedicated bandwidth to ensure network jitter and latency attributes and therefore requires guaranteed resources	2	2
VoIP signaling	VoIP traffic which contains call control traffic	Telephony service control traffic is higher in priority to allow for call setup, teardown, and class feature support	3	3
VoIP bearer data path	VoIP traffic which contains encoded speech	Speech and other encoded telephony traffic must be delivered with low latency and jitter and therefore has a higher priority	4	4
Circuit-based data service or SLA-based commercial services traffic	Commercial service which is guaranteed for delivery or which is time- and latency-sensitive and must receive network resources for system operation	These types of services require that the circuit be available at all times, even when subscriber data are not flowing—typically idle patterns or keep-alive frames are present to ensure proper circuit operation	5	5
Access system management data	Management traffic internal to the PON access system	Network operator management services required for delivery even if resources are scarce	6	6
Highest-priority traffic reservation	Reserved for the highest-priority traffic for network operator usage	Highest priority, the traffic must be delivered	7	7

priority markings required, the system may require the implementation of special filters or access control lists to implement the required prioritization. Depending on where in the FTTx access system the special prioritization is required, the implementation may take different forms. This is perfectly allowable; the important point is to ensure that the priorities are defined and the implementation complete and tested such that the system design intent is met—ensuring that higher-priority traffic will be provided sufficient resources for traversing the network, and delivered based upon the network measurement performance criteria as discussed previously: without delay, with low jitter or with acceptable packet loss, or no loss of packets depending on the type of data and the acceptable service level.

When designing the QoS mapping across the FTTx system each component of the system needs to be independently evaluated, allowing the end-to-end prioritization of each system to be recognized and documented.

Layer 3 Transport—Routing
Layer 3 Forwarding
Increasingly FTTx access systems are beginning to provide basic L3 forwarding and routing capabilities as part of their transport feature set. Examples are the DPoE compliant L3 services. The inclusion of layer 3 functionality does not preclude the usage of the very capable layer 2 transport capability that has been so widely deployed in access systems in general and PON systems in particular. Some of the driver for the addition of L3 is due to the more recently available multilayer switching platforms available to the FTTx system designers. Given that the features are available it makes sense to provide them to the network operator. At the same time the access systems which are now being fielded are increasingly large scale and the ability to support large numbers of devices (ONTs and the CPE devices behind them) is key. At some point a large L2 network can become unwieldy. Also, depending on the number of VLANs required for different services, the ability to have the VLANs terminate at the OLT operating at L3 becomes an advantage.

Additionally, as the FTTx access technology is fielded into more areas where previous technologies utilized L3 transport systems, especially for high-speed data services, standards are indicating the requirement for forwarding and routing as part of the feature set of the OLT. Ultimately, this puts more requirements on the OLT to support service models that include functionality previously provided by a router. However, with the availability of more complex switch chips and increasing capacity in OLTs, these types of requirements can be met. As an example, DPoE compliant EPON systems as deployed in MSO networks typically require L3 service capability to be backward compatible with DOCSIS cable data services.

In addition to basic feature support, the OLT can now be a peer router to the core network, or in the case of a routed transport network, a peer to the transport routers. The newer PO system equipment, typically capable of 10G PONs (10G-EPON or XGSPON), is therefore now designed in a chassis with main router blades and PON module as a linecard.

Routing Protocols
The clear requirement for OLTs providing routing functionality is that they provide not only mesh routing protocols like OSPF or IS-IS, but also edge

routing capability such as BGP. Add the requirements for multicast routing for handling IPTV broadcast video and the number of protocols supported increases considerably. Coupled with IPv6 requirements, this means the OLT is clearly becoming a capable router as well.

Depending on the architecture and size of the OLT, the L3 functionality may not always be resident on the PON-specific technology component. However, at least at the interface to the upstream network the OLT will need this functionality for interfacing to its next hop router.

L3 Prioritization

Traffic prioritization and QoS concepts at the routing layer still apply in order to differentiate traffic types and provide them the resources they require to ensure the services. Regardless of whether the OLT is L2 based or is an L2/L3 multilayer device, L3 prioritization should be appropriately handled since the OLT typically has the ability to inspect packets for access control lists. Typically, the expectation is that services which are terminating on an L3 endpoint within the access system, such as VoIP services, will be marked with appropriate L3 prioritization (marked in the IP DSCP field), which should be handled by the OLT just as easily as L2 prioritization. This capability and the necessary configuration should be confirmed by the network operator.

Access Edge Transport Considerations

Some OLT implementations also provide MPLS and other layer 2.5 and above transport schemes. This implementation may also be driven by specifications for OLT functionality that require this level of transport capability. This is typically either from vendors who have significant functionality experience in this area and can bring excellent implementations into the access equipment from general-purpose multilayer switches, when the OLT is used to provide this feature set termination beyond the transport or core and into the access network partition. Additionally, a number of the standards bodies are beginning to include L2.5 edge transport in the access partition requirements.

SERVICE MODEL ARCHITECTURES

To allow operators to develop and document how the PON and its service supporting attributes integrate into an access network, the elements of a service model need to be established. A service model is a useful abstraction that allows the identification and description of elements common to services within the framework of an access network, and the supporting upstream core or transport networks which supply the services to the access network.

Service Specification Methodology

A standard methodology for completely describing a PON access system service model is completed in two parts—in practice any service model can be mapped using these principles:

- Firstly, using the previously established unified PON access network model in combination with the layer 2 and layer 3 transport models, the standard PON system interfaces and data path partitions are defined and the important attributes enumerated.
- Secondly, the following service model supporting functions are defined and described.

PON System Service Model Partitions

Using the unified PON system model in Fig. 10.3, the following partitions of the model provides the framework and detailed descriptions for each of the data interface points, data paths, and embedded service interfaces of the PON system, to create the first part of the service model specification.

UNI Port Interface

The ONT UNI port provides the service ingress and egress point from the access network to the subscriber or premise data service device/network. As such it provides the necessary capability to provide to the premise network appropriately tagged and prioritized Ethernet frames (specific VLAN tagging modes, defined previously, depend on the data service configuration). The ONT UNI also provides the necessary addition or manipulation of incoming frames for specific tagging modes and prioritization to support the service definition. Depending on the ONT UNI implementation, there may also be rate limiting associated with this interface. Note that the ONT UNI port can encompass other physical service interfaces such as Wi-Fi interfaces and alternative distribution interfaces such as MoCA. The ONT UNI must be capable of delivering networking services as a trusted or untrusted interface into the PON system, appropriate to the networking layer it is supporting—typically as a layer 2 bridge, but there may also be an embedded residential gateway within the ONT operating at layer 3. The UNI interface is also a service ingress and egress port and therefore must directly integrate with the devices subtended to it to support the service model, as well as indirectly integrate with networking services elements in the upstream network.

- Addition or modification of VLAN tags (tagging modes), along with prioritization (adherence and manipulation of 802.1P prioritization), and placement into appropriate queues based on the modified marking. When the ONT is remarking prioritization received from subtended devices, and then acting on the updated priority, this is considered untrusted operation. Typical best practice is to employ untrusted operation. When the ONT is acting upon prioritization received from subtended devices, without using its own ability to remark the priority, this is considered trusted operation. In that case, the ONT has been explicitly told to trust the prioritization it receives with the packet. Trusted operation typically exists due to ONT's lack of QoS remark capability.

- Depending on the infrastructure of the ONT UNI, support for L3 prioritization markings, as well as trusted/untrusted L3 operation may also be available (i.e., DSCP or differentiated services code point marking).
- Secure interface functionality—capabilities of the ONT UNI to provide a secure interface within a protocol exchange, resulting in the unambiguous and controlled allocation of network resources for a specific subscriber device or set of devices. Examples include:
  - DHCP relay—the ability of the ONT UNI to insert secure elements into the DHCP protocol exchange between client and server devices.
  - PPPoE intermediate agent—the ability of the ONT UNI to insert secure elements into the PPPoE session setup exchange.

ONT Data Path

The ONT data path provides key networking resources to support triple play services for both internal service interfaces and devices subtended to the ONT UNI ports—it requires the capabilities to provide L2 switching/bridging (always provided at a minimum), IP forwarding (L3 capability to transport frames is often present in modern ONTs), and a number of other networking features.

- For L2 networking functionality, typical for bridged networking—for both residential and commercial data services—the ONT acts as a switch, managing and conserving critical resources such as bandwidth and MAC address table resources. It has the ability to adhere to the switching and priority marking of VLAN tagged frames via the placement into appropriate queues based on the priority marking.
- For L3 networking support functionality—typical for L3 routed networking (note that the inclusion of residential gateways embedded in an ONT device is a relatively recent addition to typical ONT capabilities)—the ONT has the ability to provide router/gateway features. Depending on the infrastructure of the ONT data path, support for L3 prioritization markings may also be available [i.e., DSCP (differentiated services code point) marking] independent of the residential gateway functions below:
  - Integrated NAT and firewall;
  - Packet inspection and filtering;
  - DOS attack prevention;

- URL content filtering;
- DSCP prioritization;
- PPPoE client—the ability of the ONT to act on behalf of subtended devices as a client interface in a PPPoE (Point-to-Point Protocol over Ethernet) session;
- WAN IP interface (an interface which acts as an IP client and receives an address via DHCP for example or through direct provisioning).
- In addition to switching and routing decisions, the ONT data path must allocate and enforce QoS functions and interface with upstream networking services (for example, DHCP servers). Other networking capabilities provided by the ONT for services support include the following:
  - IGMP processing (typically IGMP snooping in ONT devices)— the enabler protocol for IPTV—in which the ONT consumes and processes IGMP frames, and based upon the protocol exchanges processed, switches IPTV frames appropriately to subtended devices [typically IPTV set-top boxes (STBs)]. An ONT lacking IGMP snooping will use resources less efficiently by requiring multiple streams of the same program if more than one subtending device is watching the same IPTV show. IGMP is very common in ONTs supporting multicast distribution. Refer to Chapter 12 regarding IGMP processing and multicast distribution;
  - Quality of service is implemented by the adherence to prioritization marking (in either L2 or L3). While these resources may be dynamically allocated in various points of the network, typically they are statically reserved for the various services the ONT is designed to handle. The three mechanisms of the QoS subsystem for the ONT are defined here:
- Queuing—ability to place frames into differing priority queuing mechanisms based on marking, and the management of the differing queues based upon mechanisms internal to the ONT. Note the treatment of queues on the PON interface, spread over a number of ONT stations on the PON shared medium, would be a different subject—the current subject refers to internal queue capability within the ONT; Queue scheduling types- being strict-priority-queuing (SPQ) or weighted-round-robin (WRR)- provides additional knobs to prioritize the traffic;
- Bandwidth—capability of the ONT to provide packet processing speed (here the goal, at least internal to the ONT, is the ability to process frames at wire speed with no blocking between subsystem-level devices within the ONT);
- Rate limiting (sometimes called *policing*)—similar to bandwidth, but specifically the ability of the ONT to limit the rate of packets (traffic) transmitted in either the upstream or downstream direction, based upon an attribute of the service frames or the physical interface on which the service frames are received. For example, this would be

a mechanism to limit Internet access speed to that for which the subscriber has paid. Depending on the type of data services, single-rate or dual-rate policers may be required.

ONT Services Interfaces

Internal interfaces within the ONT which are service initiation and end points, are typically IP host interfaces which require IP address provisioning through either DHCP or direct provisioning. They require the ability to interface with upstream networking services as a client device for the transport and prioritization marking of frames (at L2 or L3) originated by these interfaces. Additionally, if they are IP interfaces they require protection at the service interface from broadcast storms, for example, so ACLs are typically available as well.

Broadcast RF video distribution is the ability of the ONT to receive downstream broadcast RF video via an RF overlay, and produce coaxial RF output into the premise. As established previously, RF overlay may contain analog or digital video. The upstream return path for the video service may be implemented in a number of ways, but in general the ONT has the ability to transmit back upstream interactive information to the service provider's RF controller. The upstream return path originates in the STB provided as part of the RF broadcast system. The PON has no interaction with it other than to transport the data (though transporting the data will require special hardware in the ONT). A useful adjunct resource is a feature which allows for remote service disconnect via the element manager. This allows you to connect and disconnect video service without rolling a truck to the subscriber. Chapter 11 has more information on broadcast RF video.

The ONT has the ability to provide packetized (and prioritized) VoIP, including the ability to perform analog-to-digital conversion of speech and modem communications and encoding and packet processing of the transformed data into a VoIP data/bearer path. It will also provide VoIP protocol interaction with an upstream call agent device (for example, a soft switch) for call setup, signaling, and tear-down, as well as the reverse operations for received VoIP from the call agent. The ONT will present itself as an IP client since the voice interface requires an IP address for operation as an endpoint. Once the speech is encoded, the entire operation becomes, in fact, a specialized data service with special delivery requirements, namely delivery with low latency and jitter. Chapter 13 has more information on VoIP.

PON Link

The (point to multipoint) PON link managed by the OLT is well understood in terms of what functionality it provides to the medium shared by the ONTs. The important aspects for defining service architectures are that the configurable attributes which differentiate the services on the PON link are specified (per the PON equipment vendor), and that each of those attributes has a well-defined value for each service.

OLT Data Path

The OLT data path is the networking subsystem which supports all data services transported on the OLT, the physical interfaces upstream to the operator network, and management of ONT devices. Typically for data services it provides considerable functionality and scalability for switching, routing, and QoS handling for large numbers of subscribers and subtended CPE devices—including L2 or L3 prioritization marking and handling—and L2 or L3 trusted interfaces, which may act as DHCP relays or perform operations based on secure provisioning actions. Depending on the complexity of the OLT architecture, the configuration and provisioning of the OLT data path for services may require a considerable element management system and/or CLI provisioning interface. Given the typical scale of an OLT, and the criticality of the data services carried over its architecture, a fully featured networking and QoS system is expected including multilayer protocols, resiliency, and high levels of scalability and interoperability with other networking devices.

SNI Port Interface

The SNI port interface is implemented in the OLT typically using multiple high-capacity Ethernet ports (40Gb/s per port are not uncommon) which interface directly to the operator's transport or core networks, providing Ethernet frame ingress and egress. Similar to the OLT data path requirements, the OLT SNI needs the ability to transport VLAN-based services with the considerable ability to manipulate type, tagging mode, prioritization marking, trust mode, ability to tag/retag VLANs, and trunk to upstream devices. To secure the data services with this architecture, expect multiple SNI interfaces with resiliency via redundant physical interfaces and higher layer protocol support for quick switchover timing, and high data rate capacities with ability to handle all service requirements for a large number of subscribers at either L2 or multilayer L2/L3.

Service Model Supporting Functions

The following supporting areas are part of the service model abstraction, with key points and considerations highlighted for each.

- Network insertion point for data service integration—The point where the service enters the network, and requirements for the service to make its way to the correct ONT and finally to other premise service equipment subtended to the ONT. Considerations: What attributes of the service are inherited from the upstream service provider? Which elements of the service must be manipulated by the access network to ensure end-to-end operation?

- Service transport—Elements of the service that allow it to be transported through the network through varying types of transport equipment. Considerations: If the service requires transformation or modification through the various types of transport systems, how is this accomplished? How does the access network utilize the transport attributes of the service when it arrives at the SNI or the UNI?
- Service assurance—Elements of the service which assure its transport through the network when combined with other services competing for resources within the network using QoS functionality. Service assurance may also include aspects specific to resilience or redundancy. Consideration: How does the access network also utilize the service assurance attributes? How does the access network device provide assurance in the upstream direction of the network?
- Secure interfaces—Provisioned attributes of the access network maintained by the service provider, are hidden or not available to outside entities in the network, and which identify the subscriber or some aspect of the subscriber, such that a service may be deployed to that subscriber uniquely and securely.
- Scalability aspects—Attributes of the service providing opportunities for the access network to grow to large numbers of subscribers. Consideration: What attributes of the access network are required to be carefully constructed such that network resources are not consumed unnecessarily as the numbers of ONT devices in the network grows? What levels of oversubscription are typical and acceptable, and based on these numbers what is the plan for network expansion? Most operators tend to keep their oversubscription levels secret, so you will probably have to experimentally figure out what is safe. This, of course, requires monitoring the amount of traffic you are handling, and cross-referencing that with customer perceptions of your service. We know that web browsing and email will tolerate very high oversubscription. IPTV may not tolerate as much, but will certainly tolerate a fair amount of oversubscription.
- Provisioning aspects—Attributes of the service model provided to the access network equipment used in the delivery of the service. Considerations: Where may the provisioning information originate, be maintained, and under what circumstances may it need to be updated? Just as important as the information is the method of delivery of the provisioning information.
- Service ingress and egress points—Elements of the service leaving the access network via the UNI and arriving at the subscriber's premise equipment and the converse—elements of the service provided by the subscriber's premise equipment and delivered by the access network via the SNI. Considerations: What attributes does the service maintain at the point of being provided to the subtended network equipment? What attributes of the service are provided as the entry to the access network from the operator's viewpoint?

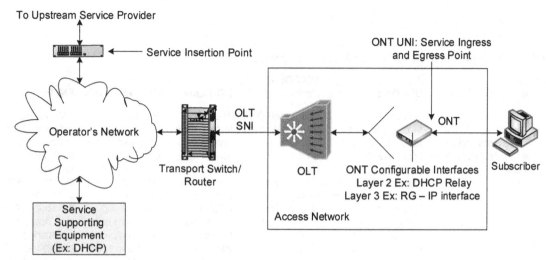

To Upstream Service Provider

Service Insertion Point

ONT UNI: Service Ingress
and Egress Point

Operator's Network

OLT
SNI

ONT

Transport Switch/
Router

OLT

ONT Configurable Interfaces
Layer 2 Ex: DHCP Relay
Layer 3 Ex: RG – IP interface

Subscriber

Access Network

Service
Supporting
Equipment
(Ex: DHCP)

FIGURE 10.5

Access network integrated to high-speed data service model.

HIGH-SPEED DATA SERVICE MODEL

Fig. 10.5 is used to describe example HSD data service models using the methodology just developed. The figure shows the access network engaged with the upstream network as well as the subscriber premise network. The OLT and ONT enable the high-speed data service by providing and participating in the network model partitions and the service support functions detailed in the following paragraphs.

Example Service Model Partitions

Here two data service types are considered. The first is a high-speed data service for residential subscribers. The second is a high-speed data service for commercial business subscribers. The system partitions for these are described in Tables 10.7 and 10.8.

Network Insertion Point

Depending on the data service type, the service insertion point may be at several points within the operator's network:

- For data services which interact with networks-at-large outside the operator's network, the northbound entrance to the operator's network is via an upstream service provider's interface.
- Within the operator's network for private services or business services which stay within the network service, insertion is typically provided by the operator's network equipment (private service model).

Table 10.7 High-Speed Data Service Model Residential

Service Model	Description	UNI Port	ONT Data Path	PON Link	OLT Data Path	SNI Port
High-speed data service residential	Best effort service for residential subscribers	Add two VLAN tags, the inner tag to identify the particular subscriber, the outer tag to identify the OLT on which the service is present. Untrust the incoming frames and mark them with a low priority marking for 802.1p. If a specific data rate is called for and the ONT can enforce the rate, then do so here	Ensure the ONT is honoring the marking of the data service frames and that sufficient resources are allocated for the service to be delivered through the ONT data path	The PON link must be provisioned for the data rate at which the service is being offered. Ensure that the PON link transport mechanism prioritizes the data frames appropriately	This subscriber's data are competing with other subscribers for the resources of the OLT, therefore the QoS subsystem must be set to enforce the markings of the data frames	If the service will be trunked to an upstream device for subscriber assurance and accounting then the VLAN tags may be maintained across the SNI. If the service is to be routed upstream the OLT may provide a routed interface and the VLANs dropped at the SNI

Table 10.8 High-Speed Data Service Table Commercial

Service Model	Description	UNI Port	ONT Data Path	PON Link	OLT Data Path	SNI Port
High-speed data service commercial	Prioritized service for business subscribers	Add two VLAN tags, the inner tag to identify the particular location of this commercial service, the outer tag to identify the commercial service customer throughout the operator's access and transport networks	Ensure the ONT is honoring the marking of the data service frames and that sufficient resources are allocated for the service to be delivered through the ONT data path	The PON link must be provisioned for the data rate at which the service is being offered. Ensure that the PON link transport mechanism prioritizes the data frames appropriately	This subscriber's data are competing with other subscribers for the resources of the OLT, therefore the QoS subsystem must be set to enforce the markings of the data frames	For the commercial subscriber, if the service is multisite, the VLANs may be maintained across the SNI to allow the secure connectivity between the locations

In either case, whether the primary insertion point does or does not interact with networks outside the operator's network, the operator may provide specific infrastructure for handling the service or some important part of the service such as:

- Rate limiting of the service (will probably be provided in the access network using the OLT or ONT capabilities or via a BRAS or specific rate shaping device at a higher point in the network);
- Tracking usage and metrics of the service (such as implementation with a BRAS or via SNMP data gathering of the ONT interfaces);
- Marking of the service for differentiated handling by resources supporting the service through the network equipment (will typically be done at the entrance to the network in the case of a northbound service model but the marking of frames appropriately is fully expected to be handled at the ingress to the ONT device from the subtended services devices in the premise);
- Capture of services data for troubleshooting and monitoring (data capture will typically be unobtrusive to the subscriber population) and will likely be accomplished at an unused SNI port by traffic mirroring;
- Layer 2 VLAN tagging or routing (depends on service model type, but will be done at the insertion point to the network and at the ingress to the network at the ONT UNI).

Service Transport

Data services in the access network are transported via layer 2 VLANs, with the allocation of VLANs to data service defined by a tagging mode or tagging model which fits a logical to physical mapping of the VLAN to a subscriber or group of subscribers. As shown in the two examples in Tables 10.7 and 10.8, there are a number of potential tagging modes (i.e., single tagged, double tagged) which fit different service model application types depending on how the service is to be used—i.e. leaving the access network and continuing on as a layer 2 service or terminating the VLAN at the access network SNI and continuing on as a routed service. The ONT may also include a layer 3 (routed) interface, and yet the services will still be transported on a tagged VLAN service. In the upstream core and transport networks, higher-level networking capabilities may certainly be implemented (MPLS, for example). In general, the OLT and ONT are flexible in providing support for the two transport mechanisms, (1) a bridge mode or switching function and (2) a routing function with an IP interface as a services endpoint as the data service may be transformed as it flows across the network.

Service Assurance

The high-speed data services are assured by the QoS handling as described in all the phases of the access network, by providing mechanisms for both adhering to and modifying as necessary either 802.1P or DSCP markings. The other supporting equipment in the network will use the same strategy. Depending on where the equipment is in the network, these markings may be changed, but they are expected to be controlled tightly within the access network (the OLT/ONT system). And certainly the access network will operate according to these markings—providing appropriate queuing, bandwidth, and rate limiting to the service.

Trusted Interfaces

To support the dynamic allocation of networking resources to subscribers in a controlled and unambiguous manner, the access equipment provides the network operator the ability to securely provision OLT and ONT. During later transactions, when the subscriber is requesting network resources, the OLT and ONT (one or both depending on exact design) inserts itself as a relay device, identifying itself and subsequently the attached subscriber via the insertion of trusted data elements into the protocol exchanges or requests for services by the subscriber CPE.

From a layer 2 perspective the ONT will typically provide either a DHCP relay function, or a PPPoE intermediate agent function. For either of these support functions a number of data elements are available to uniquely identify the relaying device. The exact specification of the relay is dependent on ONT specific implementations, but the operating team should be well aware of the options available and how they can integrate into the services infrastructure like DHCP servers. Insertion of DHCP option-82 Circuit ID and Remote ID is nowadays supported on almost all vendors' ONTs.

From a layer 3 perspective, the ONT can provide an embedded routing or residential gateway function. While providing services to the subtended subscriber devices and network, the ONT provides a secure client interface to allow the allocation of an IP address to the L3 interface via DHCP. In this case, the ONT's WAN or RG (residential gateway) interface is unambiguously identified for secure provisioning operations.

Scalability Aspects

In order for the data service model to be scalable, the OLT and ONT should provide the following:

- Broad Transport Resources—the allocation and tagging mode of VLANs required to implement the service without restriction, i.e., full VLAN ranges are supported. Note that in practice a few VLANs may be reserved for special usage and not available for allocation to subscriber services (e.g., reserved for management) but this should be a small number.
- Service assurance—the prioritization of L2 and L3 assurance markings without the need for provisioning of this capability all the time—unless the operator has identified a special handling case that needs to be provisioned.

- Trusted interfaces—these must be provisionable by the management systems, but should also contain default values which are specific to the OLT and ONT devices in their factory-fresh state, or other values which support the scalability and growth of provisioning and deployment processes and systems:
  - Topography of the network;
  - Unique and unambiguous attribute of the ONT device for a relay function (its MAC address);
  - Autogeneration of relay attribute based upon provisioning by the management system.

Other aspects of the ONT device:

- Rate limiting—the application of rate limiting must be based upon a set of criteria not specific to any subtended device which may change (for example, a specific MAC or IP address). This typically drives rate limiting based upon logical attributes (flow-based) or upon a physical interface (port-based) or a combination of both these types of attributes. ONT-specific implementations will drive the available criteria for rate limiting.

Provisioning Aspects

The access equipment parameters are to be part of the OLT and ONT basic infrastructure (especially for those attributes unique to each ONT device, i.e., client or relay identifiers), but must also be available to be controlled, maintained and provisioned by the network operator. The OLT/ONT management system can provision these or they may be driven by a higher-layer OSS system which can specify either the parameter itself, or a selection of parameter type. For example, for scalability and to support a number of different installation and deployment models, the DHCP relay function may include several selections which are provisionable.

Service Ingress and Egress Points

The ONT UNI and OLT SNI provide the service ingress and egress points from the access network to the subscriber or premise data service device/network and the operator transport or core networks. As such they provide appropriately tagged and prioritized frames (specific tagging modes depend on the data service logical attributes). They also provide the necessary addition or manipulation of incoming frames for specific tagging modes and prioritization to support the service definition. Depending on the ONT implementation, there may also be rate limiting associated with this interface in the upstream and downstream directions. With the OLT SNI, rate limiting is typically not used or required.

VoIP TELEPHONY SERVICE MODEL

The ONT supports VoIP telephony services in the PON access network by providing the ability to convert analog speech to packetized VoIP frames (and the reverse operation—packetized voice back to analog speech) and support the call signaling (setup and tear-down) interfaces with upstream call agents and media gateway functions. Fig. 10.6 provides an overview of the ONT device integrated into a VoIP service model framework. Table 10.9 summarizes important information about handling voice traffic.

Network Model Partitions

Table 10.9 describes the VoIP telephony service model network partitions.

Network Insertion Point

The VoIP service is typically inserted into the network inside the operator's network space (the concept of a VoIP service provided via call agent outside the operator's network is valid but not considered here). The call agent and media gateway equipment implementing the VoIP service will provide specific VLAN tagging and layer 2 and/or layer 3 prioritization to the voice protocol signaling and bearer paths. Or, alternatively, the directly interfaced networking equipment may provide this networking support. From the ONT perspective, this tagging and prioritization support provided by the upstream core and transport networks will be valid and typically honored directly by the ONT device.

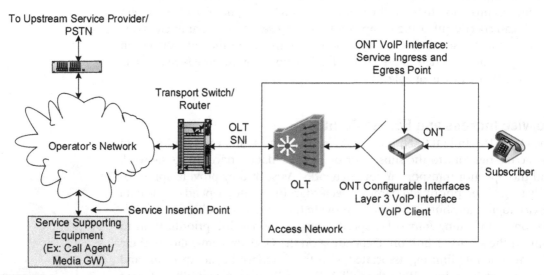

FIGURE 10.6

Access network integrated into VoIP service model.

Service Transport

The VoIP protocol is transported as either an L2 or L3 data service. Since the VoIP endpoints (call agent and ONT device) are IP interfaces, there is expected to be some L3 networking involved in the core, or transport, sections of the overall network. From the ONT perspective, the VoIP protocol is typically a single tagged L2 service (single provider network). The number of ONT devices participating in the L2 service depends on the specific OLT implementation, but would likely be a single VLAN for the ONT devices subtended to a single OLT device. Note that in the event of multiple voice service providers in an open access network, the individual service providers would be assigned to unique VLANs allowing the services to be transported independently. Of course, for that case, each transported VLAN stream would require requisite marking and prioritization handling to ensure the service.

Service Assurance

VoIP services, due to their delay dependence and time-critical nature, are treated with higher priority than other services when they are transported via networking devices which share resources with other services. From the ONT perspective, the VoIP protocol is marked with L2 and L3 prioritization when the services are packetized. This marking will typically have a default value, but is also available to be provisioned. Note that in some VoIP protocols, the call agent or media gateway may specify the L3 service assurance markings to be used, while the L2 marking is typically associated with the operator's overall networking prioritization design.

Table 10.9 VoIP Telephony Service Model Network Partitions

Service Model	Description	UNI Port	ONT Data Path	PON Link	OLT Data Path	SNI Port
VoIP telephony service	Prioritized packetized voice data service	The voice data service is not sent to the ONT UNI so external support is not required [unless the VoIP is supplied by a subtended MTA (media terminal adaptor)]	ONT data path provides critical packet marking and prioritization support as well as QoS handling to ensure the voice traffic is handled properly	There will be voice traffic from a number of ONT devices, so this traffic must be handled by the PON link as priority data and will be provided high prioritization to ensure throughput is available	Voice traffic as an overall component of the data traffic on the OLT is not large, but since the criticality of the data requires specific resources the data path must enforce QoS	Voice data traffic incoming and leaving the OLT must be tagged and marked to identify it for handling as it is incoming to the access network

Trusted Interfaces

The ONT IP interface for VoIP will present itself as a VoIP client device, which will require an IP address for operation. The IP address may be provisioned directly, but likely will require networking support to securely provide an IP resource. The client attribute of the ONT device will likely be programmed in the factory and will be unique to the ONT device. There may be provisioning aspects to change this client attribute, but typically it is not required to do so.

Scalability Aspects

Since the VoIP interface provides a client which is uniquely addressed, and since this is handled by each ONT device, the provisioning of this interface is scalable. You will typically use the default attributes of the ONT device to support scalability. The bandwidth requirement for VoIP services is, by comparison to other services in competition for resources, very minimal.

Provisioning Aspects

Provisioning the VoIP service has two distinct considerations:

- Common VoIP service provisioning attributes—components of the VoIP protocol, which are common to all the voice end-points. The provisioning may be provided via a setup file or a default provisioning function since there is not a specific, unique attribute for each ONT device.
- Unique VoIP interface component—the VoIP endpoint is unique to each ONT, and therefore requires specific handling per ONT device. However, the unique client attributes will identify each endpoint to the supporting IP address allocation infrastructure, allowing the provisioning to be handled per device, but with a common mechanism.

Service Ingress and Egress Points

The service ingress and egress points are internal to the ONT, such that the tagging and prioritization are handled internal to the ONT device and are expected to be set up as part of the ONT default provisioning, since these are common across all ONT devices (at least those subtended to a single OLT), but will also depend on the overall core and transport network design, especially if the OLT devices are in different parts of the overall network or in different networks. For the OLT, the prioritized voice traffic must be accepted and handled properly due to its critical requirements for low latency and jitter.

IPTV SERVICE MODEL

Packetized video services are delivered to the access network as multicast packets (in the case of broadcast video) or as unicast (in the case of on-demand services). Note that in specific implementations the STB may utilize unicast or multicast interchangeably, depending on some attribute that is trying to be minimized, such as channel change time, but these are implementation specific. Fig. 10.7 provides an overall architectural view of an IPTV service model integrated with the PON access network.

In Fig. 10.7, the set-top boxes which are subtended to the ONT may be connected to multiple ports on the ONT, or they may be connected to another switch which is then connected to the ONT. For the case of the ONT providing direct connectivity to the set-top boxes, the IGMP snooping and other networking services of the ONT will be sufficient for the IPTV service. In the case of another device between the ONT and the set-top box, the other device must provide the requisite network services to support the IPTV service as well. From an ONT perspective, the support required for integration into an IPTV service model is networking-related and therefore is a special case data service. However, there are some IPTV-specific services and resources which are required for this service integration and those are detailed as follows.

Network Model Partitions

Table 10.10 describes the IPTV service model network partitions.

Network Insertion Point

The insertion point of the IPTV service is typically within the operator's network, both for multicast- and unicast-based services. The interfaced networking equipment may provide the required tagging and prioritization support, but these may be provided by the IPTV origination equipment. In either case, the OLT and ONT will support these tags and prioritization markings as they are defined by the service insertion point, unless they need to override them.

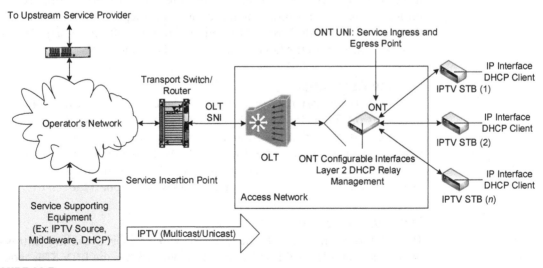

FIGURE 10.7

Access network integrated into IPTV service model.

Table 10.10 IPTV Service Model Network Partitions

Service Model	Description	UNI Port	ONT Data Path	PON Link	OLT Data Path	SNI Port
IPTV	Video delivered as packetized multicast frames or on-demand video delivered as unicast frames	The ONT UNI port must receive the IGMP protocol frames for tagging and marking, delivering the multicast and unicast frames to the subtended STB typically as untagged	The ONT data path will process the frames based upon prioritization marking, as well as supplying IGMP functionality	The PON link must ensure the upstream bound IGMP protocol frames are prioritized over other traffic to support video service availability. Typically they are prioritized just below voice traffic	The OLT will be handling extensive amounts of multicast traffic and must have the IGMP processing power as well as QoS facilities to scale to large numbers of video streams. There may also be IGMP and/or multicast routing requirements of the OLT as well	The upstream interface into the video subsystem requires receiving the multicast distribution and tagging and priority marking it (here assuming untrusted operation unless the upstream distribution can be trusted)

Service Transport

IPTV as a packet service relies on each of the components of the core and transport networks to switch the service frames through to the access network. The VLAN tagging and prioritization supplied by the service insertion point are honored through the OLT and ONT. Because it is a "networking"-dependent service, IPTV depends on IGMP as an enabler protocol, to ensure that the multicast channels or groups are switched appropriately—i.e., only when they are needed—to preserve network resources. From the access equipment perspective, this is very important, as not all multicast groups are required on the ONT device and the devices subtended to the ONT for IPTV services also are have finite networking resources. Therefore, the ability of the ONT to support IGMP protocol, typically as a snooping device, is a key integration point. Within the OLT, sometime IGMP Proxy is also required to more effectively handle IGMP control packets from the large number of ONTs on the PONs.

Service Assurance

Typically IPTV service will be prioritized at a higher priority than the data services in the network, but below the critical VoIP (and any other voice-related services), per the overall network prioritization design—also implemented in the OLT and ONT. From an upstream perspective, the ONT will provide the appropriate prioritization for IGMP protocol messages received from subtended devices for usage by the ONT and upstream networking devices which support the service.

Trusted Interfaces

The ONT supports the subtended services devices by providing untrusted interfaces in an identical fashion to data services. Since the IPTV STBs require

IP addresses for their IP interfaces, the ONT offers a DHCP relay function to ensure that the protocol transaction is secure and reliable. The inserted relay attributes are ONT implementation specific, but the design intent is common. Note that depending on the middleware support for DHCP, this function may be handled by an outside DHCP function.

Scalability Aspects

Scalability for IPTV services should include the following ONT support:

- Transport Resources—the ONT will need fewer tagging modes than for data services since the IPTV support is generally tagged per OLT device (i.e., all the subtended ONTs on the OLT may participate in the same IPTV service VLAN, although this is OLT and ONT implementation specific).
- Service assurance—the ONT will operate on the prioritization markings set up by the IPTV insertion point.
- Trusted interfaces—the ONT device must support the subtended STB devices, and can provide DHCP relay values that promote scalability and the ability to integrate with the middleware function as well (for example, if some attributes of the ONT are used to bind with the STBs connected to the ONT).
- Rate limiting—the IPTV service, since it is primarily a downstream service, will require the most significant bandwidth through the ONT device in that direction, but this bandwidth is typically set up as part of the service provisioning process and therefore is quite scalable. On the upstream side, the bandwidth requirement for incoming IGMP messages is small in comparison to the downstream. The bandwidth for IPTV is asymmetrical.

Provisioning Aspects

The provisioning of ONT attributes required to support IPTV is identical to the basic data networking infrastructure. Sometime operators will rely on the ONTs to restrict the number of active IPTV channels and/or to enforce a channel plan that the subtended STBs can request. The integration with OLT/ONT management or higher-level management systems will be the same. Typical deployment models for the IPTV service devices closely resemble data services devices, with simplified tagging and prioritization models.

Service Ingress and Egress Points

The IPTV service is generally untagged on the egress from the ONT device. The ONT is expected to provide the capability to tag appropriately and priority mark the incoming IGMP service frames for processing upstream to support the service model. The service entrance and exit from the OLT is generally more complicated since it is dealing with many IPTV/multicast streams, and in addition to IGMP operations may even be working with the upstream network via multicast routing. As the number of TV channels dramatically increase nowadays, the capacity of OLT's multicast address table and per-VLAN multicast registration become more and more important.

RF VIDEO SERVICE MODEL

RF video services for ONT devices are delivered via the conversion of optical RF overlay, on a separate wavelength on the PON from the data services wavelength, to an RF output signal which is provided to the premise devices over a standard coaxial premise plant. The ONT integration for this service type, since it is geared toward a broadcast option, does not rely on downstream networking support. In the return path or upstream direction, the ONT may or may not provide necessary networking support. Depending on the implementation of the upstream data path there are three approaches typically:

- The first is an integrated packetized approach where the RF return path is digitized in some fashion and sent upstream via an embedded IP service interface in the ONT.
- The second is available as a data service via an ONT UNI (Ethernet) interface to RF set-top boxes which are IP aware.
- The third is a fourth optical wavelength (typically 1610 nm) on the fiber, dedicated to transporting upstream traffic from RF set top boxes.

Fig. 10.8 shows the integration of the ONT into the RF service model.

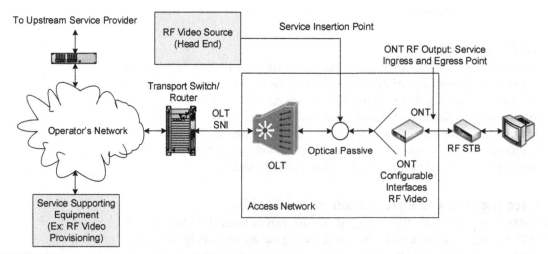

FIGURE 10.8

Access network integrated into RF video service model.

Network Model Partitions

Table 10.11 identifies the RF video service model network partitions.

Network Insertion Point

The RF video service is inserted into the services path at downstream from the OLT interface to the PON.

Service Transport

Since the RF video service is not a networking service, it does not use L2 or L3 networking, but is transmitted over an optical overlay. Of course the return will require data services if the first or the second approach mentioned above is adopted.

Service Assurance

Since the RF video service is not a networking service, it does not use L2 or L3 service prioritization markings.

Trusted Interfaces

The ONT provides a trusted management interface to allow the provisioning of the RF video port (i.e., turning the RF port on or off).

Scalability Aspects

Each ONT video port (assuming an MDU ONT with multiple video ports) is typically separately identifiable and therefore may be provisioned as the ONT is brought online or as services need to be enabled or disabled remotely. The ability of the OLT/ONT provisioning function or the upstream OSS provisioning

Table 10.11 RF Video Service Model Network Partitions

Service Model	Description	UNI Port	ONT Data Path	PON Link	OLT Data Path	SNI Port
RF video	Broadcast RF video overlay	Output is an RF port available on the ONT. If return path integrated data service operations are required, these will be provided using one of the three methods enumerated above	If integrated or IP enabled return, then RF return traffic should be prioritized and handled accordingly. Check with the set-top box manufacturer, but the data may not need to have very high priority	Same as for ONT data path for all the ONTs on the PON link if integrated or embedded return	Will be treated as a prioritized service for all participating ONTs if integrated or embedded return	The return path data will traverse the access network upstream to the service end-point. Thus the traffic must be tagged with QoS to ensure that the customer expectations for interactive services are met

function allows the scalable handling of the RF service. This so-called service disconnect feature is generally not available in HFC networks unless extra-cost addressable taps are used. It can come almost for free in FTTH.

Provisioning Aspects

Each ONT video port is typically separately identifiable via its ONT device and may be provisioned individually. This is particularly useful in multidwelling situations, in which customer turnover is often high. It is not necessary to roll a truck to connect or disconnect service.

Service Ingress and Egress Points

The RF video service exits at the ONT device via the dedicated RF interface. The RF video service return path will also ingress into the network via the RF interface, but the upstream network path may differ depending on the implementation of the return path function described above.

OVERALL SERVICE MODEL PLANNING

Using the general service model methodology for the low-level details, an access network integration strategy can be designed, resulting in services that are secure, scalable, and manageable. The following top-level design considerations are followed at a high level to guide the application service model methodology for data, voice, IPTV, and RF video.

- For each service model, define where the service will enter the core and transport networks—the service insertion point upstream of the access network. Consider the following aspects of the service insertion:
    - How will the service be transported through the network to the PON access system?
    - What prioritization markings will be used?
    - What does each piece of networking gear through the network use for transport and prioritization?
    - Where are the likely areas for resource constraints and competition for network resources? Ensure that those areas handle prioritization of the services properly.
    - Will the PON access system use the same attributes for handling the allocation of service resources? If not, what are the capabilities available?
- For each service model define what access network specific features are required to support the service:
    - Trusted interfaces where the OLT and ONT will participate in supporting the networking transactions of subtended devices.
    - Trusted interfaces where the ONT acts as a client device and must provide identification of its own trusted interface.

- Ensure that these interfaces provisioning and attributes interface into the supporting infrastructure of the upstream network.
- Ensure that the provisioning support for each of the trusted interfaces and networking support in the OLT and ONT provides a scalable solution—ensure that default provisioning or operational provisioning supports each interface in an automated fashion to allow scalability of network equipment deployment in customer premises.
- Ensure that for each trusted interface the method of delivery of the provisioning data is secure and scalable via automation.
- Ensure that the service ingress and egress of the OLT and ONT system (in both upstream and downstream directions) to the upstream and premises networks are well understood for tagging modes, prioritization marking, and rate limiting of the services. Ensure that the OLT and ONT devices support all the service model required features and are provisionable in a scalable fashion. Finally ensure that the data paths through the OLT and ONT equipment support the networking and QoS features needed to assure the services.

CONCLUSION

This chapter describes the elements of the PON system data networking architecture and the typical residential and commercial data services in a PON access network. Next the PON-specific attributes in the EPON and GPON standards for data networking are detailed as background for presenting a unified model of a PON access network for the treatment of data networking service models. Along with the definition of the unified PON access network model, other important PON-specific attributes of FTTx networks: PON system integration, forced forwarding upstream and security of the shared medium are described. Next a detailed treatment of layer 2 and layer 3 transport models provides the background for service model definition. In the final sections, the necessary design attributes of transport models utilized in practical PON access systems are defined and presented. A unified service model methodology that shows where L2 and L3 interfaces occur in the PON access system is set forth and applied, allowing the reader to design such service models with their chosen equipment vendor. Since PON access equipment is by design networking equipment, the OSI networking model is used to define the L2 and L3 transport functions of the system.

Endnotes

i. https://www.itu.int/rec/T-REC-G.984.1/en.
ii. https://www.broadband-forum.org/technical/download/TR-101.pdf.
iii. https://www.broadband-forum.org/technical/download/TR-156.pdf.
iv. https://www.broadband-forum.org/technical/download/TR-200.pdf.

CHAPTER 11

Video Overview and Broadcast Video Architecture

INTRODUCTION

Some small fiber-to-the-home (FTTH) operators, and perhaps those considering an FTTH network, have thrown up their hands and decided that offering video is too hard, and that they can exist by just selling data and maybe voice services. We strongly recommend against this approach. True, video is a little complex, particularly acquiring the programming, and because the programmers demand high payments for their product, the margin for video is lower, and shrinking, compared to other services. However, it remains an important service to be considered. Well over 90% of the population in North America still watch broadcast video many hours a day, more hours than they spend watching video on computer and portable devices. Omitting video from your service line-up leaves you vulnerable to another service provider who DOES provide video, and who can also sell data and voice services to your subscribers. The cable TV industry learned long ago that the more services you sell to a subscriber, the "stickier" that subscriber is—he is more likely to stick with you rather than go to another provider.

There are factors to consider when determining if, and how, video should become a part of your mix of services. First, how well are the incumbent providers serving the market with video services? Are they delivering an extensive line-up of programming with a sufficient array of popular features, such as high-definition programming, video on demand (VoD), video on the go (for mobile devices), multiroom DVR, etc.? If so, will you have sufficient capital to invest in developing and operating a competitive video service? Second, what is the nature of your market? Is your market mostly comprised of single-family homes, or does it have a large number of apartments and other multiunit buildings (hotels, dormitories, retirement/nursing homes, hospitals, etc.)? Is your market stable, or transient? What are the age and income demographics? A competent and experienced consultant can assist the operator in assessing all of these factors. He or she should be able to project about 10 years out, as far as your financial model for video goes.

235

FTTx Networks. http://dx.doi.org/10.1016/B978-0-12-420137-8.00011-1

BROADCAST VERSUS IPTV

Broadcast video is the older of the two video delivery methods we will talk about, the other being IPTV, in the next chapter. Why should you care about broadcast video if you have an FTTH network? Well, you might or you might not, depending on your background and comfort level with the two technologies, as well as your current plant status. One way or the other, you should read this chapter, as we will introduce a number of concepts that carry over into IPTV. We will talk about the way the television industry is generally organized and how revenue flows (rather, we will present an oversimplified model of a complex and constantly changing set of revenue flows). We will also discuss acquisition of video programming. Then we'll get a bit more technical with a brief introduction to video. So far all of what we talk about will translate directly into IPTV. But then we will talk about subjects of particular interest to those carrying broadcast video.

TV pictures are gathered together in one place called a *headend*. The headend is roughly analogous to a *central office* in telephone company terminology. Larger systems today may operate one or two headends in an area, plus a number of *hubs*, or places where video and other signals are distributed to groups of subscribers.

Broadcast Video

Broadcast video is transmitted over FTTH networks the same way that it is transmitted over cable TV networks, so you get the benefit of over 60 years of refinement of the product. You get the benefit of high-volume production of well-understood transmission equipment and techniques. Generally, in our experience, while we have seen FTTH operators be successful with IPTV transmission, we have seen people implement broadcast video with fewer start-up problems, and usually at lower cost, though this may change in the future.

A major advantage to broadcast over IPTV is also a major source of headaches for the operator, and that is the in-home wiring. Most homes in North America are wired for internal broadcast distribution today, by virtue of having coax already installed to TVs. You can use this infrastructure when you install service, eliminating a major expense for IPTV operators, the need to install category 5 or 6 wiring in the home. Installing new wiring can be very expensive. The bad news concerning the existing coax wiring is that if the installation is old, it may not be good enough to carry all of the services you offer, particularly if you use frequencies higher than those used by the incumbent service provider you are replacing. Systems today use frequencies up to 1 GHz in some cases, but wiring installed in the early 1990s, may not handle frequencies above 600 MHz or so, since that was the limit at the time of installation. So even if wiring is already installed, you may need to do some refurbishing when you install service.

You are almost certainly going to need two-way communications with one or more set-top boxes (STBs) in the home in order to provide modern services, such as VoD, programming that the subscriber buys when he or she wants it. All broadcast STBs sold in the cable TV industry have this capability, and have a headend system to control the box. But they are designed to get communications upstream using the so-called sublow (upstream) frequencies, in North America, 5–42 MHz. Cable systems have the ability to get these frequencies back to the headend, but you will have to do something special in an FTTH system. FTTH systems have no inherent way to get RF signals back from the STB to the headend. Several countermeasures have been developed to address this. One system digitizes the upstream communications from the STB and sends the communications back on the normal 1310 nm data path. At the headend the digitized signal is converted back to RF and supplied to the headend control system.

Another way to get communications back is to borrow a page from radio frequency over glass (RFoG), and include in the optical network terminal (ONT) a 1610 nm upstream laser, which is only turned on when RF from an STB is detected. This optical signal goes back to the headend, where it is turned into RF and again supplied to the headend control system. Compared with the digitized system described above, this system tends to be more expensive (though the ONT manufacturer may adsorb some expense) and complex to make work, but due to timing constraints of some STB communications systems, it works with some systems that the digitized system will not work with. Finally, STB manufacturers may offer Internet protocol (IP) communications from the STB to the ONT using a data-over-coax solution such as MoCA or HPNA. So you have solutions, but you need to talk to both the ONT manufacturer and the STB manufacturer, to make sure you have a solution that works.

Internet Protocol Television

Internet Protocol Television (IPTV) is favored by those who don't have experience with broadcast technology but who do have experience with data networks. We must be very quick to point out that a data network is not necessarily a suitable delivery network for IPTV due to the inability of IPTV program streams to tolerate the variable delay of a data network. This issue is covered in much more detail in the next chapter, but we repeat it here because of the number of people we have seen get in trouble because they didn't understand video's needs.

The other issue concerning IPTV is one we mentioned above, and that is the fact that you are going to have to get data to each TV location in the house, and very few houses have suitable wiring. So you are either going to have to provide a category 5 or 6 cable to each TV location, or you are going to have to bear the expense and headache of installing a data-over-coax solution such as MoCA[i] or HPNA.[ii] Both technologies convert Ethernet to RF, and form a network using existing coax wiring. Either can be made to work, but either can have issues with using the coax wiring in a way it was not intended to be used—every home is different; some homes will install in a breeze, others will not. Finally, some people think of using the more advanced forms of WiFi to connect TVs. This may work in some cases, but our experience is that putting video over WiFi is going to lead to problems in many (though not all) installations, not to mention security issues.

Think hard about multidwelling units (MDUs) in your service area. They will require rewiring for IPTV (and data), and will you be able to absorb the cost of rewiring? Will you have access to the units, or will the owner deny you access to do rewiring? A good consultant, who has expertise with all aspects of dealing with MDU issues may be an excellent investment.

PROGRAM AND CASH FLOW

The flow of money and programs in the television industry is a complex and ever-changing picture, but at the risk of seeming prematurely obsolete, we shall attempt to describe things as we see them now. There are two models of which you need to be aware, the broadcast station model and the cable TV programmer model. They are similar and may be getting more so, but they are not the same.

Cable TV systems are mostly owned and operated by large corporations called *multiple system operators* (MSOs). When we talk about local cable systems, we usually mean local systems owned by one of several large MSOs. There remain a few independent cable TV systems and small MSOs; more on them later. For much of the discussion in this section, we can also include satellite distribution companies, which provide essentially the same programming as do MSOs. The FCC uses a generic term for all businesses who distribute programming from many sources: *multichannel video-programming distributor* (MVPD). That terminology is not widely used except in regulatory matters, so we shall more commonly use cable TV to mean any MVPD, be it cable, satellite, or FTTH. We shall try to remember to make a distinction when the discussion is not universally applicable or where the applicability is not obvious by context.

Broadcast Model

Broadcast stations represent the older model, and at one time enjoyed pretty much 100% of the television audience. Today the figure is closer to 47% of the audience, a number which varies by season and by who you ask. Broadcast TV today is dominated by four major national networks in the United States: NBC, CBS, ABC, and Fox. In addition, a number of smaller national networks, CW Network, MyNetworkTV, ThisTV, and Bounce, are developing and are being distributed largely as secondary program streams in a broadcast station's digital signal—in large cities they may have their own affiliated stations.

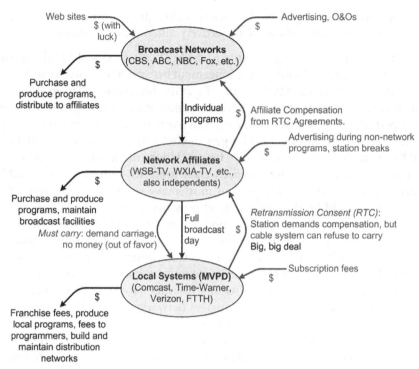

FIGURE 11.1

Revenue flow, broadcast networks and affiliates.

Fig. 11.1 seeks to diagram the main ways programs and money flow in the North American broadcast television industry. Other regions have their own models, some of which differ from this model. First we have the broadcast networks, CBS, ABC, NBC, Fox and others. These people are active in buying programs from outside producers, and they produce their own programs in-house, too. Programs are supplied to their affiliates, stations in each market which have contracted to be the network's outlet in that city. A few affiliates are owned and operated by the network (and thus are known as the O&Os), but most are owned by companies independent of the network. The programs are supplied to the affiliates, which have some (limited) leeway in when they air them, or if they air them at all. The affiliates intersperse the network programs with programs they purchase on their own, and programs such as local news and public affairs, which are produced by the local stations.

Local stations continue to own and operate transmitters for those subscribers who receive programming over the air by antenna (somewhere around 15% of North American subscribers, depending upon whose numbers you believe). The remaining subscribers either get their programming from cable TV, satellite, or FTTH systems. Recently, some subscribers have dropped their subscription to a TV service, and instead get their programming off-air and/or via the web; these subscribers are collectively called the *cord-cutters*.

Local stations provide programming to cable TV, satellite, and FTTH systems in their viewing areas. Unlike the arrangement between the networks and local affiliates, these so-called MVPDs carry the entire broadcast day from the local station without modification. There are two models of providing this programming permitted by the FCC: *must carry* and *retransmission consent* (RTC). Every 3 years, the station (not the MVPD) gets to elect which one it invokes and the MVPD must abide by the stations' choices. Under the must carry election, a station that has a cable system in its coverage footprint demands that the cable system carry it, and the cable system must make room for it. However, the station is not paid by the multichannel provider. The model of choice now, though, is retransmission consent, under which the station negotiates with the multichannel provider, who must pay for the station's consent to retransmit its signal on its system. If a station elects retransmission consent, though, the multichannel provider is free to refuse to carry it at all. However, network affiliation agreements are being structured so that a local affiliate is protected in its market from duplicate out-of-market network affiliates being carried by MVPDs. This gives the local market network station tremendous negotiating leverage as the sole source of its network programming in that market. This leverage has been particularly effective as retransmission consent fee demands have risen sharply in recent years. In exchange for the market protection, the networks are demanding a large share of the affiliate station's retransmission consent fees collected from the MVPD.

The retransmission consent model is a source of much contention between the multichannel providers and the broadcasters. The triennial negotiations pit the distribution of the broadcasters' signal by the multichannel provider to its customers against the availability of network programming from the broadcaster. Many factors enter into the negotiation, such as the number of the multichannel provider's customers (distribution), the strength of the broadcast station's programming, the availability of alternate network stations to the multichannel provider (unlikely), and the presence of competing multichannel providers in the market against whom the broadcast station can leverage its network programming. It is not uncommon for a broadcaster to withhold its consent for a multichannel provider to carry its signal after a negotiating deadline has passed, but generally agreement is reached between the two parties and carriage resumes.

Money Flows in Various Ways

Besides the capital and operational cost of running their facilities, a major expense for the networks is the purchase or production of programs. Their primary revenue stream is advertising they sell during programs they supply to the affiliated stations. As mentioned above, networks are now demanding increasingly higher shares of retransmission consent revenue from their affiliate stations, which amounts to billions of dollars annually for the networks. Of course, the networks derive revenue from their O&Os as well as their network operations. Not shown, but all of the major networks also own several cable programmers, which we'll cover below.

Besides the traditional sources of revenue, the networks have for some time been developing their presence on the web. Each network has its own website on which it promotes upcoming shows and features shows that have already aired on their network. If the show is produced on the outside, their contract must give them the right to post it to the web before they can do so. Networks walk a fine line between offending their affiliates and deriving revenue from the web. For this reason, shows are not put up on the web until after they have aired on the broadcast network. The web revenue model is a combination of advertising and charging a subscription fee for the most popular programs. In addition, several networks developed a website known as Hulu.com, which carries programming from many networks, produces some programming of its own, and acts as a program distribution facility for certain other websites. Finally, certain programs are made available to Netflix, iTunes, Amazon, and other independent websites. However, the financial model for all of these sources remains, if you will pardon the expression, up in the air. The model continues to be refined.

As this is being written, the broadcast network financial model is that no money changes hands between the networks and affiliates for shows (except, of course, for the RTC money). The network keeps the revenue it earns from advertising sold during shows, and the local affiliates keep the revenue they earn from selling advertising during station breaks and locally purchased and produced shows.

As described above, the TV stations also receive money from local cable systems and other multichannel providers. They also, of course, operate their own websites, where they may post locally produced programs (they usually don't have the right to post network shows), news stories, weather, and other material that will attract "eyeballs." Of course, they receive revenue from the advertising they sell on their websites.

Cable TV Model

The cable TV networks sprang up beginning in the 1980s, as cable TV gained enough viewers to make it worthwhile to program specifically for those viewers. When direct broadcast satellite (DBS) service came into being in the 1990s, at first the cable programmers were under extreme pressure to not make their programming available to the satellite people, but after government intervention, the programming was made available. Today, these cable networks collectively enjoy about half the viewers in the US, though the broadcast networks

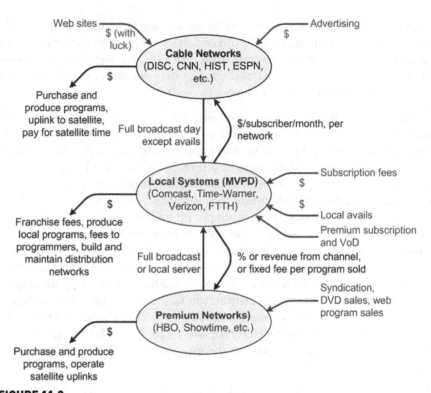

FIGURE 11.2
Revenue flow, cable networks.

each have a larger audience, since there are fewer of them. Sometimes a cable network will come out on top in the audience numbers for a particular show.

Fig. 11.2 attempts to diagram program and money flow for the cable networks. There are at least two different types of cable programming: advertiser-supported, for which subscribers are not charged an explicit monthly fee, and pay networks such as HBO, for which subscribers explicitly pay either a monthly subscription fee or a per-program fee.

The majority of cable networks supply almost an entire day's worth of programming to cable systems. Unlike the local broadcast affiliates, the local cable companies don't pick-and-choose programs and don't add their own programming to that provided by the cable networks. As shown in Fig. 11.2, cable systems pay a per-subscriber fee for programming to cable networks as well as to broadcast stations, ranging from a few cents per subscriber per month, to several dollars for the most popular stations or networks. This revenue paid by the local cable system is part of the subscription fee charged by the cable system, and is not broken out as a separate charge. At this time, about one-half of your video subscription cost goes to pay the cable networks and local broadcast stations. To partially compensate for the per-subscriber fees, the cable networks provide *local avails*, or time slot availabilities, in which the local cable system can sell and insert advertising. Typically, the local system gets a total of about 4 minutes of avails in two blocks each hour. The network transmits a signal to start playback equipment located at the local system, which is preloaded with advertising the local system has sold. For very small systems which cannot afford advertising insertion equipment and the cost of selling ads, the cable network transmits PSAs (public service announcements) during this time.

In addition to the pay programming described below, cable systems frequently have different tiers of programs which subscribers can purchase. There will be a so-called *basic tier*, which includes almost all subscribers, and most programs. Then there may be a foreign language tier or two, for which a subscriber pays an additional fee, and maybe one or two others. There is typically an unadvertised *broadcast basic tier*, sometimes referred to as a lifeline basic tier, which consists of off-air channels and maybe a few public service channels. It is established to provide a minimal level of channels for customers desiring a very low-cost service.

A particularly controversial practice is that cable programmers frequently program several networks, some of which are very popular and some of which are much less so. Programming contracts require that all of the programmer's networks be carried in order to allow the cable system to carry the popular network. At least the popular network is required to be placed on the basic tier, so that nearly all subscribers are included in the "per sub" payment to the programmer, and not just those subscribers who actually want the programming. Sports networks are particularly active with this practice. However, as subscribers continue to react against the high cost of cable TV, and as the Federal government has taken an interest in the situation, we would not be surprised to see changes in the future.

The other types of network feeding into local cable systems are the premium networks, such as HBO and Showtime, which offer movies and original programming for monthly subscription fees and/or *pay-per-view* (PPV), whereby subscribers purchase individual programs. Local systems control the sale of such programs, collect money from subscribers, and forward some of the money to the programmer. Of course, local systems also purchase the rights to show other movies via PPV. Some are offered free to subscribers, others are really "pay."

Local cable systems pay franchise fees to local governments, and of course they pay to build and maintain their physical plants. Their revenue sources are subscriber fees and the advertising they sell. Recently cable systems have been very aggressive in the "anytime, anywhere" movement, allowing subscribers access to as much programming as they have the right to offer via the web, including wireless. Large MSOs have jointly developed a national network of wireless access points available to all of their subscribers.

HOW DO YOU GET PROGRAMMING?

One thing you need to think about regardless of the way you send video to subscribers, is how you will get video. Larger operators will likely negotiate directly with each video provider, and there are many. Smaller operators seldom have the resources to negotiate with each provider, and they would not be able to get the best terms due to their size. So there are buying cooperatives (co-ops) which negotiate on behalf of their members, both for programming and in some cases for equipment. While we have known of smaller operations who have successfully negotiated their own contracts, we don't recommend that you try it unless you are ready to negotiate for tens of thousands of subscribers, maybe more.

Even if you use a co-op to negotiate your programming contracts, you will be left with a handful of program sources with which you must negotiate yourself, most notably local TV stations. See above for the options TV stations have in negotiating carriage on your system.

Most programming will be delivered via satellite, so you will need multiple satellite antennas ("dishes") to receive them. In some cases you may be able to use a special receiving antenna to receive several satellites in closely spaced orbital slots. Besides the dish, you will need receivers, which receive and descramble the satellite signals, and facilities to rescramble then modulate the signals onto RF carriers or to put the video into IP packets for IPTV transmission. Programs are scrambled over the satellite, and you will receive a descrambling key when you sign a contract with the programmer, and identify the receiver you will use. Typically programs will be rescrambled for transmission on your FTTH system, though in some cases you may choose to not scramble them so that your subscribers can receive certain channels without having to use a set-top box.

Co-ops may be able to be put you in touch with consultants who can help with headend design and other details. There are music services that you may want to carry, too. They present their music through the same set-top boxes that you use for video.

Emergency Alert

Cable TV systems and almost certainly FTTH systems are required to issue emergency alerts on every channel. There are companies that specialize in equipment that allows duly certified agencies access to putting audio or video alerts on channels you carry. A typical way this might be done today is to put a crawl across the bottom portion of the picture.

PEG Channels

As a condition of the franchise you negotiate with your city or county governments, you may be required to reserve a few channels for government use. These channels are referred to as *PEG channels*, for public, educational, and government. The government may provide the production facilities, or you may be called upon to contribute to the production facilities—it is negotiable.

Local Origination

Many cable systems operate their own TV channels, usually called *local origination* (LO) channels. Some metro areas have very sophisticated operations rivaling broadcasters, often for continuous local news. Local sports can be a big draw too. Advertising can support the better channels. Quality LO channels can be a competitive asset for an operator, but poorly done operations can be a liability. Of course, you need a large audience base for this to be practical, and if you are entering a competitive situation, you are going to have to think long and hard about your LO operation. A major factor, of course, is what the competition offers, and whether or not your pockets are deep enough to carry an LO operation to profitability.

HOW DO YOU CONTROL PROGRAMMING?

We've alluded to selling programming by the tier, or by individual channels, or by individual programs. You need a way to do this. Whether you are using broadcast video, IPTV, or a mix of both, you will use the same basic control method to deny programs to subscribers who have not paid for them. Programs are sent in *scrambled* form. In the television world, "scrambled" has a different meaning than it does in the data communications world. In data communications, the term refers to combining the data to be transmitted with a pseudorandom bit sequence, for the purpose of removing any dc content from the data, and in the process making sure there are enough transitions for reliable clock recovery. In cable television, though, "scrambling" refers to rendering the signal unintelligible to anyone who does not have the *key* required to restore it to its unscrambled form. You will recognize this as the process referred to in data communications as *encryption*. Sometimes that term is used in television, but for historical reasons, the term "scrambling" is much more prevalent.

The descrambling function is done at the STB in the home. Depending on the scrambling system in use, the key is communicated to the STB. The key applies to a program or channel the subscriber has ordered. If the subscriber has not ordered the program, the key is not supplied to his box.

An STB controller in the headend manages all communications with the STBs, interfaces with a billing system to receive information on what subscribers have purchased, and communicates with the billing system as to what programs were purchased within the STB. The purchase of programs in the STB used to be called *Impulse Pay Per View* (IPPV) or some similar name; today most people seem to have dropped the word impulse, because that is how everything is ordered. The term *video on demand* (VoD) is common today. This is the most common means of allowing a subscriber to order individual programs today; the subscriber presses keys on the remote control to order the program. The STB has an upstream communications channel through which it reports these purchases back to the STB controller. Typically, when a subscriber orders a PPV program, the STB communicates the request back to the headend. The PPV file server system determines a free channel on which to send the program, and so informs the STB. The billing system is, of course, informed of the transaction. The process is invisible to the subscriber.

Several methods of sending communications upstream are used. In conventional cable TV systems, the upstream spectrum is reserved in the lower portion of the spectrum, somewhere between 5 and 42 MHz in North America (the band extends to about 65 MHz in certain countries). Wider bandwidths are being considered in North America. The HFC distribution plant is configured to transport these signals back to the STB controller, along with upstream cable modem signals. When these STBs are used in FTTH systems, at least two different ways of sending upstream signals can be implemented. One is to digitize the upstream signal at the home, and send it upstream on the normal upstream data channel. Another way borrows a technique from RFoG (see Chapter 5), and creates a fourth wavelength on the fiber, which transmits the upstream RF signal. (Some techniques may be covered by patents.)

Sometimes a DOCSIS cable modem may be built into the STB, and it will be used to transport upstream control signals from the STB to the controller. The technique will probably not be useful in FTTH systems.

We have seen STBs with an Ethernet connector on them, which Ethernet connection can be used for two-way control with the STB controller. This can be a good technique, but does require either bringing an Ethernet cable to the STB, or using somewhat costly Ethernet/coax conversion devices (MoCA or HPNA) on either end of the coax. WiFi could conceivably be used, but it has its own installation issues—as stated above, we can't recommend it for video. Except for WiFi, all of the methods we've mentioned rely on the coaxial cable already being used to transmit video signals. Of course, if you are using IPTV transmission, you will be able to work the low-bandwidth control communications channel in with the normal Ethernet communications channel over which you are receiving video and other services. This does require that you bring a data cable to the STB, use a wireless link, or that you use Ethernet/coax conversion devices.

The scrambling system and the STB control system are typically unique to the STB you buy. However, there are some moves in the industry to expand one control system and scrambling system to work over more than one brand of STBs. In some cases MSOs have been successful at pressuring STB manufacturers to allow others to use their proprietary scrambling and control systems. At one time there was a duopoly in the cable TV market, with two companies controlling pretty much all of the STBs and scrambling systems, but this model is receding now.

An obvious question is why use an STB at all; why not integrate the functions into the TV? This has been tried and failed. One of many attempts by the cable TV industry to break the decades-long duopoly in STBs was to define a product called a CableCard, which contained the descrambling portion of an STB, but which could be plugged into either a third-party STB or directly into a TV equipped with a suitable interface. In fact, for a number of years the FCC mandated that the STBs DO NOT have built-in descrambling, but rather, rely on the CableCard for descrambling. However, the approach was a commercial failure, and as this is being written, the rules requiring CableCards have been rescinded.

Switched Digital Video

As an alternative to sending all video signals all of the time, some cable TV systems employ a technology called switched digital video (SDV). The idea behind SDV is that, on a node, or on a PON in our case, there are few enough viewers that not all television channels are being watched at any one time. In fact, consider a PON with 32 subscribers. If on the average, each subscriber has two TVs on at one time (a very, very high number), and if each TV is watching a different channel (highly unlikely), then 64 programs are being consumed on that PON, against perhaps several hundred that might be made available. So with SDV, rather than send all programs all the time, VOD-like techniques are used to only send the programs that are being watched.

In an SDV system, when a subscriber selects a program to watch, the STB sends a request to the headend. At the headend, the SDV system checks to see if that program is already being delivered to that PON. If so, then the SDV system informs the STB of how to receive the program, and it gets it. The process is invisible to the subscriber. If the program is not being delivered to the subscriber, then the headend SDV system identifies an unused channel, puts the program on that channel, and notifies the STB of how to get the program.

SDV will probably not make sense for FTTH systems as a rule, because the equipment is somewhat expensive, and all FTTH systems today have as much

RF bandwidth as do the most modern cable TV systems. Thus, it will probably be more economical to just transmit all channels all the time. The one exception we can think of is if you have a stretched FTTH plant such that RF signal levels are too low for reliable signal delivery. Then you might be able to resuscitate the plant by using SDV. Since you will be carrying many fewer channels on the plant, you can increase the optical modulation index (see Chapter 6), perhaps by as much as 7 dB. This may result in you being able to deliver reliable video. But we question why a plant would be built with too low an RF level anyway. Again, there may be a few, very few, corner cases in which you might do this, but it would certainly be unusual.

WHAT GOES INTO A MODERN HEADEND?

There is a lot in a modern headend, but don't let that scare you. For a smaller system, you may not have all of the things we are going to show, and there are lots of good consultants out there who can help you navigate the waters. We are first going to show you the options for carrying video, then we'll show what may be a super-set of a headend that you might build. Again, we reiterate, video is not that hard, but if you don't have experience with it the whole task can seem daunting. If you don't have experience with TV, regardless of the form, then hire someone who does have the experience—if you don't, that might be the most expensive money you ever saved.

Fig. 11.3 illustrates and contrasts the ways you might transmit video today. We show a camera as the source; it might be a camera or it might be a satellite feed or something else. But a camera is pretty basic, and illustrates what we can do. Video comes out of the camera as *pixels* (*pi*cture *el*ements), or individual "dots" of the picture, each having a value for each of the three primary colors used in video: red, green, and blue. The pixels come out sequentially, reading the picture line-by-line from top left to lower right. (Often the picture will be *interlaced*, meaning that every other line top-to-bottom is read out, followed by the alternate lines. This is a bandwidth-saving technique adopted in the early days of analog TV and still used a lot today.) At this point, the picture has no idea how it will be transmitted—indeed, it may be transmitted a lot of different ways.

Encoding

The camera output goes into one or more *encoders*, which format the signal for transmission. It is here that the signal "discovers" how it will be transmitted. The oldest way to transmit pictures is analog video, shown coming out of the encoder at the top. Here the picture is encoded into an analog signal level representing the brightness of each pixel, plus two color parameters, which are modulated onto a subcarrier. This *composite* signal plus sound is supplied to an

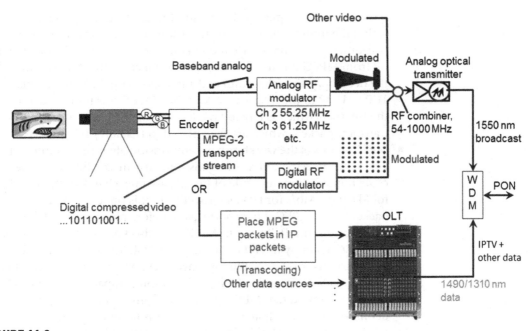

FIGURE 11.3
Options in transmitting video.

analog RF modulator, one program per 6 MHz wide channel. A large number of these channels can be combined at RF, and the output supplied to an analog (linear) optical transmitter.

We say a *linear* optical transmitter because if we tried to supply all of these signals to a digital transmitter the distortion would be unbearable and we would wind up with completely meaningless signals. Linear, or analog, transmitters are available from a number of manufacturers. A more complete description than we can provide here may be found in Large and Farmer.[iii]

Also being transmitted on the linear optical transmitter are digitally modulated signals, which would be supplied from a digital encoder. IPTV signals may be processed in the same encoder. The encoder includes compression for one of four decompression algorithms in use today:

- MPEG-2: this is the original commercially available algorithm that has been in use since the mid-1990s. As a rule of thumb, you can assume that full entertainment-grade video is available at a data rate of about 4 Mb/s for standard definition (SD) and 12–15 Mb/s for high definition (HD). While not as efficient as newer decompression algorithms, it remains in use for broadcast, most cable, and much satellite transmission. It is used in conventional DVD players, and is a required option for Blu-ray players. The reason for its continued popularity is that the number of decoders in consumers' hands (purchased by consumers in the broadcast and satellite cases) is very high, so moving on from MPEG-2 is not something to be taken lightly. MPEG-2 includes the decompression algorithm and a transport container analogous to TCP or UDP in the internet world. When MPEG-2 is transmitted on the Internet (which is rare today), it must first be placed into MPEG-2 transport packets, which are then placed in (usually) TCP packets.

- MPEG-4: this is the workhorse decompression algorithm of Internet video transmission today, and finds some use in satellite and some cable transmission. As a rule of thumb, assume a bandwidth of 2 Mb/s for SD and 8 Mb/s for HD using MPEG-4.[1] It is optional to put MPEG-4 packets in an MPEG-2 transport stream before put them in UDP or more commonly TCP packets. MPEG-4 is also known as *advanced video coding* (AVC) or by its ITU designation, H.264. MPEG-4 is also specified as a decoding format for Blu-ray players. Oh, what happened to MPEG-3? Originally it was to be the high-definition companion to MPEG-2. But people found that MPEG-2 was a perfectly competent high-definition decoding system, so MPEG-3 was never developed.

- VC-1 (*video coding 1*): this decompression standard is promulgated by the Society of Motion Picture and Television Engineers (SMPTE), and is said to be very similar in performance to MPEG-4. It is used by some on the Internet, and is included in the formats required to be decoded by BluRay DVD players. VC-1 is claimed to not be subject to all of the patents needed for MPEG-4.

- HEVC (*high-efficiency video coding*): This is a new standard which is being completed as this is being written. It is expected to yield entertainment-grade video at about one-half the bit rates stated for MPEG-4, and will likely be used for home distribution of ultrahigh-definition video (UHDTV).

Note that we have referred to these as *decompression* algorithms, not *compression* algorithms. This is an important distinction, though people do sometimes improperly refer to *compression* algorithms or standards. The standards specify how a decoder should react when presented with certain packets. It does not say how those packets are generated. This is one of the strengths of the decoding algorithms: the decoders, in the hands of consumers, are standardized, and it is very predictable how they will react. The encoders, on the other hand,

---

[1]Data rates transmitted for "high definition" on the Internet are sometimes this fast, down to one-quarter of what we have quoted here. However, there are compromises in Internet transmission that are necessary at this time, which yield picture quality less than what professionals consider "entertainment grade," though the best do not look too bad.

are largely in professional equipment, and built in much lower quantity. We anticipate that as time goes on, better compression algorithms will be found, enabling lower bit rates at a constant video quality level. Indeed, we have seen this happen with both MPEG-2 and -4.

Yes, there are encoders in consumers' hands, in video cameras and the like. But they rarely if ever compress video to the same extent it must be compressed for transmission at the data rates we have stated. Doing all of the compression steps required is too computationally complex for consumer encoders. The trade-off is a higher data rate. For example, we are working with some consumer cameras that produce good-looking MPEG-4 high definition. But while "Internet high definition" might be transmitted at around 2 Mb/s or a bit more, and "entertainment grade" might require 8 Mb/s, the data rate from the cameras is about 27 Mb/s.

In order to keep cost low, almost all TVs and STBs use hardware decoders controlled by a small microprocessor. Computers do decoding in software, which demands a much more capable (and expensive and power-hungry) processor, but does provide the advantage that another decoder can be downloaded later if desired.

Back to the Headend

Having taken that detour into decoding algorithms, let us return now to Fig. 11.3. Digitally encoded video (with audio) can be supplied to digital RF modulators. Because of the bandwidth savings, you can usually get 10 or more SD or two or maybe three HD signals in one 6-MHz wide channel (MPEG-2), and this was the original impetus in the cable industry for digital: to get more programs in the bandwidth available. Since then HD has become very big of course, and all HD transmissions are digital.

Several programs are multiplexed into one MPEG-2 *transport stream* (TS) for transmission over a single 6-MHz (North America and some other places) channel. This multiplexing process is not shown in Fig. 11.3. The modulator may add scrambling, or this may be done before the modulator, depending on the products being used. Finally, the data are modulated onto an RF carrier, today using one of two modulation methods: 64-QAM or 256-QAM. Digital modulation is covered in Ciciora et al.[iv]

The outputs from the digital modulators are supplied to the RF combiner, along with the analog signals, and the combined RF signals, each on a different frequency, are supplied to the analog optical transmitter. For FTTH, the wavelength of this transmitter is between 1550 and 1560 nm. This forms the signal transmitted on the 1550 nm wavelength. The amount of downstream bandwidth available today on the 1550 nm overlay may be calculated based on common cable TV parameters. With 256-QAM modulation, the *wire rate*, or measured data rate, is 44.884 Mb/s. After removing transmission overhead, the payload per 6 MHz channel is about 38 Mb/s. The common frequency range transmitted is 54–1002 MHz, and in this bandwidth, there is room for $(1002 – 54)/6 = 158$ RF channels, times 38 Mb/s payload for each, and you have a downstream bandwidth of 6 Gb/s, should you choose to use the bandwidth that way. (Or we could follow the lead of some marketing folks and start with the 44.884 Mb/s wire rate, times 158 channels, and say that the downstream capacity is just over 7 Gb/s.) Remember, this is on the RF-modulated wavelength: FTTH also has the data optical carriers both downstream and upstream.

Looking at the bottom part of Fig. 11.3, we see that the encoder can format the video into streams to be transmitted via IPTV, and those streams are switched to an OLT, from which they go out on the FTTH network as part of the normal data service. Since IPTV is a much newer technology than is broadcast, MPEG-4 was commercially available by the time it came along, and most or all IPTV decoders support it. We shall cover IPTV in the next chapter.

Another Look at a Headend

Just a little more and we'll move on to talking specifically about broadcast video. A modern headend can use any combination of broadcast and IPTV transmission that seems good to the operator.

Fig. 11.4 summarizes some of the elements of a modern headend. You may or may not have all of these elements, depending on the services offered. Starting with the broadcast video in the center left, this is the collection of all programming sent out on a subscription basis, either RF-modulated or via IPTV. Many but not all of the subscription channel programming will flow through an advertising insertion system, which switches in local avails, described earlier. This is done under the management of a *traffic* system, the human/machine system used to sell and insert commercials during local avails. The output of the ad insertion system might feed the broadcast set of modulators, then the optical transmitter, represented here as an electro-to-optical conversion (E/O). Alternatively, programming may be converted to IPTV and switched into the OLT interfaces. Set-top control generally follows the same path, and is used to authorize or deauthorize the set tops for certain programs, and to fetch information from the set tops as to what pay-per-view shows were watched. The control system usually interfaces with the billing system, which needs to know everything the subscriber bought, so it can send the bill.

Above the broadcast equipment is the VoD equipment, usually a file server also coupled to the billing system, which stores your inventory of video-on-demand material. Upon command from the set top, it can play out programming, either to the broadcast facility or the IPTV facility or both. The VoD file

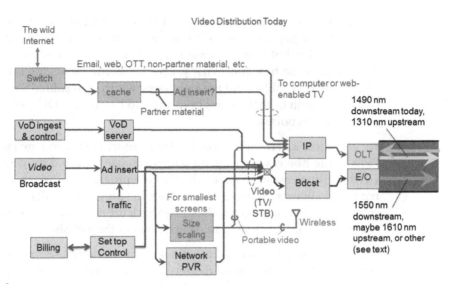

FIGURE 11.4

Video flow in the headend.

server must get programming from somewhere, usually one or more distributors from whom you buy it. The process of getting the video into your server is called *ingesting* the video. Frequently the video may be sent via satellite or maybe by a private terrestrial network, but there are times that a particular server will not get everything, so the ingest and control system must know when this happens, and must request retransmission. The server at the distributor's facility which sends the programs to you is often called the *pitcher*. Your server which receives the programs is called the *catcher*. No, we don't know what happened to the batter.

At the top is your Internet connection, which comes in through some sort of switching facility. The Internet connection will be connected to OLTs to allow your subscribers to access the Internet. You may also have one or more servers that cache popular data, such as movies from any companies with which you partner [video of this nature, which is intended to be retrieved by subscribers over the Internet, is called *over-the-top* (OTT) video]. Caching would be done where you expect a number of subscribers to access the material. By caching it locally, you save charges for Internet access, and you can improve the subscriber experience by delivering the movie faster.

We also show provisions for rescaling video for small screens. If you are delivering your local video content to pads and smart phones, you may want to reduce the bandwidth by reducing the resolution of the picture—the small screens are not capable of delivering full resolution of a big screen, and you don't want to burn the bandwidth to deliver bits that the small screens cannot display. Normally, this bandwidth reduction may be done higher up in the network today, but it is conceivable that you may do some. We show wireless access in the headend. What people are doing these days is establishing access points in public (and private) places, which their subscribers can use. So communication to these access points would be over the OLT, terminating on wireless access points.

We also show a network personal video recorder (PVR). You are familiar with PVRs in the home, which the subscriber can use to record programs for later viewing. The network PVR records all of the programs for which you have the right, and allows subscribers to play back the programs on demand. Thus, if a subscriber misses a program, she can go back the next day or two and see it. Of course, networks are often putting up shows to the web shortly after they air.

Not shown are a series of additional servers you need to do a complete data service. These include time-of-day server, a DHCP server, a management system for your FTTH network and possibly other systems.

In-Home Interfaces

We have covered RF or data interfaces in the home, but there are others you will encounter. Coming out of an STB and into a TV or other equipment, you may encounter any of several interfaces. The most common today is a digital interface, either DVI or, more commonly, HDMI. Fig. 11.5 illustrates the connectors you will find. DVI is the older standard, and contains digital and (optionally) analog video, but no audio. HDMI uses a smaller connector, and includes digital video and digital audio, but no analog signals. It is the most

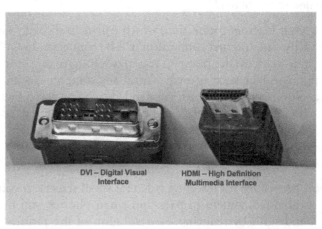

FIGURE 11.5
Common digital video interfaces.

common interface you will likely find on newer TVs and STBs, and is the preferred interface when both pieces of equipment support it.

The format for the digital video is identical for both DVI and HDMI, and you can find passive adaptors to go from one to the other. Of course, with DVI, you will need another path for audio. You can do analog audio interfaces, and you can do both coaxial (usually on a single RCA plug) and optical digital interfaces, depending on the customer's equipment capabilities.

These interfaces serve both standard- and high-definition video. There is one consumer analog interface for high definition, which consists of three RCA connections, colored red, green, and blue. All three cables should be of the same length, and making them of 75 Ω coaxial cable is recommended, though not always practiced. Other analog standard-definition interfaces include a single RCA connector for composite video, and the S-video connector, which has been used on many VCRs since the late 1980s, and is often found on STBs. Neither of these carries audio.

TV CHANNELS

OK, now for a confusing issue that used to be simple: TV channel numbers. In the beginning of television, the FCC set aside certain frequencies for analog TV transmission (analog was all that was available until the 1990s). Consumers had already become used to tuning to *frequencies* on their AM radios (FM was not popular at the time). But TV signals required a band of frequencies, set at 6 MHz wide in the US, 7 or 8 MHz in certain other countries.[2] Furthermore, unlike the radio band, the frequencies were not all contiguous for technical reasons. At one time the TV bands were 54–72 and 76–88 MHz (VHF low band, channels 2–6), 174–216 MHz (VHF high band, channels 7–13), and 470–870 MHz (UHF, channels 14–83). It was too difficult for subscribers to keep track of frequencies in this case, so channel numbers were adopted to define the frequencies. Channel 2 occupied 54–60 MHz, channel 7 was 174–180 MHz, and channel 14 was 470–476 MHz. It was possible to construct a simple table that unambiguously related channel number to frequency range.

But things were not to stay so simple. Enter cable TV. It was a closed system, so it could use frequencies not assigned to off-air broadcasting. What to call those channels? At first, cable TV used letter designators for the non-off-air channels.

---

[2]Bandwidth and other parameters were set by the National Television System Committee (NTSC), the industry body that standardized the television system in the US. The standard was later incorporated into the FCC rules.

But then when STBs got electronic channel displays, the displays didn't support letter designations. So the cable TV industry adopted its own numerical designations. After several years of confusion, the cable TV and receiver industries agreed on a standard channel designation plan, codified as CEA 542.[v] The VHF channel designations were identical to the FCC off-air designations. Above channel 13, though, the channel designations are different from the FCC off-air designations. Adding complexity, the UHF channel band edges are offset 2 MHz between the off-air and cable plans.

Adding further complexity, at one time the cable TV industry used three different channelization plans, with the frequencies shifted slightly in each plan. The reason was that distortion in distribution amplifiers produced certain types of picture degradation, which could be somewhat hidden from the subscriber if the alternate channel frequency band edges were used. With modern technology, these alternate plans, referred to as "IRC" and "HRC," have largely gone away. But we mention them because they still appear in CEA 542.

But things were not to stay so "simple." Enter digital transmission. Now a number of programs could be placed into one 6 MHz channel. Since consumers were accustomed to associating a channel number with a particular show, it was desired to retain that familiarity, but how to do it, with an indeterminate number of programs in each channel? The cable TV industry had by then developed the ability to download a table of channel numbers and the corresponding frequency and program identification (program ID or PID, the way a decoder knows which of several programs in a channel it is to decode) to each STB. So the cable industry added a third digit to their channel designations, and downloaded a table telling the STB how to tune in order to receive a particular "channel." But the "channel" tuned did not necessarily bear any resemblance to those defined in CEA 542.

But things were not to stay so "simple." Enter the broadcasters. For a long transition period that ended in 2009 in the US, broadcasters radiated their analog signal on their traditional channel, by which consumers had learned to identify a station. For digital transmission, each station was assigned a second 6-MHz wide channel somewhere else in the spectrum, wherever the FCC could pack it in. Stations built their digital transmitters on those new channels. But since consumers had learned to associate the analog channel number with the station, the same channel number was used for the digital broadcast. At the end of the transition period, when analog transmitters were turned off, stations either kept their digital channel as their frequency, or in some cases they used their old analog channel for digital. A few stations went to a different frequency. But in all cases, since the station was known by its channel number, it retained that identification, transmitting to the TV or other device, information as to what frequency to tune to when the consumer asked for a particular channel.

But things were not to stay so "simple" (are you beginning to see a pattern?). Now each off-air station could carry more than one program. How to designate a channel number for each channel? The TV stations wanted to retain their channel designations because viewers knew them by their channel number. So off-air stations use a dot system to designate programs: Channel 2.1, 2.2, and so on for however many programs they carry.

But things may not stay so "simple." As this is written, the FCC is trying to open up more spectrum for data communications, which is running out of spectrum due to the demand of mobile devices. So the FCC is hoping to get stations to either surrender their licenses and go off the air, or to get two stations to team up and use the same RF channel to transmit both of their programs. The incentive is that the government would then auction off the freed spectrum to wireless providers, and would share the proceeds with the stations that voluntarily freed up spectrum. Stations should be able to keep their existing channel designations by transmitting the correct tuning information to tuners in TVs and other devices, but the number of stations which will participate is unknown as of this writing. If this packing concept does work, we will have two stations, operating under different call signs and different channel designations, using the same RF channel, and being identified by something else on cable systems.

For IPTV, channel designations are not really necessary, but they are often used anyway, because subscribers are accustomed to using them. With the popularity of electronic program guides (EPGs), which form a scrollable tabulation on the TV screen listing current and future programs, the concept of consumers identifying with channel numbers is arguably going away. This is true for both broadcast and IPTV. Consumers may begin to identify more with scrolling through and looking for a program, and channel numbers may become less important. On the other hand, how do you order the programs subscribers scroll through if not by channel number?

So there! In 60+ years, we have managed to take the simple concept of a channel number, and we have made it into a complex and confusing concept with multiple meanings. When in doubt, we tend to refer to "RF channel" and "program channel," but this practice is far from universal. Often you have to figure out what is being referred to from the context.

BROADCAST PLANT FUNDAMENTALS AND RECOMMENDED PRACTICES

OK, now let's get down to considerations for broadcast plant. IPTV people can skip to the next chapter if they wish. So that we don't duplicate information readily available elsewhere, let us refer you to Ciciora et al.[iv] for information on assembling the programming and getting it modulated onto RF.

That reference has most of the technical information you will need regarding fiber optic transmission, so here let us concentrate on a few issues that are different in FTTH than in HFC. We'll go over key points that you need to look out for, then we'll look at a typical plant design, seeing how to use the broadcast overlay.

Those operating a broadcast overlay should avail themselves of another reference, which will be useful in the engineering and maintenance of the plant. These represent the culmination of many years of experience in the cable television industry, whose technical plants form the basis for FTTH RF overlays. One good reference you'll need is the *SCTE Measurement Recommended Practices for Cable Systems*, published by the Society of Cable Telecommunications Engineers.[vi]

Operation of the Analog Optical Transmitter

We measure the amount by which each signal modulates the amplitude of the optical transmitter using the *optical modulation index* (OMI). The higher the OMI per channel, the more output RF signal you get at the far end, but as OMI increases, the distortion of the signal increases somewhat. In HFC systems, the OMI normally used is somewhere around 2.4% per analog channel where the transmitter is loaded with a number (traditionally about 54) of analog signals to 550 MHz, with digital signals carried 6 dB down from the analog signals, at frequencies up to 1 GHz. This OMI has been found to work well for cable TV systems, where the optical level at nodes, where signals are converted back to RF, can be up to maybe +5 dBm. Both the carrier-to-noise ratio (C/N) and distortion must be very good at this point, to allow for degradation in the following RF amplifiers.[3]

The situation is a little different in FTTH networks. There are no RF amplifiers after the ONT to contribute signal degradation, so we can tolerate more degradation in the optical network. Furthermore, since we are splitting the optical signal up to 64 ways before we get to the home, we are encountering a lot of splitting loss. Amplifying the signal has its limitations and costs money, so it behooves us to be able to hit the ONT with the lowest optical level that permits us to obtain a satisfactory C/N. With modern techniques, it so happens that we can hit the ONT with optical levels down to about −6 to −5 dBm and achieve the C/N level considered good engineering practice (48 dB C/N for an analog signal). But in order to do that, we must increase the OMI at the transmitter. Experience has shown us that we can use OMI of about 3.5% or a bit

---

[3]C/N is a measure of the "snow" in an analog picture. In a digital picture, it has the effect of blocking demodulation of the signal if it is too low (a higher C/N is better). It is measured as the ratio of signal power to noise power, expressed in decibels.

more before we get into trouble with *clipping*, the thing that causes problems when you get up to that high an OMI; at clipping, the laser actually turns off when the carriers all reach one peak at the same time. For analog signals, the symptom you will see is strong horizontal or diagonal lines in the pictures. If you get this, then back off the OMI until the lines go away. Digital signals will start breaking up, or will disappear completely if you get the OMI too high. You can monitor OMI in the headend, as there is nothing later in the system that can alter it.

Thus, you want to shoot for an OMI of about 3.5% per analog carrier in a transmitter being used just for FTTH transmission of broadcast signals. Going from 2.4% to 3.5% per carrier will increase your received C/N by just over 3 dB, a significant improvement. Some transmitters may not be capable of achieving this increase in OMI. Some can be placed in an AGC mode, in which the composite (over all channels) OMI will be held constant regardless of input signal level. So discuss the issue with your proposed optical transmitter vendor, and see how you can increase the OMI, or decide that you can design for slightly higher optical signal levels to compensate for the lower OMI.

Things change a little when you go to all-digital signal transmission. While the analog signals require a C/N of about 48 dB to yield good, noise-free pictures, digital signals (256-QAM) can work down to a C/N of about 27 dB if no other degradation is present (NOT a real-world situation). The good-engineering-practice minimum C/N for digital carriers is about 33 dB. Since digital carriers are transmitted at a level about −6 dB from the analog signals on the optical network, if you are all-digital you can bring the signal levels up some in order to achieve an OMI per channel closer to 3.5%.[4] This and the lower required C/N means you can hit the ONT with somewhat lower signal levels if you are carrying all-digital signals. Consult your transmitter and ONT vendors to work out the proper levels in your situation. Note that some ONTs may generate an alarm if the optical signal level drops below where it is needed for analog signals.

Optical Transmitters

There are several types of optical transmitters used in HFC networks, but your choice is more limited in FTTH networks. At 1550 nm, your choices are internally and externally modulated distributed feedback (DFB) transmitters. Internally modulated transmitters control the amplitude of the optical signal

---

[4]Analog levels are measured in peak signal level, while digital signals are measured in average level. The peak level is about 4 dB above the average level, and it is the peak level that determines how far up you can go on level without excessive clipping. Thus, while you can increase the OMI some when you go all-digital, you won't be able to increase it as much as you might think.

by applying the composite RF signal to the laser bias pins. This works pretty well, but does cause some *chirp*, or variation in the wavelength of the optical signal with modulation. Fiber optic cable exhibits a characteristic called chromatic dispersion, which means that signals at different wavelengths reach the ONT at slightly different times, creating distortion. The chirp on the internally modulated laser output is enough to introduce some distortion in the FTTH plant.

For this reason, we recommend externally modulated analog lasers for almost all FTTH purposes. With the eternally modulated (*ex mod*) transmitter, the laser is not modulated, and thus remains at a single wavelength, with the light being passed through an external modulator. This reduces the chirp, and also arguably somewhat improves the linearity of the transmitter.

Stimulated Brillouin Scattering

We said that the laser output for an externally modulated transmitter was at a single wavelength. It really is spread out over a small wavelength range intentionally to help control *stimulated Brillouin scattering* (SBS). SBS is a property of fiber optic cable in which you are limited in how much power you can inject in the fiber. If you try to inject more than a certain amount of power, it is reflected back to the input, preventing more power from being injected and creating excessive distortion. The mechanism is a mechanical vibration of the atoms in the fiber due to the high power density of the optical signal. The SBS threshold is a function of the length of the fiber *before the signal level is reduced by splitting*.

Wavelength spreading is done intentionally and carefully in the transmitter to randomize the mechanical vibrations, thus improving the SBS threshold. The SBS threshold is primarily a function of the transmitter, even though the phenomenon occurs in the fiber itself. The wavelength spreading is a balancing act, to spread the signal enough to improve SBS threshold as much as practical, while making sure that chromatic dispersion is not a problem. Some manufacturers go farther and provide an adjustment to optimize SBS threshold based on the length of fiber. The problem with this in FTTH is that you often are using the same transmitter to feed subscribers located through only a few tens of meters of fiber, and as far away as 20 km. So there is no one optimum setting of the adjustment.

As we have alluded to, the SBS limit is specified for a particular transmitter as a maximum injection limit for a fiber of either 50 km or infinite distance. Fig. 11.6 illustrates the SBS limit as it applies to one particular transmitter, specified to have an SBS threshold of 20 dBm at a 50-km fiber distance. You can see that if you have significantly less fiber length you can launch at much higher optical levels without problems. Note that the fiber distance shown is to the point where the fiber is split. After the first split, the signal level is usually low enough that you don't have to worry about SBS from that point on.

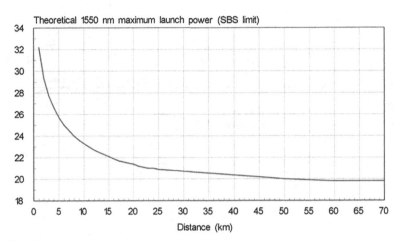

FIGURE 11.6
SBS threshold versus distance.

Having said all of this about SBS, we also note that, in those cases in which you do have problems with SBS, you can get special fiber optic cable that has improved the SBS threshold. In most cases you should not need it, but there are a few cases in which it may be advisable to use it.

Stimulated Raman Scattering

The 1490 nm downstream data carrier in a PON system can cause crosstalk into the 1550 nm RF modulated signal, creating reduced C/N. The mechanism through which the data carrier at 1490 nm causes C/N issues in the 1550 nm video carrier is *stimulated Raman scattering* (SRS) distortion in the fiber itself. Essentially, the lower wavelength 1490 nm signal transfers some of its power to the 1550 nm signal in an inefficient optical amplification process. But since the 1490 nm data signal is turning off and on with data, the energy is transferred only when a logical 1 is transmitted, and only then does amplification happen. The data pattern thus shows up as noise in the 1550 nm broadcast signal.

Several countermeasures may be applied as needed in order to mitigate the effects of SRS. These include the following.

1. Pre-emphasizing the lower-frequency channels by increasing their relative amplitude. This is easily done in the video headend.
2. Inserting optical attenuation in the OLT output prior to the wave division multiplexer (WDM) that combines the video. (Of course this will have an effect on the loss budget.)
3. Either doing the first level of ODN optical splitting at the OLT, or extending the video to the first level of optical splitting using a separate fiber strand.
4. Applying countermeasures for the idle codes.

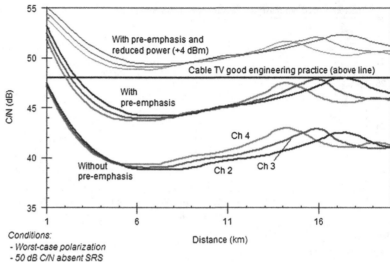

FIGURE 11.7

Effect of SRS on carrier-to-noise ratio (EPON).

SRS in EPON systems

We shall describe the quantitative effects of SRS in relation to EPON systems, recognizing that the effects are almost identical in GPON systems, with some difference in severity due to the specified differences in signal levels for the two standards. With GPON Class B+ optics, the effect is not quite as bad as we describe, but with GPON Class C optics, the effect is much worse.

Pre-Emphasis Countermeasure

Fig. 11.7 illustrates the effect of SRS on carrier-to-noise ratio (C/N) for the three lowest TV channels in an EPON system. SRS affects the lowest channels the most, which is why we look at them and not others. Lower C/N causes snow in the analog picture. For digital modulation, nothing happens until the C/N drops low enough, and then the picture goes away entirely. Good engineering practice in the cable TV industry is to maintain C/N above 48 dB for analog modulation, as shown in Fig. 11.7. Higher numbers are better. Note that, without any pre-emphasis, the C/N gets as bad as about 39 dB. When we added a certain amount of pre-emphasis, we were able to get the worst-case C/N up to about 44 dB—better but still not good engineering practice.[5] Pre-emphasis

---

[5]The FCC specifies a minimum C/N of 43 dB for analog signals delivered to subscribers. Some novice FTTH operators have interpreted this as all they must do. But remember, FCC rules are minimums and you can find yourself in trouble if you don't meet them. They are not necessarily reflective of good engineering practice.

means that we increase the OMI of the lowest channels compared with higher channels by a little bit. This allows us to provide a better C/N for those lower channels where SRS is the worst. If we are carrying digital modulation on those lowest channels, we may not need to worry about pre-emphasis, though there is a problem mentioned below that we may need to worry about.

The calculation in Fig. 11.7 assumes the maximum data carrier (1490 nm) amplitude of +7 dBm. We must make this assumption, because at some place, you will get this much optical carrier amplitude. (Well, we really could have deducted 0.5 dB for the WDM loss, but we'd still have a problem.) The power is measured where it is launched into the PON fiber. The PON stops at the first splitting point for purposes of computing the effects of SRS on C/N.

The SRS phenomenon is highly nonlinear with optical level. By decreasing the optical power from +7 dBm to +4 dBm and retaining the same pre-emphasis, we are able to improve the C/N so that it is acceptable. Note that we assumed a C/N without SRS distortion, of 50 dB. It may prove more economical to design for a C/N of 49 dB without SRS and design for even less C/N reduction due to SRS distortion. Alternatively, you may wish to achieve a competitive advantage by delivering a slightly better C/N than that delivered by a competing cable operator.

Again, note that the operative optical power level in SRS computations is the power level of the 1490 nm downstream data carrier. The amplitude of the 1550 nm RF carrier does not enter into the calculations. Also, the operative length of the fiber in Fig. 11.7 is the length from where the 1550-nm carrier is combined with the 1490 nm carrier, extending to the first split point. After that first split, the 1490 nm power level is usually low enough that there is no problem.

Optical Attenuation Countermeasure

Fig. 11.8 illustrates a countermeasure for SRS when you have excess data optical level both upstream and downstream on the link. In this case, you can add an optical attenuator as shown, in the output of the data OLT, to bring the optical level down low enough to permit good C/N with SRS. You can also take into account the loss of the WDM in calculating the optical level, as SRS is not introduced until after the WDM. This attenuator works well, and is simple and low in cost. Just be sure that you add the optical attenuator value (usually 2 dB is enough) to the loss computations.

Countermeasure of Moving the Combining Point

Fig. 11.9 illustrates a countermeasure that can be used when excess optical level is not available, in which case you can't accept the extra attenuation introduced by the optical attenuator. In this case, we have extended the RF signals on a separate

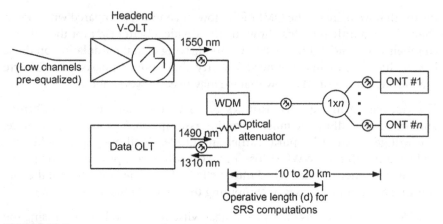

FIGURE 11.8
Countermeasure for SRS when excess optical level is available.

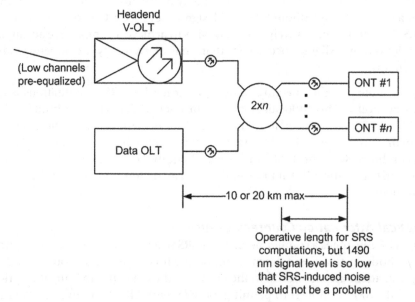

FIGURE 11.9
Countermeasure for SRS when excess optical level is not available.

fiber to the first splitting point. Then a 2 × n splitter is used, which has an integral WDM for combining the wavelengths. Multiple stages of splitting may be used; the 1490-nm optical level will typically be reduced enough after the first stage of splitting that you should not have any problems with SRS-induced noise.

Since optical level is sufficiently reduced after at least a two-way split, the first level of splitting can be moved all the way to the OLT location if you wish.

(A)

(B)

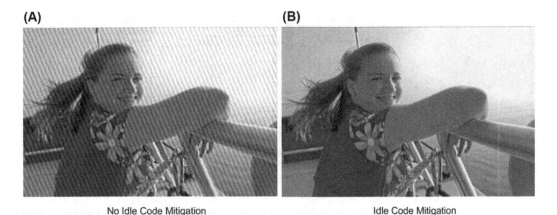

No Idle Code Mitigation

Idle Code Mitigation

FIGURE 11.10
Effect of idle code, and mitigation thereof: (A) no idle code mitigation; (B) idle code mitigation.

Then you have no field combining of the data and broadcast optical carriers. Rather, you have your first level of splitting at the OLT.

Idle Code Mitigation
There is one condition under which all of the countermeasures we have discussed so far may not be practical or sufficient to solve the SRS interference issue. When no data are being transmitted on the 1490-nm downstream data carrier, both the EPON and GPON standards require that a short code sequence, called an *idle code* be transmitted. The idle code is necessary in order to ensure that the receivers in the ONTs remain locked to the incoming data, so that they can resume reception as soon as there is something to receive. Unfortunately, the repetitive sequences used for the idle codes in both EPON and GPON mean that the power in the data signal, which is usually spread over a wide spectrum as is noise, is now concentrated in one frequency and its harmonics. For EPON, that fundamental frequency is 62.5 MHz. For GPON it is 62.2 MHz. Both frequencies are at a very bad place in RF Channel 3. Channels 14 and 9 can also be affected to a lesser extent. For analog signals, the effect is to place a so-called *beat* in the picture, as shown in Fig. 11.10A. The beat can get so bad as to potentially make a digital picture disappear under the right conditions. The solution is to replace the idle code with a pseudorandom bit pattern that goes to no ONT. One way this can be done is to put the bit pattern in a VLAN (virtual local area network) that is not directed to any end devices.

Erbium-Doped Fiber Amplifiers
Erbium-doped fiber amplifiers (EDFAs), are used extensively in FTTH systems. They accept the optical signal from the broadcast optical transmitter and amplify it. EDFAs used in HFC networks are characterized to operate from about 1535 to

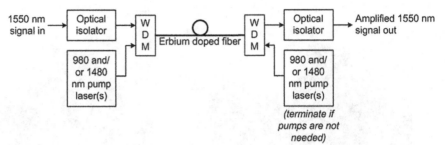

FIGURE 11.11
EDFA block diagram.

1565 nm. However, due to other wavelengths used in FTTH systems, you will find yourself limited to wavelengths from about 1550 to 1560 nm.

The heart of the EDFA is a piece of fiber optic cable a few feet long, doped with erbium atoms, as shown in the block diagram of Fig. 11.11. It is terminated on each end with a *WDM*, which separates the 1550 nm spectrum from the 980-nm and/or 1480-nm wavelengths, where the *pump lasers* operate. The number of pump lasers in an amplifier determines how much signal power you can get out. All of the pump lasers supply energy to the erbium-doped fiber, causing the valence band electrons in the erbium atoms to jump to a higher-energy state. The 1550 nm signal to be amplified is supplied through the optical isolator on the left, and the amplified signal is extracted from the optical isolator on the right. As a 1550 nm photon passes close to an excited electron in the higher-energy state, the electron drops back down to its lower-energy state, giving up energy in the process. That energy takes the form of an additional photon at 1550 nm moving in the same direction as the original photon which caused the electron to drop back to the lower-energy state.

Not shown are couplers that take a sample of the input and output power levels, and supply the level information to a microprocessor, which regulates the power supplied by the pump lasers. This circuit permits implementation of the various control modes not necessarily applicable to FTTH, and also permits interface with a management system.

EDFA Characteristics

The EDFA has a number of characteristics that are different from electronic amplifiers. They do, however, have a noise figure, and add some noise, as do electronic amplifiers. Compared with electronic amplifiers, EDFAs react much differently when you overdrive them, meaning that you drive them at excessive input levels. Under these conditions, electronic amplifiers clip, producing a lot of distortion and an unacceptable output. EDFAs, on the other hand, simply stop putting out more power, but they don't distort. When you get enough photons moving through the erbium-doped fiber to knock all of the electrons out of their higher-energy orbits, then you simply don't have any more output level you can achieve. But the signals still go through undistorted.

You can handle as many signals in an EDFA as you can pack into the 1550–1560 nm spectrum, but the total power out may not exceed the rated power output of the EDFA. That rated power out is the power you get when all available electrons are being excited to the higher-energy level, and then are knocked back down by 1550-nm photons. Because of this mechanism to limit output level, one can adjust the maximum output level by adjusting the total power output of the pump lasers. While you can operate with more than one signal into the EDFA, most FTTH applications only use one signal, and the EDFA is operated in the saturated mode. There are other modes possible, but they apply when you are amplifying more than one signal.

The maximum EDFA output power available commercially at this time appears to be about +33 dBm. However, this much power is dangerous to work with, both from an eye safety standpoint and from the possibility of damaging a connector by fusing a dust particle to the glass. Furthermore, you would not be able to transmit that much power very far before splitting it, because SBS limits the amount of power you can launch into a fiber, assuming a single carrier. Thus, very high-powered amplifiers usually include internal splitting to get the signal down to a maximum of around +21 dBm present on any one connector, about the maximum practical power you would want for an individual FTTH PON of 32 or 64 endpoints. This usually means that such a high-powered amplifier will have 16 outputs. Each output can be used for a different signal path, so long as the same signals can go on each path.

A Sample RF Optical Design

Let us look now at a sample design of the RF portion of the FTTH network. We have made a few assumptions in this sample design that may or may not be applicable to your situation. You can talk to your vendors and decide if this design is right for you, or if slightly different parameters should be applied. The PON standards tend to not have a lot to say about the broadcast overlay, as much is known from cable TV experience since the late 1980s. The reference from which we draw numbers is the ANSI/SCTE 174 2010 RFoG specification described in Chapter 5. It represented the state-of-the-art performance at the time it was written, and should be a good guide for you when dealing with either EPON or GPON video overlays. However, there may be some variations with EPON and GPON ONTs.

We start by adding up all the losses in the network. Then we look at the minimum optical level required at the ONT, which may vary depending on the signals you are carrying. By combining the loss and the minimum required level, we can determine the minimum output needed from the EDFA.

Warning

This is a good point at which to bring up an urgent important topic, the danger of looking into a fiber that is carrying laser signals. Depending on what reference you consult, any laser power exceeding about +7 dBm can be dangerous to the eye. Under no conditions should you look at the end of a fiber unless you know beyond a shadow of a doubt that there is no signal on that fiber. The wavelengths used in FTTH are not visible to the eye, so the first you will know that you have looked at laser energy is when your vision is degraded or destroyed. It is too late, as the damage is permanent. There is a reason why key locks are used on optical transmitters and EDFAs; if you are going to be working on an optical circuit, turn the transmitter off and put the key in your pocket to make sure no one turns the transmitter on. Then still do not look into the fiber, just to be sure. It is not safe to look at the fiber with an optical microscope. It is safe to look at it through an electronic magnifier, in which the image is displayed on a computer screen.

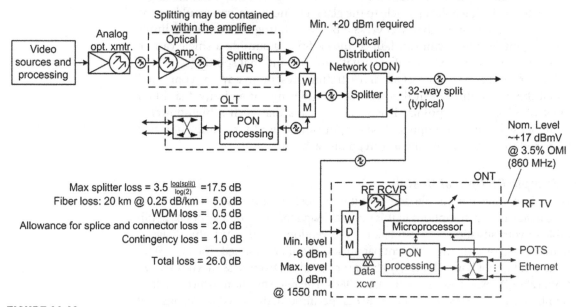

FIGURE 11.12

Example level calculations for RF optical overlay.

Fig. 11.12 shows the system with the RF laser levels shown. The loss calculations are in the lower left portion of the diagram. By far the biggest loss is the splitting loss of the 32-way (in the example) splitter. The ratio of logarithms is used to compute the number of levels of splitting required, as shown in the figure; in optics, this need not be an integer, but it is in the 32-way split case.

The 3.5 dB number is the maximum loss per two-way splitting stage. Just over 3 dB of the loss comes from the conservation of energy: if you send one-half of the power in one leg and the other half in another leg, then of necessity the power in each leg is one-half of the power you started with. To convert this loss to decibels, we multiply 10 times the logarithm of one-half, or.

$10 \log(0.5) = -3.01$ dB.

The remainder of the loss is excess loss in the splitter. Some is there just because you usually loose something in any processing of a signal, and some accounts for the variation in loss between ports. Some passive vendors are publishing lower losses now, as they feel they have a better handle on port-to-port variation and residual losses. So long as you have confidence in the numbers, you may use them, and reduce the 17.5 dB loss we show.

The fiber loss is in the fiber itself. We have assumed a 20-km fiber path to the farthest subscriber. Optical fiber has a loss of 0.25 dB/km at 1550 nm (more at 1490 and 1310 nm), so 20 km has a total loss of 5 dB. We next must allow for the loss of the WDM at the headend, which is usually on the order of 0.5 dB. Next, we will likely have several connectors and splices in the fiber between the output of the EDFA and the subscriber. From experience we have allowed 2 dB for this loss. Your loss may be more or less, depending on how many connectors and splices you have.

Finally, we add a 1-dB contingency loss. Why? Well, sooner or later, you are later going to have a fiber break: a car hits a pole and snaps the fiber, as hard as that is to do, or someone is trenching alongside your fiber and accidently cuts your fiber. (Such failures are humorously known as *backhoe fades*.) And the backhoe fade is not going to occur at 10:00 a.m. on a bright, sunny Tuesday morning. Murphy's law says that the backhoe fade will occur on a weekend night when it is raining or you have blowing snow, and your tech on call has just settled into bed. Needless to say, the repair he makes that night is not going to necessarily be of the best quality. He is not going to get the splicing machine lined up just right, because it was a big cable that got cut, and he has lots of splices to make under adverse conditions, when he was hoping to be in his warm bed getting some sleep. So that's why we recommend a contingency factor. Some people put the contingency in with the splice and connector loss.

When we add up the losses, we get 26 dB of loss. The minimum level into the ONT required for a 48 dB RF C/N is taken to be −6 dB, about right as we are writing this. So combining those numbers, we need +20 dBm out of the EDFA, amazingly, just under the number we mentioned earlier.

There is a maximum optical level to the ONT that you have to watch, too. For RFoG-compliant devices, that maximum level may be as low as 0 dBm. If you exceed this level at the input to the ONT, then you run the risk of developing distortion in the ONT receiver. So exceeding the input optical level is about as bad as going below the range. It is somewhat less likely that you will exceed the maximum level because, frankly, it'll usually cost you money in the form of more EDFA capability than you need. However, there are a couple of things to watch out for in the design. In the unlikely case that you have one or more ONTs very close to the headend and one or more at the maximum 20 km distance, then the variation in fiber loss will eat up almost all of your input level range, and you may find yourself out of tolerance on one end or the other. This may happen in a very rural environment. In such a case, it is likely that, rather than having all of your splitting at one place, you will have it spread out over several locations, and you may be using a tapped architecture, where you have optical taps of various values rather than one splitter with relatively consistent output. This can exacerbate the problem of level variation. The issue is quite controllable with proper system design, but we bring it to your attention as something to watch out for.

The above applies when you are transporting some analog signals, even if the majority of your signals are digital. When you go to all-digital, the rules can be relaxed some. It is harder to give you hard-and-fast rules in this case because practices are not well-established across the industry. These rules may or may not follow exactly the recommendations of your vendors—in case of a difference, go with what your vendors say. As time goes on, the recommendations may change slightly following improvements in the state-of-the-art.

Common practice is to carry digital signals –6 dB (256-QAM) from the analog level in cable plant. We recommend this for FTTH when you have a mix of analog and digital signals. With all-digital signals, you can raise their level to about 3.5% OMI, increasing digital RF signal levels at the ONT. Because digital carriers can tolerate somewhat lower C/N, you can also hit the ONT with lower optical signal levels. These might drop as low as about –13 dBm, but this is an absolute minimum, and we recommend keeping signal levels a few dB higher, perhaps not lower than –10 dBm, depending on what your ONT vendor says. The RF receiver in the ONT has automatic gain control (AGC), and the AGC may cease functioning below an optical input of about –5 or –6 dBm. Some ONTs may issue a low RF alarm if the optical signal drops below –5 or –6 dBm, and if this happens you may have to program out that alarm, with the concomitant loss of information. RF level goes 2:1 with optical signal level changes, so a 5-dB drop in optical signal level means a 10 dB drop in RF signal level below the AGC threshold.

RF Signal Level Issues
According to the FCC rules for cable TV, at the side of the house, the RF signal level on any analog channel should be a minimum of +3 dBmV. The units are decibels with respect to 1 mV measured in the normal 75 Ω TV RF environment. The minimum level at which you should hit the first consumer device is

0 dBmV. This is for analog signals. The FCC rules are silent on digital levels as of this writing. Digital signals using 256-QAM modulation, the highest modulation used as of this writing, are carried −6 dB from the analog signal on the cable plant, so logically, you might say that the minimum signal level is −6 dBmV, and this would certainly be a good number to use. Somewhat lower numbers would probably still work quite well.

As a practical matter, most ONTs put out much higher signal levels, such as the +17 dBmV nominal level shown in Fig. 11.12. This number comes from some very early and, frankly, of necessity limited work related to the overload characteristics of television receivers. Some early experiments performed in the 1980s by a then-active joint committee of the NCTA (cable television operators) and the EIA (TV set manufacturers, now the CEA) measured some TVs and concluded that a signal level of about +17 dBmV should not cause much problem in most TVs. Whether this is a good number today is debatable, but the test is difficult and costly to perform, so we don't expect to see more accurate numbers become available. If a technician sees poor analog signals or no digital signals when he is measuring high signal levels, a good first test is to insert 3–6 dB of attenuation at the input of the TV, in case the TV is being overloaded.

You will see some *uptilt*, or increase in signal level with frequency, in the output of some ONTs. This is to compensate for the frequency-dependent nature of the coaxial cable used to distribute RF signals in homes. The RFoG standard calls for +5 dB nominal uptilt from 54 to 1002 MHz, but this tends to be on the high side of what we have seen from early ONTs. Because of the uptilt, when the output level is specified, it is specified at a given frequency, 860 MHz in the case of the RFoG specification.

Other Issues

There are a number of other issues related to delivery of RF signals to which we are not giving much attention here, because they tend to not be limiting factors in FTTH installations. They may well be limiting factors in cable TV HFC plant. There are several types of distortion, such as second and third order, frequency response, hum modulation, microreflections, and other issues. These tend to not be as important in FTTH networks, thanks to all-fiber delivery technology. The SCTE Recommended Practices[vi] document referenced earlier gives all of the information you will need to understand the issues and to prove compliance with the rules.

SUMMARY

Key to successfully operating a broadcast overlay is understanding your equipment and how it works together, and having someone on your staff who really knows it. Of course, the same can be said for IPTV, VoIP, or any other technology. Broadcast tends to be more straightforward than IPTV in that you don't have to worry about congestion in the network, and as a result the service tends to be more predictable. In addition, you avail yourself of over half a century of experience of the cable TV industry and the TV receiver industry; we have a system that works quite well, even if the network does not look just like a data network. The infrastructure needed is available and well-proven.

Endnotes

i. http://www.mocalliance.org/.

ii. http://www.homepna.org/.

iii. Large, Farmer. Broadband Cable Access Networks. Morgan Kaufmann; 2009.

iv. Ciciora et al. Modern Cable Television Technology, 2nd ed. Published by Morgan Kaufmann; 2004.

v. Available at: http://www.techstreet.com/.

vi. http://www.scte.org/default.aspx.

CHAPTER 12

IPTV Architecture

INTRODUCTION

Radio frequency (RF)-modulated broadcast TV, covered in the previous chapter, is the way television has been transmitted since the beginning of television—that chapter includes a lot of prerequisite material you will want to review before reading this chapter. The broadcast, or *linear*, model has worked well and arguably has a place even in today's environment. However, "the Internet has changed everything," or at least it has changed a lot of things, including people's expectation of what they want to see when. The mantra today is "what I want, when I want it, where I want it," and this paradigm is often best satisfied with video sent using the Internet Protocol, *Internet protocol television* (IPTV). A video stream can be sent to one and only one person, with everyone getting individualized programming, what he or she wants, when she wants it, using a protocol called *unicast*, covered below. Of course that's not very efficient use of data facilities, but we're in the business of giving people what they want. We can also send linear (*appointment TV*), the conventional TV model, as IPTV, using a protocol known as *multicast*, which we'll also cover in this chapter, and multicast is more efficient with data facilities than is unicast.

With IPTV, compressed video is gathered into packets and transmitted using *Internet protocol (IP)*, the predominate suite of protocols used to transmit information over the Internet. Data transmission is usually analyzed using the ISO (International Standards Organization) 7-layer model, with layer 1 being physical transport, up to layer 7, the applications layer, where user software resides. If you are not familiar with the 7-layer model, there are any number of references, including a basic introduction in the Ciciora reference.[i] Here we shall be most interested in layer 3 (IP being the most interesting but not the only protocol) and layer 4 (TCP and UDP being of greatest interest). We will stray above or below these layers at times. Note that video transmitted via IPTV may or may not be transmitted over the Internet. Some operators are using IPTV as the delivery vehicle for their subscription video and pay-per-view video services rather than using broadcast. In this case, the video is not actually moving over the Internet, but rather is moving through the end fiber-to-the-home (FTTH) network from headend to home using the same or similar protocols as used

273

by video delivered over the Internet. In this case IPTV packets are intermingled with packets delivered via the Internet (e.g., web surfing and email) in the FTTH system.

OTT VERSUS TV SUBSCRIPTION SERVICE: TWO TYPES OF IPTV

When we say IPTV, we usually mean one of two things. Either we mean video that comes to the subscriber over the Internet, or we mean a video service that you the operator provide, which just so happens to use the same protocols and data path from your headend to the subscriber as does data from the Internet. Internet data may be video or it might be something else, such as web surfing or email. We're here to talk about video now. We'll try to remember to use *over-the-top* (OTT) when referring to video that comes over the Internet and *IPTV* when it is a service you provide. But even those lines blur at times. If the lines are blurred or we forget, you may have to deduce the meaning from the context.

Over-the-Top

An increasing number of video program providers are providing their programming over the Internet directly to subscribers, bypassing the local system operator (except for using the local operator's Internet access service). This type of service is collectively called *over-the-top (OTT)*. Usually this is done on demand, after the program has been broadcasted on the linear channel if the video is a TV show. The OTT showing is controlled by the people who own rights to the show. Some program networks are providing their programming "streaming" in real time or later, but only to people who subscribe to the linear channel via a distributor such as a cable TV or satellite system. Several companies are practicing a business model of selling old TV shows and/or movies via the Internet, and some are also producing original material. Probably the best known OTT video product is video uploaded by ordinary people to services such as You Tube. Cisco has said that if you watched video every minute for 2 years, you would be able to see all of the video uploaded in 1 second![ii]

Well, "bypassing the local system operator" is even complicated in this case. It is true that OTT programs are not provided by the local FTTH [or cable TV or telephone company digital subscriber line (DSL)] system, but they do use the local system's data delivery network to deliver the program to subscribers. The local system does not derive revenue from the OTT video, except for the normal data revenue. An OTT-supplied program will not carry the local operators' branding, and will not appear in the operator's program guide. However, as of this writing, we are seeing the beginning of guides to which a viewer can subscribe in order to locate some or all available programming. Some OTT programming services are starting to aggregate programming as cable TV and satellite programmers have done for a long time, and they will provide a guide (and charge for that services). Not all programmers are participating.

The target display device for IPTV may be a television receiver. Most televisions cannot receive IPTV directly, so a set-top box (STB) of some sort must be used. A few but increasing number of "smart" TVs do have the capability to receive OTT video directly, though from a limited number of OTT suppliers. Other devices used to receive IPTV include all the usual suspects: computers, pads, smart phones, and gaming devices. In some cases, wireless transmission may be used for the last part of the program's journey, though wireless can be problematical at times.

Broadcast TV is called *linear video* because it is intended for consumption when offered, and the consumer has no control over what program is presented when. Of course, recording the program on a personal video recorder (PVR) is common today. Much, but not all, OTT programming is called *nonlinear video*, because the subscriber can request the program she wants, when she wants it. She can usually pause the program, rewind, and fast-forward it. Some providers make it impossible to skip the advertisements. Some OTT programming is "streamed" in real-time, and, in addition, may or may not be made available on-demand after the real-time streaming.

Since we are talking about programming delivered over the Internet, there are potential problems involving available data rate: sometimes there will be a very open connection with lots of bandwidth, so that perhaps a TV can get very good video (for the Internet). At other times the Internet will be more crowded and the highest-quality video will require more bits than possible to transmit. The old way of handling this would be to let the video freeze when the bit rate cannot be supported. Some vendors of OTT video now support multiple data rates, and a mechanism for detecting if the data path is good enough for the highest data rate. If so, then the highest data rate is transmitted. But if that data rate cannot be supported, then a lower data rate (lower-resolution) data stream is substituted. The philosophy is that a lower-resolution picture is better than no picture at all. The bandwidth testing is dynamic, and if the path again clears such that bandwidth for the higher-resolution picture is available, then the higher-resolution video is sent.

Subscription IPTV

There is another type of IPTV that is not OTT, but which uses the same Internet technology for delivery. Traditional programming services offered via IPTV would be linear video as well as pay-per-view (PPV). They are offered by the service provider, carrying that service provider's brand name and identified in the service provider's program guide, with the service provider charging a monthly fee. This service is functionally comparable to conventional broad-cast video service, except that it is offered over the operator's data capacity as opposed to a traditional broadcast capacity. The user may not be aware of the difference. If channel numbers are used at all, it is just to aid the consumer in finding recurring programs that he wants, or possibly to give a common identification with off-air channels or cable channels to which the viewer is accustomed to tuning.

The technical advantages of subscription IPTV delivered via FTTH as com-pared with OTT IPTV are those of capacity and *quality of service (QoS)*, described below, as well as improved picture quality and less tuning delay because higher bandwidth is available. For programs delivered via the Internet (OTT), you are at the mercy of the bandwidth available between where the program is inserted into the Internet (somewhere in "the cloud") and where it is consumed. No one controls that bandwidth; it is what it is at any moment. All packets on the Internet are treated equally, so it is possible for a path to have a lot of, say, web surfing traffic or file transfers, which are not time-critical, but which hold up a time-critical video packet. In your local FTTH system, you have a lot of bandwidth, and if implemented properly, you have the right QoS mechanisms in place to ensure timely delivery of video packets. Of course, if you have a slow Internet segment somewhere, it is hard for the average consumer (or regulator) to tell the difference between that and slowing in your plant.

If we remember to do it, we shall differentiate between the two types of IPTV as OTT and subscription IPTV when necessary. However, we noted above that people are starting to aggregate programs to sell them in a traditional subscrip-tion model, but over the Internet. And of course, a subscription (traditional) operator does offer PPV and variations, which are individual programs to indi-vidual subscribers. So the field is confusing. Mostly though, we'll talk about subscription IPTV, since that is pretty much the only thing you can influence. As we shall see, the mix of different types of video makes both terminology and capacity planning difficult.

Subscription OTT as Your Service

There is a hybrid model out there today that you should strongly consider supporting. When your subscribers are not at home watching your service, be it IPTV or broadcast, they still want to see your shows. So some operators are working with their program suppliers and providing a rich line-up of subscrip-tion TV shows as OTT for their subscribers when the subscribers are not at home. They can also watch on their portable devices when they are home. In order to avail themselves of this service, they must be subscribers to your video service, and are asked to put in a user name and password before accessing your content when they are not on your IPTV network. This gives a strong competitive advantage to the operator providing the service, as your subscribers can get service anywhere there is a good Internet connection, just as if they were home.

COMPRESSION AND BIT RATES

All digital video transmitted to consumers must be compressed in order to make transmission feasible, and several standards are in use today. To be more precise, there are several *decompression* standards in use; there are no compression standards, despite common usage of the term. The distinction is important, though: since consumers all have decompression equipment and that equipment must be very low in cost, standards have been written saying that when the decompressor receives a certain command, it will react in a prescribed manner. Encoders, on the other hand, are primarily used at the professional, transmitting end, of the link. Or compression may be done in general-purpose computers, many of which still have problems implementing transmission-ready compression in real time.[1] Over time compression algorithms get better, yielding lower transmission bit rates for the same quality level. This is the reason we don't want compression specifications: the compressor manufacturers need the freedom to adjust compression algorithms, so long as the output makes the decoder do what it is supposed to do. There are several different decompression algorithms in use.

MPEG-2

This is the original commercially available algorithm that has been in use since the mid 1990s. As a rule of thumb, you can assume that full entertainment-grade video is available at a data rate of about 4 Mb/s or a little less for standard definition (SD) and 12–15 Mb/s for high definition (HD). While not as efficient as newer decompression algorithms, it remains in use for broadcast, most cable, and much satellite transmission. It is used in conventional DVD players, and is a required option for Blu-ray players. The reason for its continued popularity is that the number of decoders in consumers' hands (purchased by consumers in the broadcast and satellite cases, owned by the operator in the cable TV case) is very high, so moving on from MPEG-2 is not something to be taken lightly. MPEG-2 includes the compression algorithm and a transport container analogous to UDP in the Internet world. When MPEG-2 is transmitted on the

---

[1]It is true that consumer video cameras put out compressed video, but it is at too high a data rate to be considered "transmission-ready." In order to keep costs and battery usage within the realm of consumer electronics, consumer cameras put out video at about 25 Mb/s. They do not implement the more computationally intensive compression steps. Professionals usually handle uncompressed video at over 1.1 Gb/s because it can be edited easier with higher quality, and because picture and sound can be corrected more accurately. The video is compressed only when it is prepared for distribution.

Internet (it is rare on the Internet today), it must first be placed into MPEG-2 transport packets, which are then placed in TCP or UDP packets.

You will get some of your video streams in MPEG-2, from broadcast stations and some programs delivered via satellite. You have the choice of either carrying them in MPEG-2 on your network, or transcoding them to MPEG-4 (see below) in your headend. Transcoding equipment is available, and you will probably want to do this—even if you do have the capacity on your passive optical networks (PONs) to carry MPEG-2 (and you do), doing so will place more burden on your switching equipment and may require more bandwidth to your OLTs. Most or all IPTV STBs (let us use STB as generic for any connected device) today include MPEG-4 decoding, but they will also do MPEG-2 decoding. If you anticipate using any other decoding standard as defined below, check with your STB manufacturer to make sure that you can decode it.

MPEG-4

MPEG-4 is the work-horse compression algorithm of Internet video transmission today, and finds some use in satellite and cable transmission. MPEG-4 is also known as advanced video coding (AVC), or by its ITU designation, H.264. As a rule of thumb, assume a bandwidth of 2 Mb/s for SD and 8 Mb/s for HD using MPEG-4. It is optional to put MPEG-4 packets in an MPEG-2 transport stream before putting them in TCP or UDP packets. MPEG-4 is specified as a decoding format for Blu-ray players. Oh, what happened to MPEG-3? Originally it was to be the high-definition companion to MPEG-2. But people found that MPEG-2 was a perfectly competent high-definition decoding system, so MPEG-3 was never developed.

You will see so-called HD streams transmitted over the Internet at speeds approximately one-quarter to one-half those cited above. True, you can do that, but the amount of compression required is such that a good video engineer would argue about the picture really being HD. We recently referred one such stream to an experienced video engineer with a major programmer, and he described it as being "a little better than SD, and wide screen." This seems to be the story with much of what passes for "HD" on the Internet today, but many subscribers don't know the difference.

Some OTT programmers detect the device being used to receive the stream, and send a stream with resolution (and speed) appropriate to the device in use. Thus, they will send a faster stream to an STB, and a much slower stream to a phone. The phone screen is so small that you would not see the higher resolution if you could get it into the phone. People will call them all "HD" streams, because that is what the public is expecting, and frankly many don't know the difference.

Video Coding 1

The Video Coding 1 (VC1) decompression standard is promulgated by the Society of Motion Picture and Television Engineers (SMPTE), and is said to be very similar in performance to MPEG-4. It is based on, but not identical to, Windows Media Player 9. VC-1 is used by some on the Internet, and is included in the formats required to be decoded by Blu-ray DVD players. VC-1 is claimed to not be subject to all of the patents needed for MPEG-4.

High Efficiency Video Coding

High Efficiency Video Coding (HEVC) is a new standard which is nearing completion as this is written. It is expected to yield entertainment grade video at about one-half the bit rates stated for MPEG-4, and will likely be used for home distribution of ultrahigh-definition video (UHDTV—see below). However, UHDTV involves four times the pixels (picture elements) of regular HDTV, and pixels make the difference in transmitted bandwidth. So with four times the pixels and an improvement of two times transmission efficiency compared with MPEG-4, you are still at a transmission rate twice that of MPEG-4 if you transmit UHDTV. There are other improvements in HEVC, such as more colors transmitted, that may slightly add to the bit load.

Ultrahigh-Definition TV

Ultrahigh-definition TV (UHDTV) is thought to be the next big thing in video (after 3D TV was thought to be the next big thing a few years ago, but has so far not lived up to that promise). UHDTV has been used in some variants in theater projection for a while. As commonly accepted, UHDTV is twice the horizontal and twice the vertical resolution of HDTV, with the same 16:9 aspect ratio (ratio of picture width to picture height). Some TV sets are on the market, and some material is being shot in UHDTV, though as of this writing, transmission is still in the planning stages. Some programs are being shot in UHDTV (some are still shot in film, which is good enough to support UHDTV) in order to future-proof them, providing a ready source of material if and when it is time to transmit UHDTV. Now it so happens that perceived picture quality depends on a lot more than just the number of pixels (the resolution, or sharpness of the picture), but the commercial race has settled on this metric as being the easiest to express, and the easiest to sell to the public. So that is where the race is run.

Other Improvements

Among the other picture improvements that are likely to appear with UHDTV include improved black performance. New display technologies can produce better contrast for portions of the scene near black, and this can improve the picture. Better blacks can and may well be incorporated into standard HDTV sets too.

Another improvement is that conventional TV, including HDTV, is limited in the color spectrum it can put out. Not all colors that can be perceived by the human eye can be reproduced by television. New technology is improving the spectrum of colors that can be displayed, but this will also require the transmission of more colors, so we expect this to be phased in over the next number of years as UHDTV becomes mainstream (if it does).

IPTV TRANSMISSION OPTIONS

There are two common protocols for transmitting IPTV, unicast and multicast. *Unicast* video is intended for one and only one subscriber. A video stream is generated at the source, be that in your headend or somewhere in the Internet, "the cloud." This video stream goes only to that subscriber. Obviously this is not too efficient with data capacity, but it is often required. For video transmitted over the Internet, it is the only practical solution, since the Internet does not support the alternative, *multicast*, which we shall cover below. Also, there are very many types of video that are customized for an individual subscriber. The most obvious example is video from online sources such as NetFlix, Hulu, You Tube, or Vimeo. A user expects to watch whatever video he or she wants, when he or she wants it. So if two people are watching the video but one starts 1 second after the other, then there is no way except to unicast two separate streams. Also, video on demand (VoD), a staple of cable TV, is just what it says: on demand. Accepted practice is to allow the viewer to have "VCR-like" control over the playout, meaning that the viewer can control start, stop, pause and resume, rewind, and fast-forward. Obviously this means that each subscriber needs an individual program stream.

But even with the emphasis on "what I want, when I want it, where I want it," much video viewing remains appointment, or linear viewing, meaning that the program is broadcast by the programmer, intended for consumption (or recording) by all subscribers at the same time. If we just had a way to support this with IPTV, we could send one program stream for all subscribers, obviously much more resource-efficient. It so happens that we can do this over an FTTH network, using a protocol called *multicast*, which is very analogous to broadcasting in conventional TV environments. We'll describe both unicast and multicast in more detail, but first let us set the stage with a simplified FTTH network.

A Simplified FTTH Network
Fig. 12.1 illustrates a simplified FTTH network, showing only the pieces necessary for the present discussion. At the headend, linear video is readied for IPTV transmission using an *encoder* if it is not already suitably encoded for transmission.

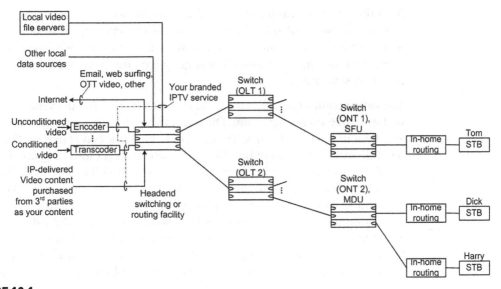

FIGURE 12.1
Reference FTTH network.

This may be the case for satellite-delivered video you purchase today from certain suppliers, as it is intended for delivery to cable TV headends. If video is suitably compressed and encoded, then it just needs *transcoding* to IPTV packets, a simpler (and cheaper) process—more video is becoming available in IP form now, reducing the need for encoding. This might represent satellite-delivered video from a program wholesaler who has prepared the video for IP dissemination before uplinking it. Sometimes video content will be supplied in IPTV format from third parties, ready to go into your switch, as in the bottom-most input to the switch of Fig. 12.1. Implied is that the video is delivered via an IP network, hopefully not the Internet. If video is delivered over the Internet, you probably will want to buffer it to compensate for Internet delay and jitter. Better but more expensive, the video may be delivered over a private network designed for video delivery. This may be very attractive for smaller operators, since operating an IPTV headend is not necessarily cheap. To the extent it is practiced, the practice of obtaining third-party content via private IP network seems to be more common in Europe than in North America. We are seeing equipment intended to allow several smaller operators to share a bulk program feed, with each being able to make the content appear to be its own service.

If we are dealing with VoD or a similar service, then the program will be supplied presumably correctly packetized for IPTV, from a video file server (or in some cases you may be purchasing it from another supplier). If you have arrangements with OTT vendors to buffer their content, that content will also come from video file servers. You will also be handling OTT video directly from the Internet as well of course, plus all nonvideo applications. All of these sources are switched suitably in your headend switching or routing facility, which we have represented as a single switch. It may be this single switch, or it may be much more complex. If a large system, the switching may be distributed over several states.

The switch connects to all of the OLTs in your network. In our example system, we have three subscribers, Tom, Dick, and Harry. Tom is connected via OLT #1 and lives in a home. He has his own ONT, #1. Dick and Harry, on the other hand, live in an apartment building and share one multidwelling unit (MDU) ONT. Their ONT, #2, is fed from a PON attached to OLT #2. Each subscriber has some sort of in-home routing network, no two of which are alike in all probability. But the in-home network doesn't play much of a role in what we are talking about here, assuming it is fast enough to be up to the tasks involved, and that its firewall doesn't block any necessary packets. Of course there are a lot of other subscribers, but this is enough to explain the principles and some problems. Let's see how unicast then multicast would work in this scenario.

Unicast

Fig. 12.2 shows an even more simplified signal flow when we are sending unicast video to Tom, Dick, and Harry. We show it coming from the local video file servers, since most if not all of what comes from a video file server will be unicast by its nature. So even if all three viewers are watching the same movie or TV show, they are each pulling their own stream. Let's assume they are all

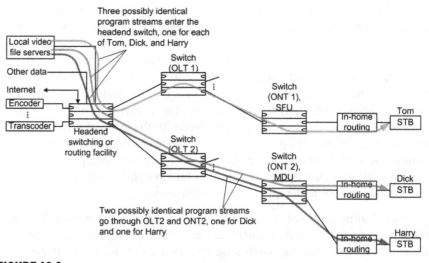

FIGURE 12.2
Unicast scenario.

watching a high-definition movie at 8 Mb/s. This means that the three of them are burning 24 Mb/s from the file server to the headend switch. Tom is burning 8 Mb/s on the connection from the headend switch to OLT 1, and the same on his PON to his ONT.

Dick and Harry, because they share an ONT, are burning 16 Mb/s between the headend switch and OLT 2. The data continue to flow on their PON to their ONT, and it is only at the output of the ONT that the two program streams split to different interfaces.

Unicast uses the maximum bandwidth at any point in the network, since it must travel from the headend (or from anywhere on the Internet) to the subscriber, as a unique stream. This is pretty much universally the way video is carried on the Internet today. If we just had a way to use the bandwidth more efficiently when possible....

Multicast

Fig. 12.3 begins our journey into multicast. This is the same scenario as in Fig. 12.2, except that now the video is being sent as a multicast, the IPTV equivalent of broadcast. Each subscriber is seeing the same part of the program at the same time. Our story opens with Tom watching the hit film *The Uninformed*, while Dick and Harry are napping. So the program is coming from a transcoder in the headend (the movie may be transmitted via satellite). The transcoder converts the packets to suitable IP packets and sends them to the headend

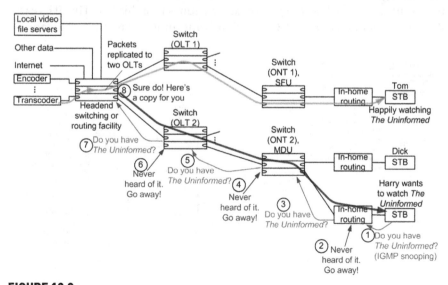

FIGURE 12.3
Multicast, first scenario.

switch, which sends them to OLT1, the next switch in the path. OLT1 puts the packets on the PON that feeds Tom's ONT (ONT1), and his ONT sends the packets to Tom's in-home routing and finally to his STB.

Having established this basic scenario, we can wake Harry from his nap. Harry decides that he wants to watch *The Uninformed*, so he tunes it on his STB. This initiates a series of actions, which also happened when Tom first started watching—follow the circled numbers to see the sequence of events as we describe them. Harry's STB sends a command, called an *IGMP request*, to his in-home routing. We assume that all boxes in the network support a protocol called *IGMP snooping*, in which they monitor the IGMP requests, and act upon them as appropriate, as we show below. In essence, the IGMP request asks the in-home router, "Have you got *The Uninformed*?" Well, since no one else is watching that movie through the in-home routing equipment, the answer is "No, I don't have it." So the IGMP request continues upstream, encountering the next switch, MDU ONT 2. The same scenario is played out here, since ONT 2 doesn't have the program, pushing the IGMP request to OLT 2, where yet again the same scenario is played out.

Finally the IGMP request reaches the headend switch, and a different scenario unfolds! Because Tom is already watching the multicast of *The Uninformed*, the headend switch DOES have the movie, so it replicates the packets and sends them toward Harry's STB. Now two people are watching the same program, yet only one set of packets needs tie up bandwidth between the transcoder and the headend switch, because the switch replicates the packets.

Now let's go a bit farther, and wake up Dick (Fig. 12.4). Dick decides that he, too, wants to watch *The Uninformed*, and he tunes it on his STB. His STB reacts the same way that Harry's STB reacted, sending an IGMP request upstream, to

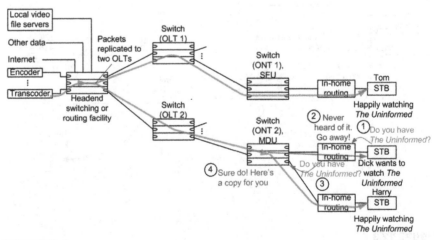

FIGURE 12.4
Three subscribers watching the same multicast.

the first device that might have the movie. It doesn't, but the next box upstream, ONT 2, does have it, by virtue of it already feeding it to Harry. Thus, ONT 2 replicates packets and sends a set to Dick as well as to Harry. Recall that Tom is getting his packets from a different route, coming through a different OLT.

So looking at the big picture now, Fig. 12.5 illustrates the same scenario, except that Tom, Dick, and Harry are all watching the same *multicast* program. Multicast is the IPv4 equivalent of broadcasting,[2] since everyone is watching the same program at the same time. Note that multicast is much more efficient in terms of bandwidth utilization than is unicast. Assuming that all equipment supports multicast, then the program needs to be sent from the headend only one time, regardless of how many people are watching it. Each switch in the chain duplicates the packets and sends them out where they are needed. In the example of Fig. 12.5, the headend switch duplicates program packets and sends them to OLT 1 for Tom and to OLT 2 for Dick and Harry. We only burn 8 Mb/s between the transcoder and the headend switch. Each OLT handles one data stream. In this case, OLT 2 does not need to duplicate the packets for Dick and Harry, because they are on the same PON. If they had been on different PONs, then OLT 2 would have duplicated the packets for the two PONs. But since Dick and Harry share ONT 2, then ONT 2 will duplicate packets, sending them out the ports serving the two subscribers. In the somewhat unlikely case

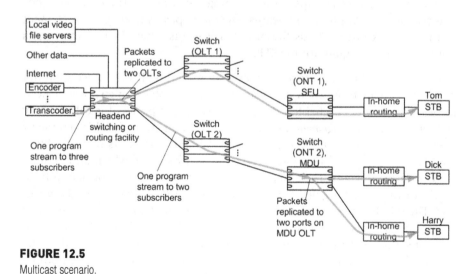

FIGURE 12.5

Multicast scenario.

---

[2]*Broadcast* has a different definition in IPv4 than elsewhere. In IPv4 the term *broadcast* means to send the same data to each and every receiver on the network without the receiver soliciting it. Elsewhere, including IPv6, *broadcast* means to make available the same signal to all receivers which are interested in receiving it.

that ONT 2 doesn't support multicast, then OLT 2 would have duplicated packets and sent the duplicates on the same PON to the same ONT.

This is our answer to the bandwidth efficiency dilemma! We only need to launch the program once from the headend, and let the network duplicate the packets. Comparing Figs. 12.2 and 12.5, we see that when each viewer is watching a multicast, we burn 8 Mb/s (in our example) from the video source to the headend switch. Then from the headend switch to OLT 2 we burn 8 Mb/s to serve the two customers in our example. This may not seem like much, but multiply it by the number of customers served by the OLT (potentially 2000 to 8000, based on the OLT capability), and the bandwidth starts to add up. Fortunately, too, statistics are going to work for us, and not every subscriber will be watching TV at the same time.

In Fig. 12.5, we see that no matter how many subscribers are watching the same multicast program, we only burn 8 Mb/s *for this program*, as the duplication of the packets occurs in the network. But as usual, we don't get something for nothing. The complexity of multicast is significant—a colleague in the IPTV business once estimated that a simple channel change by one subscriber is touched by as many as 17 vendors! If an STB watching a multicast changes channels, it will first send a LEAVE message that tells the network to stop sending it packets of the old program. The receiver of the LEAVE message, maybe the ONT or the OLT, must decide if anyone else needs the program, and if not, it sends a LEAVE message upstream, stopping the program. Then the STB sends a query for the new program it wants. The query passes through each element in the network until it finds the program it wants. That element then starts duplicating the program for the STB.

There are a number of protocols involved in providing IPTV, but we shall not emphasize them more than necessary to establish the framework you need in order to provide a reliable IPTV service. The basic protocol is called *IGMP* (*Internet Group Management Protocol*) in IPv4 and *MLD* (*Multicast Listener Discovery*) in IPv6.[iii] Among other things, it handles requests by an individual STB (or IP-enabled TV, or game console, or whatever), which knows of an IPTV program it wants. The STB gets program identification information from an electronic program guide (EPG), and requests the program from the headend. The IGMP request progresses from the STB toward the headend, but stops as soon as it finds the requested program. For instance, in Fig. 12.5, if Tom has not started watching the show that Dick and Harry are watching, then the request from his STB will have to go to the headend switch, because nothing closer to Tom has the program.

Each routing element in the chain periodically sends out a downstream query checking to see that the program is needed further downstream. If it does not get a positive reply, then it stops sending the program. But if an STB leaving the channel sends a LEAVE command, why does each element need to check to see if the program is still needed? Well, there is always the possibility of missing a LEAVE command. More likely, there is a possibility that the STB was disconnected from the Internet, or it lost power. Under either of these scenarios it would not be able to send a LEAVE message.[3] And we don't want packets moving through the network unnecessarily, because that wastes bandwidth— even though we have a lot of bandwidth on an FTTH network, we don't want to waste it. Often in the headend, we tend to work more closely to the bandwidth limit—more on this later.

Delivering Program Streams to the Headend

Let's back up a moment and talk about delivering IPTV program streams to the headend router. If you are receiving signals by satellite or locally, they will likely go through some sort of grooming equipment (not shown in the figures), to support advertising insertion, possibly the addition of IP multicast addresses and ports (if not added at the router), and possibly for other reasons. You will need to add scrambling to most channels. Start with your STB vendor to define ancillary systems needed, as different vendors configure things differently.

Recall that video packets can be sent on either UDP or TCP, depending on the application. If a packet is a multicast packet sent via UDP, that protocol does not try to keep track of whether or not all packets are received, and if so if they were received in the correct order. In a multicast session, in which packets go to a number of different STBs, it would be impossible to make corrections for individual STBs anyway, so the STB is left to its own devices to handle any packet errors it encounters.

Unicast streams may be transmitted using either TCP or UDP, but, if TCP, you need to think about whether an error in reception of the packet is correctable by reordering or retransmission or not. Most OTT video transmissions over the Internet today seem to use TCP, and the buffering intervals are long. This translates to long tuning time for the customer when he tunes to the program—we have seen tuning times approaching 1 minute. We have also witnessed differences this great when pulling two unicast streams of the same program to two different devices. For OTT video, your subscribers will need to live with these issues. If you get any of your branded content delivered over the Internet (perish the thought), you probably want to consider buffering it at the headend in order to shorten tuning time for your subscribers, then sending it out using UDP.

---

[3]Some ONTs have the capability of sending a "dying gasp" message when they lose power. A filter capacitor in the ONT is sized to be large enough to power the ONT for long enough for it to send a message saying it is going off-line due to loss of power. But this dying gasp message may not include a leave command.

Estimating Network Requirements

Thinking through the information above, you might conclude that it is hard to plan your required IPTV bandwidth. You would be correct. How many streams of unicast will subscribers pull at one time? And how many subscribers will be pulling how many multicast streams? How many programs will be standard definition (at maybe 2 Mb/s in MPEG-4) and how many will be HDTV (about 8 Mb/s, maybe less since some webcasters play a little loose with the definition of "high definition")? We might be able to estimate the percentage of TVs tuned in at each house (about one-third of all TVs connected at peak hours), but how many TVs are connected? How many STBs were left on when the TV was turned off? You don't know. Many STBs are always left on and the TV turned off—in fact, some low-end STBs don't even have the capability of being turned off.

But it gets more complicated. Not only do you need to contend with TVs, but a number of people are viewing on computers, pads, and phones, as well as game boxes. Some OTT providers offer their programs in high definition (the ones we've seen, we'd call pseudo HD) and standard definition. Some providers claim to be providing UHDTV over IPTV, though we are again skeptical of the real quality level. In general you will need at least three streams at different data rates to satisfy all of these platforms: large-screen ultrahigh-definition TVs demand very high bandwidth. Phones are very small screens, and may not even be able to ingest the number of bits per second demanded by large-screen TVs. Certainly they cannot display the same number of bits, so there is no use transmitting that many bits. Many streaming providers detect the type of device being used for receiving a unicast program, and supply an appropriately sized data stream.

But it gets more complicated. Because of congestion on the Internet, some IPTV OTT providers monitor the network speed available to each subscriber. If they are sending out more data than a particular subscriber can receive (for example, due to congestion on the Internet), they switch that one subscriber to a lower-speed data stream. If the subscriber can utilize a higher-speed stream, and the bandwidth is available, the data rate is increased. The idea is that a lower-speed, lower-resolution picture is better than a picture that is breaking up, or no picture at all. But, of course, this can add another source of uncertainty into your system.

The writer recently set up a test of a streaming service he was originating and sending to a reputable content delivery network (CDN), an outside company that replicates our one stream into as many unicast streams as needed to satisfy all viewers. We were on the phone with a representative of the CDN, who was monitoring our stream at their ingest point, on the other side of the US from our location. He confirmed that he was seeing our stream coming in at a respectable (for the 720p material being handled on the Internet) 3+ Mb/s. Yet we could see the return stream coming back at varying speeds from 3 Mb/s and dropping to below 1 Mb/s as congestion in some part of the Internet limited our bandwidth. As the speed changed, we could easily see the change in resolution of our picture.

But it gets more complicated. You are sitting pretty on a fall Saturday afternoon, with half of your subscribers watching the favorite football team. Of course, this is a multicast stream, so the bandwidth consumption is a minimum. Now all of a sudden, the network switches to commercials. Maybe 20% (and I'm pulling numbers out of thin air) of your subscribers get up to take a break and 50% sit and watch the commercials. The other 30% start channel-flipping to see what else is on, waiting until the commercial break is over. Some are just flipping channels randomly, and some have programmed in favorite channels and are flipping through them. Remember the complexity we discussed above regarding tuning a multicast? All of a sudden, 30% of your subscribers are flipping channels as fast as they can flip them (which isn't very fast for IPTV). Now your entire network is going crazy handling IGMP leaves and joins at each point in your network. We have known systems located where football is bigger than just about anything else, which systems worked perfectly except during commercial breaks in football games featuring the #1 college in the state.

But it gets worse: some middleware providers attempt to speed channel change by operating servers which cache the program stream, always holding an output queue with the most recent i-frame at the head of the queue. When someone changes a channel, the server begins unicasting with the current i-frame. This avoids the need for the STB to wait for the next i-frame, which has all of the information to start displaying the picture. The program is unicast to all STBs needing it, and the multicast stream is also sent to these boxes. The STB gradually brings the two streams into synchronization, and when they are synchronized, switches over to the multicast stream, dropping the unicast stream from the local server. But this adds bandwidth, doubling the bandwidth to each STB upon a channel change by that box. If a subscriber is channel surfing, this can happen over and over again until he finally settles on a channel. While this technology for speeding channel change was developed by a very well-known company, and since sold to others, we are not a fan of the technique. It does improve channel-change time, but is rather complicated, and it can add significant load to the network.

You need rules of thumb as to how much bandwidth you require in order to support all of the services you will need to support. We have not seen any issues with EPON systems providing 1 Gb/s to 32 subscribers, though the systems sometimes are loaded more than 50%. We are not sure what will happen in the future, as more IPTV gets consumed but compression gets better. For the headend-to-OLT links (see Figs. 12.2–12.5), and with close to 2000 subscribers on an OLT, and with good QoS (see below), we know that a 1 Gb/s link (network-side of OLT) is insufficient, but 10 Gb/s works. One way to allocate bandwidth is to assume all available programs are being handled by the OLT, so provide for that much video bandwidth to the OLT. Whether or not all channels are provided to the OLT depends on the particular OLT and switch/router vendor. Redundant links are strongly recommended at this point in the network. Programs must be properly tagged with their priority level (described below) *at the entrance to your network*, and this tag must be carried throughout your plant.

Fig. 12.6 summarizes the capacity issue based on experience with a number of customer installations on several continents. Let's start at the entrance to the headend switching facility. Remember, we have illustrated this as a single switch or router, but it may be much more complex. There may be a number of different video inputs to the switch, depending upon how you get your video. Video may be coming from satellite receivers at your headend, and either being

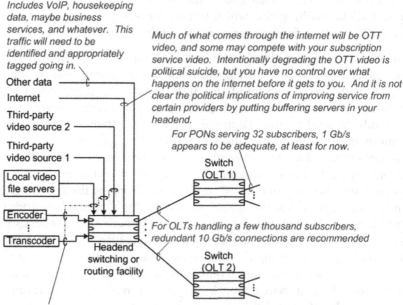

FIGURE 12.6
Suggested capacity planning issues and tagging.

encoded or transcoded to IPTV for input to your switch. You will have a VoD server which supplies video (we are not showing the upstream control in these diagrams, but of course it exists). Sometimes you may be getting video from other suppliers via a data network. We show two inputs here. This video may be coming over the Internet, but it is more likely coming from a private data network which can ensure adequate capacity.

In addition, of course, your subscribers will be pulling data from the Internet, and much of these data will be OTT video. Finally, you will have other data, VoIP, housekeeping data, and possibly business services. Your switching facility should have the ability to identify and tag these packets as they enter the switch, or the first point where you touch the packets. The tag needs to be carried all the way to the ONT, where it is usually stripped off before the packet is sent to equipment outside of your control. Similarly, upstream packets must be tagged appropriately at the entrance to the ONT, and the tag retained until you hand off the packet to some other system.

You need to make sure that you can prioritize packets appropriately, because you will get conflicts, and the correct packets must go first when multiple packets present for transmission at the same time. Below we shall present two different methods of making sure packets are dealt with in the proper way as they go through your system. Either approach can work, and each has advantages and disadvantages.

INDEED, A BIT IS NOT A BIT IS NOT A BIT

In the early days of the Internet, proponents of sending video via IP used to say, "a bit is a bit is a bit," meaning that you could treat all data, be it part of a web page, part of an email, or part of a video, the same. This has proved to be far from the truth, though, and many problems have arisen when people didn't understand the concept. For email and web surfing, if there are delays getting bits to the customer, no problem. But it can be devastating to delay video or voice, both of which are time-critical.

Transmission Control Protocol

Let's talk in terms of packets, collections of up to around 1500 bytes sent as a group to one receiver, or in multicast, to multiple receivers—more on that below. If the packet is part of an email or a web page, and if it gets lost, corrupted, or delayed en route to the receiver, it is no big deal. Those packets are sent using a layer 4 protocol called *TCP* (*transmission control protocol*), which keeps track of packets sent and received. If a packet is received out-of-order with respect to others because it got delayed for some reason, that's no problem. TCP will put it back in its rightful place at the receiver, before passing it on to higher-level processing. If a packet gets lost or corrupted, then TCP requests that the sender resend the packet, and puts it in the correct packet order at the receiver. The user is unaware of these operations. The problem with these functions for video (and audio) is that they take time, and when a decoder needs the information in a packet, it needs it then, not a few milliseconds later.

User Datagram Protocol

We have shown that TCP is appropriate for certain types of packets, such as most web page access and email. But as we have implied above, it is not always appropriate for very time-sensitive material such as video or audio. The problem is not just the handling of delayed or missing packets as we described above, but there is another problem. As we described above, much video material is sent on your network (not on the Internet) using a method called *multicast*, in which multiple receivers get and use exactly the same packets. This is analogous to broadcasting video, in which all receivers are tuned to the same program. If we were to try to use TCP with multicast packets, we would create a mess; different receivers will experience loss or corruption of different packets, and if TCP tries to request retransmission of each, we could create quite a traffic jam with the retransmission of packets that will arrive at their destination too late to do any good anyway.

So there is a different layer 4 protocol that can be used for real-time video and audio on your network, called the *user datagram protocol* (UDP). We refer to TCP as a *connection-oriented* transmission model in that it makes every effort to get the message through in spite of the things that can go wrong in data transmission. By contrast, UDP is considered to be a *connectionless* transmission model; it is best-effort only. If a packet makes it through, which fortunately is the norm, all is fine. But if a packet does not make it intact, then it will be passed (or not if it didn't make it at all) to higher layers of processing the way it was received. The higher layers of processing will have to deal with it. This makes more sense for real-time transmission, since retransmission or waiting for a late packet doesn't work, as we have argued above.

In some cases, incorrectly received packets can be masked at higher layers in the ISO stack. For example, if a packet representing certain pixels of a picture is not received intact, thus rendering a certain part of the picture incapable of being displayed correctly, then the corresponding pixels from the previous frame might be substituted. Of course it is not a perfect solution, but the pixels change relatively little from one frame to the next, so repeating pixels from the previous frame can do a decent job of masking errored information. A more sophisticated decoder might look at the previous frame and the following frame, assuming it was received correctly, and interpolates correctly received pixels.

Since multicast is rarely used on the Internet as of this writing, we don't see much UDP—all of the OTT traffic we've monitored has been unicast using FTP[4], and this agrees with what little survey information we have found. But delays from the time you request video until the time you get it are high. Five or six seconds delay from requesting a video until it starts seems to be generally the low end, though we have found a few low-bandwidth videos that started faster. We have seen delays approaching a minute on some services. Once the video starts, delay really makes no difference. By contrast, if you are channel surfing on your TV, you probably think 1 second is too long to wait for video after a channel change.

The Internet does not support multicast, only unicast, and it is in multicast that UDP makes the most sense. On your network, from the headend to the home, then multicast makes a lot of difference in programs you are distributing to many subscribers at once. But this is on your network, not the Internet, even though your network is using Internet protocol and in many ways looks like the Internet (such networks are sometimes called *stubs* off the Internet). You have several advantages that the Internet does not have when it comes to delivering packets successfully. For one thing, you have a lot of bandwidth per subscriber compared with the Internet. Also, you can prioritize traffic such that more critical traffic will experience less delay, at the expense of less critical traffic. The Internet can't do this.

Jitter

Packets can be delayed not only due to missed and out-of-order receipt, but even absent these problems, any Ethernet-based system is going to introduce a certain amount of variation in the time a packet is received versus when it was sent. The reason goes back to the shared path nature of Ethernet-based systems. Normally, when a packet presents itself at the input of a router, it is forwarded as soon as the router has finished forwarding packets presented earlier. But packets can be of different lengths and there might be several higher-priority packets already in queue, or there may not be any packets in queue. So at every element in a network, the delay encountered by a packet is indeterminate. Thus, the variation in time a packet is received at the set-top box. This is called *jitter*, not to be confused with *clock jitter*, a time base instability which is more in keeping with jitter as understood by traditional video engineers.

Buffering

This problem of jitter can be mitigated to an extent by *buffering* the data at the STB. Buffering is accomplished by putting the incoming data through a

---

[4]FTP is a transmission protocol that keeps track of data packets received. If they are received out of order they are re-ordered, and if any are missing, they are requested to be sent again.

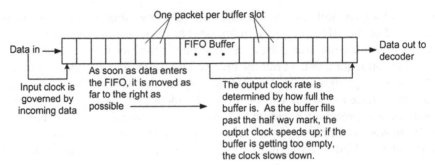

FIGURE 12.7
FIFO buffer in STB.

first-in-first-out (FIFO) shift register. At one time, literal shift registers were used, but today it is more likely that you will find the function accomplished in software, but using a shift register to explain what is going in is convenient and accurate.

Fig. 12.7 illustrates an FIFO function in an STB. The FIFO is divided into a number of slots or cells, each of which can hold one incoming packet (or we can look at it in terms of bits, not packets). The packets are clocked into the FIFO by the receive data clock, which causes a transfer each time data are received by the STB. As data are received, they are moved as far to the right in the FIFO as possible, so that they are adjacent to previously received data, and as data are shifted out to the decoder, the more recent data move farther to the right.

There are several ways to clock data out of the FIFO, but the one we have shown is that the "fullness" of the shift register is measured, and that fullness controls the speed of the output clock. As the buffer fills past a certain point, perhaps the 50% fill point, the output clock speeds up. As the buffer empties, the output clock slows down. Thus, the buffer stays more-or-less half full, and if a packet is delayed, it has time, within limits, to "catch up" in the FIFO.

So why is this not a 100% solution to the packet jitter problem? The longer the jitter we have to deal with, the longer the buffer has to be in order to accommodate it. And there is no cap on the delay that may be experienced, though as the delay gets longer, the probability of a packet getting delayed that much goes down. The longer the buffer, the longer it takes to fill it to the half-way point, so when you first tune to a program, it will take longer before the picture appears. A common complaint against any digital video system, and especially against IPTV, is the delay between when you tune a channel and when you get a picture. So the more a designer protects against packet jitter, the more complaints he or she gets about tuning time.

There are things you can do in your headend to minimize the packet jitter, and we'll cover them later in this chapter. But you have little to no control over packet movement on the Internet, so you are pretty much stuck with whatever jitter you get in OTT video. You can buffer the video in your headend, though this does cost money. It is sometimes practiced that you may team with certain OTT video providers to store their popular material in local servers or caches, so that when a subscriber requests certain material, it is played out locally. This saves Internet access bits, since you only download to a local server once, and it improves the subscriber experience by eliminating any Internet-induced jitter. But it does cost money, and you have to work that out with the OTT vendors. We are not in the business of giving legal advice, so consult your attorney, but there have been some cases in which operators were accused of favoring one OTT vendor over others. If you buffer locally, you will want to make sure you are not perceived as violating some rule in existence at that moment.

Quality of Service

Quality of service (QoS) can also be called quality of experience (QoE). QoS problems can be due to dropped packets, corrupted packets, packet jitter, or other issues in the network. But they all show up pretty much the same to the subscriber: frozen pictures, pixilation ("blocky" video), stuttering audio, or no program at all. QoS remains a problem over the Internet, which doesn't have end-to-end QoS implemented. But you can make it good in your plant, at least for video over which you have control—OTT video will do what it does; your task with OTT is not to degrade it further. You can use deep packet inspection to identify incoming packets that contain video, and you can give them QoS from the entry to your system. Will it do any good? Maybe, maybe not. But for relations with your subscribers and regulators, we recommend doing it—it shows that you are not favoring your own service over others, even though it may be hard for some people to understand.

At least two different QoS schemes have been used: intserv (integrated services) and diffserv (differentiated services).[iv] We shall explain both below.

Differentiated Services

Ethernet-based services, including most FTTH protocols, have traditionally used *differentiated services*, also called prioritization or diffserv. Different types of services are assigned different prioritization levels (*priority queues*), of which there are between four and eight available, depending on the equipment. Packets of more than one priority may go in the same priority queue. When two packets present for transmission at the same time, the one in the higher priority queue gets to be transmitted first. A common prioritization scheme has the highest prioritization assigned to system control messages, because these need to get through no matter what. They don't take much bandwidth, but if you are having congestion problems and need to get into your network to control it, the last thing you need is to have your control messages blocked by something else.

The next highest priority of service is usually voice, because voice packets, while taking only modest bandwidth, must not only get through with low jitter, but also low delay (latency). If you have excessive delay in a telephone conversation, one talker will grow impatient waiting for an answer from the other end. Lower delays (a small fraction of a second) are usually not noticeable. (If you want to experience delay, set up a cell phone conversation with both ends in the same room, and see how much delay you are getting. The cell phone companies try hard to keep the delay within tolerable limits.) Back in the 1980s, when many overseas voice calls were made via satellite links, sometimes multiple hops, it was not at all unusual to experience a maddening delay, in which you ask a question, and it seems that it takes forever to get a reply. What was actually happening is that you were getting a second or so of delay in each direction of the phone call, and that was very noticeable, and irritating.)

The next bandwidth priority is IPTV. You can stand some delay in the IPTV packets, but you are limited in the amount of jitter you can stand—we have discussed this some above and will return to it below. IPTV is by far the highest consumer of Internet bandwidth, so this is a big deal in setting your QoS parameters. If you are also handling commercial traffic covered by service-level agreements (SLAs), which require that you provide a certain minimum bandwidth at all times, you may put them in this same queue—more on that below.

After IPTV, you still have web browsing and email. These can be low priority, because if there is delay in receiving a packet, or even if a packet is dropped and resent due to congestion, it is not a problem and will not even be noticed by the user. As for OTT, you could (and probably should) put it in the same prioritization level as IPTV, but there could still be problems due to jitter and other delivery problems that happen before you get the packet.

This should cover the vast majority of needs for consumer data, but there could be a few more considerations in handling commercial data. You may be handling commercial data on the same network over which you handle residential data. For commercial accounts you may well offer (and be tested on) a guaranteed bit rate, either at all hours or at specific hours. The agreements are called *service-level agreements*. We show one way of handling it in Fig. 12.8, but there are other ways as well. You will need to make sure that you have enough

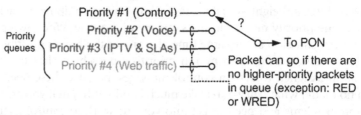

FIGURE 12.8
Packet prioritization in differentiated services.

capacity to provide for the SLAs you have signed, AND have enough bandwidth left over for all of the other services.

There is an exception in some systems to the strict prioritization scheme shown. If you get into a capacity problem (not likely on the FTTH portion of your network, but possible in your routing), you (or your switch) may have to make some tough decisions as to what to drop. This can alert you that there is extreme congestion in the network, and cause you to look into doing something about it. The dropping of higher-priority packets is called *RED* for *random early detection*, the improved version being *WRED* for *weighted random early detection*.

RED and the improved WRED come into play when more than one priority of packets is in one queue. For example, in Fig. 12.8 you might have IPTV packets, which really, really need to get to their destination on time, and you might have packets covered by an SLA, which if they do not go in will cost you money. So if you get a total congestion on the output such that you just can't send all of the packets, the switch may be programmed to discard enough IPTV packets that the packets covered by the SLA get through.[v] This is going to make one or more TV viewers mad, so you want to do your capacity planning so that this never happens, or happens so rarely as to be hardly noticed. If it happens very often, you are going to have to add more capacity at that point in your network.

Note that capacity problems can crop up in a number of places in your network. Depending on the configuration of your network, they can happen at the input of the network, or they can happen between the switch and the OLT, or they can happen when the OLT makes up the packet stream for each PON. So you may have to implement WRED at any of several places in your network.

Integrated Services

The other QoS mechanism is *integrated services* (Fig. 12.9). In telephone-speak, this was referred to as a "nailed up connection." This is more analogous to the traditional telephone-oriented bandwidth reservation system, which was adapted to DOCSIS protocols for cable modem service. When a service needs bandwidth, some intelligence in the network must be aware of the need, and must reserve the bandwidth during each cycle of data (often called a *frame*, *super frame*, or *master frame*). Enough bandwidth is reserved to accommodate

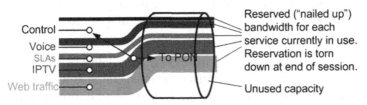

FIGURE 12.9
Integrated services QoS mechanism.

the need, and during the time that the service is active, no other service can use the bandwidth. If the service that reserved the bandwidth is not using it, no other service can use it.

It stands to reason that integrated services-based QoS is not going to be as efficient with bandwidth as is differentiated services, because unused but reserved bandwidth cannot be used for some other service. Also, differentiated services QoS does not require intelligence in the network to set up and tear down a "virtual circuit." With integrated services, each virtual circuit must be set up (in each direction) when needed, and "torn down" when it is no longer needed. There is no doubt that integrated services QoS will offer more reliable bandwidth, as there is no possibility of oversubscribing the bandwidth. (It is, however, possible for a service to get the equivalent of a "busy signal" if there is no room for the service in the data stream.) Jitter can be controlled better, too, since the reserved bandwidth can occur at the same time in each frame. Most or all FTTH systems we have seen to date do not use integrated services-based QoS, but some extensions to FTTH will likely use it in the future, though it may be restricted to PONs used more for business than for residential applications.

Tuning Time

Several times we have alluded to tuning time for IPTV. In the old days of analog video, it was possible to tune from one channel to another and have video displayed within well under a second. People got into the habit of channel surfing, just holding down the UP or DOWN button on the remote control to flip through channels, stopping if they saw something interesting. Or even if you knew which channel you wanted next, it was sometimes easier to just hold down the UP or DOWN button until you reached the channel you wanted. This doesn't work too well for digital video, though, for a number of reasons, some of which we have and will describe. Fortunately there are new methods for finding the channel you want (electronic program guides), which might make channel surfing less important than it used to be. But complaints about tuning time with either broadcast digital or IPTV abound. Systems have been developed to reduce the tuning time, but they tend to be complex and add cost to the headend. In this section, we'll mention some of the things that tend to increase tuning time. Maybe this section is getting a little deep for a practical book on setting up systems, because there are only a few things you can do to affect tuning time. But we present it because it has gotten to be such an issue in some situations, so you may want to understand it. If you don't care, skip to the next section.

Note that tuning time is not the entire delay from transmission of the signal to reception—this can run much longer due to encoding times. But we assume that these encoding times are of no interest in the present context, because they don't affect the subscriber. For live over-the-air events, the entire delay from program origination to reception can easily run 5–10 seconds (did you know that you didn't know about the winning touchdown until 10 seconds after it happened? Your buddy found out about it 3 seconds before you did.). For live OTT video delivered via the Internet, we have personally witnessed delays approaching a full minute. "Tuning" delays for OTT can be in the tens of seconds for reasons we'll mention below.

Program Request

Regardless of whether you are dealing with multicast or unicast, the STB must request the program, and the request must propagate to the place in the system that has the program, and is capable of sending it to the STB. Particularly with multicast, there could be a fair amount of processing along the way to determine whether or not a particular switch had the program, and there is some time required to start duplicating packets. If another program is being left, then the packets associated with that program must be stopped, else twice the required bandwidth is consumed until the program does stop. This can under some conditions create a transient condition in which the demanded bandwidth exceeds that possible, or at least exceeds that authorized to a particular subscriber. This can slow the time that packets for the new program begin to arrive at the STB.

Error Correction

It is possible to transmit redundant information in the data such that errors in transmission can be corrected within limits. This allows systems, even FTTH systems, to operate at lower signal levels, improving economics and making the systems more forgiving of problems. The downside is first that more data must be transmitted in order to effect error correction, and second, at the receiver, the data are delayed. A block of data is covered by extra bits (*error correction* bits) that allow most errors not exceeding a certain length to be corrected, using a technology called *forward error correction* (FEC). But at the receiver, all of the bits in the correction block plus the extra bits used in correction must be received and the corrections, if any, made before the block of data can be passed to the next stage. This adds more delay to tuning.

Your video service should not need as long a buffer as does OTT video. Jitter on an FTTH network should be low compared with what OTT video experiences. Most modern FTTH equipment does include error correction, and this can let you operate safely at lower optical signal levels. However, you should not operate your system at such low optical levels that you depend on error correction too heavily. Video still will not tolerate as much error correction as will other services. Generally you don't have control over the length of buffering used in the STB—that is set by the manufacturer and doesn't change.

Packet Reordering

In order to improve the effectiveness of error correction, often the order of packets will be changed for transmission. The reason is that error correction can be used to fix certain transmission errors by transmitting some redundant information as described above, and if a fairly long block of data is corrupted, the forward error correction can often fix it. A block of data is covered by a set of error correction bits—any error in the data block can be fixed by the extra error correction bits, within limits. Frequently errors come in bursts, and it is possible that the error burst is too long to be corrected. By intelligently changing the order in which bits are transmitted, it is possible to make the error burst cross two blocks of data such that the errors in the burst can all be corrected, because they occur in multiple correctable blocks. But then the receiver must put the bits back in the correct order, and that takes more time.

Jitter Buffer Fill

Above we described the need for a jitter buffer, to compensate for inconsistent arrival time of packets, and in the case of OTT video, to allow for out-of-order and missing packets to be corrected. Before the STB can start decoding video, the buffer must fill to its nominal fill level, and depending on the buffer depth, this can take significant time. The manufacturer designs the length of the jitter buffer to take into account the longest jitter expected, but that number can differ from one system to another. In some cases there can be more than one jitter buffer that must fill, one at a time, before the video can start. Especially in systems receiving video over the Internet, OTT video, the buffer fill time can sometimes take 30 seconds or so. This long buffer fill time is due to the way programs are sent over the Internet. Packets can encounter some very long network delays, as well as delays for error correction, reordering, or retransmission. Also, even programs sent for simultaneous consumption by many people must be individually sent to each receiver, because there is no concept of multicast on the Internet itself. So the server must generate an individual packet stream for each viewer.

Waiting for the i-Frame

This gets us into a bit of awkward semantics. There are several uses of the word *frame* in the world in which we live. A frame can be a block of data in some systems, but here we are talking about television frames. Each complete TV picture presented to the viewer is called a frame. This is what we are talking about now.

Analog video consists of a series of complete frames, usually 30 (or really 29.94) frames per second in North America. Analog TV can start displaying video when it gets a full frame, so it has about 30 times a second to get started displaying the picture. Digital video works differently, though. Since there is considerable redundancy between frames, one of the methods to reduce the data rate is to eliminate this redundancy. But it means that the TV will have to wait longer in order to get enough information to display a picture. Several types of frames are transmitted, one of them being *i*-frames. An *i*-frame contains all of the information needed to reconstruct a picture. So the TV has to wait for an *i*-frame before it can start displaying a picture—the other types of frames only include difference information and thus do not have enough information to generate a picture. There are choices in how often the encoder transmits an *i*-frame: since *i*-frames are big, you don't want to transmit them too often, but the longer you delay between transmitting *i*-frames the more error correction information that has to be transmitted and the longer the TV must wait before it gets an *i*-frame. There are no standards for how often *i*-frames are transmitted, but transmitting two *i*-frames per second is fairly common in MPEG-2, longer between *i*-frames in advanced systems—we have seen 8 seconds intervals. This means that a TV may have to wait at least 0.5 seconds before it can start decoding a picture, and this is after it requests and receives the data stream, finds the data it needs, fixes any errors, and fills its jitter buffer.

Some STBs wait until they have a complete picture built prior to display, and others build the picture in real time. While this does open the door for a "blocky" picture right after a channel change, it reduces the time before the STB is showing some sort of picture of the channel.

One vendor does sell a solution to the tuning time delay related to waiting for *i*-frames, as we mentioned above. In this solution, a server (or servers) at the headend captures each frame of each channel, and keeps the most recent *i*-frame at the front of a buffer, so that when a subscriber tunes to that channel, the server is ready to immediately play out the most recent *i*-frame, which is unicast to that subscriber. Over the next number of seconds, the video being unicast to that subscriber is brought into synchronization with the multicast being sent, and when the two are in sync, the STB is switched over to the multicast stream and the unicast stream is discontinued. You can see that this is a rather costly solution for one part of the delay problem, costly both in the servers and in the bandwidth used on the FTTH network. Only relatively large systems are able to afford it.

Reordering Frames

We talked about *i*-frames, which include the most data because they have all of the information necessary to reconstruct a picture. They are transmitted maybe twice a second, plus at every scene change. Another type of frame transmitted is the *p*-frame, which predicts the next frame based on the previous frame. Since there is a lot of redundancy from one frame to the next, a lot less information needs to be transmitted in a *p*-frame than in an *i*-frame. The third type of frame is the smallest of all: the *b*-frame (bidirectional), which allows the decoder to decide what a given frame looks like based on the preceding and following frames.

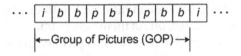

FIGURE 12.10
Group of pictures.

This takes a picture to comprehend. Fig. 12.10 is a typical so-called *group of pictures* (GOP), one of our more amusing acronyms. The GOP starts with an *i*-frame, followed by two *b*-frames, which estimate a picture from the *i*-frame and the next *p*-frame. But here we have a problem: we are trying to estimate the two *b*-frames using the *i*-frame and the next *p*-frame, but when we need the two *b*-frames, we have not yet received the next *p*-frame. So the order in which the frames are transmitted must be the *i*-frame, the *p*-frame predicted from it, then the two *b*-frames. This means that the encoder must send the *i*-frame, followed by the *p*-frame, then the two *b*-frames that preceded the *p*-frame. The decoder in the STB receives the *i*-frame, then the *p*-frame, then the two *b*-frames. Only then can it start to decode and display anything, because only then does it have the information it needs.

AD INSERTION

Many systems offset the cost of purchasing video by inserting advertising in the channel. Typically national cable TV networks (but not local broadcast outlets) provide two blocks of 2 minutes per hour of *local avails*, or time available for local systems to insert advertising. The network sends a signal to the local system activating and stopping the avail time, so inserting the ads is automatic for the local system. Of course, the local system sells and bills for the advertisements, and may or may not produce the ads. The value of this for smaller systems must be compared with the cost of purchasing the ad insertion equipment, the cost of selling and possibly producing advertising. It may be that you can join an advertising consortium of systems that share some or all facilities.

MPEG encoding includes *presentation time stamps (PTSs)* individually for both video and audio, telling the receiver when it is to present each video frame and each snippet of audio. The PTSs are normally put on at the encoder (usually not under your control), and ride through the system. However, there are times that the PTS must be re-established, one of those times being when an ad is inserted locally. This breaks the timing being used by the TV, so the ad insertion system will need to reset the PTSs based on what the ad does. This is one of several opportunities to develop *lip-sync* problems in the video. Lip-sync problems arise when the PTSs for the video and audio do not follow each other correctly. It is manifested as what the name implies, a time error between when you see a speaker's lips move and when you hear the words.

SIGNAL GROOMING

Another common situation encountered at headends also can produce lip-sync problems. Common practice is to multiplex several programs on the same satellite transponder, so what you have coming out of the receiver is the program multiplex. But you may well not want to carry all of the programs, and over IPTV there is no concept of multiplexing several programs on a single RF carrier. Rather, every program is transported in its own packet stream with its own program identification. Perish the thought, but if you are also operating some slower-speed delivery networks, such as DSL, you may decide to reduce the data rate of the programs as they come off the satellite. This will reduce the resolution, or sharpness, of the signal, so please don't do it to your FTTH customers! But if you do change the resolution, this may well mean that PTSs need to be changed in the headend, which is the job of the local multicast router or specialized video equipment. So check lip-sync.

SCRAMBLING

It is common practice in cable TV systems to scramble some or maybe all signals transmitted. Certainly all high-value content, such as video-on-demand and premium channels will be scrambled. We may be moving to more of an â la carte world, in which consumers have more choice in the channels to which they do or do not subscribe, and this will encourage more systems to scramble more channels. Typically, a scrambler is used in the headend to encrypt the signal. What cable TV calls *scrambling* is called *encryption* in other fields, and scrambling has a different meaning. We are using the cable TV definition here, meaning to render the signal unwatchable by anyone who has not purchased the channel and thus received the key to descramble it.

A number of scrambling systems are in use, some based on standard encryption algorithms, some based on proprietary scrambling systems. All must have some mechanism of securely getting the descrambling key to the set top(s). For unicast material (e.g., video-on-demand), key distribution can follow usual methods. But for multicast, some sort of key distribution must take place that delivers keys to the set-top boxes ordering the service, and not to others. This is frequently a part of a manufacturer's "claim to fame."

SO IN SUMMARY, HOW DO WE OPTIMIZE IT?

The first issue with IPTV is to make sure you have enough capacity to make all of your customers happy. Video can suffer some delay, but it is not very forgiving of packet arrival jitter. If you put longer buffers in your set tops (usually not under your control), this can make up for more jitter, but at the expense of slower channel tuning, and this makes subscribers angry. The problem is that this is a hard number to predict: you have a mix of unicast and multicast, you have pictures going to big-screen TVs that take lots of bandwidth, and you have pictures going to phones with very small screens, and correspondingly less need for data.

Often the biggest usage time will be during station breaks, and commercial breaks in highly watched sports events. At those times, subscribers are going to start channel surfing, and that will place quite a load on your system. The best guideline we can give you is that you need more than 1 Gb/s just for video, in order to serve an OLT with a couple of thousand subscribers. Ten Gb/s works well, and redundant connections are important. One Gb/s on a PON with up to 64 subscribers seems to work fine. We strongly recommend that you monitor your capacity utilization at every interface possible, and be prepared to add facilities as you see usage creep up. You should consider a bandwidth increase as soon as peak utilization reaches 80% in order to prevent congestion.

For the downstream streaming signal, you must give it the correct priority, usually below control packets and voice priority but above everything else. The priority must be added at the entrance to your network, not part way through; don't let nonprioritized video go through your router and put prioritization on at the OLT—the OLT may do it, but you can get into trouble in your router. Strip the prioritization off at the ONT at the home, and not before. Every device that handles the IPTV must honor prioritization (or another QoS mechanism if you are using something else).

Probably the biggest mistake we have seen systems make when it comes to IPTV goes back to the old untruism, "a bit is a bit is a bit." We say it is an untruism because, well, despite what folks said in the beginning, it is not true. This manifests itself in a manager assuming that just because he has a great IT guy, that the guy is qualified to configure IPTV. "It ain't necessarily so." IPTV is enough of a different animal that you need someone who knows it to configure it. Larger systems may have an IPTV engineer on staff. Smaller systems may send their IT person to their FTTH vendor's training to learn how to configure IPTV, or they may rely on an outside consultant. But if you rely on the outside help, make sure that the help is qualified. We have seen consultants who claimed to understand IPTV do quite a number on unsuspecting systems, things that ultimately cost the system a lot of money; they paid once to have it done wrong, paid a second time to have the wrong undone, and paid again to have it done right by someone who knew what he was doing. Your FTTH vendor or your video system vendor may be able to train your person, or may have someone who can do the required configuration. It'll be real expensive to save the money and not hire them to do their thing for you.

OTT video presents an interesting conundrum. Your subscribers are likely to expect the same performance from OTT as they do from your video service. Yet there is no concept of prioritization or of multicast on the Internet, so you have no control over what happens to packets before you get them. You can and probably should do *deep packet inspection* in order to determine what packets contain OTT video, and assign them to the same priority as to your video. But the results are not likely to be as good because of what happens before you get the packets. Explaining this to customers or regulators may be difficult. As this is written, the FCC has said that they intend to regulate IPTV and OTT as a data service, which probably means some expectation of quality. But how this will really play out is still up in the air. The saving grace may be that this book may be obsolete and you may be retired before all of the expected court challenges run their course <grin>.

If you are a larger system, then some popular OTT vendors may be interested in setting up servers in your system which capture their more popular content, then stream it to your viewers from the local server. This improves the experience for the OTT viewer, and it reduces the amount of data that you have to get from the Internet, so it seems like a win–win situation. However, keep your ear to the ground regarding regulations coming from the FCC or elsewhere in the government—we are not sure if this practice will be found to be legal or not.

Regarding scrambling (meaning, rendering the video and audio unintelligible without having the descrambling key), it is true that FTTH systems can and do scramble data sent to subscribers. Some operators like to use this scrambling to control who gets what video, and to save the cost of video scramblers in the headend and descramblers in the home. We do not recommend this approach. While you might make it work, the scrambling done in the set-top box market works seamlessly with billing systems, and can respond to high loads of people tuning to an event at the same time. It is designed to work well with both unicast and multicast. The same cannot be said for the scrambling of the PON system. Its purpose is to give comfort to each subscriber that his or her data cannot be seen by anyone else. Let the FTTH system do what it does well, and let the set-top box system do what it does well.

CONCLUSION

Well, we hope that between this chapter and the one on broadcast video, that you have a decent feel for what you need to do to get video up and running. We have avoided details that tend to be manufacturer-specific, because, well, they are manufacturer-specific. You will need to make sure that you have someone available who understands all aspects of your video product. Just because someone is a good IT person does not necessarily make him a good video person. We have worked with many a system which proved this to us in no uncertain terms. Hire or train someone on your video configuration—it'll be the cheapest money you ever spent.

Unfortunately, video is not going to be your biggest profit center due to what you will have to pay your suppliers for programming. But it can be profitable, and will be the most visible part of your service offering. So it needs to be good, better than that of the competition. People who have gone about video the right way have been successful with broadcast video (on which the entire cable TV industry was built), and they have been successful with IPTV service when they have done it right. Just remember, "a bit is not a bit is not a bit."

Endnotes

i. Ciciora et al., Modern cable television technology. 2nd ed. Elsevier, Inc.; 2004.

ii. http://stor.balios.net/Live2011/BRKEVT-2614__Designing_a_Video_Sharing_and_Delivery_Environment.pdf.

iii. Currently the governing document is RFC 4604 from the Internet Engineering Task Force, https://www.ietf.org/. This document may be superseded by another in the future.

iv. Weber J, Newberry T. IPTV crash course. McGraw Hill; 2007.

v. Cisco IP Telephony Flash Cards: Weighted Random Early Detection (WRED), see http://www.ciscopress.com/articles/article.asp?p=352991&seqNum=8.

CHAPTER 13

VoIP Architecture

INTRODUCTION

There are many ways to send voice over the Internet. Collectively they are called, very creatively, voice over internet protocol (*VoIP*). While each of the standards is different (and incompatible), they have this in common: a central intelligence, called a *softswitch* or something similar, sets up the call at the request of one of the telephones on the network. The calling telephone (endpoint) notifies the softswitch that it wants to call a certain party. The softswitch sets up the call by talking to the two (or more) endpoints and telling them how to communicate with each other. During the actual conversation, the softswitch is out of the loop; it plays no role in the endpoints talking to each other. At the end of the call, one endpoint may communicate with the softswitch again, telling it that the conversation is over. The softswitch then *tears down* the call by telling the endpoints to stop communicating, and it records that the endpoints are again ready for another call. In some systems (e.g., DOCSIS cable modems), the softswitch has a role to play in setting up the quality-of-service features that ensure a high-quality call. In most fiber-to-the-home (FTTH) systems this is generally not necessary.

Besides the softswitch, you will need an interface to the *public switched telephone network* (PSTN), since not all calls will reside entirely on your network. You will need a way to handle long-distance calls. This may be most economically provided by keeping the call in VoIP form until it reaches the location of the other party, then getting on the PSTN there. Many competitive phone companies offer included domestic long distance. You will need a way to complete and bill for international calls.

The softswitch (known by other names in some standards) is not necessarily located in the served system, and may well not be owned by the entity operating the network and branding the service. It is not uncommon to contract with a third party anywhere in the world for softswitch services. If you do this, we strongly recommend that you establish a connection between you and the softswitch that has quality of service features not offered over the open Internet. Many times contracting for softswitch functionality and PSTN interface is done

307

FTTx Networks. http://dx.doi.org/10.1016/B978-0-12-420137-8.00013-5

by smaller FTTH companies who have a hard time justifying the expertise to operate a phone system. It is also practiced to permit nonaffiliated companies to sell voice services over their FTTH network, in the name of the nonaffiliated company. And it is possible to have more than one voice provider on the network. One of the providers may or may not be the operator of the FTTH network.

While we usually speak of VoIP in terms of voice calls, it can be used for video calls as well. VoIP systems can usually provide all competitive calling features, including voice mail, call forwarding, emergency (E-911 in North America) services, PBX support, fax and security system support, etc. Frequently you will use a gateway at the home to convert from VoIP to analog plain old telephone service (POTS) in order to interface with a subscriber's existing telephones. This feature is usually built into the ONT, and in FTTH networks, we usually just refer to voice ports on the ONT. The cable TV people have a name for the POTS interface; they call it an MTA, or *media terminal adaptor*. When it is part of a cable modem, the more common configuration, it is called an EMTA (*embedded media terminal adaptor*). As a subscriber acquires IP phones that work *with your chosen protocol*, they may be attached directly to the data network in the home. But note that, say, an MGCP phone will not operate with a session initiation protocol (SIP) phone system—these are two of the more common yet incompatible VoIP standards.

The phone may be hidden behind a firewall in the subscriber's home—you may or may not be able to call out, you probably will not be able to call in. At a minimum, most residential firewalls use network address translation (NAT) to convert an incoming address (the public address of the ONT) to a private address used by the SIP device in this case. A calling party will not necessarily be able to see the phone behind the firewall. There are some IETF protocols (e.g., STUN, TURN, and ICE) developed to accommodate firewalls. If you have a problem, your softswitch provider or your outside softswitch contractor will be your best resource to resolve the issue.

Just as we discussed in the IPTV (Chapter 12), there are "over-the-top" voice providers, though we rarely hear them referred to as such. Skype is the best-known of many. It is prudent to handle their traffic with the same prioritization as you handle your own VoIP traffic, using the best of your ability to identify their packets.

VOIP STANDARDS

A number of different standards have been used for VoIP. An early entry was the ITU's H.323 standard, which was conceived mainly as a video conferencing standard, though it works fine for voice too. SIP is similar but incompatible—it has been described as a simplified version of H.323. It was developed by the Internet Engineering Task Force, the IETF, and is probably the most popular protocol used in FTTH systems. The controlling document currently is RFC 3261. MGCP, or *media gateway control protocol*, was used in early FTTH installations as well as in early cable TV VoIP applications. You will still find it in use, but most newer installations, both FTTH and cable TV, seem to favor SIP. Thus, we shall concentrate on SIP in this chapter. H.248, Megaco, was originally a joint development of the IETF and the ITU, but is now being promulgated only by the ITU, for use in carrier networks. SIP uses Megaco to control gateways to the *public switched telephone network* (PSTN). SCCP, sometimes called *skinny*, is a proprietary Cisco protocol, which is being replaced with SIP.

A MODEL SIP SYSTEM

In SIP systems, the endpoints of the communication, SIP phones or adaptors, video conferencing systems, or what have you, are called *user agents*. The user agents communicate by using common Internet protocols. During a voice or video call, the user agents communicate directly with one another, but they need a central intelligence to tell them how to set up a call; the user agents are rather "dumb" boxes that have to be given specific instructions at every step along the way. This is not to denigrate the user agents, but rather it was done intentionally to keep user agents (of which there must be at least one for every user) low in cost while capable of implementing advanced functions. SIP has an infrastructure of network hosts (called *proxy servers*) to which user agents can send registrations, invitations to sessions, and other requests, and from which they can receive "do this next" instructions. SIP is an agile, general-purpose tool for creating, modifying, and terminating sessions that work independently of underlying transport protocols and without dependency on the type of session that is being established.

The SIP Trapezoid

Fig. 13.1 shows the so-called *SIP trapezoid*, so-called because the four elements used in the illustration form something of a trapezoid. The proxy servers provide the intelligence needed to allow the relatively "dumb" endpoints (softphone for Alice in Atlanta and SIP phone for Bob in Biloxi) to start talking to each other. Once the call is set up, though, communication is directly between Alice and Bob, and the proxy servers don't see the packets.[1]

---

[1]In some cases, it may be useful for proxies in the SIP signaling path to see all the messaging between the endpoints for the duration of the session. Each proxy can independently decide to receive subsequent messages, and those messages will pass through all proxies that elect to receive it. This capability is frequently used for proxies that are providing mid-call features.

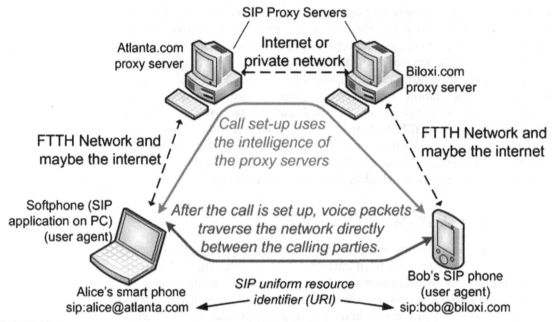

FIGURE 13.1

SIP trapeziod.

We are using the term *softphone* to mean a phone based on software in a computer. It uses the computer's microphone and speakers (or headphone interface). We use the term *SIP phone* to mean a self-contained phone that is on a network, probably wirelessly but maybe wired, which is self-contained so far as the SIP functions are concerned.

Note the similarity between the SIP address and an email address. The SIP address, called a *uniform resource identifier* (URI) will be preceded by either *sip:* (no security desired) or *sips:* (encryption desired). Since Alice's smart phone doesn't know Bob's location (i.e., his IP address), it sends the request to talk to him to the appropriate server, Atlanta.com. Either Atlanta.com has been programmed into Alice's smart phone, or the smart phone discovered it using DHCP, the same way it probably discovered other information it needs in order to communicate.

Communications between the user agents and the proxy servers is done through text messages. By design, the user agents are as "dumb" as possible, relying on the proxy servers to prompt them at each step of placing a call. This reduces cost for the user agents (UAs), and makes it easier to add more capabilities in the future. The UA converts audio and control information (such as dialed digits) into packets that can be routed through a data network to call servers and other UAs.

What SIP Does and Does Not Do

SIP does not provide services. Rather, SIP provides *primitives* (basic communications functions) that can be used to implement different services. For example, SIP can locate a user and deliver an opaque object to his current location. (An opaque object may be defined in this case as a packet that the SIP protocol cannot understand, but which can be understood by another protocol involved in completing the call.) If this primitive is used to deliver a session description written in SDP (*session description protocol*, used for describing multimedia sessions), for instance, the endpoints can agree on the parameters of a session. If the same primitive is used to deliver a photo of the caller as well as the session description, a "caller ID" service can be easily implemented. As this example shows, a single primitive is typically used to provide several different services.

SIP does not offer conference control services, such as floor control or voting, and does not prescribe how a conference is to be managed. SIP can be used to initiate a session that uses some other conference control protocol. Since SIP messages and the sessions they establish can pass through entirely different networks, SIP cannot, and does not, provide any kind of network resource reservation capabilities. The nature of the services provided make security particularly important. To that end, SIP provides a suite of security services, which include denial-of-service prevention, authentication (both user to user and proxy to user), integrity protection, and encryption and privacy services.

SIP works with both IPv4 and IPv6.[i]

Other Protocols Required

SIP is not a vertically integrated communications system. SIP is rather a component that can be used with other IETF protocols to build a complete multimedia architecture. Typically, these architectures will include protocols such as the real-time transport protocol (RTP, RFC 1889) for transporting real-time data and providing QoS feedback, the real-time streaming protocol (RTSP, RFC 2326) for controlling delivery of streaming media, the media gateway control protocol (MEGACO, RFC 3015) for controlling gateways to the PSTN, and the session description protocol (SDP, RFC 2327) for describing multimedia sessions. (We met RTP and RTSP in Chapter 12.) Thus, SIP should be used in conjunction with other protocols in order to provide complete services to the users. However, the basic functionality and operation of SIP do not depend on any of these protocols.

A MORE DETAILED LOOK INTO SIP

Fig. 13.2 is a complicated expansion of Fig. 13.1, showing more elements and physically how they might talk to each other. We shall follow the dashed lines, starting with #1. We assume that you have FTTH networks in Atlanta and

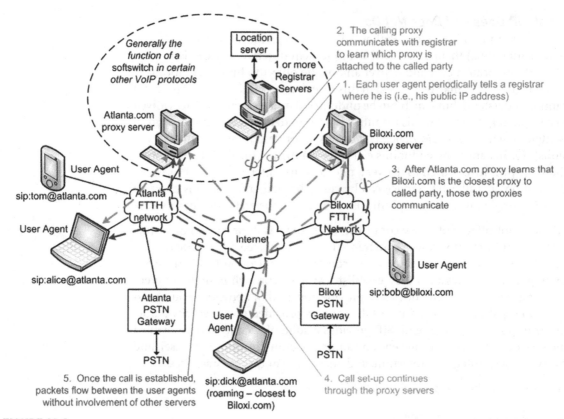

FIGURE 13.2
A more detailed look into SIP.

Biloxi, each individually connected to the Internet. Each location also has a connection to the PSTN. In the example we have one of your Atlanta customers, Dick, roaming somewhere on the Internet—you don't know where he is, but as long as his user agent can point to your *registrar server* (of which you have at least one and probably more if you have multiple locations), you can provide voice service to him.

Registrar Server

Registration is one way in which the system can learn the current location of Dick. Upon initialization and at periodic intervals, every SIP user agent sends REGISTER messages to a server known as a *SIP registrar*, as in dashed line #1 in Fig. 13.2. The REGISTER messages associate the SIP or SIPS URI (sip:dick@atlanta.com) with the public IP address currently assigned to Dick's user agent. The registrar writes this association, also called a *binding*, to a database, called the location service, where it can be used by the proxy in the atlanta.com domain. Some people talk about a location server in which the binding is stored. While logically the location server may be shown as a separate machine, physically it will probably be the same machine as the registrar. Obviously each proxy must have a registrar from which it can obtain information as to how to direct a call. (Often, a registrar server for a domain is colocated with the proxy for that domain, and it is likely the same machine. It is an important concept that the distinction between types of SIP servers is logical, not physical—that is, the same server may be serving as a proxy and a registrar.)

In this figure one of your Atlanta customers, Dick, is roaming and is connected to the Internet. He periodically notifies the Registrar server of his whereabouts (i.e., his public IP address, which will likely change as he roams to different locations). While RFC 3261 doesn't use the term, some references show a *location server* which stores bindings, a data base of users, and IP addresses.[ii] We could also look at this information as residing in the registrar.

Returning to a description of Fig. 13.2, in #1 we showed that each user agent periodically talks to a registrar to give it his whereabouts (defined by the public IP address). In #2 we start the process of calling from Alice to Dick. Alice is the calling party, and goes to her proxy server (Atlanta.com) seeking Dick. Proxy server Atlanta.com communicates with the registrar in step #2 in order to learn that Dick, despite the fact that he is registered in the Atlanta domain, is in fact traveling now, and happens to be closer to the Biloxi proxy server (#3).

In #4, after Atlanta.com has learned that Dick is reachable through Biloxi.com, then those two proxy servers relay the several messages necessary to establish the call—but remember, the call has not started yet. Alice is hearing a ringback at some point, and Dick is hearing his phone ring. After Dick picks up, we move to #5, at which time the call is established, and both user agents know the IP address of the other. Thus, they can communicate directly without involving the proxy servers or the registrar. Only if the call is modified (such as conferencing more people onto the call) are the proxy servers involved.

Dick is not limited to registering from a single device. For example, both his SIP phone at home and the one in the office could send registrations. This information is stored together in the location server and allows a proxy to perform various types of searches to locate Dick. Similarly, more than one user can be registered on a single device at the same time. Also, note that Dick might be anywhere. This has implications for emergency calls, as described below.

We have marked in Fig. 13.2 that the proxy servers, the registrar, and maybe some other ancillary functions comprise what some VoIP standards call the *softswitch*. This term is not used in SIP. However, the functions are there.

Multimedia and Conferencing

We have described SIP in terms of a voice call, but it is just as capable of setting up a video call. SIP can also cause data files to be transferred, so for instance if you are holding a conference call, you can also transfer slides or recorded video to each participant.

Conferencing is easy with SIP. So long as all of the participants are on your network each user agent sends multicast packets of data to all other user agents in the conference. However, it will be common that some participants are to be reached through the PSTN. For those participants, your PSTN gateway will need to manage the conference, using the facilities of the PSTN.

LAWFUL INTERCEPT

As a telephone provider, you are likely subject to the requirements to provide certain records to law enforcement with proper court orders. The original Communications Assistance for Law Enforcement Act (CALEA) was signed into law in 1994, as a way to ensure that law enforcement personnel had access to telephone call information (from/to records and, if appropriate, call content) upon execution of proper authorization. The law has since been expanded to include most traffic handled on voice over Internet protocol (VoIP) systems, and also packet data (any data traffic) in most cases. By May 14, 2007, all affected telecommunications providers (meaning almost all facility-based telecommunications providers) were to have been in compliance. The Federal Communications Commission (FCC) is charged with enforcing the law. As of this writing, their controlling documents are FCC 05-153, adopted August 5, 2005, and FCC 06-56, adopted May 3, 2006. Both are in the matter of Communications Assistance for Law Enforcement Act and Broadband Access and Services, ET Docket No. 02-495, RM 10865. As of this writing, most of the requirements concern voice intercepts. Requirements for data intercept are not as well defined, at least not in the United States. Similar requirements exist in many other countries.

CALEA requires you to provide for lawful intercept (LI) of telephone traffic, which may mean either who-called-who and/or the actual content of the phone call(s). It also requires that you provide for lawful intercept of data packets related to Internet traffic (email, IM, etc.). You are responsible for making available the required information to the appropriate law enforcement agency. There are several places in your network where you may obtain this traffic, but each system is a little different, so this should be discussed with your SIP provider and with your FTTH electronics provider, maybe others. You will probably set up mirror ports to mirror the subject traffic. Deep packet inspection (DPI) techniques have become important to the lawful interception of VoIP communications.

As an alternative to making all of your own arrangements for CALEA compliance, it is possible to use a so-called trusted third party (TTP), with whom you develop interfaces for providing both voice and packet-based lawful intercept. This generally simplifies your task, as you have one outside party with which to deal, rather than an unknown and large number of law enforcement agencies who may make demands on your system. The TTPs are experts in interpreting the law, in extracting the required data, and interfacing with law enforcement agencies.[iii,iv]

MAKING YOUR VOICE SYSTEM WORK WELL

While we have talked about SIP, this section applies equally to any VoIP system. There are a number of issues of which you need to be aware in order to make your voice system work well, and to provide service superior to that provided by traditional POTS. The good news is that you can provide superior service. The first ace up your sleeve is that you are digitizing the voice right at the home. So the distance the voice travels in analog form is very short. In the traditional POTS environment, the voice stays in analog format back to the central office (CO) over a distance that can go to 12,000 feet or more in some cases. In many cases now, the analog voice will go to a digital subscriber line access multiplexer (DSLAM), a field-mounted device located within a few thousand feet of a subscriber, which digitizes the signal for the remainder of the trip to the CO. But the voice travels in analog format over much more distance than it does in a VoIP system. While analog voice can sound very, very good, there are more things that can degrade it than there are when you are using digital transmission over fiber—that's the gold standard for quality!

The Dumb Stuff is the Biggest Problem

One of the biggest problems we have seen in voice-over-FTTH is something we would not have expected. We call this the dumb, simple, stupid stuff that has caused many headaches. As well as components in the traditional telephone system are specified, this one caught us by surprise. There are cheap telephones out there that do not meet specifications for ringing voltage, and for the accuracy of their touch tones. Also, there are in-home wiring issues that produce more loss than expected. But the phone companies have learned to live with the problems, so you must live with them too. You create problems when you bring in the latest-and-greatest FTTH system and one or more of the subscriber's phones will not ring or will not dial. You will never convince the subscriber that his phone is the problem, because it worked with the telephone company. And in some cases, while the cheapest way out might be to buy the subscriber a new phone, sometimes the subscriber likes what he or she has, and is not interested in a new phone; they'll just go back to their old voice provider, thank you.

Over the past couple of decades, those of us in the FTTH equipment business have gained a lot of experience with these issues during sleepless nights. The industry has learned a lot about dealing with the problems, and there is test equipment out there that will help you to track down such problems. So we hope it will not be such a problem for you if you are building a new FTTH system today. But we mention this to make sure you are covered if it comes up. Equipment vendors have considerable experience in dealing with the problems. Ask your proposed vendor(s) about their experience with nonconforming phones, and what they have done to mitigate the problem. Usually this will entail providing somewhat higher ringing voltage than what the standards say you need, and making the DTMF decoder more sensitive and more forgiving of frequency errors. In addition FTTH equipment vendors must implement country-dependent ring tones correctly, typically on the ONT; the VoIP country code configuration is important for the ONT to interoperate with in-home telephone sets.

Voice Quality

Voice quality is often graded using a mean opinion score (MOS), which is a numerical grading of perceived quality, ranging from 1 to 5, with 5 being perfection. While the MOS score was originally subjective, there are machines today which purport to automatically grade a call such that the machine score reasonably correlates with the subjective MOS score. We have seen MOS on reasonably short analog lines in a new suburban area measure around 3.5, while a line used in an FTTH system measured in the neighborhood of 4.5 using the same machine. And since the voice signal is transmitted digitally over fiber for FTTH, the MOS will not change with distance.

Ground Loops

We once saw a problem in which the ONT power supply manufacturer had improperly connected the negative 12 V line to the primary safety ground (the green wire in a North American power cord). Then, properly according to code, the ONT itself was grounded to power ground. But there was a ground loop in the home, causing the neutral potential at the power supply ground to be different than at the ONT ground. This created significant alternating current in the negative lead going to the ONT, resulting in hum on the negative lead, which in turn caused hum in the telephone. The problem was fixed by lifting the ground in the power supply. This was the way the power supply was supposed to have been wired in the first place, and it was not hard to fix once we found the problem. But it cost your author a cold supper.

Voice Compression

Compression of voice transmission is used where it is important to reduce the amount of data transmitted due to a limited-bandwidth channel. This is usually the case for cellular voice communications, and may well be the case for communications via DSL or cable modem. However, for FTTH, you have a lot of bandwidth available, of which voice takes little, and because compression always reduces quality, we urge you to not do it in FTTH. The only concession we may make is that if the other end of the call originates using a severely band-limited channel so that compression is needed on that end, and if it is possible to carry that compression through to the FTTH end without having to decompress and recompress, then it may be best to keep the compression the other end needs.

All compression systems used in voice, such as the popular G.729 specification, use *lossy* compression. That is, some characteristic(s) of the voice signal are changed in a way that the exact voice signal you started with can never be reconstructed. An object of compression is to "throw away" information that the human ear will not notice is missing. But as you get more aggressive with compression, this becomes impossible to do. The native data rate for most voice communication is 64 kb/s, comprising 8000 samples per second at 8 bits per sample. In the POTS world, when this is transported almost no overhead is added. But in the VoIP world, where we have to add Ethernet and IP overhead, this 64 kb/s transmission becomes 110 kb/s or more, depending on how long a sample we put in a packet. This is nothing for an FTTH network, where the slowest possible speed on the fiber is 1 Gb/s, but it could be significant on a cellular network or a DSL network, or even some older cable TV modem standards. Thus, the pressure to compress.

The compression methods used in voice work use a technique called *linear predictive coding* (LPC). We shall provide but a brief overview of the technology here. It assumes a model of human speech that is pretty accurate, and allows speech (not music) to be encoded using minimum computational power. It models the vocal system as a frequency generator that, over a short interval (e.g., 32 ms), produces a carrier frequency and modulation on that carrier frequency. The "carrier" is produced in the vocal cords, and the "modulation" is produced by the throat and mouth. So, for a short sample time, the "carrier frequency" (and of course its amplitude) is measured, then the time modifications are encoded. This information is transmitted to the receiver, where the speech waveform is reassembled as best possible, given the estimates involved in the compression process.

Note that LPC assumes a single dominant frequency in the sample. This is an accurate model for voice but not for almost all music, where multiple tones are the rule rather than the exception. Listen to music-on-hold through a cell phone, or put a phone in front of a radio or other music source and listen on a cell phone located where you cannot hear the original. The extremely distorted sound is a result of LPC trying to compress a multitone signal. (On rare occasion we have heard specially manufactured music-on-hold material that was designed to work with LPC by virtue of it consisting of single tones.)

Now each time you go through a compression and decompression process you lose quality. If you do this several times, you lose a lot of quality. So, for instance, if a phone call originates on a cell phone and is compressed according to that standard, then it is decompressed to go over the POTS system, then it is recompressed to be delivered over an FTTH (please don't compress) or DSL or cable plant, then you have two steps, each of which damages the audio quality, and the multiple compression/decompression steps make a bad situation even worse. So since it is not necessary from a bandwidth-conservation standpoint to compress over FTTH, we urge you to not do it. Not compressing will almost certainly get your MOS above that of a competing POTS system.

Fax Compression

Fax is still in use, as is telephone modem service from security systems and from a dwindling number of point-of-sale (POS) terminals used for sending credit card information. We have a simple answer for compressing these signals over FTTH or any other medium: don't. Don't ever compress them. You will almost certainly destroy the transmission. Fax and telephone modems use multiple carrier frequencies in the audio band, and the LPC compression technology used in voice transmission assumes a single carrier frequency in each time increment. Furthermore, the transmissions are susceptible to the jitter of any IP system, though we would expect good buffer management at the receive end to ameliorate this issue.

Sending uncompressed fax or telephone modem traffic over an FTTH VoIP system should work. There is an alternative in the ITU T.38 fax relay standard. When a fax call is detected at the originating end, then at that user agent (SIP terminology—see Fig. 13.1) the fax call is demodulated to the baseband bits that made up the fax signal before modulation (usually at a data rate not exceeding 14.4 kb/s). This baseband signal is transmitted in IP packets to the receiving end, either the location of the receiving fax or where the signal is put on the PSTN, and there it is converted back to the multitone fax transmission format that came out of the fax machine. Again, this should not be necessary on FTTH plant except maybe for compatibility with something else you are doing, but some voice interfaces may support T.38.

If echo cancellation is provided for voice calls, it must be disabled for fax and modem transmissions. This should be automatic and transparent to you, but you should be aware of the need. Echo can develop in the telephone itself, and is canceled by processes in the ONT or voice adapter. Those processes should detect a fax or modem transmission and shut off the echo cancellation.

Quality of Service

We wrote quite a bit about quality of service (QoS) in Chapter 12, IPTV. You might want to go back and review that information, as it also applies to voice, maybe even to a greater extent than it does for video. Video is very sensitive to packet jitter (the uneven arrival time of data packets), though to an extent jitter can be compensated with buffering. Voice, on the other hand, is sensitive to jitter *and* it is sensitive to *latency* (the absolute delay from the transmitter to the receiver); that is, voice packets cannot be delayed anywhere between the sender and the receiver. When you are talking on the phone and you ask the person on the other end for a response, even 1 second of delay seems long, and makes you wonder just what is wrong with that other person, that they take so long to respond. Because of this sensitivity to latency, we must give voice packets the highest priority of any packets except system control packets. Fortunately, voice takes little of the abundant bandwidth in FTTH networks.

We are limited in our ability to use buffering to compensate for packet jitter with VoIP because buffering adds to the latency of the link. Latency for voice is even more of a problem than is increased tuning time for video due to a longer jitter buffer. If your system uses integrated services as its QoS mechanism (a packet reservation system described in Chapter 12), make sure that you are actually reserving bandwidth for each phone call in each direction (each direction must be treated individually), and tearing down that bandwidth at the end of the call. In the more common case of using differentiated services, a packet prioritization mechanism, make sure that you prioritize voice packets above all others except control messages. In both directions.

Packet Size

You may have a choice of the size of voice packets that you transmit. That is, a packet may contain 4, 8, 10, 20, or 30 ms worth of speech. Or some other length of speech may be in one packet. There is obviously a trade-off here in that the more data you put into a packet the more efficient your transmission because one packet header is used for all of the data sent in the packet, be that 4 or 30 ms of data. But the more data you put in the packet the more of that bad latency you will get, running a risk that the users will notice delay between when one party speaks and the other speaks. Since the data in the entire packet must be accumulated at the transmitting end before the packet can be transmitted, and since at the receiving end we may need to get the entire packet before we start decoding it, we may introduce one-way latency equal to about twice the length of speech in the packet, depending on the implementation of the decompression. The table below illustrates the net bit rate for transmitting a packetized 64 kb/s voice channel using different sizes of voice packets (the *block size*).[v] For severely limited channels, this is an issue, but for FTTH we are not talking about much of our total bandwidth, so you may opt for lower block sizes in order to introduce less latency. Ten ms block size may be good. You certainly don't want to get carried away and use blocks larger than 30 ms.

Block Size (ms of Voice in the Block)	Bytes of Data	Total Bytes with Overhead	Blocks per Second	Data Rate (kb/s) for One Voice Channel
		(Bytes of Data + 62 Overhead Bytes)		(Total Bytes × Blocks per Second × 8)
(A Component of Delay)	(Block Size × 8)		(1000 ms ÷ Block Size)	
4	32	94	250.0	188.0
8	64	126	125.0	126.0
10[a]	80	142	100.0	113.0
20[a]	160	222	50.0	88.8
30[a]	240	302	33.3	80.5

[a]PacketCable Standard.

Uninterruptible Power

As this is being written, uninterruptible power in FTTH systems is a big deal, at least in Washington. What happens to phone service when commercial power is lost? POTS, which you are likely replaced with FTTH-based voice, uses copper wires up to and going inside the home. The copper wire is bad because it conducts electricity. It is good because it conducts electricity. We say it is bad because it conducts electricity, because this means that any power disturbances on the network can get in the house. But it is good because this allows the telephone company to supply power to operate corded phones in the home. Indeed, the phone company traditionally supplies 48 V when a phone call is not in progress and also when it is in progress (though the voltage may drop due to loss in the cable). The phone company provides back-up power for its equipment, and this back-up power is available to corded phones in your house. Traditionally the phone companies provide for at least 8 hours back-up power, though this does not appear to be a standard written down anywhere— it is just what has traditionally been done.

With FTTH, we have a nonconductive drop to the house, so there is not a good way to get power from the network to the home. This is analogous to a situation that existed when the cable TV industry first got into the telephone business in the mid-1990s. There was a lot of concern about emergency powering for in-home telephone equipment. Even though there was a conductive drop, and often there was power in the plant passing homes, there was no way to get the power from the plant to the home because the *tap* used to extract RF signals for individual homes was not designed to pass power. Besides, there was concern that the power used on the plant (90 Vac in most cases) would be dangerous to put on the drop. There were designs for power-passing taps that would remove power if they detected an open drop cable. But, in the end, the industry decided that the most practical solution was to use rechargeable batteries to back up the in-home voice equipment. It is this decision that drives our discussion of powering for FTTH networks.

Concerning back-up power, you have several choices:

1. Do nothing. Most people have cell phones now, so let them use their cell phone for back-up.
2. Do nothing, but provide for an indoor power connection, and let the subscriber provide an uninterruptible power supply (UPS) if so desired. Then management of the UPS and its battery is not your problem.
3. Provide (or offer to sell) a battery inside a power supply that you supply with the ONT. Most of the power supplies used with ONTs will allow you to monitor back-up battery condition through your element management system (EMS). If you do this, you have several choices for battery maintenance:
   a. When you detect an end-of-life backup battery, make an appointment with the subscriber to come out and change it.
   b. When you detect an end-of-life backup battery, mail a new battery to the subscriber, with instructions for changing it, and a mailer in which to return the old battery to you for recycling.
   c. When you detect an end-of-life backup battery, send a notification to the subscriber that she needs to change the battery. Either offer to sell her one, or refer her to a local or web retailer who has the battery. Recycling the old battery becomes the subscribers' responsibility.
4. While not being done as of this writing, some operators are looking at the possibility of providing a power supply that uses nonrechargeable D cells for backup, and defaulting to (3c) above. Nonrechargeable cells have a longer shelf life than do rechargeable cells, they cost less, and you save money by not having to buy a recharging circuit. You would still need to monitor the battery condition and notify the subscriber when new batteries were needed.

We won't presume to tell you what to do, but our nightmare scenario is that for whatever reason, the back-up battery is not available when needed, and while commercial power is out grandma has a heart attack and dies because emergency medical services could not be called. Is this realistic? You decide. Just remember that we live in a litigious society.

The Cordless Phone Trap

Cordless phones have been popular for many years. But a lot of people are unaware that cordless phones do not work if you lose power; even if they are connected to a powered phone line, that power is not intended to power the cordless phone, and indeed, the cordless phone will not use it. So if you provide for any type of emergency power, we suggest that you educate your customers that their cordless phones will not work if commercial power goes out. For that reason, we recommend that each home keep at least one corded phone, which will be the only functioning phone during a power outage.

Emergency Calls

As a phone company, you are expected to be part of the emergency calling system (E-911 in North America). Your softswitch/proxy server vendor should be able to assist with setting this up. As opposed to the situation with POTS providers, though, a phone number is not attached to a physical address (by way of the phone switch), but rather is attached to a device, be it a smart phone on the SIP (or other standard) network, or a gateway serving analog phones in the home. That device is in turn attached to a physical address in the emergency database, but in practice this presents a problem. Particularly in the case of a smart phone, it is possible to take the phone with you to another location. If that phone is then used to contact emergency services, then the incorrect address may be displayed. This is another case of subscriber education.

CONCLUSION

Some people are using their cell phones as their only phone now, but other people still need that home or business fixed phone line. When you are operating an FTTH system, adding voice service is relatively low in cost, and thanks to modern VoIP technologies, you can offer a staggering line-up of features for very low cost. But there are traps you might fall into, so make sure you have access to someone with extensive experience in VoIP.

Endnotes

i. Internet Engineering Task Force, Network Working Group, *Request for Comments: 3261, SIP: Session Initiation Protocol*. June 2002.
ii. Harte L, Bowler D. Introduction to SIP IP Telephony Systems. 2004. Available from: ALTHOS Publishing.
iii. https://www.fcc.gov/encyclopedia/communications-assistance-law-enforcement-act.
iv. http://www.etsi.org/technologies-clusters/technologies/security/lawful-interception?highlight=YTozOntpOjA7czo2OiJsYXdmdWwiO2k6MTtzOjEyOiJpbnRlcmNlcHRpb24iO2k6MjtzOjE5OiJsYXdmdWwgaW50ZXJjZXB0aW9uIjt9 (or go to etsi.org and search for lawful intercept).
v. Ciciora W, et al., Modern Cable Television Technology. 2nd ed. Elsevier; 2004.

CHAPTER 14

Network Management Architecture and Design

NETWORK MANAGEMENT ARCHITECTURE

As long as there have been telecommunication systems providing services to residential and enterprise subscribers there have been management systems. These telecommunication systems have become more sophisticated today, with multiple heterogeneous platforms each with their own independent element management system (*EMS*). Operators have been forced to move from simple command line interface *(CLI)* management interfaces to large-scale distributed platforms providing a common view across each EMS platform. The expectation of the higher-level management platform is to provide a common solution for monitoring, maintaining, and monetizing an operator's network.

In the early 1990s the International Telecommunications Union (ITU) defined a series of standards beginning with X.700, titled "Management Framework for Open Systems Interconnection (OSI) for CCITT Applications". X.700 formalized a structure of network terminology and framework for the management of these heterogeneous platforms. The OSI management framework was defined into five functional areas including (1) fault management, (2) configuration management, (3) accounting management, (4) performance management, and (5) security management. In addition to the five functional areas, as fiber-based access networks start to offer subscriber-facing services, the capability of an FTTx management system to perform troubleshooting and routine or on-demand maintenance becomes more and more useful. Therefore we have decided to extend the framework for the purposes of this book to include a sixth functional area, troubleshooting and maintenance.

More recently the Broadband Forum *(BBF)*[i] has started the effort to address the management architecture and operational process requirements for PON-based network deployments. Many concepts thereof have been derived from the copper digital subscriber line (DSL) access network (see Fig. 14.1) that has existed since the 1980s. Included in these efforts is extending the management architecture to include a further functional area of service quality monitoring (in addition to providing additional structure around configuration management and fault management).[ii] This chapter provides details on each of these functional areas.

323

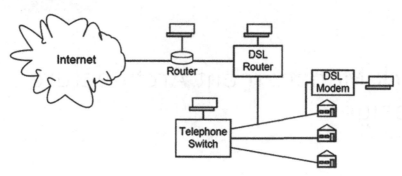

FIGURE 14.1
A DSL access network.

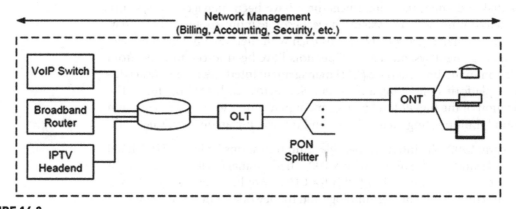

FIGURE 14.2
Network elements that form the PON access network.

We have done our best to make sure the terms EMS and network management system *(NMS)* are not used interchangeably. As we use the term EMS, we are indicating a system or toolset whose responsibility within the network management system is to manage a single autonomous system. Examples of these systems may be a cable modem terminations system (CMTS), GPON optical line terminal (OLT), or possibly a voice softswitch. Fig. 14.2 illustrates network elements that form the PON access network to deliver voice, Internet, and video services. As we use the term NMS, we are indicating a system or toolset which aligns with the roles and responsibilities defined in this chapter typically across multiple EMS platforms. The X.700 definition is a framework for an NMS platform to utilize. Fig. 14.3 illustrates the reference points both the EMS and NMS have to one another and how they fit into the overall system management.

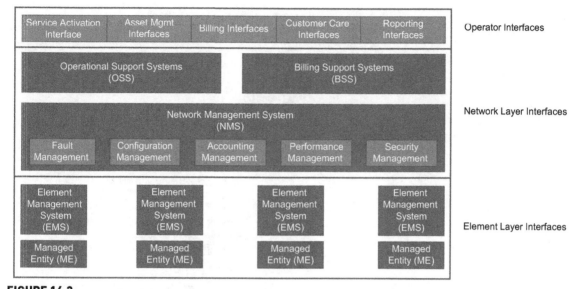

FIGURE 14.3
Relationship between management systems.

Network Management Protocols and Interfaces

Within a managed system we tend to define two geographic terms identifying the direction to which we are referring. The term *south-bound* (as in *south-bound interface [SBI]*) is used to define the reference from the operator's network looking towards the subscriber's equipment. The term *north-bound interface* (NBI) is used to define the reference from the subscriber's equipment looking towards the operator's management network. Within a given managed entity of a management system (network management system or element management system), both south-bound and north-bound interfaces are "managed" through a series of protocols. Over the years these protocols have transitioned from "back-in-the-day" archaic protocols such as TL-1 to modern-day protocols such as XML and SOAP.

The SNMP (Simple Network Management Protocol) is perhaps the most popular management protocol adopted for the network management system (NMS) and EMS platforms within an FTTx network. The NMS/EMS and each managed entity maintain an MIB (management information base) indicating the specific managed elements. The MIB defines a series of managed objects within the managed entity, the type of values (string, integer, etc.) the object represents and whether the entity has read-only or read-write access. SNMP is also used within the management system to alert an operator of an expected event occurrence within the system. One such event is a *trap* which offers a

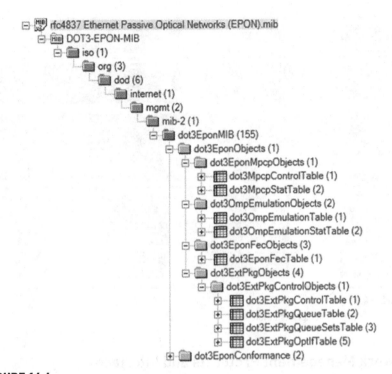

FIGURE 14.4

A simple MIB for EPON ONTs used for their MPCP, FEC, and extended capabilities control and status.

simple way for sending a notification from the network element to the NMS/ EMS. For example, if an ONT detects that its upstream laser is not able to put out the minimum required light level, indicating end-of-life for the laser, then the ONT might "throw a trap," meaning that it sends a message defined in the MIB, to the element management system, informing it of the problem. As an example, Fig. 14.4 shows MIB objects for managing ONU interfaces that conform to EPON standard as defined in the IEEE Std 802.3ah-2004 and specified by RFC 4837.

Recently XML (Extensible Markup Language)-based protocols such as SOAP (Simple Object Access Protocol, defined by World Wide Web Consortium, W3C)[iii] have become popular and are especially welcome in web-based management platforms. Typically the SOAP envelop is encapsulated in the HTTP payload. These protocols have evolved as network management platforms moved more to an HTTP-based architecture, as well as the need for much more complex management information to be passed between managed entities.

A legacy command-line-based management interface is TL1 (Transaction Language 1). TL1 is defined in Telcordia Technologies (formerly Bellcore) document GR-831-CORE.[iv] The protocol consists of a set of ASCII-based instruction messages passed between the management system and the network elements. The protocol is widely supported in digital switching digital cross-connect, optical and SONET networks in North America. TL1 provides an industry standard CLI, which may also be used as a protocol for the NBI interface of a management system.

It is worth mentioning that the NETCONF (NETwork CONFiguration; as defined by the IETF in RFC 6241)[v] protocol has been gaining great attention recently in datacom and access networks because it offers management security. In addition, NETCONF is much more powerful than SNMP in terms of number of transactions. NETCONF is able to configure 100,000 managed objects in a single transaction.

Finally, many managed networks provide the trusted CLI, allowing an operator to use a simple command-line infrastructure to access the managed elements. The CLI is typically hosted as part of each managed element, differs usually in structure and format across different platforms, and may be accessed through protocols such as TELNET and SSH. Today, CLIs are used typically for diagnosis and scripting purposes. They are sometimes preferred by network management experts, who can type them faster than they can go through a graphical menu tree.

Fault Management

Within the ISO framework, fault management is responsible for detecting, correlating, and providing the necessary interfaces for correcting a failure within the managed devices. A failure may be defined as an event within the network causing the system to operate outside its normal operating conditions. The failure may be defined as *transient* or *persistent*, requiring the management system to have the capacity to detect either condition under all operating environments.

Upon detection and correction of a failure condition it is critical the management system is capable of recording all events surrounding the event to permanent record. Once the system has been restored to normal operation, each failure condition should be evaluated in detail to make sure all events leading up to the failure are well understood. Any possible corrective action to prevent the conditions from occurring again should be put into place.

Events and alarms are typically displayed within the management system as a sorted table listing each of the conditions the system has detected.

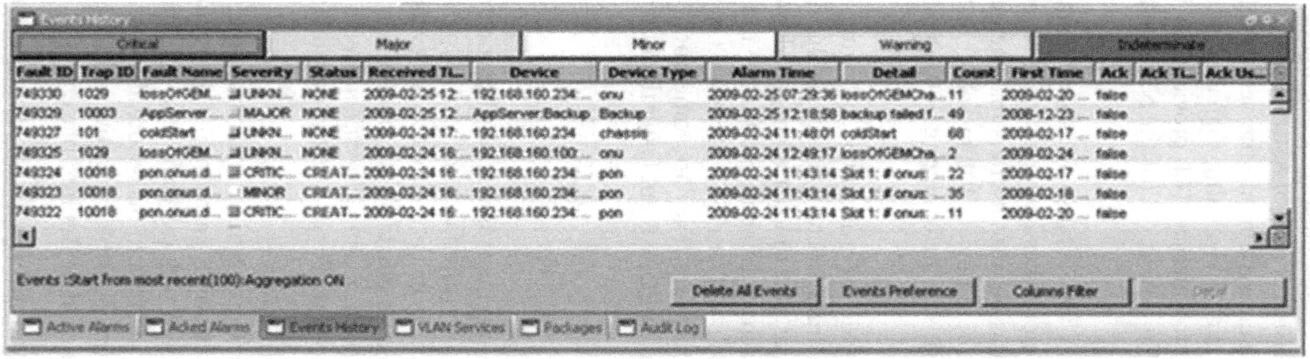

Event History

	Critical			Major			Minor			Warning			Indeterminate	

Fault ID	Trap ID	Fault Name	Severity	Status	Received Ti...	Device	Device Type	Alarm Time	Detail	Count	First Time	Ack	Ack Ti...	Ack Us...
749330	1029	lossOfGEM...	UNKN...	NONE	2009-02-25 12...	192.168.160.234 ...	onu	2009-02-25 07:29:36	lossOfGEMOf na...	11	2009-02-20 ...	false		
749309	10003	AppServer...	MAJOR	NONE	2009-02-25 12...	AppServer Backup	Backup	2009-02-25 12:18:58	backup failed f...	49	2008-12-23 ...	false		
749027	101	coldStart	UNKN...	NONE	2009-02-24 17...	192.168.160.234	chassis	2009-02-24 11:48:01	coldStart	66	2009-02-17 ...	false		
749325	1029	lossOfGEM...	UNKN...	NONE	2009-02-24 16...	192.168.160.100...	onu	2009-02-24 12:49:17	lossOfGEMOf na...	2	2009-02-24 ...	false		
749324	10018	pon.onus.d...	CRITIC	CREAT...	2009-02-24 16...	192.168.160.234 ...	pon	2009-02-24 11:43:14	Slot 1: # onus...	22	2009-02-17 ...	false		
749323	10018	pon.onus.d...	MINOR	CREAT...	2009-02-24 16...	192.168.160.234 ...	pon	2009-02-24 11:43:14	Slot 1: # onus...	35	2009-02-18 ...	false		
749322	10018	pon.onus.d...	CRITIC	CREAT...	2009-02-24 16...	192.168.160.234 ...	pon	2009-02-24 11:43:14	Slot 1: # onus...	11	2009-02-20 ...	false		

Events :Start from most recent(100)-Aggregation ON

Delete All Events   Events Preference   Columns Filter

Active Alarms | Acked Alarms | Events History | VLAN Services | Packages | Audit Log

FIGURE 14.5

Alarm and event table.

Fig. 14.5 shows an example alarm and event table in an FTTx NMS/EMS.

The key attributes of an alarm or event include the ID of the condition, the severity of the problem as defined by the operator (critical/major/minor), the source of the condition including the device name and type, the time the condition was received by the management system and finally the number of times this condition has been reported by the network element.

In today's environment of a distributed management system it is important for a network operator to *ACKnowledge* each alarm they are working to resolve. This tells the operator's staff that a colleague has already begun taking action on the condition received by the system. Enforcing this discipline is critical in order to avoid one of two undesirable outcomes: either two people start working on the same problem and work at cross-purpose, or everyone assumes someone else has it, so no one works on it.

Alarm and event notification is critical to a fault management system in order to facilitate automatic reporting to staff. Notifications are typically set up for particular alarm/event, severity level, frequency, and device types through email, SMS text message, voice message, and system alarm. These features are critical to allow for indications of various conditions and escalated problems within a managed system to be easily communicated to the staff.

Accounting Management

If there was a component of the overall system architecture which could be considered critical to the success of the entire system at all times then we would have to say that accounting management is that component. Accounting management provides far more than just visibility and processing of revenue streams within the system. Below is a listing of components which may be incorporated into the accounting management system. Depending upon the service models deployed some of these may not be necessary or you may include additional over time.

- Differentiated service tiers among subscribers, defined by different revenue tiers;
- Differentiated service tiers between residential and commercial customers;
- Bandwidth metering, allowing subscribers to use a defined data-rate and/or a defined amount of total data, charging additional if they choose to go over their defined limits;
- Differentiated on-network services hosted by the operator, such as on-network gaming.

Philosophically, accounting management should be considered as managing the expectations of the consumer on the costs he or she is incurring each billing cycle, based on the services requested. This is your primary view of revenue streams and how these revenue streams are generated based on services defined within the system. From here you can define the more popular tiers, how the tiers are being consumed, and how to predict your network growth and investments.

Configuration Management

The primary goal of configuration management is simple enough: provide the tools necessary to enable and disable services as required to ensure smooth routine operation of the system. One of the key tasks for which configuration management is responsible is taking those marketed network services and mapping them into the various managed objects within the active equipment. In other words, configuration management provides the key interface for enabling and disabling network services.

Now, this sounds simple enough; however, there are usually many managed elements that must be set up, some as simple as residential-grade Internet services or a voice line. Further, as network services change over time or new network solutions are integrated into a network, the configuration management must be capable of adapting to those changes. This may include service offerings to current network tiers (e.g., increasing data speed to all subscribers) or entirely new network architectures such as adapting a commercial services offering or the rollout of carrier Wi-Fi services.

Another artifact of the configuration management subsystem is visibility into the demand that provisioned services are having on the capability of the systems offerings. Many OSS (operational support system) platforms target the configuration management system as the responsible interface, given the knowledge of the rules justifying service creation and intimate knowledge on capacities provided by each network interface or element.

When deciding on the integration of a new OSS-based platform, a key is to make sure the configuration management solution provides interfaces which are easily adaptable to new hardware implementations. The solution should provide clean interfaces to guarantee network changes, whether this includes new service models being put into place, enabling or disabling subscriber services, or adding new network capacity.

The configuration of services within an FTTx network is rather extensive given the number of network endpoints being configured. Each of the subscriber services has a number of configuration elements required to ensure the services purchased align with the services experienced by the subscriber. The service configurations typically have configuration details as illustrated in Table 14.1.

Table 14.1 Configuration of Services Within an FTTx Network

Service Type	Service VLAN, QoS priority, Bandwidth	Additional Configurations
Data (Internet)	Must specify	Client IP address management (ex. DHCP relay option 82 or IPv6 LDRA)
Video (RF)	N/A	Video enable/disable, optional RF return parameters
Video (IPTV)	Must specify	IPTV channel plan enforcement, maximum active channels, IGMP or MVR configurations
Voice	Must specify	Embedded VoIP client IP address management, VoIP signaling type (ex. SIP, MGCP, H.248), soft-switch or call-agent configurations, voice call features

For other types of services such as business data (e.g., MEF E-Line and E-LAN), TDM over IP (PWE3 for T1/E1), data service for mobile-backhaul (MBH), TR-069 management, and RG (residential gateway) and WIFI, service configurations can have very different parameters.

Advanced FTTx NMS/EMS systems must allow flexible service configuration for service addition, service removal, service suspension, and service modification. Configuration tools such as the ones below are very welcome.

1. Structural service configurations
   FTTx service requires many levels of configurations in order to fully function. For example, a data Internet service requires a networking profile providing details such as VLAN and IP address configuration, a security profile defining artifacts such as MAC limit and DHCP snooping (to protect network L2/L3 resources), and an SLA profile defining bandwidth and QoS parameters. The structural service configuration approach means that many profiles in each category (networking, security, and SLA) above are created in the management system, allowing for different service levels based on subscriber needs.
2. Bulk service application tool
   A service package can be applied in one action to many subscribers at the same time with a live indication of progress. This tool is very useful when bulk service provisioning requirements are necessary or service modifications are implemented.
3. Service configuration scheduler
   Many times service changes are performed during maintenance windows; however, the configuration of the bulk service changes take time. As configuration changes are made, a method to schedule these changes during a normal maintenance window is necessary to ensure a stable live network environment.

Fig. 14.6 shows an example of an FTTx NMS/EMS GUI that has IPTV and data services configured on an ONT. Notice that on the left of the GUI window are displayed all ONTs on a specific PON.

Service Provisioning and Software Management

The activation of services to a subscriber should be flawless and scalable. This allows the operator to bill customer services immediately upon installation of the ONT. A method which makes this possible is having the ability to preprovision all services within the network prior to the installation of the ONT. We describe preprovisioning below, and strongly recommend this operational model.

Service preprovision and *auto-configuration* speed up service turn-up. Prior to the installation of the ONT, the network operator should consider including within their management system the option for preprovisioning what can be termed as a *logical ONT*. A logical ONT is the exact instance of the ONT to be deployed; however, the deployment of the physical device has not commenced. All services which are to be configured to the ONT are made including all northbound systems such as voice platforms, network servers, and IPTV platforms. Upon first connection of the physical ONT, the ONT is discovered within the system and matched to the ID of the logical ONT using unique elements such as an MAC address, serial number, etc. Once the match is completed the management system automatically activates the ONT and configures the preassigned services.

Another major step in the commissioning of an ONT is to ensure the software running on the equipment is the current revision. Many times an operator will make this change to the ONT hardware prior to sending the ONT on the service truck. The does enable a much faster field installation; however, the effort to unpack, download the new software, then repacking is enormous. Another option is to automatically update the software installed on the ONT upon installation of the ONT at the subscriber's premise. This provides an easy and automated activity allowing for significant time savings and guaranteeing the software running is consistent with the network on which the ONT is installed.

The process of upgrading software is crucial for bug fixes and for introduction of new features. A robust software management solution of the OLT and ONTs requires dual software images and backward or forward compatibility in the design. Dual image storage on the OLT and ONT assures that in the event of unforeseen software crash and network outage in the new software version just introduced, all network elements can revert to the previous known-working versions. This is typical in most carrier-grade access equipment, allowing for immediate restoration of services upon detection of a major fault detected after a software upgrade.

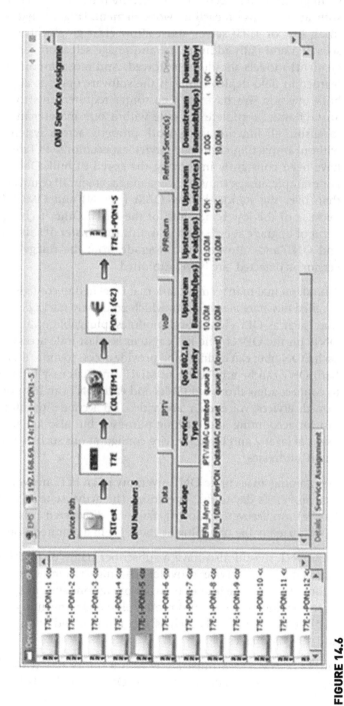

FIGURE 14.6

Example FTTx NMS/EMS GUI with IPTV and data services.

Configuration management for software must record active/backup/running software versions on each network element. Upgrade paths, typical pointing to an FTP or TFTP server, must allow clear graphical user interface (GUI) selection and path addition. Invalid image selection based on NE (network element) models should be enforced. And most importantly from what we learned in field deployments, is the software upgrade efficiency when using bulk upgrade. We have seen customer requirements that all ONTs under an OLT must complete upgrade within one maintenance window. This is to ensure all functionalities work properly across system software entities without impacting customer service expectations. FTTx equipment vendors have been constantly improving the speed of bulk ONT software upgrade. For example, image transfer over a management IP connection is much faster than over the standard PON OAM (EPON) and OMCI (GPON) channel because of the low bandwidth of the latter. Other techniques for improvement of upgrade speed, such as multicast transfer of software image to ONTs and ONT and software auto upgrade from the image server when a new version is detected, are being exploited.

A fundamental management task that is related to configuration management is called *inventory management*, which accurately tracks deployed system hardware such as OLT chassis and modules, pluggable optics, and all connected ONTs on the ODNs. The FTTx system is a last-mile access platform in which each ODN fiber can connect and provide access to more than a hundred ONTs. Each ONT can be an SFU or an MDU unit. It is easy for a chassis-based OLT to connect a few thousand ONTs and each ONT can have one to many provisioned services, voice, data, and video. An accurate inventory is necessary not just for accounting and tracking purposes, but also key in reporting level of usage of layer 2 and layer 3 service configurations such as bandwidths, VLANs, and IP addresses.

Maintaining an accurate ONT inventory in an FTTx network is key for the service provider's day-to-day operation. The active state of an ONT [discovered (active), undiscovered (down), fault, or discovered (disabled)] under every PON is usually the first thing to check for in a reported trouble ticket.

Each ONT should also have a subscriber name or location address that is mapped to the service provider's billing system. Inventory management information also facilitates network operations such as spare inventory, software upgrade planning, and product life cycle. Inventory management must record hardware records such as part number and revisions, serial numbers, and MAC addresses.

The FTTx NMS/EMS must allow an inventory report to be generated. The report typically includes selectable ONT or OLT blade models and their quantities, running software versions, and preferably the location information (e.g., OLT/slot/PON/ONT ID numbers).

Performance Management

Network operators are faced with challenges when it comes to understanding those possible artifacts which may cause a decrease in performance experienced by subscribers. When a network is architected, the operator must make decisions on how the service provisioned will be "oversubscribed." What this means is that an operator must make a capital decision on how much capacity will be available to all subscribers within the network compared to how much bandwidth is "offered" or "provisioned." The concept of oversubscription has been around for generations, even well outside of the telecommunications world. For example, when a road is to be built a decision has to be made on how many lanes need to be provided, and in Atlanta, GA, with all the traffic there is never enough. However, it would not be prudent of the local governing authority to build a road such that there is never congestion. The governing authority just needs to continually monitor the situation such that if the situation becomes overbearing then the road must be expanded or new roads constructed. Planning is crucial because construction work takes time and taking too much time could present a series of other challenges and delays in completing the road.

The same concept must be employed by a network operator. A network must be continually monitored at all potential congestion points to determine traffic utilization. Many times operators find their highest network utilization starts around 7:00 p.m. and does not begin to taper off until much later into the evening, around midnight. People are home from work, school, and sporting activities and looking to watch the news or browse the Internet or possibly do some gaming. Performance management is the key to ensuring the network is performing at all times across the defined set of "oversubscription" levels the operator is expecting.

The performance management activities must be reviewed on a regular basis and consistently compared during each review period. Changing how data are reviewed can only mask certain data unless historical information is available to show trends. This exercise allows an operator to plan accordingly in understanding when additional capacity is required at different points in the network. Many times the addition of capacity could take a lot of time and money. This importance of tracking capacity utilization, predicting how usages may change over the next 6 months, must be part of performance management. The trick is to provide enough capacity so that subscribers don't notice congestion, while not overprovisioning the network, which will raise cost for no offsetting revenue. Chapter 8 discusses oversubscription and the effect of quality of service (QoS) management. It suggests some good-practice numbers you might consider.

An FTTx NMS/EMS typically supports the following performance management functions:

- Give the status of platform resources such as CPU usage and memory usage.
- Gather real-time per-port or per-service transmit/receive frame and byte counts. For example, a service provider may want to verify that its business data subscriber can actually reach the contracted bandwidth throughput. Many FTTx NMS/EMS systems now support 15-min and 1-day performance management counters at the ONT subscriber ports.
- Gather aggregate OLT data usages—service providers will need to know the percent data usages of each PON or network interface port over a day, a week, or a month. It is also desirable to have such PM data on a per-service basis.
- Modern deep packet inspection (DPI) technologies make it possible to report subscriber data usage across selected URLs, protocols, and other user-defined metadata fields. These collected metadata statistics can be used to optimize network usage based on applications, lawful interception (e.g., within emails), or for marketing or research purposes.

Security Management

The final functional area should not be considered the least important. Security management is just as important as each of the other functional areas. Without a strong security policy set forth within a management system all other aspects of the system will be compromised. Over the past two decades more and more of peoples' lives have become digitalized. As much as we would like to hope that everyone is good out in the Internet, as my mother used to say, "if there is a mud puddle in the yard, I was going to find it and make a mess of things regardless."

An operator must take this advice from my mother to heart, understanding how critical it is that a well thought-out security policy is put into place. An operator many times may allow a subscriber to pay for services using credit cards, and that data must be carefully protected. An ambitious gamer may look to exploit all aspects of the network for possible ways to prioritize his or her data to win in a combat game. An avid but cheap sports fan may look at ways to enable the sports networks without paying for the service.

Each of these scenarios and many others are all possible opportunities for a network to be exploited. The function of a strong security management policy is to not only protect the network from those who do not have access, but also ensure those who do require access have it as required when required. A strong security management solution provides visibility as to when a network is accessed externally, as well as identifies clearly when an unauthorized or unexpected security breach is detected.

The FTTx NMS/EMS typically supports the management user security by login security control for feature and device access rights.

Fig. 14.7 show an FTTH EMS screen that allows the administrator to define a user group and permit or deny access right to nearly every management function.

Access rights are defined typically by a system administrator user. "View-only" access right is a read-only privilege (not service affecting) that can be, for example, assigned to tier-1 support staff who only need to verify configurations. Access rights of "Add", "Edit", and "Delete" can modify the service configurations and should only be assigned to higher-tier support staff for troubleshooting or service enabling/disabling.

User groups can be allowed or denied for access to any device in the system via editable device lists.

Similarly, a system admin user can assign device access rights (as defined by the system device filter in Fig. 14.7) based on ownership of the hardware on the per-PON, per-blade, or per-chassis basis. Fig. 14.8 shows that devices inaccessible to the current user are shown up as disabled (grayed out) in the GUI. This can, for example, be the case for a login user who only handles residential subscribers and does not need to see the hardware associated with the business customers.

Other security features can include *view current users* and an *audit log viewer* that displays all previous user actions in the system. Fig. 14.9 shows an example of *audit log* that has the attributes of action time, user name, category, and detailed description of action.

TROUBLESHOOTING AND MAINTENANCE

As FTTx platforms are deployed for mission-critical services, trouble-shooting and maintenance features are now being requested. Many technologies have matured for such purposes, and equipment vendors are beginning to include them in their product offering. The following are a few solutions which assist in troubleshooting an FTTx deployment.

Ethernet OAM CFM and Y.1731 Management

Connectivity fault management (CFM) as defined in IEEE802.1ag is an end-to-end per-service-instance Ethernet layer operation, administration, and management (OAM) protocol. It includes proactive connectivity monitoring,

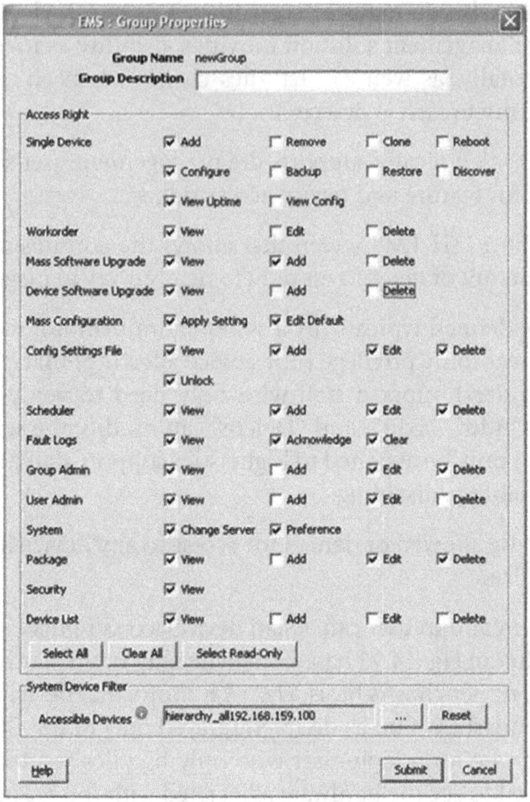

FIGURE 14.7
Example EMS screen defining user group.

fault verification, and fault isolation for large Ethernet metropolitan-area networks (MANs) and wide-area networks (WANs). ITU-T Y.1731 defines similar functionalities and adds performance management. In comparison, IEEE802.3ah (the original EPON standard, now subsumed into 802.3) EFM only defines link-layer fault management.

Fig. 14.10 shows where MIP (in circles) and Up MEP (up arrow) and Down MEP (down arrow) are defined for three MD (management domain) levels for CFM application in GPON network as defined in TR-156 Sec. 6.1 for 1:1 VLANs.

The FTTx NMS/EMS must support:

- CFM MD (management domain) creation, MIP (management domain intermediate point) and MEP (maintenance association end point) creation.

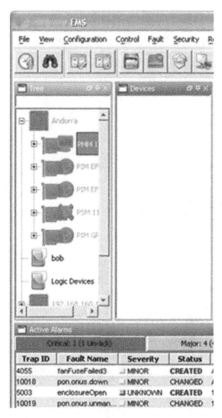

FIGURE 14.8
Assignment of device rights.

- CCM (continuity check message) statistics—An MEP generates CCM messages to announce its local port and interface status. When CCM is enabled, an MA (maintenance association) tracks CCM messages from all MEPs, and is performed at a defined interval.
- LBM (loopback message) and LBR (loopback reply message)—An MEP generates an LBM message when the CFM loopback test is performed. An MEP/MIP responds with an LBR message when it receives an LBM message destined to its own MAC address.
- LTM (linktrace message) and LTR (linktrace reply message)—An MEP generates an LTM message when link trace is performed. An MEP responds with an LTR message when it receives an LTM message.

When Y.1731 is supported, the management system also needs to report management performance counters, including frame delay (FD), frame delay variation (FDV), and frame loss ratio (FLR).

FIGURE 14.9
Audit log viewer.

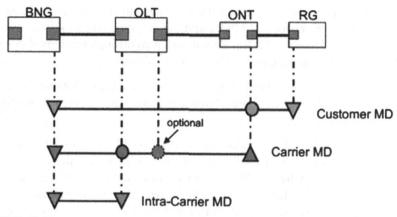

FIGURE 14.10
Connectivity fault management in GPON networks.

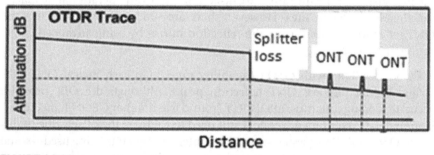

FIGURE 14.11
Sample OTDR trace.

For example, when CCM monitoring is enabled at the BNG, it can monitor at a defined interval the CCM messages from the MEP on the customer MD. This assures the L2 connectivity across the FTTH segment.

As another example, on the carrier MD an MEP can generate a CFM LBM message when the CFM loopback test is performed. The MEP/MIP on this MD responds with an LBR message when it receives an LBM destined to its own MAC address. As can be seen this is similar to the L3 "ping," and why the CFM loopback function is called "MAC Ping."

OTDR Monitoring (for Physical Layer Debugging)

OTDR (optical time domain reflectometry) provides a very convenient way to troubleshoot problems in the fiber plant itself. It gives you a picture of how the light propagates through the fiber, and can show splices, connectors, splitters, and breaks or other fiber faults. You will find that an OTDR is your best physical-layer troubleshooting tool. A typical PON OTDR trace will look like the one in Fig. 14.11. A simple single-stage splitter is in the ODN.

The industry has converged on the OTDR wavelength as 1650 nm, considering current and future versions of EPON and GPON, plus point-to-point overlay and RF video and return. This wavelength will pass through modern fiber optic cable, but is not used for transmission to subscribers.

Note that if two or more ONTs happen to be at the same distance from the OLT, within the distance resolution (typically 2–3 m) their reflection peaks will collide with each other.

In a PON network with a maximum of about 30 dB ODN loss (1 × 64 plus 20 or 40 km fiber), it is a challenge for the OTDR to see the ONT reflection peaks. This is why the Broadband Forum TR-287 (*PON Optical-Layer Management*, Issue 1, June 2014)[vi] still leaves a few specifications for the "drop fiber reflection event" as for-future-study (FFS). A workaround is to use a reflection mirror at the input of the ONTs. This reflects much more light at the OTDR wavelength back to the OLT, improving the signal-to-noise ratio of the measurement. Technically it works, but it creates an operational headache for already deployed sites. However, there are vendors who can detect the ONT reflection without using the reflection mirror by using advanced single processing techniques.

A PON NMS/EMS with OTDR capability must map each logical ONT subscriber to the physical ONT reflection peaks. Although the OLT provides accurate ranging distances, EPON RTT (round trip time) or GPON EqD (equalization delay), equipment vendors still need to calibrate the offsets due to different ONT PON SoC (system-on-a-chip) integrated circuits being used—some may add more delay than others to the ranging signal, introducing errors that must be calibrated out. Proper calibration must be included in the embedded software to use a unique offset time constant for RTT or EqD based on the SoC type or the ONT model being discovered.

PON OTDR tests can be on-demand or routine (scheduled) tasks, depending on the needs. When a subscriber reports service outage, the OTDR capability can clearly sort it out if the issue is physical-layer related. The FTTx NMS/EMS must be able to launch an OTDR test for any PON, report fault location, stored history test results, and trigger alarm and notification.

Forced Protection Switch

ITU G.984.1 [Gigabit-capable passive optical networks (GPON): General Characteristics. 03/2008] defines four types of protection. These can be used to protect high-value customers from physical layer faults and some electronic faults, at the expense of extra equipment and fiber routing. The most common two types that FTTH vendors have implemented are type B and type C. Protection is only defined for GPON and may or may not have been implemented by a given manufacturer, and certain EPON manufacturers may have implemented their own protection, which may or may not work as shown below.

In both types of PON protection, *automatic protection switching* (APS) is typically enabled by default. For type B normally one OLT PON port is active (Tx/Rx both on) and the other is in standby (Tx off, Rx on) (Fig. 14.12). APS is controlled by the OLT. For type C protection, both PONs are always active and software on the ONU controls which PON is active (Fig. 14.13). When failure is detected on the active PON, the embedded software will automatically switch to the standby PON. Traffic protection with less than 50 ms interruption can be achieved. For type B protection a switch-over requires reranging of the ONTs to the new OLT port, which could take many seconds. There are methods of sharing the ranging distance values between the primary OLT and the secondary OLT such that the convergence of ranging takes place faster, but 50 ms is still difficult to achieve. One method is using the GPON POPUP message for faster ONU state transition. Obviously type C is more expensive and therefore typically deployed for business customers and at the emerging MBH (mobile backhaul) ONT sites. Note that real installation will prefer the

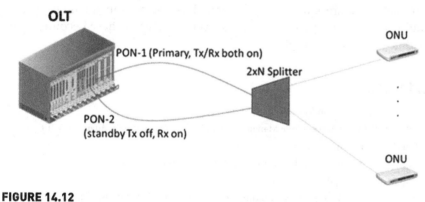

FIGURE 14.12

Type B backup—OLT-only duplex system.

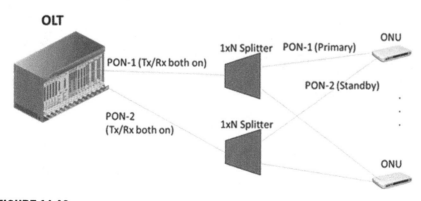

FIGURE 14.13

Type C backup—full duplex system.

two PON ports are on different OLT line cards, which can protect line-card hardware failure.

When RF video overlay on FTTx is deployed, additional protection-switching mechanism needs to be installed to protect the video light signal (typically 1550 nm) when this is ODN fiber cut.

While switching is normally automatic, there will be need to use the FTTx NMS/EMS to issue a "force switching" to the standby facility, for example, for planned ODN network upgrade or transceiver swapping in OLT or ONUs.

SUMMARY

The management of telecommunications systems has been in place since the birth of nonverbal communication. Over the years the industry has defined a series of functional areas which all should be considered regardless of the size of the network or the complexity of the services put into place. Although these functional areas were defined some time ago not much has changed in defining the importance of these areas, even as networks have become highly integrated and more complex.

Endnotes

i. https://www.broadband-forum.org/.
ii. BBF WT-312 PON Access Node Management Requirements, Revision; August 4, 2014.
iii. http://www.w3.org/.
iv. https://telecom-info.telcordia.com/ido/AUX/GR_831_TOC.i01.pdf.
v. http://tools.ietf.org/html/rfc6241.
vi. https://docs.google.com/viewer?url=https://www.broadband-forum.org/technical/download/TR-287.pdf&embedded=false&chrome=false&dov=1.

4

FTTx Network Operation

CHAPTER 15

Production Operations

INTRODUCTION

FTTx networks, regardless of technology type and business focus, rely on the same key technical areas when it comes to operating an effective long-term network. In fact, what are considered major differences in PON networks, such as providing commercial or residential services or FTTx technology type, are minimized when we consider the technical challenges involved in operating such a network. For example, consider a technology choice of EPON, GPON, or Active Ethernet (Active), which primarily describes the OLT to ONU/ONT link—far more important is the specific vendor implementation. As another example, consider residential versus commercial services. In most cases, both service types transport over the same network—with distinct service model implementations based on the service delivery requirements being the primary differences. More important than the previous examples, are the following aspects of developing and operating the network.

- End-to-end inside plant design to support the multiple, specific service types (data, voice, video) from insertion point through the core, transport, and access networks to the subscriber end-point. Consider such aspects as service implementation, network scale, equipment internetworking and integration, and service models that are unique but interrelated.
- Effective management framework supporting the network, service, and subscriber through *performance management* (correlating the health of the network by "listening" to the markers it provides and "asking" what is going on), *support systems* (the utilities which enable the services, monitoring, and provisioning system to operate), and *provisioning* (applying subscriber-specific services configuration to the customer premises equipment (CPE) and networking gear transporting the services).
- Production engineering processes which support the technical business management of the network—"how" activities get done and "how" requirements and opportunities are identified; the technical evolution

FTTx Networks. http://dx.doi.org/10.1016/B978-0-12-420137-8.00015-9

of the network—equipment and software systems that will change and improve over time and readiness of the network for new and improved products and services; and next-generation network investment—as the FTTx standards, technical capabilities and vendor offerings march on, an effectively managed network will support where and when these investments get applied.

- Cohesive teams, strong and successful, are needed to pull the pieces together in building and operating the network. These teams need the right mix of skills, using in-house resources which can "train and gain," or with the judicious use of outside consulting services. From a technical perspective, the team requires services experts and networking experts who together must own the end-to-end development and delivery of services. From a business perspective, the team needs to drive the evolution of the product offerings. Ultimately with the right business and technical leadership, the right team can help the FTTx deployment business beat the competition and well serve the subscriber customer base.

In this chapter we will take a close look into the production operations view of running the network and how it touches on each of these important key areas. In this chapter we will focus on:

- Developing the business and technical leadership of the program management office—Its goal for oversight and models for operations in building the network, taking control of the network, and maintaining the network over time.
- Operations team—Making sure engineering and operations teams are separate, allowing the two teams to focus on the appropriate work areas, the engineering team on planning and designing solutions for the network and the operations team on running the network. Specifying what the operations team needs from the engineering team. Defining where the operations team should be engaged as the network is managed over time, and what personnel and skill sets should be in the operations team.
- Process book—Which processes are required and what is the activity each one is covering? The necessary processes will be covered each in their separate section as follows.
  - Process: Network documentation—The as-built documentation of the network from initial deployment and over time how the network changes. How the network is documented and the nature of the repository (where and how is the network documentation book kept).
  - Process: Configuration management—The managing of the hardware and software revision history of the components of the network. In particular, which revisions of components are compatible together

in order to provide services to the network subscribers? How the configuration is managed over time and, importantly, how are changes to the baseline deployed to the production network?

- Process: Troubleshooting, problem resolution, and working with vendors—The mind-set and methodologies required for operations teams to identify, troubleshoot, and apply solutions that resolve issues (not just Band-Aid them) while engaging with their vendor counterparts to maintain the network's existing hardware and software products, as well as adding new equipment and services to it.
- Process: Production engineering—Defining the engineering activities taken on by the operations team and how the other operations/performance management activities play into them. The operations team needs the right tools (hardware, software, and equipment) to assess, maintain, and upgrade the network. The ability of the operations team to understand the network and provide information back to the planning and engineering functions and senior management team to allow sound decisions for network investment, is key to making the network successful long term. This is the integration aspect of network operations— the intersection of people, technology, processes, and tools.

PROJECT LIFECYCLE PROCESS OVERVIEW

Fig. 15.1 details the expected project lifecycle for a network deployment project. It is expected that in general most projects follow this typical lifecycle with minor adjustments required for individual project specifics. Thus the project lifecycle process may be tailored to any type of project. This project lifecycle process has been developed over a number of years of customer engagements with various organizations in network deployments. Given the number and different types of customer experiences, the process has been adjusted over time and for that reason is quite flexible. An overview of the process follows.

Project Phases and Deliverables

The overall project timeline which will govern the expected milestones and project phase start and end milestones will be developed as part of the overall project planning phase, occurring after the project starts. The following general project phases are expected to occur.

Project Planning Phase

During this phase of the project, the overall project plan and overall timeline are developed. The project team and roles and responsibilities are assigned and project goals are reviewed to ensure that the timeline and the project plan

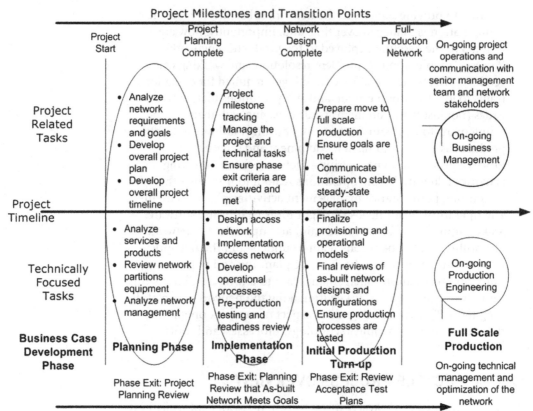

FIGURE 15.1

Project lifecycle overview.

supporting that timeline are consistent and can be met. During this phase the following project-related criteria are reviewed:

- Analyze and review network requirements:
  - Services and products to be deployed to subscribers;
  - Equipment to be used in the project which must interoperate with the FTTx equipment;
  - Premise installation requirements and processes;
  - Operational support system (OSS)/business support system (BSS) integration and provisioning support;
  - Network assurance and monitoring strategies;
  - Any additional customer/operator requirements;
- Develop overall timeline for the project:
  - Detailed milestones for project checkpoints—when are the milestones and what are the success criteria;
    - Core, transport, and edge network deployed;

- Services insertion deployed;
- Access network integration;
- Services integration with access network;
- Provisioning testing;
- Access network acceptance testing;
  - Develop risk, contingency, and critical path planning;
- Develop project plan which supports the overall timeline for the project.

Before leaving the phase, as a gate to transition to the next phase of the access network deployment project, a planning review is completed to ensure that the developed timeline and plans meet all goals for the project. The stakeholders involved in the project are identified and included in the review.

Project Implementation Phase

During the project implementation phase, the major focus of the project work turns to the design and implementation of the access network and its integration into the overall network topology.

- Engineering design of the access network requirements;
- Implementation preparation for the access network;
- Design and implementation of operational processes and planning for initial production testing and ramp-up;
- Implementation of the access network;
- Preproduction testing (to enter phase 0 production)—acceptance testing of services and services integration.

Before leaving the phase, as a gate to transition to the next phase of the access network deployment project, a design review is completed to ensure that the developed and implemented design have met all goals for this phase of the project. The stakeholders involved in the project are identified and included in the review.

Initial Production Turn-Up

During the initial production turn-up phase of the project, the focus turns to operational aspects of the network deployment in preparation to proceed to full-scale production. The results of robust project planning and disciplined engineering and implementation efforts are now in place, and the milestones of initial turn-up of early customers (many times friendly or beta customers) proceeds because services are now in place and operating. Key aspects of provisioning and operational processes are tested and refined. During this phase, typical tasks that are completed are the following:

- Finalize and review the provisioning processes and operational models to be followed in the full-scale production phase;
- Review, test, and finalize the production engineering processes and procedures;
- Finalize initial-production testing (to exit phase 0 production).

At the end of the phase 0 activity the acceptance test plans for provisioning are reviewed and completed.

Project Phase Closures and Transitions

As a closure to each phase and as a clean transition to the next phase of the project, the project managers both at the equipment vendor organizations, the FTTx network operator organization, and any agencies contracted for installation and implementation will be required to review and complete milestone lists and successes to ensure each phase of the project is completed successfully and that transitions to new phases do not occur without proper assurance that the objectives for each phase and the project overall have been met.

Project Reviews and Communications

As an assurance that the project and all related project specifics, technical activities, and deliverables are on track, and that project milestones and objectives are being met, it is expected that the project management counterparts at both companies, equipment vendor organizations, and the FTTx network operator organization (including any contracted installers) are engaged in periodic reviews and communications. As this on-going communication is crucial to the efficient sharing of information, issue tracking and resolution, risk identification and mitigation plans, it is critical that such a communication plan and periodic review cycle be agreed upon at the beginning of the project and followed through until project completion and transition to full-scale production.

Transition to Full-Scale Production

During this phase of the project, the network enters what is considered the full-scale production phase. During this phase, the operations of the network are supported by production engineering processes. The production engineering processes are built upon the solid project and engineering activities of the earlier project phases. While this phase of the project (the long-term operations phase) is typically marked by stability and repeatable processes, occasionally there are technical support requirements for issues that may arise which are not covered by the production processes, or the need may arise for software upgrades, hardware migrations, or bringing additional systems online. Thus, the FTTx network operator organization's network will be supported through the technical assistance center of the equipment vendor organization. The levels of support available through the equipment vendor organization are through service-level agreement (SLA) contracts which are typically renewed yearly.

OPERATIONS IN THE NETWORK LIFECYCLE

The activities involved in the design, development, and implementation of the FTTx access network to fulfill the requirements and vision of how the network should serve its technical and business purposes is the purview of the program management office (PMO). The PMO provides oversight on the deployment of the network, strategic releases of baselines, new product introductions, and overall customer support and management. For a new network deployment, this includes the full project implementation phase, defined as from network build start (with day one support from all of the vendor organizations) to production network operational (when technical assistance center (TAC) and on-going customer support processes take over).

Within the PMO, a given project team will be composed of subject matter experts from different disciplines as required for the successful completion of the project. The project team is managed and directed by the designated PMO project manager who is the primary network advocate and interface during the implementation phase of the project. This project manager provides a central and single point of communication for the project. This designated project manager will work with his or her counterparts within the vendor organizations, including contracted organizations providing plant construction or equipment installation services, to provide overarching oversight and rules of engagement for the project. Thus the working relationship between the project management counterparts (at the vendor organization, the network organization, and any contracting organizations) is key to the successful conclusion of the project.

Project Oversight

The following project attributes provide oversight for the project and allow all project management counterparts to fully understand and provide status to their respective organizations. These attributes ultimately describe how the project is managed—reviews, documentation, configuration management (both as-built network and software baseline configurations), and change management (how changes are requested and made in an organized fashion). A detailed description of the project oversight attributes follows:

- Project milestone reviews—As agreed upon in the overall project schedule, the project management counterparts will prepare and hold reviews at predefined milestones to complete a project phase, provide closure, and ensure that the next project phase begins at the appropriate time, with the level of completeness of the previous phase intact.
- Project documentation—As agreed upon in the list of project deliverables, the project management counterparts will ensure the timely completion and submission of required deliverable documentation and manage reviews of the documentation as appropriate.

- Configuration management—Configuration management of network deployments is critical. The project management counterparts ensure that the project proceeds with well-defined release procedures, and change procedures for all components of the project including: software baselines, as-built documentation baselines, hardware revision baselines, project review baselines.
- Milestone tracking—The project management counterparts agree on and track the project based upon milestones and completion of those milestones.

FTTx Equipment Vendor Expectations

The network build organization should expect the following capabilities from their FTTx equipment vendor:

- The interconnection via Ethernet technologies of the subject OLTs with third-party transport systems.
- The interoperation of the access network OLT and ONTs with the gear supplying services and any hardware and software supporting the services.
- The integration with various network management systems and operational support systems.
- The combination of ONTs with various third-party CPE, including residential gateways, set-top terminals for IP and RF video, integrated access devices for TDM transport, and analog telephone adapters for POTS into voice over IP.

If the FTTx equipment vendor organization is an independent part of the build process (i.e., has been chosen separately from the other vendors of the network) then this integration phase can occur as a proof-of-concept phase at the beginning of the network build process, otherwise it will be part of the overall project build.

Network Build Models

As for the majority of the network integrated with the FTTx vendor solution, several models of oversight are possible for the PMO:

- Build-operate-transfer (turn-key) managed—In this model the entire project is completed as a turn-key effort with the resulting production network transferred to the owner/operating organization. This oversight model is useful when the owner/operating team does not have the requisite resources or skill mix to build the network.
- Consultant or build organization managed—In this model the owner/ network operator utilizes a dedicated consultant or build organization to help manage the end-to-end vendor organizations (external stakeholders) in creating the network and launching it into production.

The intent is that the consultant with experience building FTTx networks can provide valuable experience with helping the network owner have a seamless experience in getting the network implemented and released to production.

- Network operator managed—In this model, the owner/network operator fully controls the equipment vendor organizations in producing the network. The expectation is that the owner/operating organization has the requisite skills and experience necessary to bring the network to production.

Regardless of the network build model utilized, the expectation is that the lifecycle process can be tailored to fit the work of bringing the network project to fruition.

Build Operate Transfer (BOT) Model
Build Operate Transfer Organizational Structure

In order to proceed forward in a timely manner with all phases of the project—once the contract is awarded and purchase orders are received to begin work—the BOT organization should initiate and maintain the following project organization to ensure efficient, complete, and robust operations throughout the lifecycle of the project.

- BOT program management office—Provide the organizational, project management, and technical capability of a network equipment supplier and integrator with experience in FTTx projects, ensuring that the overall project is successful and that ongoing support operations are monitored and fully supported.
- BOT organization local project office—Provide project and technical support in close contact to the customer site to ensure that all project and technical objectives are met and provide ongoing program office operations.
- BOT technical support organization—Provide local technical support at the customer site ensuring that all technical objectives are met and on-going support is provided.

BOT Organization Program Management Office (PMO)

The BOT organization program management office is the point of contact for the owner/operator for all design and deployment operations related to the FTTx network project. The PMO is responsible for the following activities:

- Fully support the owner/operator in providing project management support for the FTTx network equipment vendor project teams in all phases of the project (the project lifecycle was described previously).
- Fully support the owner/operator by providing as-required design and production engineering guidance and leadership on system integration efforts.

- Fully support the owner/operator by providing as-required on-site support from technical applications engineering resources from FTTx network equipment vendors' corporate locations.
- Fully support the owner/operator by providing as-required on-site support from technical training department from the FTTx network equipment vendors' corporate office.

It is expected that in fully supporting the owner/operator that the BOT PMO will provide support and guidance to ensure that all objectives are met through the network transition into full-scale production, and finally the transition into post-sales support from the network equipment vendor's organization.

In order to support the local management and engineering teams of the equipment vendors, the BOT PMO will initiate and conduct an on-going series of project planning and oversight activities to ensure that the project proceeds on pace and that risks are identified and mitigated accordingly. Given the responsibilities of the BOT PMO it is expected that they have a depth of experience with FTTx projects, making them uniquely suited to provide such project support and oversight.

BOT Organization Local Project Office
The BOT organization project office is the point of contact for local project support of both the BOT support organization and network equipment vendor teams. This office is empowered to provide timely assistance and support from both a project and technical perspective and will be fully backed and supported by the BOT organization PMO. The BOT organization is well-placed to provide on-site logistics and spares management, local level 2 technical support engagement, and other focused project support as required by the BOT support organization and FTTx network owner/operator organization. The methods and procedures for obtaining level 2 support from the network equipment vendor organizations should be detailed in the overall project plan at contract award.

Support
The BOT support organization is the on-site, local presence for technical and project support to ensure the day-to-day success of the project. They are backed up by the support of the BOT organization project office and by the BOT organization PMO as required. It is expected that the BOT support organization will provide significant on-site resources and will be trained to provide level 1 technical support of the FTTx network owner/operator organization's network deployments. The format and procedure of invoking level 1 support from the BOT support organization will be detailed in the overall project plan.

Build-Operate-Transfer Phases

In the build-operate-transfer model the network integrator will propose a full-service solution consisting of several serial phases. The first is the network build or design and implementation phase. During the rigorous implementation phase, the network build team should leverage their extensive practical deployment knowledge of their professional services team.

- Choose technologies and solutions for each component of the network (note that the FTTx network owner/operator may have some choices which the BOT organization must use).
- Design the access network [including IP addressing, virtual local area network (VLAN) assignments, QoS functions, and networking services such as DHCP] and its integration with the transport and core networks—they may even design and implement the transport and core networks, especially in a smaller network build.
- Design the management integration (including definition and management of services).
- Install EMS and other management solutions and integrate them with SNMP NMS and OSS/BSS as required to ensure seamless provisioning and management workbench.

The second is the network operation phase where the network build team recommends production engineering processes and capabilities and ultimately implements those operational processes.

- Train FTTx network owner/operator organization personnel;
- Determine sparing strategy;
- Install OLTs, OSP, and distribution as required, plus ONTs as required;
- Insert services solutions;
- Interoperability testing of networks and services;
- Provision subscribers and services as required.

In the final phase, the network is transferred to the owner organization, with the implementing BOT organization providing support.

- In the implementation phase, a solid network that minimizes the impact of failures through resilient operation will have been created, thus the BOT support organization's role should be more of training and providing guidance to the owner/operator teams who will take over and manage the network long term.
- Technical assistance center—the technical assistance center may provide 24 × 7 × 365 availability, or a lower availability may be required depending on the size of the network and the familiarity of the owner/operator organization. Ultimately, the owner/operator organization should require lower levels of support over time as their

training and experience allow them to independently operate the network long term.

- Warranty and postwarranty Return Material Authorization (RMA to invoke equipment repair and replacement services). The FTTx and network vendor organizations should have been chosen to design and manufacture extremely reliable products. For those few products that do fail, the support process provides a replacement unit based on the sparing strategy and to close the loop on field performance, analysis of the failures for future quality improvements should be part of the process.

Consultant or Build Organization Managed

The administration, project management, design, and implementation of the FTTx network project will be a combined and focused effort of the network owner/operator and equipment vendor organizations. The combination of vendor equipment companies provides the technical experience and on-site technical capability to accomplish each of their component pieces of the project. However, in order for the project to be successful, the network build project must have the requisite management oversight and organization so that the integration of the equipment vendor solutions comes together appropriately. This project oversight may be accomplished in a model where either a consultant or a contracted build organization offers comprehensive service and support programs for its network owner/operator customer. In this build model, the consultant or network build organization provides the following service components:

- Design and implementation phase management—The services provided by the consultant or build organization include a subset or all of the following: project management, network design, ISP and OSP design, implementation strategy and support, services insertion integration and access network integration, OSS/BSS and provisioning integration and support, on-site turn-up and hands-on training. At the time of contract award, the build organization's program office personnel help to determine the right mix of services and support for the initial network turn-up and operational goals.

- On-going operations support—For the in-production network, the build management consultant organization can provide additional services, based on the need of the owner/operator organization: production network engineering consulting and implementation, operational procedure development and consultation, training, technical assistance center, on-site engineering for access network optimization and services deployment, VoIP and IPTV interoperability services. Any or all of these may be provided. However, the owner/operator of the network may ultimately provide the post-implementation phase operational capability, depending on the skills and capabilities of their own internal organization.

Regardless of the scale of the assistance from the consultant or build management organization, the network owner/operator goals should be first fielding a well-defined and implemented production network which is fault-tolerant with resiliency and robust operation built-in. The second is developing a local depot sparing strategy which allows the ability to place spares into production rapidly and the additional ability to replenish spares supplies when required in a seamless and predictable fashion. The design of both of these strategies is accomplished at the initial project planning and network requirements planning phases of the project. The project management, implementation engineering, and long-term operational processes provide the predictable and well-known process for bringing the network into production.

FTTx Network Owner/Operator-Managed Build Model

A third model for the build out of an FTTx network allows the owner/operator of the network to manage the equipment vendors through the design and implementation phases and lead the efforts to integrate the equipment, services, and management solutions resulting in the as-built network. Additionally, the owner/operator of the network will be responsible for creating and deploying the production processes supporting the long-term operation of the network.

In this model, the network operator does not take a very different approach from either the BOT or consultant/build group approach, rather they take full responsibility for all aspects of the network build, overseeing the project to successful network launch. In this model, the network operator must utilize the service resources of each of the equipment vendor organizations and ensure that the integrated network meets the expected requirements, using the best from each vendor to produce the final result. In this model, the network operator should have a good level of experience leading the building of a complex technical system. If the operator does not feel that such technical experience exists within their present organization, a single or multiple consultant(s) can be engaged to provide guidance, with the responsibility for execution of the project staying with the network operator. Typical professional services provided by equipment vendor organizations are detailed below.

Vendor Organization Professional Services

Equipment vendor organizations often provide a field engineering, or professional services group that can provide focused technical consulting on their own gear and related interoperable products, protocols, and deployment methodologies. The types of consulting and services are to be determined in consultation with the FTTx network operator based on the project timeline, project requirements, and/or requests for focused technical assistance. Typically these services are delivered in the implementation and initial production phases. However, once the network enters the full-scale production stage, professional services may still be rendered to the FTTx network operator as required. Such professional services in any phase of the network lifecycle may include but not be limited to:

- Network design and implementation;
- Services design integration and testing;
- Interoperability assessment and testing of voice and IPTV solutions;
- OSS/BSS integration and flow-through provisioning integration and testing;
- Project management for access network planning, integration, and implementation;
- Development of production engineering processes and procedures specific to the vendors' equipment.

Such consulting can be undertaken and completed remotely—especially planning and design activities. Where the vendor organization must be involved in equipment deployment and commissioning such consulting is undertaken on-site and completed at the customer site.

Vendor Organization Training

Part of the training regimen for the operator team running the network will be specific product-level training for all the deployed equipment, including the FTTx solution. This training should contain several levels that can be mapped to specific roles within the operator organization:

- Introductory FTTx product training—This training should provide an introduction to general PON networking and should also provide some specific introduction to the PON technology used to implement the selected product line. The training should also contain hands-on material allowing the student to successfully commission and configure the OLT, then add ONTs to the system and apply provisioning for services to the system. The course should also cover management of the system using the dedicated management software system. Basic troubleshooting should also be covered allowing the technician or engineer to learn and apply PON access networking concepts and provide the basis for additional technical training on the platform.
- Advanced product-level training—This training level should provide network engineering product-level knowledge transfer using the FTTx platform at a detailed level. Additional deeper topics addressing advanced concepts such as QoS design and configuration, system troubleshooting and management system concepts should be covered. Typically, the operator's technical staff who are working with the FTTx system on a daily basis, as well as those designing the network engineering of the deployments using the equipment, should benefit from this training level.
- Product certification training—Training at this level is for operators and designers who must be experts in all aspects of the system in order to

be certified by the vendor organization as a qualified operator-expert. The training should include deep immersion into all aspects of the FTTx platform for advanced-level network engineers and provisioning personnel. Previous classroom and operational experience with the FTTx system would typically be helpful as this training should provide as many topics and as much depth as necessary to allow the students to pass certification examinations as part of the training experience.

The FTTx equipment vendor instructors will be subject matter experts on various aspects of their solution. Network integration and deployment of services including data, voice, IPTV, RF video, along with outside plant design and deployment considerations should all be covered as part of the curriculum in the training, which should be as in-depth and hands-on as possible. The intent is that the individuals receiving the training, who are engaged with the network deployment have the ability to successfully design, deploy, and maintain their network, working with their equipment vendor over time as new features and capabilities are added to the system.

Table 15.1 represents a generic, standard introductory curriculum offering which an operations team member should receive for their selected FTTx product platform.

Vendor Organization Technical Support

Technical support is an important part of the overall package of assistance services provided by the vendor organizations for both the FTTx solution and other equipment in the network build-out.

In order to carry out the maintenance of the full-scale production network, where the FTTx network operator requires support for operations and production engineering, the FTTx equipment vendor must provide a comprehensive support capability. This capability consists of a number of components supporting the efficient and uninterrupted operation of the FTTx network. Depending on the lifecycle phase of the FTTx network the number and type of support components may change, but at each stage they are a critical aspect of the relationship between the network operator and the equipment vendor.

It is expected that the network operator take advantage of this assistance for the full service lifetime of the FTTx system, whether this is included with the equipment purchase, available during the standard warranty period at no additional cost, or is a purchased service that is renewed on an annualized basis. It is critical that technical assistance be available to the operations team who are responsible for deploying the FTTx system. The network management team should consistently provide a support package to the technical operations team. The support package should be part of an overall support service agreement which may have a number of aspects to support the operations team.

Table 15.1 Introductory FTTx System Training

Training Topic	Content Details	What Students Should Learn	Notes
Introduction to the FTTx system	1. OLT and ONT devices 2. Planning and designing a network with the OLT and ONT 3. Modeling the network 4. Network scalability	Student should learn the physical and logical interfaces of the OLT and ONT devices, the operation of the PON link, how to design a network for desired split ratios, and the desired bandwidth capabilities based on those split ratios	Basic FTTx system information transfer is the goal
Outside plant design techniques	1. Network topology 2. Split ratios and optical budgets	Student should achieve the ability to understand the optical budget of their PON technology, physics of loss in fiber and design a basic optical plant	Note that ISP personnel may not be the primary OSP designers, but must understand the concepts to troubleshoot the FTTx system properly
Data service integration	1. Networking design 2. Secure interfaces	Student should learn the networking capabilities of their FTTx system (depends on the switching and routing supported) including L2 VLAN allocation and mapping and L3 IP routing architecture. Should also include IP address scalability, VLAN mapping to WANs MAC address limiting	Student should be familiar with the basic networking concepts at L2 and L3—if not, the course may need to provide basic capability training required to understand the FTTx system
IPTV service integration	1. IPTV service design 2. IP multicast and scalability 3. Internet group management protocol (IGMP) and IGMP snooping 4. IP video network architecture 5. IGMP metrics	Student should learn the basics of IPTV operation as implemented in the FTTx system and where applicable the basics of IPTV transport systems in general, including the design of an IPTV system end-to-end	Details regarding the measurement of IPTV transport to ensure customer experience should be covered as well as troubleshooting techniques
Voice service integration	1. Introduction to VoIP 2. VoIP architectures 3. VoIP protocols	Students should learn the end-to-end architecture of the VoIP system and be familiarized with a basic level of call flow and protocol support for their selected solution	Material for VoIP should include basic telephony information which will help the student with troubleshooting voice issues, especially with identifying where the likely area of voice trouble exists. This can be difficult for network operators without backgrounds in telephony or VoIP systems
QoS subsystem introduction	1. QoS features 2. Access control lists 3. Configuring QoS templates	Students tasked with setting up and maintaining the QoS configuration for their network will need considerable depth in this knowledge area	Other students will need at least rudimentary coverage as they may be involved in troubleshooting QoS issues as the network build-out is completed and new subscribers added
Troubleshooting	1. Troubleshooting principles 2. Mechanics for logging 3. Typical FTTx issues	Student should learn to use the FTTx system built-in capabilities to detect troubles. They should also be exposed to troubleshooting methodologies using the system tools and knowledge of FTTx systems, with directions on how FTTx troubleshooting adheres to general networking troubleshooting principles, such as starting with the physical layer and moving upward through the networking layers. Additionally, typical FTTx system issues, and steps to quickly find and resolve them should be covered	Students with basic networking troubleshooting skills will be well-equipped to master this topic

Category	Subtopics	Student learning objective	Notes
Maintenance	1. Hardware maintenance 2. Software maintenance 3. Software upgrades 4. Management of system configuration	Students should learn the required software and hardware procedures to maintain the system in steady-state operation, as new components are added to the system to replace failed components, or as hardware and software upgrades are added	Key information for the procedures of performing maintenance should form the basis for some aspects of the production processes book for the FTTx portion of the network
Management system capabilities and operations	1. Management system features overview 2. OLT configuration and commissioning 3. ONT discovery 4. Service and device provisioning 5. Troubleshooting support 6. Integration with northbound systems 7. Backup and restore configuration 8. Software upgrades 9. SNMP system and traps 10. Security and administration	Students should learn the feature set of the management system whether CLI or server application based, and the typical operational procedures the management system enables	Where possible advanced management system capabilities should be explored and details of the management system itself discussed, with recommendations for best practices in operating the FTTx system
ONT	1. Physical interfaces and powering 2. Logical interfaces: IP services (voice, RF, gateway) and management 3. Configurable trusted interfaces	Students should learn all physical and logical interface of the ONT devices in use as these will be the primary points of offering services	Both configuration and provisioning of the device should be covered
Resiliency and quality of service (QoS)	1. QoS (quality of service) 2. ACLs (Access control lists) 3. LAGs (link aggregation groups, LACP protocol for port interfaces) 4. STP (spanning tree protocol, L2 resiliency) 5. Higher layer resiliency protocols	Students should learn to design and configure resiliency solutions and quality of service-related mapping for the FTTx system, end-to-end	Resiliency strategy is highly dependent on the system design and implementation and may vary greatly from vendor to vendor. The QoS and resiliency strategies will likely be interconnected
Turn-up and operations	1. Turn-up and operational best practices 2. OLT/ONT CLI turn-up 3. EMS turn-up (depends on management system)	Students should learn to commission (configure and deploy) the OLT and ONT system, along with typical operational procedures using the management system	Understanding typical management operations prepares for understanding services provisioning in the context of the PON system
Services turn-up and customer activations	1. Discovering and managing ONTs and bringing them into management 2. Provisioning services	Students should learn the processes related to discovering ONT devices and bringing them into management, as well as provisioning of services on both the OLT in preparation for the ONTs to be discovered and on the ONTs when they are brought into management	Data service—Create VLANs for residential and business services and provision the ONTs for operation IPTV—Create IPTV VLANs and provision services on the ONTs Voice—create voice VLANs and provision services

The components of the support agreement may contain some or all of the following attributes:

- A comprehensive sparing strategy (specifying which spares must be stocked and the locations of the stocking). This sparing strategy must be developed as a part of operational process deployment and production engineering requirements and may include advanced replacement of some components depending on their criticality. Advanced replacement agreement parameters may include timing of the shipping and receipt of components covered by the equipment vendor's support agreement.
- The selection of options for phone-based support programs which provide the flexibility for the FTTx network operator to choose $24 \times 7 \times 365$ or other options for assistance availability.
- Availability of on-site support by qualified applications engineering resources to assist the FTTx network operator with initial deployment activities or in the longer term of a production network to assist in targeted troubleshooting, network optimization activities, training, or deployment of new equipment and services.
- Options for other value-added support services such as system and network design, technician premise turn-up support and optimization, system documentation, and process development.

OPERATIONS TEAM

Table 15.2 describes the network operator's project team members' responsibilities in detail, along with their equipment vendor organization project counterparts in the process of designing, implementing and operating the FTTx network.

PROCESS BOOK

Process: Network Documentation

A critical work output of the design and implementation of the FTTx network is the creation and maintenance of the network documentation kit. This repository of information represents the physical layout of the network, inside plant and outside plant, as well as the logical configuration of all the programmed elements within the network. Note that this can also include the customer provisioning information which is configuration related to the allocation of subscriber services. If not, the logical configuration certainly details how the services are built in a general sense. The network documentation will fall into one of several categories defined below.

Physical Configuration

The physical configuration represents the implemented physical connections between active and passive elements as part of the inside plant or outside plant.

Table 15.2 FTTx Network Operations Team

FTTx Network Operator Project Team Member	Equipment Vendor Project Team Member	Expected Communication	Note
Project manager—overall project oversight for the FTTx network organization	Project manager—overall project oversight for vendor organization	Frequent, direct communications via email, conferences, and face-to-face meetings	The two project managers must work in lock-step tandem, especially during the design and implementation phases of the FTTx network build. Once in steady-state operation, their roles may change to include other aspects of the network lifecycle
FTTx network engineer lead—technical leader for the network operations team, typically an engineer leader with experience in multiple disciplines related to access networking such as switching, routing, VoIP, video, optical plant, or other related disciplines	Field engineer lead—provides technical oversight on all aspects of the project, including overall design responsibility for the access network and its integration into the core network, will be a technical expert on the FTTx equipment systems and operations	Direct as-required during design phase and at beginning of implementation phase	The FTTx network lead engineer will provide technical leadership to engineers representing multiple disciplines as a one-to-many contributor
FTTx network or operations engineer—technical specialist with training and experience in one or more disciplines or technologies required to build and operate an access network. These individuals may be at the junior or senior level depending on skills and experience	Field engineer—provides hands-on configuration, implementation and troubleshooting services for the project	Direct as required during implementation and steady-state operations	Individuals in these roles will represent deep technical knowledge of one or more technologies or disciplines including the operation of the FTTx system
FTTx network technician—an inside or outside plant specialist who will perform technician-level operations and maintenance on the FTTx system including customer premise operations and outside plant work as required	TAC engineer—provides remote technical support to the FTTx network organization team	Direct as required depending on the phase of the network and issues which require resolution	
	Escalation engineer—TAC resource which provides escalation of technical issues into R&D within the vendor organization and drives problems to resolution—provides feedback to customer on resolution and expected timeframes for deployment of solutions	Direct as required depending on the types of issues encountered during network operations	

Items such as the connections between device ports, cables, or fibers used in a connection, location, and setup of patch panels, for example, should all be documented in this information repository (Table 15.3).

Logical Configuration

The logical configuration represents the current as-built configuration which is then implemented and saved in programmable or configurable devices typically in the inside plant either in primary or secondary facilities or equipment cabinets or hardened enclosures of some type. This includes the as-built-to specifications and implementations for the PON access network design, but also may include supporting logical configuration for the transport and core networks and even should include, where possible, services supporting equipment. This vital repository must include the complete network logical design implemented in the device configurations. Examples of documents which make up the logical configuration of the network are included in Table 15.4.

Table 15.3 Example Physical Configuration Documentation

Example Documents	Description	Detailed Information
Outside plant diagrams	Physical location and identification of the fiber plant	Contains the detailed description of the outside optical plant for main fiber feeds, trunks, and drops to individual locations including patch panels, splicing points, and enclosures for craft work, testing, and maintenance. This repository will also include power readings and other levels taken over time as the plant is maintained through cleaning and testing. These data may be contained in specialized tools designed for the storage and maintenance of such operational outside plant information.
Inside plant diagrams	Physical location and identification of the inside plant equipment	Contains the facility and frame locations for the OLT and other equipment contained in primary or secondary facility locations (could also include cabinets). May also contain basic wiring, powering, cooling, and other environmental documentation. Note these may also be called equipment elevations. However, they should be the accurate as-installed elevations for the purposes of the production network
Network diagrams	High-level physical connections of the inside plant devices	Documents which diagram the physical topology of the inside plant network, allowing for discussions of design and maintenance. Note these may also contain the physical connection points at the detail of network wiring diagrams. However, the wiring diagrams may contain information at a level too detailed to allow for protocol and other topology discussions
Network wiring diagrams	Detailed physical connectivity of the inside plant devices	Low-level detailed information regarding port, wire/fiber, small form-factor pluggable, and other physical level details of equipment interconnectivity. Allows for exact location of physical attributes by engineers and technicians who are performing maintenance or commissioning new equipment

Table 15.4 Example Logical Configuration Documentation

Example Documents	Description	Detailed Information
FTTx access network (OLT and ONT) design document	Access network design includes the physical interconnectivity and logical configuration to integrate the OLT and ONT northbound into the upstream network and southbound into the customer premise. Includes all aspects from physical layer to upper-level protocol layers. Also provides the engineering design to specify the specifics of PON implementation including traffic characteristics, expected loading, resulting split ratios, and support for services models	This document or set of documents covers the following aspects of the overall logical design of the access network: Redundancy and resiliency requirements, open access requirements, physical interconnects and supporting resiliency protocol interfaces to the transport and core networks. The comprehensive design may include some aspects of the network at large in order to completely describe the FTTx design, such as "core or transport network design supporting the PON access network" or design of outboard gear such as "DHCP application design supporting the PON access network" as two examples. This design must ensure the seamless integration of the access network into the transport and premise networks
Services specification	Services specifications derived from high-level network system requirements	Services specifications include guidance to design and implement the network to support services taking into account redundancy and resiliency requirements, physical interconnects, protocols, L2 VLAN allocation, L3 routing protocols and configuration, QoS design and implementation, IP networks and their allocation of addresses to subscribers
Services design document	Logical network design for services (per service from insertion point through core/transport/access networks and customer premise)	This document provides the services design which will be implemented in the access network equipment. This document may also cover other services-related configuration where required to fully design the service delivery. This will typically be a very detailed view of the services and the configuration which will support them
Design of network monitoring solutions	Design of systems to provide telemetry on network operation	Provide guidance on specification, design, and network integration of best practice systems and tools for network capture/monitoring, services testing and monitoring tools (i.e., IPTV assessment equipment), and OSP health monitoring tools
Design of network management and provisioning solutions	Specification, design, and network integration of required supporting network solutions for element management systems, northbound provisioning systems, and other supporting management integration such as SNMP information gatherers, DHCP servers, and event notification systems	Creating a specific design for the management system will foster the creation of seamless integration across supporting software systems and intentionally avoid the creation of a hodge-podge management system on non-integrated components

Methods of Procedure

The methods of procedure (MoP) are step-by-step processes for how to achieve certain activities successfully when maintaining the network. These important documents are necessary to ensure that the knowledge of how to perform required maintenance on the network is not dependent upon the specific memory or written information of any one individual, but is organized and maintained as an organizational resource which is available to any members of the production operations team to accomplish their objectives. The number of MoPs necessary will vary from network to network. However, there are some which are expected to be available for any FTTx production network and these are provided as examples in Table 15.5.

Documentation Repository

The network documentation may be in a number of forms including spreadsheet, PDF, and word processor files. Depending on the type of information, there may also be custom applications with their own proprietary database repositories for the data. In either case, the repository should be able to control documents and supporting data, along with managing the revisions to data and documents ensure that changes are tracked, controlled, and can be audited as required (depending on internal quality and auditing processes). The intent is to understand that the network documentation is a living representation of the design and implementation of the network equipment and its configuration. As with any large set of distributed engineering information on a project as complex as an access network, having a logical representation with which to understand and manage the network equipment is key. Without such information, the as-built network would be difficult to understand and maintain on its own.

Each set of documentation should have a lead author or change control manager who is responsible for those data. In order to make changes to the repository, there should be a control board, along with a configuration management system officer who maintains the repository. For an access network design document, for example, the control board would be the team of network engineers charged with designing the network. Changes to the documentation kit must be reviewed and signed-off by this board before they are added to the repository. Therefore, along with the task of maintaining the repository over time, there must be processes in place to review and sign-off on changes to the network documentation, to ensure the quality of the information. Ultimately, to support the number of persons who work on a system such as a large access network over a potentially very long period, the information regarding that network must be maintained in careful and thoughtful manner.

Process: Configuration Management

Managing the configuration of the production network is a key process area which will ensure greater success with keeping customer services operating over

Table 15.5 Example Methods of Procedure

Example Documents	Description	Note
Method of procedure to commission an OLT	Procedures for setup of the PON access network's primary traffic device	Required for access equipment integration into the transport and core networks
Method of procedure to commission an ONT	Procedures for bringing an ONT device online and preparing it for management and provisioning	This set of procedures may become well known since it will be commonplace for these devices to enter and exit the network. However, specific indicators, logs and state-machine knowledge may be critical at some points
Method of procedure to troubleshoot network issues	Procedures specifying how to locate and determine the root cause of service and network affecting issues	Important information for training new operations individuals. These procedures will be modified over time as new tools and techniques become available and new problems are encountered
Method of procedure to replace OLT components	Procedures specifying the maintenance window operation to replace OLT cards and restore known working configuration	This MoP will likely contain separate sections for each integrated component or field replaceable module in the OLT
Method of procedure for deploying new software baseline	Procedures for receiving the new software from the vendor organization, assessing readiness to deploy it on the production system and the instructions for doing so	This may be a single or a series of MoPs specifying how to load and bring up new software releases on the FTTx equipment
Method of procedure for services creation	Procedures to implement the configuration of services in the management system and access equipment infrastructure	Procedure may touch many systems as the support for any given service will touch aspects of all the network partitions and involve a number of equipment vendors and devices including core, transport, and access network systems. The traffic engineering and quality of service aspects which are key factors in the logical network design are part of the access network and services design documents
Method of procedure for baseline release testing	Procedures to prepare and validate all services and provisioning in test network's production-ready environment before releasing the new software baseline element	Baseline release testing provides a readiness assessment and recommendation go/no go on making a change to the documented FTTx production baseline
Provisioning of customer services	Provide procedures to operationally provision customers who are brought online—may be engineering-level or customer service-level documentation, depending on intended audience	Provisioning may be performed using a number of layers of software applications, especially if the provisioning information is a flow-through operation. If so, there may be several levels of MoP documentation which cover all aspects of this information flow (at both an engineering and operations level), not only the final operational steps

a long period—despite the numerous changes which naturally occur in the life-cycle of the network. The configuration of the production network is defined by the following collections of code, configuration, and provisioning (Table 15.6).

Configuration Management Processes

There are a number of important process areas and activities related to the configuration management of the previously defined asset collections, either contributing directly to configuration management or supporting the deployment and maintenance of the managed assets. Consider the following key processes and activities:

- Development of the configuration documentation methodology—Documentation of the asset configuration baseline as well as processes to identify and track the configuration baseline as new assets (ex: executable software loads) are incoming to the production operations team.
- Development and deployment of the configuration management repository—The creation or (purchasing) and deployment of a system used to manage assets which are subject to revision, such as documents, configuration files, executable code, etc.
- Development of processes to identify, track and deploy configuration baselines—Development of the strategy on a per-asset basis to manage the revisions of the assets—to answer such questions as, where do the assets reside, under what circumstances do they change, how are

Table 15.6 Definition of Assets to Be Configuration Managed

Asset Collection to Be Managed	Description	Examples
Executable code	Released executable from the equipment vendor for OLT, ONT, or any other active device which requires a software executable to operate	These code files should be either the generally released (GA) or specific customer release code for a particular site. The executable code generally is disbursed with a package of release notes indicating features, changes, and known operational issues which must have specific workarounds
Running configuration	Configuration which represents the implementation of the network design documents	Saved configuration in device flash memory, configuration files which are provided to network devices via TFTP or FTP transfer and maintained in file systems, supporting DHCP configuration
Service provisioning	Configuration which represents the allocation of specific resources to a particular subscriber	Saved configuration in device flash memory, configuration files (for example, TR-069), other supporting device configuration as necessary to implement the service. Depending on the implementation of the provisioning system, the service provisioning information may be stored in its own distinct database separate from running configuration storage

revisions deployed to the production network, how is a set of revisions compiled into a configuration baseline set? There are a number of other considerations related to the deployment of configuration baselines.

- Testing procedures to certify a new configuration management baseline or a change to an existing configuration management baseline before releasing it to the production network. These testing procedures can also be utilized when deploying a new hardware or software system to the production network. Since the tests should be inclusive of all activities that are enabled by the network such as providing subscriber services, provisioning subscribers, enabling network management, etc., by demonstration and testing they can ensure the new system is prepared for operational readiness.
- Development of procedures for deployment of the new or partial configuration management baseline to each piece of vendor equipment subject to update, based upon vendor best practices for deployment new code or configuration.
- Development of the internal process of staged deployment including success criteria for each stage resulting in the ramp-up process for introduction of a configuration baseline into production. The step-up phases should include, for example, a beta period where the configuration is applied to beta customers who can certify that services are working.

The Test Network

Creating and operating a test network which mimics on a smaller scale the exact equipment used in the production network is the most cost-effective method of supporting a number of production network activities:

- Providing a test bed on which to perform configuration management baseline testing prior to moving new hardware or software to production, and validation of other hardware before moving it into the production network. Hardware may also be preconfigured before commissioning by using the test network.
- Providing an easily accessible location to recreate issues or problems with a system running at the exact production configuration baseline so that data can be collected for the vendor organization's analysis.
- Proactively maintaining a set of hot spares for critical items which are in known working condition at the current production baseline code revision for quick deployment into production, replacing failed modules.
- Providing a location for interoperability testing of various service components such as—VoIP interactions between CPE end-points and soft switch, IPTV CPE and middleware, TR-O69 provisioning servers and CPE of various types—to support assessments of new products or planned implementations of new software or hardware solutions.

Backup and Restore Capability

Development of the configuration and provisioning backup and restore strategy maintains the security of the running configuration of the active devices in the network and the subscriber provisioning information—both of which are required to recreate the network's operating environment. Typically for active devices there will be a software facility to periodically and automatically transfer the running configuration to a back-up file system for storage and retrieval when required. For critical databases used for provisioning, there should be a strategy in place to have periodic back-ups of the data, along with a resiliency strategy to protect the data at all times, as well as having it available at all times, along with periodic back-ups for catastrophic situations. Regardless of the specifics of the processes developed for the network, there must be a periodic testing exercise in which the stored backups are retrieved and restored to representative network devices to assure that back-up processes are working.

Process: Troubleshooting, Problem Resolution, and Working With Vendors

Large and complex systems like an access network are going to have problems and issues over time, whether related to hardware failures, software bugs, incompatibilities between equipment, or unusual issues caused by equipment introduced into the network by subscribers. In order to get past these types of issues and ensure the network continues to function properly, eventually every operations team must interface with their equipment vendor organizations—sometimes, depending on the problem, multiple vendor organizations simultaneously. Previously, we defined the expected technical support function that vendor organizations should at a minimum provide to their customer operating organizations. In order to make the best use of these resources from the vendor organizations, each operations organization should develop the following capabilities within their operations team.

Working With Equipment Vendors

Each operations organization should develop their own internal procedures for working with vendor TAC resources. As issues are encountered and reported to TAC, they will need to be tracked internally. Work products and data associated with the issue will need to be collected, maintained, and likely turned over to the vendor TAC in order for them to solve the issue. If possible, a best practice is to determine with the individual equipment vendors which data sets they will likely require as part of a problem investigation and have these available when the problem is reported, thus avoiding a second round of problem initiation and data collection.

As issues are resolved, the necessary configuration changes or executable code changes will need to be prepared for introduction into the production network at large. These are typically planned as the GA executables are provided by the vendor organization as a released baseline. Once these are received, the operations team will use their test network, baseline testing procedures, and deployment process to move the code into the production network, thus revising the current running baseline in production.

Periodically an equipment vendor will release code which contains new features and bug fixes which were not driven by errors or problems in the operators network (presumably these were driven either by another customer network or found in internal testing by the equipment vendor). In this case, typically there are features or updates that would be beneficial to the production network. Therefore, it is a best practice to review the release notes for these baselines to understand what new content is available in order to make a determination of whether the release should be made part of the current network baseline. Of course, the process to revise the production baseline and bring new code into the network is costly and, therefore, it is best to review the new code content with the vendor organization to understand fully the implications of the software upgrade before planning to undergo the process of updating the network.

Another aspect to consider regarding new code from equipment vendors is the support provided to previous code revisions. The vendor's policy on how many previous code revisions are supported may drive the network operator to make the upgrade to keep current with latest supported code—this typically is the best option since this is presumably where the vendor organization is focusing their time and effort for new feature content.

Troubleshooting

Troubleshooting network issues is both art and science. However, for the most part effective troubleshooting is an engineering or scientific skill that is learned and through experience becomes what appears to be an art in the hands of a skilled practitioner.

When it comes to troubleshooting, the access network devices should be treated as any other network device. For this reason, troubleshooting should start at the lowest layer of the networking hierarchy as possible (the physical layer) and move upward through the higher-level network model layers. For each layer, confirm that the error is not occurring there, before moving on to the next higher layer.

In order to quickly either rule out problems in a particular part of the network, or confirm where a problem is occurring, a best practice is to have a network monitoring strategy as part of the network management infrastructure, with the ability to quickly gather port statistics, network packet traces, and protocol exchanges between devices when required. In addition to allowing for quick data collection in the event that a problem is occurring, this will allow the operations team to practice collecting data to ensure the network is operating correctly on a regular basis. In the best case, the data collection can be done automatically and reported to the operations team as a report or graph to help spot network issues as quickly as possible.

Depending on the type of error being encountered—something periodic which repeats on a regular basis or an error that occurs seemingly randomly and infrequently—the network operations team will need to rely on their local engineering counterparts and the equipment vendor TAC to collect data, pinpoint the issue, and provide testing and investigation that resolves the anomalies—they should be proactive in asking for assistance, especially when their efforts do not quickly lead to a resolution path. The most important thing is to regain the network to best operating order.

Resolving Problems

Once the troubleshooting process is able to provide an answer to the cause of the network problem, the operations team will need to quickly move to implement a problem resolution.

- The issue at hand may be the result of a hardware failure in a component, which requires an immediate replacement. Providing a sparing resource in the network operations facility via the test network is a best practice to have spares in a known ready state with the current network configuration baseline installed on them. Typically these will not have beta or customers provisioned on them, but may be configured to provide production services to the operations facility to provide a quick check that the network is operating correctly. At a minimum an OLT and up to 10 ONTs should be prepared for a quick swap into service.

- The problem may be resolved by making a workaround to specific configuration parameters—considered an operational workaround— with the expectation that the vendor organization will be making an executable code release which will resolve the issue using proper configuration for the affected functionality. In this case, the operations team will need to track the existence of the workaround and the code release from the vendor and into production before they can fully close the resolution of this type of problem.

- The error in the network may be such that a quick change to executable code is required—often called a patch. In this case, the vendor organization reacted quickly to a specific situation and minimized the amount of code change required to resolve the problem, producing a release based upon the current GA baseline with the single change added. In this case the production network may be forced to use this release until a new GA baseline can be received from the vendor organization. Once again, the operations team will need to track the new release of code and the required changes into the production network before fully closing on the resolution to this problem.

In either of these types of cases, or a case which is a combination of these, the operations team will need to provide the discipline to fully document the resolutions to the problems, and use their processes to methodically release new code and configuration changes into the network, ultimately securing its operation.

Process: Production Engineering

Production engineering is defined as the set of technical operational techniques required to continuously maintain, troubleshoot, and upgrade the software systems, electronics, and fiber plant implementing a production FTTx access network deployment. This body of knowledge and practice is an intersection of a fully trained, organized, and well-led team, a complete set of network management technologies and tools, and a realized group of processes which guide the work of the team. The three areas of this framework: team, technology, and processes are the drivers for organizational excellence, and thus production engineering excellence:

- Team—with specific networking skills, trained in the equipment that makes up their access network, and prepared to troubleshoot and resolve issues;
- Technology—network management systems providing performance management telemetry to identify issues, areas for maintenance and expansion;
- Process—development of processes and procedures to allow the team to work efficiently and guide both longstanding and new members of the team.

Periodic Network Assessment

A best practice of the network operations team is a periodic assessment of the network. During these assessments, which can be planned and scheduled to occur over a calendar year, the team should undertake the following types of maintenance and verification activities:

- Confirmation of baseline configurations;
- Confirmation of baseline code revisions;
- Gathering of network traces to confirm prioritization markings;
- Forced failovers to secondary northbound providers to ensure network recovery;
- Recovery of configuration from saved back-ups;
- Review of recovery procedure to replace hot spare components;
- Forced failovers to resilient systems to ensure network services recovery;

- Validation of outside plant power levels and match to design levels;
- Cleaning and replacement of fiber connector patch panels and test points;
- Review of services design and requirements versus current network operation (ex: voice features validation, video validation).

Operations Team Toolkits

In addition to the network data-gathering systems, monitoring systems, and management system tools which will be in place in the production network, each operations team member should be equipped with or have access to a set of FTTx specific tools:

- OTDR—for making measurements of outside plant fiber;
- Network protocol tracers—can be either PC workstations or standalone high-capacity network protocol devices;
- Network test sets—handheld test sets which can generate packets and test received packets per Internet standards;
- Optical meters—handheld meters which can be inserted into an optical path and used to make power measurements. Meters are available that go in the optical line and make measurements individually at each wavelength in use, and in the appropriate direction;
- Laptop PCs—additional laptop PCs for collecting data, collecting logs, or generating traces—especially in customer premises where an additional computer is required;
- Fiber cleaning kits with known jumpers, attenuators, and splitters.

CONCLUSION

An operations team which has the key roles fulfilled, the right training to build their skills, and the essential management tools is key to a successful production network. If the vision and goals for the project in the business plan were followed with a careful plan and design, then assembling the team to protect and thoughtfully maintain the resulting set of solutions is just as much an investment as the inside and outside plant implementing the network. It means that the result of the hard work in getting to a production launch—selecting the best in class vendors, the network build model, and running the implementation project—will be successfully maintained, upgraded, and continue as an asset for further investment. The operations team running the network with their management technologies, processes, and vendor relationships, provides the technical management that will ensure the success of the network long term.

CHAPTER 16

Performance Management

INTRODUCTION TO PERFORMANCE MANAGEMENT

Operators designing and implementing FTTx access network solutions need a comprehensive strategy for using performance management concepts during the lifecycle of the network. This includes defining performance management and the functions it encompasses, how it can be described, modeled and implemented, and how it can be used. A major aspect of performance management is considering it during the whole process of building and the full lifespan of the network.

Delivering services seamlessly in an FTTx deployment using network-generated telemetry for performance management requires not only sufficient tools and techniques, but an effective overall strategy. While performance management is directly related to the operation of the final as-built network, it should be taken into account during all lifecycle phases of the network realization process:

- Planning;
- Requirements;
- Design;
- Implementation;
- Production Operation.

Starting with the early concept phases, on through planning, gathering requirements, selecting vendors for each component of the network, designing and implementing the network, and getting through the early integration and testing and finally to production operation—there is (what can seem at times) an overwhelming amount of work and focused effort. Part of this effort must be the considerations of how the operator will monitor, measure, and control this overarching network system of integrated subsystems. Since of all the phases of the network realization, the longest phase will be production operation, where the work of managing the network over the long haul will be required, the ultimate goal should be optimization of the access network—allowing the operator to have the most efficient and well-executed collection of subsystems for delivering services to customers.

FTTx Networks. http://dx.doi.org/10.1016/B978-0-12-420137-8.00016-0

In order to embark upon the realization of an effective performance management system we need to consider the following objectives:

- Objective one—Define a unified description of performance management.
- Objective two—Identify and prioritize which elements (physical and logical) in an FTTx network should be monitored and measured.
- Objective three—Select what data and information should be gathered—based upon a survey of the types of performance management data available and backed by the industry standards for performance management—including how the data are obtained from the network.
- Objective four—Apply the performance management data to the day-to-day operation of the network using standards and potentially proprietary methodologies to measure and make decisions about how the network is managed and optimized.
- Objective five—Develop a set of recommendations for network operators, with takeaways they can use moving forward—wherever they are in their network lifecycle.

DESCRIPTION OF PERFORMANCE MANAGEMENT

First we will embark on a "unified" description of performance management, encompassing a number of concepts.

Performance management allows the FTTx network manager to collect and analyze data regarding the operation of the network in order to make sound decisions regarding the management of the network.

Performance management is distinct from other activities that are performed in managing the network, but is interrelated to those other activities. We will see this concept when examining performance management in context with the other management activities defined in the *FCAPS* (*fault, configuration, accounting, performance, security,* the management categories into which the ISO model defines network management tasks) model for network management defined in the ITU-T X.700[i] recommendation, which is a reference for the ITU-T M.3000[ii] series of recommendations for management networks (see in particular ITU-T M.3010[iii] Principles for a telecommunications management network and ITU-T M.3400[iv] TMN Management functions).

Clearly, performance management falls in the "management of the network" arena but considering the many aspects of managing a network, we can say of performance management:

- It clearly is part of the steady state operation of the network, but in order to get it right, that is, to get a performance management strategy and implementation that works for us, we need to consider it from the beginning of the network lifecycle—if we don't, for example, we may make implementation choices that limit us later.

- What we will see as we continue to analyze and consider performance management in FTTx networks, is that many of the tools, techniques, and standards were developed for other similar networking technologies but are being applied to FTTx networks either because they need to be embedded in the FTTx gear, because the FTTx gear interacts with elements "higher" up in the network, or because the FTTx network has some unique features.
- It contains elements of what is enumerated in the FCAPS network management framework from the ITU, not only for performance management, but in the other areas covered by FCAPS.

The FCAPS Model for Network Management

Applying the ITU FCAPS Network Management Framework as it applies to FTTx performance management provides a view of how this functionality sits within the industry expectations for network management in general. Reviewing the FCAPS standard and how this applies (the framework is straightforward and easy to map) provides a good way for network operators and builders to think about the overall management of the network. The different FCAPS areas of concern and a description of their primary functions, along with their relationships to performance management are:

- Fault management—find and correct network problems—by nature this seems like a reactive response, so it is better to be proactively identifying areas for maintenance. This proactive approach is directly related to performance management.
- Configuration—control of the revision of the network—including the inventory of hardware and software components and their operating level. This also includes the application of configuration information to the network devices in order to achieve delivery of services, or provisioning. The configuration of the network is peripherally related to performance management as it is important to understand how the revision of resources affects the ability of the network system to do its job.
- Accounting—allocation and accounting of network resources based upon the subscriber's share of resources, and the recording of resource usage to allow proper billing. Allocation and accounting are both related to performance management through the collection of information about the network. Also, the use of performance management for optimization comes into play—in how we are going to allocate resources across the network in the manner that allows the network to perform best.

- Performance management—collection of network data to guide the allocation of resources through shared components and proactive identification when network changes or maintenance are required.
- Security—having networks operate securely from intrusion, protecting subscribers, their services, and their data. In this discussion of performance management the intent is to understand the operation of the network and through that understanding to protect the elements of the network.

This provides us with two complementary views on performance management.

- The first is operator/network-focused: as an operator how can I measure what I am managing so I can make sound decisions in the operation of the network?
- The second is customer-focused: how to manage the network performance to get a flawless customer experience?

From a technical standpoint, these two views define the performance management component of FCAPS for our discussion moving forward. Our goal is to use performance management to support the sound engineering practices used in operating and maintaining the network as well as ensuring the services customers receive fully meet their expectations for excellence.

Thus the management of the network and the services it is providing are nearly as important as the services themselves…and thus the planning for performance management of the network is just as important as the planning for the services, through all phases of the network lifecycle.

FTTx Network Phases

Fig. 16.1 indicates, in a waterfall model, the different phases of the FTTx network lifecycle, and the activities that are included in each phase. Note that at the bottom of each phase the distinct activities for performance management are included.

- PM goals—strategic objectives for the performance management system;
- PM requirements—what is required of the performance management system to meet the strategic objectives;
- PM design—design of hardware and software systems, integrated to create the performance management data collection and reporting requirements;
- PM implementation—deployment of the solution which implements the design, resulting in a system which the network operations team can use to proactively manage the network;

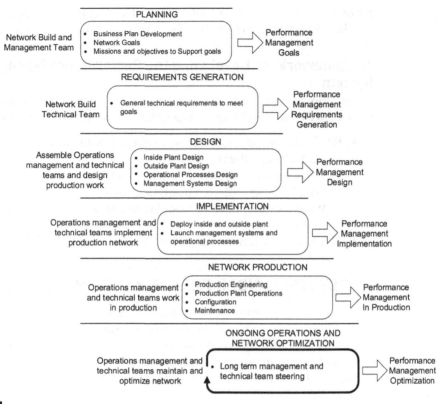

FIGURE 16.1

FTTx network lifecycles.

- PM in production—ongoing operations using the performance management solution which allows the network operations team to accomplish production engineering activities.

Using this approach, the performance management of the network will not be left to the end, but will be just as important as every other component of the network during the design, implementation, and production phases.

On the top of the waterfall, the status and types of teams involved in each of the phases are specified. Once the network goes into production, the on-going operations and management of the network is aided by the performance management system, which is also designed and implemented during each of the phases. Even if the network you are involved in operating is in a later phase than the beginning planning phase, or any of the other phases, you can still work on creating a performance management solution for the network. This is especially true if you are faced with a network which is beset by technical problems and is difficult to control. Part of getting the network under control is a data-driven approach enabled by a performance management system.

A Framework for Developing the Performance Management System

To develop an effective performance management system to control an FTTx services network in all lifecycle stages, the following framework is used:

- Firstly, define the system under performance management (SUPM);
- Secondly, define the set of network telemetry available
  - What data the network provides or pushes;
  - What data are collected from the network;
  - What data are collected from instrumentation or appliances attached to the network;
- Thirdly, define how to gather and apply the data.

THE SYSTEM UNDER PERFORMANCE MANAGEMENT

In this section, we explore the components of the SUPM. This provides a model for thinking about the system we are measuring and controlling, and allows us to partition the system so its control interfaces can be defined. Ultimately, if we are successful in creating a model of the SUPM, we will realize the goal of controlling it most efficiently, expending the least effort and resources to do so.

Integrated Network System

Think of the network—including the FTTx access component (OLT and ONTs), the upstream components for transport, aggregation switches and routers, and the services integration equipment—as the entire integrated system under performance management. Consider this integrated SUPM then, as a set of interrelated and connected subsystems providing services to customers and requiring measurement and management, through the use of network telemetry. Network telemetry is performance data provided by two distinct sources in the network:

- The first is data generated by the network components themselves, as part of operating and providing services. These data may be sent proactively to the measurement and control system or they may be periodically measured, then collected through sampling or querying the network equipment directly.
- The second is data generated by instrumentation and appliances used to "measure" the network. Here the data will be set up for gathering or sampling and then either saved or sent at a certain interval to the management and control system.

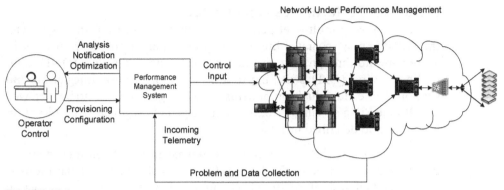

FIGURE 16.2
Integrated SUPM.

There are numerous types of network-generated telemetry built into the network systems, and considerable sets of data available from network measurement tools if you have the methodology, gear, and techniques to gather and analyze it. Both these areas will be explored in depth.

Fig. 16.2 shows this integrated SUPM system. In this figure, the integrated SUPM is represented by the "network cloud" and is built up of a number of components. The performance management measurement and control system is provided problem and data collection points, where it is able to collect data about the network and receive telemetry generated by the network. It is also afforded points where it can add control back into the network through the control inputs.

Through the control and instrumentation interfaces, the performance management system is collecting and analyzing data and telemetry. The performance management system then provides the network operator analysis reports of the data from the SUPM, notifications when data indicate that certain thresholds or levels have been reached by monitored attributes of the SUPM, and thus opportunities for optimization of the SUPM. With these management data the operator is able to make informed judgments about the control and maintenance of the SUPM.

Similarly, the network operator, based on what their PM management system is able to collect and provide to them in terms of actionable information, is able to make control input changes back into the network. The operator can use the information from the performance management system for tactical purposes (solving immediate problems), or for strategic goals (making longer-term decisions) regarding the SUPM.

Ultimately our goal is to meet both our performance management goals—one operator-based and the second customer experience-based using the SUPM model. To do this we will break down the SUPM into its requisite components, allowing us to consider performance management at more detailed levels within the SUPM, resulting in a multilevel performance management system view.

Multilevel Performance Management

Fig. 16.3 shows a multilevel performance management view. In this system, the SUPM is now separated into its component parts (moving from the subscriber upward through the network)—optical network terminal (ONT), optical line terminal (OLT), switching/routing, transport, services integration, and support. These individual components of the integrated system to be managed are allocated to a specific performance management segment. This allocation is defined and described in Table 16.1.

In Fig. 16.3, we see that the performance management and control system has the ability to receive network telemetry from each of the network partitions as well as send control information back into the network components to act on the results of the telemetry analysis. The performance management levels are defined based on which partitions support the activities of that performance management domain. The expectation is that performance management activities for each of the levels includes telemetry and analysis for the network partitions encompassed by that level, as follows.

- PON system—Performance management data and processes specific to the FTTx access system, for sets of subscribers (per PON) or individual subscribers (per fiber-drop) including the health of the shared PON medium, which includes the outside plant.
- Network system—Performance management data and processes specific to the distribution of services and management data to specific regions of the network and to aggregated sets of access networks. At this level, the performance management can include thousands of subscribers and equipment that serves large numbers of access networks.

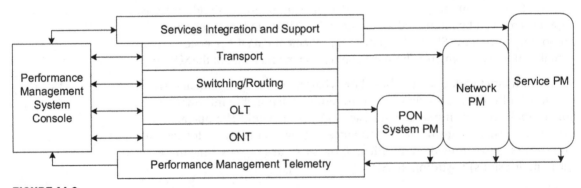

FIGURE 16.3

Multilevel view of performance management.

Table 16.1 System Component to Performance Management Level Allocation

Performance Management (PM) Level	System Partition Allocated to PM Level	System Description	Performance Management Focus
PON system PM	ONT	FTTx CPE and interface to the subscriber	Use subscriber-specific data to manage the health and services optimization of the individual customer
	OLT (this includes internal to the OLT and the plant between the OLT and ONTs)	FTTx access primary networking device and system interface	Use aggregated data of all subscribers on the chassis to ensure the access network is functioning properly
Network PM	Switching/routing (i.e., the network side of the OLT)	Operator network aggregation devices responsible for services management and deployment to the locally attached access networks	Use the network appliances to assess and manage the health of all subscribers' services and the health of the overall network
	Transport	Operator network devices responsible for projecting services into regional areas	Use the network appliances to assess and manage the distribution of services data
Services PM	Services integration and support	Operator network devices which support services deployment	Use the network devices and any associated monitoring devices to assess the health of the services applied to the network

- Services system—Performance management data and processes specific to the generation and deployment of services into the network system and ultimately the access network and to the individual subscribers. Performance management at this level can include very detailed information germane to an individual subscriber or services support appliances, such as DHCP servers that handle large sets of subscribers.

Now that the levels of performance management are defined, the next step is to specify the telemetry available from the allocated system components.

NETWORK TELEMETRY

In terms of network telemetry, there are rich sets of data generated by the network, available at defined collection points. Grouping the performance management data sets gathered and derived from the integrated network into categories based on the previously defined performance management areas:

- Information generated by the PON equipment—PON equipment PM;
- Information generated by upstream extended network equipment—Network equipment PM;

- Information generated by devices in the services infrastructure. This is typically provided by devices so involved in the implementation of the services that they have specific information about those services—Services PM;

For each of the categories of network telemetry that are available, the following details need to be answered:

- What comes from the network itself (embedded in the equipment and built-in)?
- What comes from adding instrumentation to the network through probing and monitoring?

Data From the PON Equipment

The PON equipment, based on one of the FTTx standards, provides performance management data as part of its operational attributes. Note that while the standards do provide guidance on the types of data which should be generated, the implementation will be vendor-specific. The OLT/ONT system will have some or all of the following types of data available through self-generated telemetry or through network probes or monitors:

1. Management indicators via SNMP: Alarms and events/traps. The SNMP (Simple Network Management Protocol; the various revisions of such are defined in the following IETF RFC's: SNMPv1 [RFC1157][v], SNMPv2c [RFC1901, 1905, 1906, 1907][vi], and SNMPv3 [RFC2271–2275])[vii] events include alarms that are stateful (meaning that they set a state and clear that state when the condition is no longer valid), traps which are not stateful in that they represent a one-shot event notification and may continue to trigger at some rate as long as the condition is detected. The number and type of traps are considerable, and they are extremely useful indicators of system health. But in many cases the traps will need to be managed due to the sheer number of SNMP messages that can be received on a medium to large network installation. Some of the trap operations that can be used are roll-ups (showing only one trap when a large number of identical traps has been received), grouping (showing sets of identical traps based on some matching criteria), sometimes suppressing noisy traps (equipment generating multiple traps which cannot be filtered or suppressed) where necessary—these are all features that a good performance management system can provide to the network operations team.

   At the PON link management layer, SNMP traps are used to assess the health of the ONTs in link, indicating faults due to a loss of PON data link. They also indicate links with detected errors during transmission upstream. In terms of a state machine, the traps indicate state changes (coming into and out of link) and from the detection of error rate in the transmitted signal, the traps indicate threshold crossings, with the error values of the threshold configurable by the vendor of the PON equipment.

So this set of network telemetry as an example would be collected by an SNMP trap collector and analyzed to assess the health of OLT to ONT links and to make decisions as to which ONT's optical link to investigate further. Hopefully the further investigation can be carried out proactively before services are affected.

As an example of further drill-down into detail on the PON standards, the SNMP trap data bases for GPON and EPON:

a. ITU-T G.984.3[viii] GPON transmission convergence layer specifies the following traps
    i. Loss of signal (LOS)
    ii. Loss of frame (LOF)
    iii. Drift of window
    iv. Signal fail (BER)
    v. Signal degrade (BER)
    vi. Loss of GEM channel delineation
    vii. Remote defect indication (ONU)
    viii. Transmitter failure
    ix. Startup failure
    x. Loss of acknowledgment
    xi. PLOAM cell loss
    xii. Error message.

b. EEE 802.3ah[ix] EPON Traps specified the following traps which provide BER information
    i. errSymPeriodEvent—defined number of errored symbols in a defined period
    ii. errFramePeriodEvent—defined number of errored frames in a defined period
    iii. errFrameEvent—defined number of frame errors in a defined time period
    iv. errFrameSecsSummaryEvent—defined number of symbol errors in a defined time period.

c. PON system will provide standard SNMP traps for networking devices
    i. Equipment status (ex: cold start)
    ii. Protocol specific indicators (ex: STP events).

Use the vendor's management system or send the traps and gathered telemetry to a specific application for central collection and analysis.

2. Counters of various types on specific physical and logical interfaces or flows. The most common counter types are:

   a. RMON (remote monitoring of SNMP MIBs) interface counters which are polled on a specific interval.

   Interface counters are instrumental in both troubleshooting faults and in determining how much capacity is flowing into, out of, and through the network (even across the backplanes and internal PON interfaces of the OLT, for example). These counters can be very detailed in terms of information regarding packet sizes and types of data being transported in the access system. Collecting and measuring or graphing this information over time is important to understanding the overall data flow of the network.

   b. SFLOW and net flow statistics (per data flow counters, which are "pushed" or sent proactively to a collection server).

   Flow counters provide a view into individual subscriber statistics for data flow "through" the network gear. The devices capable of this level of network view are typically the higher-level devices in the network such as OLTs, large switch routers, etc.

   c. Ethernet interface link status (link reported via standard traps, and counters polled at regular intervals).

   Ethernet interfaces provide status of their link state via SNMP traps. The link status can also be polled on a regular basis to determine the status of the connectivity—this can be important for critical connections between OLT equipment and the upstream switch or routers.

   Counters which are also associated with the Ethernet interfaces are covered next. There are counters available on the ONT service-specific interfaces (Ethernet data ports, Wi-Fi statistics).

   The vendor may provide a management solution that provides derived statistics based on the counter polled values. However this may need to be something that the operator develops through third-party applications as part of their own performance management strategy. In either case the performance management system can derive statistics based on the sampled counter data, and graph resulting history and trends.

3. Other logs (typically proprietary) which are available from the devices but which are not usually required unless there is an error or troubleshooting situation—in which case there must be a method available to collect those data, typically with a dedicated server.

   a. SYSLOG is the industry standard for logging subsystem information. The vendor will provide guidance on which logging levels should be activated for a given system—and under what conditions to enable logs. For example, some systems leave logging enabled continuously for levels which indicate trouble or faults.

b. The PON equipment will generate other logs which provide very product-specific, proprietary information about the operation of the PON equipment. This information may be extremely useful in debugging issues or resolving problems, but may be turned off or ignored when an issue is not present.

4. Optical devices in the network which generate data regarding power levels sent and received into the outside plant, and increasingly seen in later-generation optics, the ability to provide burst mode measurements as part of the optical link. Measurements from individual ONT stations can be obtained by the OLT.

a. SFP/optics measurements such as launch and receive power as part of the digital diagnostic monitoring (DDM) interface in the SFF-8472^x standard specification for optics, both in the uplink and PON sides of the OLT

b. Received signal strength indicators (RSSI) built into the PON SFP can provide burst mode measurements of individual ONTs on the PON link. This is very useful because a measurement of the PON link efficacy for an individual ONT can be obtained without inserting an optical power meter into the link and disrupting communications with other ONTs on the shared PON medium.

c. The ONT optical components increasingly provide the ability to provide launch and receive power readings for all wavelengths they handle, and provide those via SNMP direct query to the ONT or even report them through the PON link to the OLT

d. All the optical devices in the OLT and ONT typically provide indicators when the laser has begun to degrade or is operating outside its normal range, indicating the laser may be reaching its end of useful life.

5. From the PON OLT control chips (individual ASICs which perform the PON link control upstream and downstream), BER measurements per ONT device are available. These are available either as part of trap indicators (as seen previously) or through command line or MIB interfaces, depending on the vendor-specific implementation. Note that interoperability of the PON ASICs for OLT and ONT needs to be confirmed for these measurements as part of the equipment/vendor selection process.

Data From the Networking Equipment

Available from the devices in the network is higher-level services information based on standard data collection as well as individual probes or information-gathering devices for different service types.

Here are the data available from the networking equipment:

1. Counters and MIBs—large networking gear such as switches and routers provide a rich set of counter data for various interfaces, as well as frame

types and sizes. Additionally, the MIB database for the gear will provide a status of the overall management and performance of the device, and this is available to polling devices via SNMP, including such internal resources as CPU and memory usage.

2. SNMP traps and alarms—similar to the FTTx access network equipment, the upstream networking equipment will proactively send SNMP traps and alarms to alert the operator to various events and stateful status information, such as the operating state of fans and other hardware components.

3. SYSLOGs and other proprietary logs—similar to the PON equipment, the upstream networking equipment will provide a logging subsystem that will provide both standard SYSLOG and proprietary logging (typical—depends on vendor specific implementation).

4. Instrumentation/probes—in order to do network troubleshooting and analysis a network probe is a useful device. Note that many times a PC or workstation with readily available networking software can be used to gather network traces from Ethernet ports which are configured for port mirroring (using SPAN, switched port analyzer, to send a copy of all packets seen [ingressing or egressing] to a network port to another port), and provide useful traces of network transactions. In many cases a network operator will seek to deploy dedicated network probes at specific points in the network to be able to troubleshoot and proactively gather traces at various times to confirm services prioritization marking, and service-specific protocol exchanges. Depending on the interface to the network, these data may be gathered with a passive probe such that port mirroring would not be required (occasionally port mirroring will have some limitations on data collection activities).

5. In addition to the ability to set up specific probes for data networking analysis, the data services equipment, depending on vendor implementation, is able to collect and forward (also referred to as "push") statistical and data flow information to collectors for analysis and reporting.

Services-Specific Telemetry

Services-specific telemetry is either generated by the equipment providing the services or through instrumentation embedded in the network for probing and monitoring. External collectors are used to receive logging and statistics from the services equipment to aid in troubleshooting or to gain an assessment of the health of the particular service.

- IPTV service instrumentation to provide protocol statistics and throughput of IPTV frames;
- Voice service instrumentation to provide call statistics;
- Data service instrumentation to gather traces of particular transactions, protocol exchanges, or networking sessions;

- Log collection servers (specific to equipment vendor and generic in the case of SYSLOG, for example).

Applying Network Telemetry

We have established the definition of performance management in the context of our FTTx access network and the surrounding and supporting network at large, that PM is part of each of the entire realization phases of the network, how a system under performance management can be modeled, and the different types of information to be gathered. Let's turn to the areas of application for these data and determine the tactical and strategic application of performance management.

APPLICATION OF PERFORMANCE MANAGEMENT

So we have these rich and somewhat overwhelming sets of information, "telemetry" available from the network. There are a number of performance management applications in which to use the data. Consider the following operational and service-related practice areas, supporting the production engineering processes of managing and maintaining the production network.

Network Health

The first example is using performance management to determine how the network is doing (its health) based firstly on what is happening at certain key interfaces in the network and secondly looking at incoming SNMP trap and alarm data that indicate trouble. From these data we can perform the following activities:

- Fault detection and recovery—which interfaces are active and operating properly and which are in a fault state, including what types of data and data throughput flowing across those interfaces in order to determine if the current data transmit and receive levels are meeting expectations.
- Monitoring and maintenance (using fewer resources)—through long-term data collection, looking at trends in network capacity and the mix of types of data flowing over the network, determine where maintenance may need to be performed, where to target more in-depth collection of network traces to assist with:
  - Determine which points in the network are trouble spots;
  - Network security and protection, by looking for sudden changes;
  - Understanding the expense of maintaining the network (where to apply scarce resources).

Network Capacity

The second example is determining the current network usage as a fraction of the capacity, to help us determine the current scaling of the network and the trend toward requiring additional resources. Determine where the loading hotspots in our network are (especially the FTTx area) to:

- Provide knowledge of network's loading at key interfaces between equipment, and if the counters are available, internal to the equipment.
- Scaling—knowing when to increase capacity—by adding additional physical interfaces to the connection between equipment or to increase bandwidth available to certain service types (for example, at a loading of 80% capacity on current interfaces in a connection LAG group, then a new interface needs to be added).
- Apply network engineering—refine QoS settings for certain services or data types, to block certain data types which are consuming excessive resources.
- Planning and implementing changes (configuration management) for new service types, or new service levels requiring changes in QoS settings.

Services Health

The third example is determining the current services health, to ensure the customer experience, and to proactively seek to manage the network to protect it. In addition to the information that the services implementation equipment provides, deploying probes and instrumentation gathering equipment can be extremely helpful to:

- Manage services based upon the performance management data (hopefully before customers are aware there is a problem);
- Troubleshooting when there are problems to quickly get the services back to full operation;
- Planning to add new services or modify the services over time;
- Services efficacy by proactively monitoring services or during network assessments, making specific services-related network traces and tests.

In order to implement these objectives, the following sections detail a number of the services-specific standards and measurement techniques, helping assure these services using performance management.

Voice Service

For the voice over IP (VoIP) service implementation a large expenditure of design, implementation, and operational budget is placed on providing quality of service (QoS) to ensure the service. In many cases, this service is the most critical since problems with voice services can be quite serious for operators and subscribers. Many aspects of the voice service can be measured and assessed including packet loss, packet delay, and network jitter—typically this is done by the equipment involved in providing the service, including the voice call agent (soft switch typically) and the end-point, which is many times embedded in the ONT. Additional types of measurements through the call agent are availability, including connection setup time, percentage of successful call transmissions, speed of fault detection and correction.

For voice services, there are a number of industry standard performance measurements that characterize the quality of the voice service. These measurements are made more practical by the soft switch and network packet monitoring equipment which can help to determine the scoring. Usually such measurements of voice quality should be made when the voice service is initially put into production to ensure that the network engineering supporting voice has been sized and configured properly. Then, over time, the measurements should be repeated to ensure that as more subscribers are being brought online and network loading increases, that the voice service is being protected properly.

Standards/metrics of PM measurement (subjective and objective) which are available to measure the quality of the voice service include:

- MOS (ITU P.800)[xi]—Mean opinion score—subjective human-based measurement, provided by test equipment algorithms, based upon historical perceptive tests.
- PSQM (ITU P.861)[xii] and PESQ (ITU P.862)[xiii]—Perceptual quality scores: perceptual speech quality measure and perceptual evaluation of speech quality (measure of quality based on comparison of input to output speech, looks primarily at distortion effects).
- E-Model (ITU G.107)[xiv]—Using network impairment measurements (packet loss and delay) along with the VoIP system attributes (i.e., codec type) to estimate voice quality based on an R-value which is related back to MOS score.

The MOS and PSQM/PESQ measurements are typically provided by test and measurement equipment which can send and receive tones over the VoIP sessions and determine the received voice quality. The E-Model measurement can be measured using the services equipment (soft switch and CPE endpoints in the VoIP exchange) and the measurement tied back to a related quality score by the soft switch. As noted above, for most systems this quality measurement would be made during the production launch of the network and retested periodically over time to ensure the measurement is consistently good.

The applicable PM protocols which support the above standard measurement of voice services while the service is being deployed (in use) include:

- RFC real-time control protocol (RTCP)[xv]—a control protocol which provides service quality-related information such that network delay, jitter, and packet loss of a VoIP conversation can be determined.
- RFC3611 RTP control protocol extended reports (RTCP XR)[xvi]—an update to the RTCP protocol which defines the XR packet type and their usage

within the RTCP protocol to provide information that supplements statistics contained in RTCP reporting. This update contains additional types of reports other than those in the initial RTCP standard.

The performance management telemetry gathered in the implementation stage of the network based upon these standard measurement and enabling protocols includes the network protocol traces and data gathered by voice test analyzers and embedded protocol probes within the soft switch and CPE devices. From the collected data, analysis based upon the standards is used to generate scores of the voice quality in real time, enabling a view of the network's capability to support the VoIP service.

Data Service

Data services for residential and commercial subscribers represent a significant expenditure of networking support, transport capability, uplink expense, and end-to-end QoS to assure the services. In order to securely deploy these services the operator needs to understand the scale of the services within the network, loading of the network, and specific interfaces of special interest—those most important to shared resources and scaling. All the available metrics must be gathered from the PON, network, and services systems to get a full view of the network performance. With the number of types of data traversing the network increasing on a regular basis, the ability to collect metrics and statistics and determine how the network is performing over time, is critical—especially at points in the daily operation when subscribers and businesses are most active and the network is therefore most active.

Available standards for performance management to gather data for measuring the quality of the data service include:

- RMONv1 (MAC layer monitoring)[xvii]/RMONv2[xviii] (monitoring traffic on all network layers), IETF RFC1757 RMON MIB[xix]—Allows the standardized collection and gathering of statistics for network monitoring using SNMP. This is an extension of the SNMP MIB, with extensive statistical data generated by the generating and transmitting host. A collector device polls the RMON capable network equipment, and receives the RMON data which are used for network utilization, future planning, and performance management. RMON data consist of ingress and egress statistics on all interfaces, broken down into unicast, multicast, broadcast, errored and discarded packets, and frame size.
- NetFlow (IETF RFC 3954)[xx]/IPFIX (IETF RFC 7011)[xxi]—Defines the protocols for exporting from switches and routers, internal information regarding data flows, to other collector devices where the data may be gathered and analyzed. The NetFlow records contain numerous rich data points regarding the data traversing the data device. There are a number of vendors supporting NetFlow.

- SFlow (IETF RFC 3176)[xxii]—Defines a methodology for sampling traffic in switched and routed networks, by sending sFlow records to collectors. A view of data flows across a number of devices can be built using a central sFlow collector receiving sFlow records at the interfaces of the switches and routers. There are a number of vendors supporting sFlow.

The performance management data—gathered from the OLT, switches and routers providing the data services, either polled by an SNMP application or a collector receiving pushed NetFlow or sFlow records—are used to establish the health of the data services and the network in general by the following:

- For SNMP data, there are numerous applications for gathering and manipulating the collected data. For example, the data can be graphed for a visual representation of the network loading in real time, or reports generated and saved. Another example is creating notifications on the detection of certain events such as threshold crossing. These collection and monitoring tools are available as third-party applications. However, the equipment vendor may provide some level of support in their management applications if one is available. Either way, integration of these capabilities into the management workbench available to the network operator should be the goal.
- For flow-based data, there are again numerous applications and open-source tools to collect and analyze the data. Third-party vendors or open-source products provide workbench applications for this type of data collection and analysis, typically. However, the vendor of your networking equipment may provide some monitoring capability for their equipment. However, it is understandable if the vendor-supplied application is not necessarily designed to integrate with other products.
- For both of these cases, the network operator needs to be aware of which standards are supported in the data equipment and plan accordingly for those. Most network management applications are well-designed to handle SNMP, and many of the flow-based collection and analysis tools can handle both protocols for flow-based information transfer. The best solution provides an integration of this type of data for all devices in the network if it is available.

IPTV Service

The IPTV service, using packet-based video distribution for broadcast and on-demand services, requires considerable network planning and implementation including QoS constructs and services hardware. Transport mechanisms include unicast and multicast distribution, and therefore, the tools and techniques to ensure efficacy of the service are network-centric.

In the area of standards-based organizations actively working in the area of objective video quality measurement and assessment there are several (besides these focused groups, other general standards organizations, such as the IETF and the Broadband Forum, have also published some video- and IPTV-related RFCs and standards documents):

- Alliance for Telecommunications Industry Solutions (ATIS) IPTV Interoperability Forum (IIF)[xxiii]—Doing work in the area of analyzing and assessing video quality metrics in the area of IPTV;
- ITU-T Study Groups 9 and 12 and other initiative groups—Working in a number of areas of video quality assessment;
- Video Quality Experts Group (VQEG)[xxiv]—A group formed out of ITU participants working in a number of areas including video metrics evaluation;
- Video Services Forum (VSF)[xxv]—Concerned with video delivery for telephone company (telco) organizations, has numerous committees working in a number of areas including IPTV metrics.

For these industry standards groups, which cover a wide range of activities related to video, their work is not always IPTV-centric and network-centric performance management (measurement and analysis) standards, so a review of their considerable bodies of documentation and work products is in order to find the relevant publications. For the FTTx network with IPTV deployment, performance management measurements which allow the operator to ensure efficacy of the service should be objective, practical standards for measuring video quality in steady-state production environments—not depending on human assessment or on comparing the original video with resultant received video. This narrows the number of objective-based evaluation standards and vendors with implementations for the specific technologies of steady-state (production) measurement, analysis, and quality assessment of IPTV services. These technologies will typically require deployment of specific software and hardware probes to make the quality assessments, but can be invaluable in having a real-time assessment of the IPTV service at various point in the network.

- IETF RFC4445 Media Delivery Index (MDI)[xxvi]—A Codec independent IPTV monitoring methodology based only on network impairments, providing an assessment of jitter, traffic rates and lost packets to characterize an IPTV stream (or set of streams);
- V-factor—Related to MPQM (moving picture quality metrics)[xxvii] but does not require the reference video as full MPQM—typically proprietary video quality measurement calculated using content attributes and network impairment factors to arrive at a quality rating.

STRATEGY FOR DEPLOYMENT

With the large number of performance management-related measurements, standards, tools, and technologies available, defining the strategy for implementation and deployment can be confusing. However, creating a strategy is simplified by using the multilevel performance management model from Fig. 16.3.

Start with the PON system performance management basics, making sure the PON system-level performance management data are collected, monitored, and used to manage the PON system. The PON equipment vendor will be the most knowledgeable of their own equipment and will assist in understanding what performance management support their FTTx system has built-in. Part of the implementation of the FTTx system should be specific technical discussions and training regarding best practices for gathering information from their equipment and recommendations for adding probes and collectors to assist the collection of data from the PON equipment. In addition to the gathering of telemetry from the FTTx system, the PON management system provided by the vendor should be considered in the overall performance management strategy. For example, it may have the ability to perform some of the gathering and monitoring or notification functions. However, it may make more sense to send the data from the management system and equipment collectors to a higher-level management system that will be the performance management central control for the entire network: access, core, transport, and services.

Next move to the performance management of the network system, pulling in the data services equipment. Using what is available from the devices via flow-based push protocols and what is available via SNMP polling, define the locations in the network where notifications and data reporting will help to detect trouble areas and proactively discern where updates are needed to the infrastructure to support higher-scale data services.

Next define the service-level PM needed based upon the services supported by the network. Ensure customer services are managed, to the full extent capable by the services equipment and the network performance management function. The most important factor is to create a performance management system which does not rely purely on customer feedback to give the network operations team the notification that there is trouble with the services (although customer feedback is certainly useful, having angry customers who are struggling with their services is too late a notification for most network operators). To ensure the service performance over time, measure service performance and quality when they are first deployed and in a periodic fashion thereafter—don't assume that the network will stay static, it will not, especially when new equipment and services are added, and as inevitably more subscribers are added to the network.

This strategy can be applied to all or any of the network lifecycle phases, regardless of where the implementation of the network currently resides. The reasoning is that performance management is too critical a function to leave out of the network build, even if the network is already in the production phase. The remaining lifecycle of the network will still be enhanced with a performance management solution.

Performance Management Workbench

As part of the deployment strategy, consider the performance management tool integration with the overall management system in the creation of a performance management workbench. Certainly each level of network performance management (PON, network, services) is complemented by the management system of each piece of equipment, with vendors providing their own management solutions for their products. However, the goal is an integrated performance management workbench that allows the operator to gather and manage the entire integrated access network system. Creating the performance management workbench requires integration with the equipment vendor supplied management subsystems where possible, potentially direct integration with vendor equipment for performance management data collection, or possibly the receipt of exported data from the vendor management system into the integrated performance management workbench.

Ideally, the workbench would be able to handle the two primary activities for most of the equipment being managed: data collection and reporting. Data collection is the gathering of incoming telemetry and the sampling of the equipment for periodic data, and reporting includes not only notifications, but also the ability to set thresholds for those notifications, allowing the network operator to get real-time proactive information about FTTx, network, and services performance. Reporting is the ability to generate graphical and other types of reports ensuring the operator can visualize the network performance over time, both in real time and historically.

The additional ability of the workbench to automatically and on-demand generate reports of interest to the operator, such as the following basic reports, is important. The assumption here is that for a given implementation, the vendor would have a set of very specific and useful reports available, and that the ability for the operator to design their own reports would exist.

- The current link state of the ONTs in the network—especially those that are not available and are considered nonoperational (on a per-OLT basis).
- Sets of alarms/traps with the ability to associate devices with specific traps (or specific traps with certain devices).
- Amount and type of FTTx equipment in the network, with sortable inventory lists.

Of the network management tools for gathering data, performing data analysis and alerting the operator with notifications and reporting, there are third-party tools which are readily available. In the areas of performance management there are also numerous vendor-supplied/supported tools in the network system level and services level which are available. Ideally, the network operator will be able to acquire or develop an integrated system which is able to integrate with other systems to make the usual operations of performance management both easy to do in an interactive fashion and also in an automatic or programmatic fashion.

References for Further Study

For study and reference of performance management, as shown previously, the standards bodies provide guidance regarding protocols, techniques, and technologies for performance management of networking equipment, services evaluation, and product-specific tools and techniques.

Standards development typically comes through study and working groups chartered for the development of standards for technology and practice, including key performance management technology developments, and recommendations for best practice. Specific tools and technology implementations are generally vendor-prepared to support their products. Occasionally, vendor-specific technology is adopted into standards or becomes a standard. However, sometimes there is not a lot of information on proprietary technologies.

Almost every networking standards body provides performance management definitions (at least) for the technology area they are working in, some delving further into what would be called implementation-guiding specifications. For example, providing specific measurements that should be captured in order to determine the performance of certain attributes specific to that measurement. Some standards provide detail on how to actually implement the measurements and analysis. As you read the different standards you get a sense of some interrelationships and crossover or blurring of boundaries of influence. Guidance from a number of sources, including the following providing information on which data should be monitored, how they are generated, measured, and the results evaluated (some of which were detailed in previous sections). Since standards in these areas are constantly being updated, changed, and improved upon, the network operator is urged to keep abreast of them:

- For FTTx performance management, the primary PON standards bodies provide guidance not only for the standards themselves, but the supporting management and measurement applications up to and including the services level as well (IEEE, ITU/FSAN). The broadband forum also provides crossover standards which provide good work in the PON and services spaces, which complement the basic PON standards.
- For data network equipment, the IETF set of requests for comments (RFCs) provide strong and influential standards across numerous networking technologies, the Metro Ethernet Forum provides strong

specifications for data service definition, evaluation testing, and performance management.

- For services equipment, such as VoIP and IPTV, there are standards for protocols to support performance management as well as specific standards for measurements and evaluation of those measurements.

In addition to the standards-based literature, additional reference information from vendors on specific implementations is available via white papers, specific vendor product or tool user manuals, and data sheets.

CONCLUSION

Performance management is a necessary part of the full lifecycle of FTTx access network implementation. It encompasses more than just the PON portion of the access network system, it is part of the overall network and services implementation, and is necessary for a successful deployment. Therefore it should be treated with the same level of depth in the planning and implementation stages as the rest of the network. The FTTx standards bodies and vendor community have been successful with performance management implementations. Additionally, data network equipment vendors and services equipment vendors also have performance management solutions. For the network operator, the challenge is to create a performance management solution that allows the integration of performance management systems for the entire network system—allowing it to be applied to the management of production networks long term. The available breadth and depth of standards and literature for performance management promote the awareness of performance management as an overall science and engineering discipline.

Endnotes

i. https://www.itu.int/rec/T-REC-X.700/en.

ii. https://www.itu.int/rec/T-REC-M.3000/en.

iii. https://www.itu.int/rec/T-REC-M.3010/en.

iv. https://www.itu.int/rec/T-REC-M.3400/en.

v. https://www.ietf.org/rfc/rfc1157.txt.

vi. https://www.ietf.org/rfc/rfc1901.txt, https://www.ietf.org/rfc/rfc1905.txt, https://www.ietf.org/rfc/rfc1906.txt, https://www.ietf.org/rfc/rfc1907.txt.

vii. https://www.ietf.org/rfc/rfc2271.txt, https://www.ietf.org/rfc/rfc2272.txt, https://www.ietf.org/rfc/rfc2273.txt, https://www.ietf.org/rfc/rfc2274.txt, https://www.ietf.org/rfc/rfc2275.txt.

viii. https://www.itu.int/rec/T-REC-G.984.3/en.

ix. https://www.ieee802.org/21/doctree/2006_Meeting_Docs/2006-11_meeting_docs/802.3ah-2004.pdf.

x. ftp://ftp.seagate.com/sff/SFF-8472.PDF.

xi. https://www.itu.int/rec/T-REC-P.800-199608-I/en.

xii. https://www.itu.int/T-REC-P.861/en.

xiii. https://www.itu.int/T-REC-P.862/en.

xiv. https://www.itu.int/T-REC-G.107/en.

xv. https://www.ietf.org/rfc/rfc1889.txt.

xvi. https://www.rfc-editor.org/rfc/rfc3611.txt.

xvii. https://tools.ietf.org/html/rfc2819.

xviii. https://tools.ietf.org/html/rfc2021.

xix. https://tools.ietf.org/html/rfc1757.

xx. https://www.ietf.org/rfc/rfc3954.txt.

xxi. https://tools.ietf.org/html/rfc7011.

xxii. https://www.ietf.org/rfc/rfc3176.txt.

xxiii. http://www.atis.org/iif/index.asp.

xxiv. http://www.its.bldrdoc.gov/vqeg/vqeg-home.aspx.

xxv. http://www.videoservicesforum.org.

xxvi. https://tools.ietf.org/html/rfc4445#ref-i12.

xxvii. http://www.eetimes.com/document.asp?doc_id=1298245.

CHAPTER 17

Identifying Network Threats and Security Vulnerabilities

INTRODUCTION

As an operator begins deploying services to subscribers there are a large number of factors which may cause a lack of sleep. An operator is typically faced with issues such as IPTV pixilation or voice quality issues or maybe even the random Internet point-of-presence failure. Each of these issues may be quickly resolved and services restored within an acceptable timeframe. Many times operators feel their network is secure with iron-clad firewalls capable of keeping the bad guys out and the good guys in. What is often ignored is the fact that many times the bad guys "live" within the network. This chapter provides a high-level view of the issues of which an operator should be aware, pointing you to possible agencies or organizations who are experts in securing an access network.

DEFINITION: DENIAL OF SERVICE (DOS) ATTACK

Before we can dive into the realm of network protection we should probably lay some groundwork on what we are trying to guard against. The term denial of service (DoS) attacks tend to become the buzz word used when there is a wide-scale network outage. Unfortunately, the publicity of a DoS attack tends to be rather negative many times pointing the finger at the network operator or service providers' lack of security. So, let's begin here defining what a DoS attack encompasses.

A denial of service attack can be thought of as an attempt to make a machine or network resources unavailable to its intended users. This may cause a temporary or indefinite interruption or suspension of Internet services. Plain and simple, a DoS can be simply defined as someone preventing your network from operating at the expected service level. The service outage may impact a single subscriber from making a phone call or watching TV or impact a complete service offering, such as Internet TV or access to services such as NetFlix. A DoS attack on an operator's network is NOT a condition in which resources outside the operational boundary are impacted, thereby reducing service quality to subscribers. Unfortunately, this may impact the perception of the operator by their subscribers.

403

FTTx Networks. http://dx.doi.org/10.1016/B978-0-12-420137-8.00017-2

An organization which will greatly assist operators in not only helping to better understanding the current threats from DoS attacks but also to assist in recovering is the United States Computer Emergency Readiness Team (US-CERT). The US-CERT is part of the US Department of Homeland Security responsible to "improve the Nation's cybersecurity posture, coordinate cyber information sharing, and proactively manage cyber risks to the Nation" (https://www.us-cert.gov/about-us).

An attempt to add an exhaustive list of DoS attack types would not be possible, given the rapid change in tactics. The remaining sections detail some considerations on the prevention of DoS attacks while also protecting the integrity of the operational network.

MANAGEMENT NETWORK SECURITY

Before the first services are activated on a network, the ability to control and manage the equipment providing services to subscribers under all conditions is absolutely critical. This requires a well-protected and stable management network throughout the network architecture. In many cases the management network is connected over the same interfaces to which subscriber services are provided in order to help minimize network construction and connectivity costs; however, major considerations should be made as your network is built and services are architected.

Even with an industry-leading secure management network in place, once an employee is given rights to make changes to the network, errors in configuration will occur, intended or not. Unfortunately, human nature is difficult to secure. The best an operator can do is track how changes are made, by whom, and to control and understand access rights and privileges. The next few sections will walk through these topics in more detail to provide a better understanding of how to better prepare your management network.

Management Network Architecture

More often than not, when an access network is designed and put into operation the primary goal is to ensure services are delivered as efficiently and deterministically as possible. Consideration for the management network is at times placed as a secondary consideration, which may lead to stranded equipment not operating efficiently, or unreliable reports or logs. Typically issues with the management network are not exposed until a major software upgrade is pushed out to the system or an outage is experienced.

One of the more reliable but also more expensive management networks put into place is a parallel physical layer network with dedicated interfaces, as shown in Fig. 17.1. By securing the physical management network separate from the

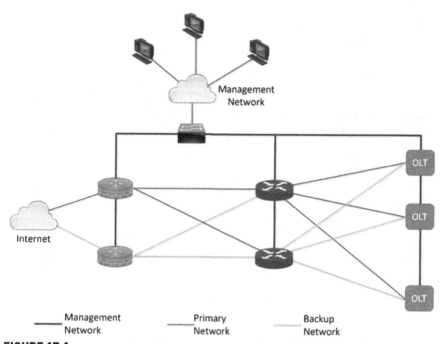

FIGURE 17.1
Dedicated network management.

subscriber services network, on dedicated interfaces, the overall network reliability will increase in the event of a service outage. A DoS attack such as an Internet Control Message Protocol (ICMP) flood, whereby interface bandwidth is consumed by malformed broadcast packets, may be easily and reliably diagnosed if a separate management network is used to access the network equipment. Equipment logging and event/trap notifications may be sent out to the operator reliably, possibly before subscriber services are heavily impacted.

Although this may be practical for equipment residing within a central office or headend this is not practical for the access equipment distributed deep into the network and out to the customer premises equipment (CPE) gear residing at the subscriber's premise. If we take into consideration the impacts of the networking gear at your headend/central office many thousands of subscribers would be impacted by such an attack and deploying a dedicated network for this equipment should be a priority. However, when talking about distributed equipment or CPE gear, the level of exposure to subscribers is much smaller, thus the deployment of a dedicated management network is not practical.

In such instances, in any case in which the development of a parallel management network is not possible, an operator should pay careful attention to ensure network accessibility and management is achievable in the event of

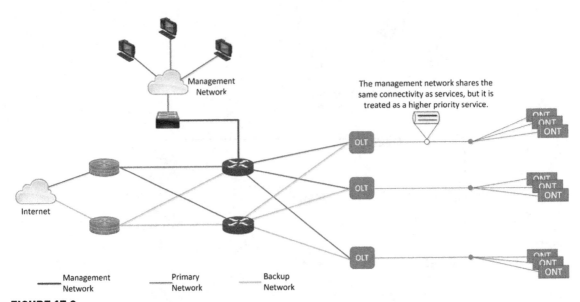

FIGURE 17.2

Integrated network management.

a network attack. At a minimum, the management network should reside as an independent virtualized network within a dedicated virtual local area network (VLAN) architecture as in Fig. 17.2. This VLAN architecture must have privileged access to all network interfaces, both routed and switched, allowing management access to the network elements. Further, the deployment of the VLAN architecture must be taken with care to ensure security from external or noncontrolled interfaces.

Finally, care should be taken to prevent management protocols such as system logging and event/trap notifications from causing a services outage. During major network events there could be a possibility for these management activities to overload or congest network interfaces. If the virtualized network is not prioritized accordingly, such management activities could themselves become a major cause of inaccessibility to the network equipment. Techniques such as throttling should be considered to help control traffic congestion.

Managing Those Who Manage the Network

There is usually an innate trust by a management organization to believe the people working for them have the best interest of the organization in mind at all times. Unfortunately, there are factors which may be considered accidental, such as the proverbial fat finger, and others which are just naïve, and finally those which are more intentionally harmful in nature. The question isn't which one of these will occur; the question is what checks are you putting in to help mitigate the impact these actions have on your network operation *when* they occur.

To start, a clear management of permission levels should be established within the system. Each user should be assigned a permission level based on their job function and system knowledge. The following table provides a minimum guideline of users' levels to be defined within the system and their relative access levels.

Read-only	User has read-only access to all service-level tables within the system including routing/switching tables and service provisioning
Provisioning	User has read-only access to all service-level tables within the system and capable of provisioning/activating subscriber services
Provisioning and configuration	User has not only the ability to provision services but also make configuration changes to network elements such as routing protocols and voice server addresses. This user typically also has the ability to initiate a software upgrade to the network elements as necessary
Admin	Although this user does not have super-user permissions, this user does have access to make changes to user permission levels, create/modify usernames and passwords and commission network elements to name a few

A key element to manage each of the assigned users in the system and their service levels is to have a centralized authentication server that services all platforms. As a user "logs into" a platform or network element, the network device would be required to check back with the centralized platform to validate the user's authentication credentials as well as privilege level. Many times these platforms are capable of not only authentication but also able to log user activity within the system. The ability to log user activity is highly recommended. These logs will be key during a root cause analysis after a network outage or misconfiguration occurs, in order to rectify the immediate problem and to help prevent further occurrences.

Finally, any network appliance or service which will touch the network should also use the same authentication tools. Network appliances such as performance management platforms continually poll network elements, providing visibility into possible areas of congestion. Given the level of network traffic these tools are capable of generating, using the same authentication and logging methodologies is key to ensure internal platforms do not cause problems or security holes.

NETWORK ROUTING SECURITY

With the deployment of a wide-scale network architecture there is a belief those network peers themselves are trusted networks. Unfortunately, as a network operator you are only able to rely on that which is under your control, and everything else should be considered suspect. It is critical for a network operator to protect these network assets by only allowing those protocols within your network which are necessary for routing of services and management of the network.

The scale and dynamic behavior of network routing security should be treated with the highest level of consideration. External influences have the capability to impact networking services. These external influences include domain name services (DNS), routing protocols such as OSPF and their respective route tables, which can cause various forms of networking irregularities such as temporary routing loops and unnecessary network failovers. The use of defensive techniques such as access control lists (ACLs) control what traffic types are allowed on the network. Disabling services such as ICMP and Ping will only increase the overall stability of the core network architecture.

There are a number of organizations and forums which provide guidance on how to protect a network. There are also other organizations providing updates on current threats detected throughout the world. It is key as an operator to engage with the various organizations, such that a comprehensive and updated security policy is in place, allowing for a stable services model. These threats are continually changing their impacts and new threats are identified daily. There is no such thing as a completely secure network, only a network which has yet to be compromised.

CONCLUSION

The topic of security and networking threats by itself is large enough to fill volumes. Furthermore, as network security becomes more complex and intelligent, those looking to exploit the holes are keeping up. Security experts patch a network hole only to allow those looking to hack the network to identify a new network vulnerability they can exploit. It is essential that a network operator be aware of the possible areas of vulnerabilities within the network, establishing a base level of security policies from the first day of operation. Once a series of bad practices and uncontrolled access commences, the difficulty of re-establishing a more restrictive policy is nearly impossible and only adds to confusion and frustration by the staff.

Data Flow in a PON

Fig. A.1 represents data flow in any passive optical network (PON) or similar systems such as DOCSIS; it applies to just about any point-to-multipoint system. In the downstream direction, the optical line terminal (OLT) puts out continuous data with no gaps. In this simplified diagram, there are three optical network terminal (ONTs), each of which gets its downstream data during a time slot of variable length, depending on how much data is available for that ONT and how much bandwidth the subscriber is allowed. The data for each ONT are preceded by a header (not shown) embedded in its data, which identifies the ONT and usually the port on the ONT which is to receive the data. It is essential that the downstream data never stop, even if there is nothing to send. This is because, in order to maximize efficiency, the downstream receivers at the ONTs have a clock locked to the downstream signal, so there is no need to waste time synchronizing with the downstream data. Thus, when there are no data to send, the OLT sends *idle code*, a short sequence of bits that keeps each ONT locked to the downstream data. This continuous data transmission is commonly called *time division multiplex* (TDM) transmission.

It is possible to keep each ONT locked to the downstream data because all data on the PON, regardless of the ONT for which they are intended, go to each ONT, by virtue of the nature of the passive splitter used in the network. Note that each ONT will stop the data not intended for it, not passing it to any outputs. However, this is the motivation for using encryption in the downstream direction: suppose one is somehow able to "trick" the ONT into passing the data for one or more other ONTs. Or, even more far-fetched, suppose that someone was able to tap into the fiber ahead of his ONT and watch the data from other ONTs. While these situations are improbable, we cannot totally guarantee that they will not happen. The solution is to encrypt each user's data with a unique encryption key known only to that ONT and the OLT. Thus, if someone were to be able to look at another subscriber's data, it would be gibberish—totally meaningless. Appendix B provides a light overview of encryption.

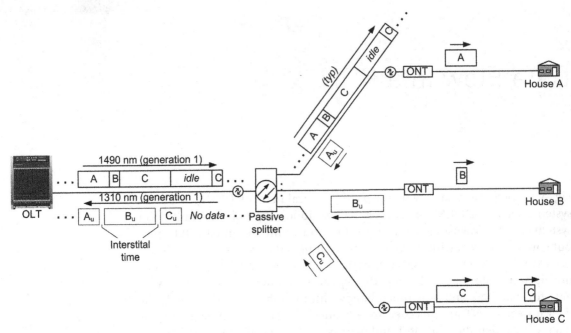

FIGURE A.1
Data flow in a PON.

The idle code transmitted when there are no downstream data available for transmission can create a problem when video overlay is used. As explained in Chapter 6, there is a distortion product in the fiber itself called *stimulated Raman scattering* (SRS), which can cause the data modulated onto the 1490-nm optical carrier (first-generation systems) to modulate the 1550-nm carrier bearing the RF-modulated signals (a form of what RF engineers would call *cross-modulation*). As long as data are being transmitted, there is enough transition randomization that the power of the crossmodulated signal in any one channel is low, resulting in some degradation in the carrier-to-noise ratio (C/N) of the RF signal, but not to a degree that cannot be managed. However, when an idle signal is present on the 1490-nm optical carrier, the signal power "bunches up" at a few frequencies, resulting in enough power to cause problems. The signal power "bunching up," or peaking at one frequency and its harmonics, is due to the short, repetitive data sequence that is the idle code. With first-generation EPON systems, the frequency affected is 62.5 MHz, falling into channel 3 of North American video frequency plans, and to a lesser degree, harmonics of 62.5 MHz. For GPON, the frequency is 62.2 MHz, not that much different; both frequencies are extremely damaging to an RF signal transmitted on channel 3. If the RF signal is analog-modulated video, the effect will be moving diagonal lines in the picture, very distracting. We have seen the

SRS interference level high enough that even digital signals modulated using the common 256-QAM modulation could be rendered undetectable, resulting in no signal whatsoever under worst-case conditions. The solution is to NOT transmit the idle code specified in the standards, but rather to transmit a (usually) longer random data sequence addressed to no ONTs. Different vendors have somewhat different solutions, and some early equipment didn't have a solution for this problem, but most modern systems do handle it.

The upstream transmission technique is called *time division multiple access* (TDMA). Since data must originate at each ONT, and since one ONT cannot "hear" data from any other ONTs, it is not possible to use TDM transmission in the upstream direction. Rather, at the beginning of a transmission cycle, each ONT reports the amount of data it has to transmit upstream—obviously the data must already be in a buffer in the ONT for the ONT to know this. The OLT looks at all the data that are to be transmitted upstream from each ONT, and decides how much time to allocate to each. (While the ONTs usually are able to transmit all of their data, there are some conditions that may preclude an ONT from getting as long a transmit time slot as it needs.) The OLT then assigns each ONT a time slot and duration for transmitting its data. The ONT gets a reference time message from the OLT, and counts from that time to when its transmit window occurs.

Because different ONTs on a PON can be different distances from the OLT, the *propagation delay*, that is, the time required for data to transit the fiber, can differ significantly from one ONT to another. If nothing was done about this difference in time delay, then either there would be collisions between data from different ONTs, or there would be a lot of time wasted because no ONT could transmit in certain time blocks without risking "stepping on" another ONT. In order to prevent this, during initial acquisition of a new ONT (sometimes called *registration*) the round-trip time from the OLT to the ONT and back is measured, and this tells the OLT how much time compensation should be supplied to each ONT in order that its transmission arrive at the OLT at the expected time. Thus, an ONT located far away from the OLT will be told to transmit its data a little sooner than would an ONT located close to the OLT.

Note in Fig. A.1 that there is still a little dead time (we called it *interstitial time* to be more upbeat) between upstream packets received from different ONTs. This is needed to compensate for errors in the delay time measurements and, more so, to the time needed to turn off the laser in one ONT upstream transmitter, and to turn on the laser in the next ONT. Each ONT also transmits a run-in sequence that allows the receiver at the OLT to set its gain according to the received optical level, then to synchronize its receive clock to the transmitter in the OLT.

In order to discover new ONTs when they are installed on the network, there must be a *discovery window* that occurs every few seconds to few minutes, in which any and all ONTs new to the PON can announce their presence. Since the OLT doesn't have any propagation delay information for the new ONT, the discovery window must be large enough to make sure that, no matter what the propagation delay, the new ONT doesn't step on a transmission from another ONT. In fact, the discovery window may be large enough for more than one new ONT to announce its presence. This means that the discovery window is relatively big, reducing the upstream throughput of the system. For this reason, we don't want discovery windows occurring too often. But we also want them to occur frequently enough that waiting for a new ONT to get discovered is not a burden.

Introduction to Encryption

By no means will you be an expert in encryption from reading this short introduction, but it is intended to give you a feel for what is going on in your passive optical networks (PONs) when we discuss encryption.

Downstream encryption is considered important in PON networks because all data packets go to each optical network unit (ONT) at each customer's home or business, as shown in Appendix A. Granted, the ONT only passes traffic intended for that one subscriber. However, there is always the lingering fear that someone may hack an ONT and get it to pass data intended for someone else. While improbable, there is also the fear that a subscriber may tap into the fiber in front of the ONT and recover data that way. Tapping into a fiber undetected is not easy due to the nature of the transmission and the characteristics of fiber, but we cannot unequivocally say it is impossible. Interception of upstream transmission is much less probable than is interception of downstream transmission, as the splitter(s) used in the fiber-to-the-home (FTTH) network do not pass significant signal from one subscriber port to another. So while there have been systems made with upstream encryption, this is generally not considered important to the security of the network.

THE FUNDAMENTALS

There are many encryption schemes used today, each with strengths and weaknesses. Many books have been written on the subject, so it is not necessary for us to go into a lot of detail here. There is a limited but fairly readable general description of encryption in the Ciciora book,[1] and we shall only summarize some of the information here for the convenience of the reader. There are several elements related to encryption that must be addressed, and we shall

---

[1]Walter Ciciora et al., Modern Cable Television Technology, 2nd edition, Morgan Kaufmann, 2004, Chapter 22. The presentation here is in the context of transmitting video from a set-top box to a display, but it can be applied to transmission from an OLT to an ONT, or for other transmission systems. Note that it is not an exhaustive dissertation on the subject.

provide a basic introduction to each. In traditional cable TV use, *encryption* is called *scrambling*, as applied to rendering a video signal unintelligible to an unauthorized viewer. In data communications parlance, *scrambling* has an unrelated meaning, to remove the dc content from data. One has to ascertain the meaning of the word *scrambling* from the context. Here we use the term *encryption* to mean rendering any data signal unintelligible to all except the intended receiver.

Fig. B.1 illustrates one common method of encrypting data, though it is by no means the only way. It is not necessary to understand the details of encryption in order to use it, but it is helpful to understand some basic concepts. The encryption method of Fig. B1 is based on the *exclusive OR* (XOR) operation, a fundamental logical operation defined in Fig. B1(A). An exclusive OR logic element has two inputs and one output, whose value is a function of the two inputs. For the present discussion, one input (the *pseudorandom bit stream*) is derived from the *key*, or secret shared between the sender and the receiver (the optical line terminal [OLT] and the ONT), and the other input is the data to be sent. Before encrypting, the data are called *plaintext*, and after encryption, the signal actually sent on the fiber is called *ciphertext*. The plaintext and the key are both dealt with on a bit-by-bit basis, clocked (moved) by a common clock signal. As shown in Fig. B1(A), if the pseudorandom bit at a given time is 0, then the output of the XOR is the same as the input plaintext. If the pseudorandom bit is 1, then the output of the XOR is the opposite of the plaintext input.

Fig. B1(B) shows how the XOR function is used in encryption. A *shift register*, a hardware (or software) device, holds 1 bit of data at a time in one element (a shift register *stage*), identified as b4 to b1. When the shift register receives a clock pulse, it moves its data to the next stage to the right.

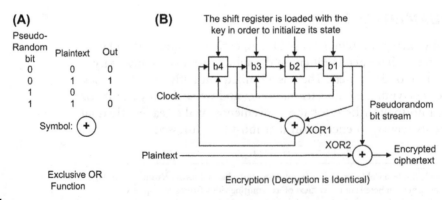

FIGURE B.1
Symmetric key encryption and decryption.

The input to the left-most stage is calculated from some combination of bits from different elements of the shift register, illustrated as the XOR of the output of the first and last stages. At the beginning of an encryption cycle (which might encompass some number of Ethernet frames), the shift register is loaded (initialized) with the key.

At the receiver (ONT), the same function shown in Fig. B1(B) can be used again to recover the plaintext, so long as the key used in scrambling is known to the receiver. The key thus is the shared secret needed by both ends in order to effectively encrypt and decrypt a signal. The method shown here is called *symmetrical key encryption*, because the same key is used at both the transmitting and receiving sides. It is popular because of the low computational complexity involved. It can be very secure so long as the key is long enough—we show a 4-bit-long key for illustration, but 128-bit keys are common today, and 256-bit keys are used. Assuming that the key can be securely agreed to between the OLT and ONT, and we shall show a way to do that below, the main way to break the encryption is to try all possible combinations of bits and see which one works (this is called an *exhaustive search*, and is exhausting for reasons we are about to show). With 128-bit keys, we have 2^{128}, or about 340 with 36 zeros following, combinations to try. Assuming you could try 100 keys a second, it would take about 108 followed by 27 zeros (108×10^{27}) *years* to try all possible combinations! (If it is any comfort, on average, it will only take half this long.)

KEY EXCHANGE

So we have established a way to encrypt data such that they are very difficult to decrypt unless the transmitter and receiver share a secret key. The next problem is to find a way to share that key between the two devices in a manner such that, even if someone is able to "listen in" on the conversation, it would not be possible to figure out the key. Fortunately there are ways to do this. Some are based on an *asymmetric key*, as opposed to the symmetric key shown above. We shall not go into the mathematics now, but they are briefly outlined in the Ciciora reference cited above. These are so-called *public–private key pairs*. A device picks a *private key* known only to that device. This can be done, for example, by a random number generator built into the software of an ONT. Using certain mathematical operations frequently involving exponentiation, a *public key* can be computed such that plaintext encrypted with the public key can only be decrypted with the private key or vice versa. Computing the public key from the private key is relatively easy, but going the other way, computing the private key from the public key, is difficult at best. Letting each end of the conversation do partial computation of the key and exchanging information between the two sides, it is possible to construct a symmetric key that is never transmitted completely on the insecure network (the PON). Thus, if there is an interloper (highly improbable with FTTH, but not necessarily impossible), there is no way for that interloper to learn the symmetric key used to transmit data.

The computations involved in the public–private key exchange are too complex to use them for real-time data exchange at 1 Gb/s or faster. However, they lend themselves to exchanging key information for a symmetric key that is then used for encrypting the actual data. Thus, periodically, a new symmetrical key can be computed, and used to encrypt data. If it is going to take 54×10^{27} years on the average to break a key, and the key is changed once a month, you can see that the data are pretty secure.

AUTHENTICATION

Encryption consists of hiding the data by passing it through some process known to the sender and the receiver, but not to anyone else. But suppose you are the sender; how do you know that the receiver you are sending to is a legitimate receiver (in this case, a legitimate ONT or OLT), rather than some rogue box? This brings us to the first step (which we are presenting last) in the encryption process, *authentication*, or making sure that you are talking to the box you think you're talking to. Authentication involves a manual step, which is normally hidden from you, the system operator, but which is very important to secure operation of your system. The first step in authentication involves a manual process normally performed by the manufacturer of the ONT and OLT.[2] The manufacturer will go to a third-party company called a *certificate authority* (CA). There are several companies which provide CA services. The CA verifies, using whatever means it finds appropriate, that the manufacturer is a real equipment vendor who intends to provide legitimate equipment, as opposed to someone who is setting up a business to try to break the system.

Once the CA determines that the manufacturer is legitimate, it provides him with a *digital certificate*, unique data sequences stored in each and every copy of the box being built. The same digital certificate is not used twice. Rather, the CA has a so-called *private key* (defined above), which is used to encrypt a unique digital certificate for each box. The CA provides the manufacturer with a whole series of digital certificates, each encrypted with the CA's private key, and which can only be decrypted by a *public key* provided by the CA.

---

[2]In general, the OLT and ONT do not have to be manufactured by the same entity, but at the current stage of maturity of the industry, you will probably want to obtain both ends from the same manufacturer. As the industry matures, this may change.

Not the only solution, but a common digital certificate is the ITU's X.509 certificate.[3] Among other data, the X.509 certificate includes a plaintext number generated by the manufacturer and sent to the CA. The CA returns the completed X.509 certificate, which includes the number and the number encrypted with the CA's private key, plus other data. The other end of the pair trying to talk (the OLT and ONT both go through this process, so each knows that the other is legitimate) must have the CA's public key, and uses it to decrypt the encrypted number found in the certificate. It then compares the decrypted version with the plaintext version, and if the two match, it knows that it is talking to a legitimate device. The information in the X.509 certificate is used in computing the symmetric key information used to encrypt and decrypt data.

Suppose an interloper is sitting in the middle of the data path (the so-called *man-in-the-middle* attack— improbable, but not totally beyond physical possibility). He could pass, unaltered, the certification information exchanged between the legitimate OLT and ONT, neither of which would know that an interloper is in the middle. However, doing so would not do him any good when it comes to intercepting data, because the complete symmetrical encryption key information is never passed on the network, so the man-in-the-middle can listen to the data, but cannot decrypt them.

Suppose that a mistake is made and a manufacturer who gets legitimate certification turns out to be a rogue manufacturer. Or maybe a legitimate manufacturer is sold to an unscrupulous owner, who decides there is money in intercepting users' information. To our knowledge, this has not happened, but it is not beyond imagination. Or suppose that the CA's private key is compromised for some reason (maybe an employee with access to it gets mad and quits). Then all certificates associated with the compromised equipment must be revoked. For equipment connected to the Internet, such as pretty much all OLTs and ONTs, the existing certification can be revoked and a new certificate issued (if appropriate) through communications. There are some pieces of equipment that use authentication and encryption that are not connected to the Internet. One example is Blu-ray players. Revocation of certificates in these devices is accommodated by having all new DVDs that come out after the problem is discovered, carry a certificate revocation notice. The rogue machine may work for a while, but presumably sooner or later the owner will try to play a newer DVD with the revocation information, which will permanently yield the rogue machine inoperable.

---

[3]http://www.itu.int/rec/T-REC-X.509-200811-I/en, http://en.wikipedia.org/wiki/X.509. There is a later version of the standard in prepublication state as of this writing, and it may become generally available at any time.

Forward Error Correction

Another key concept applicable to just about any fiber-to-the-home (FTTH) or other data system is *forward error correction* (FEC)—the ability to detect and correct errors in the transmission of data. FEC allows us to transmit at lower signal powers and still get data through, as well as to sometimes get flawless data delivered even in the event of momentary interruptions in data (if the interruption is short enough), such as in the case of a burst of noise in a network. FEC doesn't come for free, of course, in that in order to reap the benefits, we need to add processing to both ends of the network (not necessarily too burdensome today), and we lose some efficiency of communications, because we sacrifice some data bits to the redundancy of FEC in order to get the advantage. But in many cases, the sacrifice is well worth the effort. As with other appendix subjects, our object here is not to make you an expert on the subject, but rather, to give you enough understanding of the underlying technology that when you see FEC referred to, the reference will make sense, and you will understand the trade-offs.

PARITY

Before we get to FEC per se, we need to review an older technology that is used in FEC, *parity*. Parity has been around in data communications systems for decades, and serves by itself to detect that a transmission (or storage) error has occurred, without being able to do anything about it. This is done by appending an additional bit to a transmitted bit pattern, such that the total number of 1s transmitted is odd (for odd parity) or even (even parity).

Suppose that I want to transmit a 7-bit word. I transmit the 7 bits and then I transmit an 8th bit, such that the total number of 1s is odd. If I want to transmit 1010101, I have four 1s, so I will add one more 1, transmitting 10101011. On the other hand, if I transmitted 0101010, I already have an odd number of 1s, so the 8th bit will be a 0, and I transmit 01010100. The receiver looks at the bit pattern it received, and if it gets an odd number of 1s, then it assumes that it received valid data—no bits were changed in the transmission. Parity does, indeed, correctly identify data corruption if 1, 3, 5, or 7 bits are received incorrectly, but if an even number of bits are corrupted, then parity will come up with the wrong conclusion about the integrity of the received data. On the other hand, in any viable transmission system, the probability of 2 bits being corrupted is less than the probability of 1 bit being corrupted, and so on. Thus, parity provides a valid error detection scheme, though by itself it does not allow you to correct any errors that develop—you know that a bit has been changed between a 0 and a 1 but you don't know which bit was changed. And there is a data penalty for transmitting the parity bit—in the illustration, it takes 8 bits to transmit 7 bits worth of data, so I am reducing my throughput by 1/7th (14.3% overhead) in order to have the benefit of usually knowing when data have been corrupted.

So what do you do if you detect an error in transmitted data? Well, depending on the type of data, you might be able to ask for a retransmit, and this is commonly done. If the data are part of an email message or most web pages, there is no harm in asking for a retransmission, and the user will not be aware of it. The *transmission control protocol* (TCP) does this: if it detects an error (across many more than 7 bits, of course), it will ask the sender to resend the packet, and it will replace the bad packet with the good. But there are other times that you can't ask for a retransmission. For example, if the botched packet was part of a voice (VoIP) session or a video (IPTV) stream, then by the time you could ask for and receive a retransmit, it would probably be too late; the decoder would have needed the information and not had it. So in this case, you might mark the packet as bad, or you might discard it. In some cases, the decoder will try to "cover up" the mistake, maybe by repeating information that "should be" a lot like the missed information. For data for which it is not reasonable to ask for a retransmission of a botched packet (or to take time to reorder packets received in the wrong order), *user datagram protocol* (UDP) will be used in the place of TCP. There are other differences between TCP and UDP.

BASIC ERROR DETECTION AND CORRECTION

We can get an intuitive view of FEC by considering Table C.1, which represents 49 bits of data we wish to transmit, arranged in seven rows and seven columns. We read in all 49 bits at the transmitter, then we calculate the parity bit for each row (shown in the 8th column), and the parity bit for each column (shown in the 8th row, at the bottom). We now transmit the 49 data bits and the 14 parity bits, for a total of 63 bits transmitted.

Now suppose we receive the data, and find that we have a parity failure in the third row and the fourth column, as shown in Table C.2. We have placed an "X" in the boxes with the two failed parity bits. From the failed parity bits, we know that there was an error in row 3 and column 4. Only 1 bit can cause that

Table C.1 Error Correction on a 7 × 7 Matrix

							Row Parity
1	0	1	0	1	0	1	**1**
0	1	0	1	0	1	0	**0**
1	1	0	0	0	1	1	**1**
1	1	1	0	1	0	0	**1**
0	0	0	0	1	1	1	**0**
1	1	0	0	1	1	0	**1**
1	1	1	0	0	0	0	**0**
0	*0*	*0*	*0*	*1*	*1*	*0*	*Col. Parity*

Table C.2 Data of Table C.1 With 1 Bit Corrupted

							Row Parity
1	0	1	0	1	0	1	**1**
0	1	0	1	0	1	0	**0**
1	1	0	1	0	1	1	**1 X**
1	1	1	0	1	0	0	**1**
0	0	0	0	1	1	1	**0**
1	1	0	0	1	1	0	**1**
1	1	1	0	0	0	0	**0**
0	*0*	*0*	*0*	*1*	*1*	*0*	*Col. Parity*
			X				

error, so we know that the bit in both row 3 and column 4 is bad. We received it as a 1, and the only other value it can have is 0, so we will change it from a 1 to a 0, and we have corrected the error! Some reflection will show that there are certain other failures involving more bits that we can also catch. For example, if we have a parity failure in row 5 as well as row 3, then the most likely explanation is that the bit in row 5 column 4 is also bad and needs to be changed. Of course, there is some ambiguity at this point, because there could also be a failure of either row parity bit itself, which would lead us to make one or two improper corrections. We shall leave it to the statisticians to calculate the probability of correctly identifying and correcting multiple bit errors. We have transmitted a total of 63 bits for the ability to correct errors in 49 bits, so we have 14 bits of overhead for 49 bits transmitted, or just over 28% overhead.

Note that, besides the bit overhead, we have sustained certain other penalties for the privilege of correcting errors. Most notably, we have incurred a time delay penalty. We must load all 49 data bits in registers before we can calculate the row and column parities at the transmit end, and we must load them in registers at the receive end before we can do the parity checks and error correction. Of course, we could maybe speed things up some by transmitting the data bits while we are loading them into the parity check matrix, then we could calculate the parity check and send it after we send the data bits. This would speed things up at the transmit end, but we will still have to load all 49 data bits into a matrix at the receive end, then get the 14 parity bits and do the checking. So we are going to lose some time to error correction. This may not be too much of a penalty with a lot of data, but if we have data requiring low latency (such as a telephone call), it is one more source of latency that we may want to keep an eye on.

REAL FEC

What we've discussed above is merely an intuitive introduction to real FEC. There are a number of FEC technologies in use today for a lot of different purposes. One that has found a lot of application in FTTH and other systems is Reed–Solomon (R-S) coding. It, as with all error-correcting codes, is rather computationally intensive and well beyond the scope of what you need to know in order to deal with FEC in FTTH systems. The FEC is usually optional, and may be turned on or off, depending on the needs of the network.

Communications networks are evaluated partially in terms of *bit error rate* (BER), or the fraction of transmitted bits that are received in error at the receiving end. BER is usually expressed in parts per million, or parts in 10 raised to some negative number (1% BER would be expressed as one part in 10^{-2}, but such a poor BER would be unusable in any event). You will hear reference to pre-FEC and post-FEC BER. Pre-FEC BER would be the bit error rate of the raw communications channel, before FEC has done its magic to improve BER. Obviously post FEC BER is the error rate of the data after the FEC has been applied. Post-FEC should be better than pre-FEC by a number of orders of magnitude.

R-S coding is often expressed as, for example, R-S (255, 239, 8), meaning that it is applied to 8-bit symbols. There are 239 data symbols and a total of 255 symbols, meaning $255-239=16$ parity symbols are added to 239 data symbols, for an overhead of 6.7% (certainly better than our oversimplified example, and with better results). Recently, in a quest to raise the efficiency of a communications path, a different FEC technology has started to be used in some systems, such as DOCSIS 3.1. This is termed *LDPC, low-density parity check*, a technology known since the 1960s but not used much until now due to its computational complexity.

INTERLEAVING

A final topic we should mention in conjunction with FEC is *interleaving*. In some systems it is common to have transmission errors occur in bursts. This might be due to noise, such as from an electric arc, or from any other event that occurs once in a while, but which can destroy communication for some short time. If a noise burst occurs for too long, then the FEC will not be able to correct the errors because too many occur over too short a time. One solution is to create the FEC, then "mix up," or interleave different blocks of FEC-protected data, so that any one FEC block is transmitted over a longer interval, with other blocks interspersed. Then when the FEC blocks are put back in the correct order, presumably the noise burst that caused loss of data, will affect multiple FEC blocks, but none to the point that the FEC cannot recover data. FTTH is probably not the ideal communications medium for interleaving, and we are not aware of its use within the standards, but we mention it because you may hear of it with respect to error correction.

Motivation for Quality of Service

This brief appendix states the motivation for, and techniques for, *quality of service (QoS)* in passive optical network (PON) or other systems. Very similar terminology, sometimes used interchangeably with QoS, are *class of service (CoS)* and *quality of experience (QoE)*. All of these terms refer to getting packets needed by a user to that user at the time he needs them. One might argue that QoS is the broadest term, CoS refers to how it is delivered, and QoE refers to what the subscriber experiences.

In the early days, when people were just starting to deliver text files to subscribers over telephone lines, and digital audio and video were gleams in a few people's eyes, the advantage of delivering everything digitally was explained by its simplicity: "a bit is a bit is a bit." That is, you could send any type of data on one network and you didn't have to worry about what you were carrying when. Well, it sort of turned out that way in the early days, when there was not that much data to transmit and if data were delayed, no one would know it anyway. However, as we started to actually use the bandwidth to deliver the plethora of services envisioned originally, we began to realize the fallacy of the "a bit is a bit is a bit" philosophy. Think of some of the things that can go wrong with the delivery of packets of bits to a user:

- If the packets are pieces of an email or of most web pages, a delay of even a second or two (a long time in data communications) will be unnoticed. Almost any message of useful size is divided into many packets, each having as much of the information as can be packed in that packet.[1] Such data are delivered by a protocol called TCP (part of the TCP/IP verbiage that was so popular a few years ago, even by people who didn't know what it meant). TCP makes sure that all packets making up a message arrive at their destination. Because of the vagaries of the Internet, not all packets may arrive one right after the other. Some may be dropped along the way, and some may arrive before others

---

[1]The nominal maximum length of an Ethernet packet is 1500 bytes, or 12,000 bits, not enough for the average email or web page.

that were sent first. But no matter, the TCP protocol will keep track of such problems, and will fix them without the user knowing there was a problem. Packets received out-of-order will be put back in order, and packets not arriving will be requested to be sent again and placed in the right order before higher layers of software interpret the message. So this type of traffic is pretty easy to handle.

- Now suppose the packets are part of a streaming video clip or program (*IPTV—internet protocol television*). Now we have a bit (pun intended) of a different problem. The decoder in the computer, TV, or whatever device you are using to watch the program, uses the information in a packet to reconstruct part of the picture and/or sound. After that part of the picture or sound is decoded, the decoder needs more information, since it takes lots of packets to make up the picture. What happens if the decoder is ready for the next packet, and that packet has not yet arrived, perhaps due to congestion or loss on the Internet? You get a picture freeze or a pixellation, either way, an unusable picture. And that makes you mad! If a packet has been lost, or even arrives out-of-order, there is usually no time to recover before the packet is needed. A way to say this is that packet *jitter*, the differential time from the arrival of one packet to the next, must be small. The situation can be mitigated to an extent by employing *buffering* at the receiver. Buffering in this context simply means that you store a number of packets before you pass them on to the decoder. That way, if there is a delay in getting a packet, you have something for the decoder to use while awaiting the arrival of the next packet. But buffering doesn't come for free. Obviously it takes memory at the receiver, though memory is not that expensive any more. The other thing it costs is that when you start receiving a new stream, the buffer must fill maybe half way before the decoder can start decoding the stream—if you don't let this happen, you defeat the purpose of having the buffer. And waiting for the buffer to fill means that after you tune to a new channel, you have to wait some time before you start to get your picture. You have experienced that tuning any digital signal takes longer than tuning an analog signal. While not the only thing causing the delay, filling the signal buffer can be a major component of the delay you experience.
- Now we come to the service that really takes good QoS: old-fashioned voice. Voice doesn't require nearly the bandwidth required by video, but the QoS requirements placed on it are more extensive than those for video. Not only do you have to keep the packets coming to the receiver when they are needed, as with video, but you cannot tolerate much absolute delay in the transmission. It is very irritating to have much round-trip delay in voice transmission, because you ask the party you are talking to a question, and you expect an answer right away, not a second later. Those of us old enough

to have been traveling internationally back in the 1980s remember well overseas phone calls via satellite. Even a one-hop link caused a noticeable and irritating delay in getting a response from the other end, and the round-trip delay for a one-hop communication works out to a little over half a second—twice that if you needed two hops to communicate. So voice not only requires even lower jitter than does video, it also requires low *latency*, or delay in delivering the signal. Low latency works against the use of buffering to compensate for jitter.

- Oops, there is yet another service that requires the highest QoS of all, though it tends to be very low in its bandwidth demand. Control information you need to pass in order to manage each part of your network must get through no matter what, and it can't be delayed too long. Suppose your network gets flooded with high-priority traffic. To be kind, suppose you have subscribers pulling more IPTV bandwidth than you have available in your network, and you have to go into your network to manage the bandwidth. To be more realistic if not as kind, suppose you get hit with some sort of denial of service (DoS) attack you didn't protect yourself against, per information elsewhere in this book. In a DoS attack, someone floods your network with more traffic than it has the capacity to handle, so communications slow to little or nothing, and your customers get really angry. If you have not made provision for your control traffic to move through your network regardless of what else is happening, it is going to be hard for you to stop the problem. So it is not wrong to think of your needs first. (By analogy, first responders, police, fire, and other rescue personnel, are instructed to see to their own safety before rescuing others. This is not selfish or wrong; if a first responder gets himself into trouble and needs help, he has taken one rescuer out of the picture, and created one more victim needing rescue, so he has swung the balance of capability in the wrong direction by two people.)

So depending on the type of data, we have different needs for QoS, which are handled by dividing the traffic in the network by CoS, and resulting in subscribers experiencing the QoE they expect. Rather, we hope the subscribers never think about the quality of their experience because it is always so good that they don't need to think about it.

There are several ways you may manage QoS with EPON, but probably the most common involves assigning data to *virtual local area networks* (*VLANs*), which are assignments of different types of data to different "pipes," called *local area networks* (*LANs*), in which all devices on the LAN can talk directly to each other. This is common in business (enterprise) or home networks, but when we talk about a *virtual* LAN, we mean that there are multiple isolated LANs which happen to share the same physical "pipe," in this case a PON. The data travel on a common network, but data assigned to different VLANs are isolated. It is possible, and often the practice, to put a VLAN inside a VLAN. Frequently the first, or *inner* VLAN *tag* is used by an organization using your network to connect several locations, and the second or *outer* tag is used to prioritize the traffic in your network.

One thing that VLANs can be used for is to define a QoS priority level. There are eight possible priorities that can be assigned to any VLAN, though not all equipment may recognize this many levels. The highest priority is usually reserved for network control, ensuring that your control packets get through first. Next comes a priority level for voice, then for video, then, in decreasing order, everything else.[i] When two or more packets present themselves for transmission at the same time, for example, at the OLT input, obviously one is going to have to wait for the other. The packet with the highest priority gets to go first.

GPON uses VLANs too, but it has yet another QoS mechanism in that it can embed packets of like QoS level within T-CONTs. Five levels of T-CONTs are assigned one of five QoS levels, as shown in Fig. 4.2. The highest priority T-CONT, always guaranteed to be moved to the front of any queue, handles OAM (control) messages and queue-length reporting. Next is a fixed bandwidth T-CONT, which reserves bandwidth that is always guaranteed to a user, whether that user is consuming the bandwidth or not. Next is assured bandwidth, which is guaranteed to be available but is not reserved, so that bandwidth is available for other users when not being used by the user(s) for whom it is guaranteed. Then at the bottom of the priority are nonassured bandwidth and best-effort bandwidth, which contain traffic that might be dropped if there is not enough bandwidth for everything. Often the decision as to which T-CONT a packet goes into is based on the packet's VLAN and the priority assigned to that VLAN. So does the use of T-CONTs add additional value to the prioritization associated with VLANs? That question is left for the reader to ponder.

Before we leave the subject of QoS, we might mention one other method of providing for QoS, which is somewhat different than any described above, and that is the method of QoS provided in DOCSIS, the cable modem standard. Its QoS is based on the concept of service flows, which are set up and torn down on an ad hoc basis when needed. Something in the network must request service flows of the CMTS (which serves an analogous function to the OLT), then the CMTS reserves, or *nails up*, the required bandwidth for the duration of the service needing the QoS. At the end of the session, such as a phone call, the service flows are released, and the bandwidth becomes available for other uses.[ii]

Endnotes

i. http://pic.dhe.ibm.com/infocenter/powersys/v3r1m5/index.jsp?topic=%2Fp7hatl%2Fiphbl-configvirtethqost.htm.

ii. Walter Ciciora, et al. Modern cable television technology. 2nd ed Elsevier; 2004. [chapter 5].

Index

429